Sacred Objects and Sacred Places

Sacred Objects and Sacred Places
Preserving Tribal Traditions

Andrew Gulliford

University Press of Colorado

Published by the University Press of Colorado
5589 Arapahoe Avenue, Suite 206C
Boulder, Colorado 80303

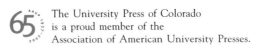 The University Press of Colorado
is a proud member of the
Association of American University Presses.

The University Press of Colorado is a cooperative publishing enterprise supported, in
part, by Adams State College, Colorado State University, Fort Lewis College, Mesa
State College, Metropolitan State College of Denver, University of Colorado,
University of Northern Colorado, University of Southern Colorado, and Western State
College of Colorado.

The paper used in this publication meets the minimum requirements of the American
National Standard for Information Sciences—Permanence of Paper for Printed Library
Materials. ANSI Z39.48-1984

Library of Congress Cataloging-in-Publication Data

Gulliford, Andrew.
  Sacred objects and sacred places : preserving tribal traditions / Andrew Gulliford.
    p. cm.
  Includes bibliographical references and index.
  ISBN 0-87081-560-1 (alk. paper). — 0-87081-579-2 (pbk. : alk. paper)
  1. Indians of North America—Material culture. 2. Indians of North America—
  Antiquities—Collection and preservation. 3. Indians of North America—Ethnic
  identity. 4. Indians of North America—Government relations. 5. Cultural prop-
  erty—Repatriation—North America. 6. Sacred space—Government policy—North
  America. 7. Ceremonial objects—Government policy—North America. 8. Historic
  preservation—North America. 9. United States. Native American Graves
  Protection and Repatriation Act. I. Title.

E98.M34 G85 2000
973'.1—dc21   99-088350

Designed by Laura Furney
Typeset by Daniel Pratt

09 08 07 06 05 04 03   10 9 8 7 6 5 4 3 2

Author's note on photographs: The exact location of sacred sites cannot be determined
from this book's captions, and for other sensitive photographs tribal permission was
requested and granted. Out of respect for the ancestors, no photographs of human remains
have been included.

To the elders
and to all native peoples
struggling with repatriation
and protection of their sacred sites

Contents

Illustrations

Acknowledgments

Though this book recounts some unbearable tragedies, it is essentially a work of affirmation about the ways in which Native Americans have maintained their cultures against all odds. As we enter the twenty-first century, tribal identities grow stronger, and the native peoples of America continue to teach the rest of us the valuable lessons they have learned from living on this continent for millennia.

This book could not have been undertaken without the help and encouragement of dozens of tribal people, historians, archaeologists, and museum professionals throughout the United States. I am deeply indebted to my friends and colleagues for their wisdom and assistance. I am honored that so many Native Americans have explained critical issues to me and that they have opened their hearts to discuss very difficult, emotional topics. A book of this scope will inevitably have errors and omissions, and I apologize for omissions or for any cultural mistakes on my part. I have tried to be as accurate and inclusive as time and space would allow.

I would like to acknowledge the trustees of the James Marston Fitch Foundation in New York City, who awarded me the Second Annual Mid-Career Grant in Historic Preservation in 1992 to pursue the primary research for this book. Fitch funds enabled me to travel to distant Indian reservations and to Alaska to speak personally with tribal elders and cultural leaders concerned with issues of tribal preservation and cultural identity. My warmest regards go to Richard Blinder and Eric De Lony, Fitch Foundation trustees.

As the Wayne N. Aspinall Visiting Chair of Public Policy and History at Mesa State College in Grand Junction, Colorado, for spring 1997, I honed my thoughts and ideas while teaching a short course on sacred objects and sacred places. My own institution, Middle Tennessee State University, granted me a noninstructional assignment for fall 1997 so that I could do additional research and have time to write, and my colleagues in the Department of History have granted me course releases to work on this book. I am also indebted to the Charles Redd Center of Brigham Young University for a travel grant to assist with expenses during my sabbatical. Redd Center funds gave me the opportunity to visit with tribal preservation officers in the Southwest and to locate valuable photographs. In May 1999, I had the pleasure of being a Smithsonian Study Leader aboard the stern-wheeler *Queen of the West* for a week on the Columbia River. Lively dinner table discussions, a visit to the Tamastslikit Cultural Institute of the Confederated Tribes of the Umatilla, and local updates on Kennewick Man and Makah whaling added texture and depth to this book.

In early August 1999 I led a Smithsonian Study Tour on the Lewis and Clark Trail by raft, horseback, and canoe in Montana and Idaho, and we visited Nez Perce sacred sites on the Lolo Trail in the Bitterroot Mountains. The view from The Smoking Place is the same now as it was two centuries ago for Lewis and Clark.

In my work on the Ute Indian Trail in Colorado, I have enjoyed learning from Ute cultural consultant Kenny Frost, Northern Ute elder Clifford Duncan, Northern Ute cultural protections officer Betsy Chapoose, and Sun Dance chief Alvin Pintecoose. I have also learned from White River National Forest Heritage Resources Manager Bill Kight and archaeologist Mike Metcalf. I have enjoyed my friendship with Cathy Wright, director of the Taylor Museum of the Colorado Springs Fine Arts Center, and I have profited from talks with Carol Gleichman and Alan Stanfill of the Advisory Council on Historic Preservation in Denver. Among the Eastern Shoshone at Fort Washakie, Wyoming, I have worked with Shoshone Tribal Cultural Center directors, the center's board members, cultural resources adviser Haman Wise, and Pat Bergie, grants coordinator. I particularly want to thank my friend Fred Chapman, Native American liaison for the Wyoming State Historic Preservation Office, for his wealth of insight and personal dedication to tribal preservation. I also gained valuable information in my interviews with Lawrence Hart from Oklahoma and Curly Bear Wagner from Montana.

Washington, D.C., scholars who helped me learn about the politics of Indian culture include Richard West, director of the National Museum of the American Indian; Rayna Green of the National Museum of American History; Nancy Fuller of the Smithsonian Office of Museum Programs; Suzi Jones of the National Endowment for the Humanities; Patricia Parker of the Interagency Division of the National Park Service; consultant Thomas F. King; and Susan Harjo of the Morning Star Foundation.

In Illinois, Margaret Brown, director of Cahokia Mounds Historic Site, was most helpful. I also learned about human remains issues from Kit Wesler, director of the Wickliffe Mounds Research Center of Murray State University in Kentucky. Robert Archibald, director of the Missouri Historical Society, and T. J. Ferguson, from Tucson, helped clarify issues about the return and protection of Zuni War Gods. Richard Hart explained much about Zuni sacred sites, and Leigh Kuwanwisiwma spent a day with me at the Hopi Cultural Office in Kykotsmovi, Arizona.

In New Mexico, I was aided by Edmund Ladd, of the Museum of New Mexico; Peter Garcia, a student at Western New Mexico University; Robert Schiowitz, archaeologist for the Gila National Forest; Paul Lucero of Laguna Pueblo; and David Vackar, manager of Vermejo Ranch.

A number of people in Alaska provided important information to me. They include Barbara Carlson, of the Aleut Institute; Rachel Craig, of the Northwest Arctic Borough; Judith Bittner, the state historic preservation officer; Rosita Worl and Walter Soboleff, of Sealaska Heritage Foundation; the late Chris Makua, of the Tongass Tribe; the eloquent Robert Sams; Ellen Hays, of the Southeast Alaska Indian Cultural Center; and Gordon Pullar, of Alaska Native Human Resources.

In Washington State, I was privileged to meet Adeline Fredin, of the Confederated Colville Tribes, and William Yallup, the former cultural manager of the Yakama Nation, as well as Yakama Museum Registrar Marilyn Malatare. Michael Hammond, former executive director of the Museum at Warm Springs, Oregon, explained the process of creating a tribal museum, and Scott Stuemke, cultural resources officer for the Confederated Tribes of Warm Springs, discussed tribal archaeology and preservation ordinances.

Hawaiian hospitality was extended to me in my talks with Sara Collins, Elaine "Muffet" Jourdane, and Nathan Napoka, of the Hawai'i State Historic Preservation Office, and Valerie Free and Noelle Kahanu, from the Bishop Museum. Advice on Maui cultural sites, particularly the ancient King's Highway, came from Lance Holter and Rosemary Kuulei. Information on the island of Kaho'olawe came from Daviana Pomaika'i McGregor.

In Tennessee, I have profited from professional advice offered by historians Fred Rolater and Lorne McWatters of Middle Tennessee State University, and a host of my graduate students who wrote term papers or master's theses on tribal cultural preservation and museum topics; these students include Jennifer Martin Maxwell, Tirri Parker, Lisa Nichols, Jay Smith, Kara Mills, Judi Birkitt, Kristina Fusco, Bethany Berlejung, Shelley McCollough, and Heather Fearnbach. For transcribing, I am indebted to Trish Travis, Terri Ferrell, and Marge DeBoer. Thanks go to Jack Ross and his staff at Photo Services of Middle Tennessee State University for their excellent processing and printing of my black-and-white photographs. Appreciation is also extended to Linda Illingsworth, Jeff Gulliford, and Paula Wenger for their editorial suggestions. Joan Sherman has done a superb job in copyediting my manuscript; she truly understood my intent. All remaining errors and omissions are, of course, my own.

I am especially indebted to Luther Wilson, director of the University Press of Colorado, and to his experienced staff, as well as to fellow historian and preservationist Tom Noel, who urged me to send the manuscript home to Colorado. I am also grateful to Canadian photographer

Courtney Milne, who allowed us to use his magnificent medicine wheel photograph for the book's cover.

Finally, I wish to acknowledge my wife, Stephanie Moran, who believed in this book, and my two sons, Tristan David and Duncan Jewett, who have shared in tribal visits and long walks to very special places.

—ANDREW GULLIFORD
Silt, Colorado, and Murfreesboro, Tennessee

Author's Note

Half of the proceeds from the sale of this book will be donated to the National Museum of the American Indian, which curates Native American artifacts and collections from throughout the Western Hemisphere, and to the Keepers of the Treasures, a national organization devoted to preserving, affirming, and celebrating native cultures through traditions and programs that maintain native languages and lifeways, as well as protecting and preserving places that are historic and sacred to indigenous peoples.

Sacred Objects and Sacred Places

Introduction

Nationally, as a group of people we all seek preservation. . . . Tribal preservation will be the key to enhanced social development and growth for all Indian people. To know what you are, and where you came from, may determine where you are going.

—ARLY YANAH, Yavapai-Prescott

When we think of historical preservation, I suppose that you think of something that is old, something that has happened in the past and that you want to put away on a shelf and bring it out and look at every now and then . . . I'm not really sure that that's the way we want to look at these things at all. In our way of thinking, everything is a significant event, and the past is as real as us being here right now. We are all connected to the things that happened at the beginning of our existence. And those things live on as they are handed down to us.

—PARRIS BUTLER, Fort Mohave

This is a book about the ways in which Native Americans seek to preserve tribal traditions and a sense of Indian identity after decades of misguided federal attempts to force them into the cultural mainstream. Given the size and diversity of America's native population, with over 550 federally registered American Indian tribes (including Native Alaskan villages), this volume cannot be inclusive. Instead, it offers an overview, outlining an important native revival movement to preserve sacred sites, to retain dance and song traditions, to pass on languages, to identify and use sacred plants, and to repatriate human remains and sacred objects to their tribes of origin. Ultimately, *Sacred Objects and Sacred Places* demonstrates the resilience of native cultures.[1]

I have tried to make the exceedingly complex information in this book readily accessible so that general readers may begin to understand why tribal peoples are so passionate in defending their sacred objects and sacred places. To that end, academic and professional jargon has been reduced as far as possible. In addition, many native voices are heard in the pages that follow. My goal is to increase public support for tribal preservation without revealing secrets or sensitive cultural information.

I approached this work as a community and public historian who believes that we have much to learn from native peoples about the land and landscape—if only we will listen. Certain Indian values and concepts differ profoundly from those of the mainstream culture. For native peoples, as an example, time is often neither linear nor narrowly circumscribed by decades or centuries; rather, it is circular and without boundaries. Thus, a sacred landscape spoken of in ancient myth is as sacred today as it was when the spirits were creating it. Similarly, Indian guides at a century-old massacre site or battlefield, such as Washita in Oklahoma or Big Hole in Montana, can hear the keening of the bereaved as if the shooting had just ended. And for American Indians, Native Alaskans, and Native Hawaiians, respect for the dead is as important as respect for the elderly and reverence for life itself.

At congressional hearings on tribal historic preservation, Mary Proctor of the Cherokee Band of Oklahoma stated, "We do need help in all areas of preserving our culture, our heritage, our language, our burial grounds, and a multitude of things from trees to birds and animals."[2] Her words remind us that though historic preservation frequently focuses on buildings, Indians look at culture and landscape in much broader terms. As Robert LaBatte of the Cheyenne River Sioux explained, even rocks are sacred: "They are people. They are nations. They are there to help us. . . . I think that many people think that just plants exist alongside of us as relatives and animals. But also the rocks."[3]

Native peoples can reshape the American preservation movement and lead us to think deeply about the relationship between place and spirituality and the convergence of myth and landscape because they bring to historic preservation and archaeology an entirely different perspective—a perspective that must be both respected and supported. They are concerned about the preservation of places as diverse as Canyon de Chelly in Arizona and Serpentine Hot Springs in Alaska, which they believe were given to them by the Creator to protect. To truly appreciate the rich diversity of American history, we must think about heritage preservation not only in terms of structures but also in terms of the ancient Hawaiian hula dance, the annual Crow Fair at Crow Agency near Harding, Montana (the largest seasonal tepee encampment in the world), and the Ute Trail in western Colorado, possibly the longest and highest Indian trail left intact in the United States.

Much of the Native American past has been saved, but even more has been lost. Consequently, even as we support the preservation of tribal traditions, we must also acknowledge the tragedies of massacre sites and the theft of sacred property. As a nation, we must reconcile a brutal past with the present because for native peoples time cannot be divided into "then" and "now." American Indians once roamed and hunted on two billion acres of the American landscape; today, they own less than 2 percent of the land they once inhabited. In the Northwest Ordinance of 1787, Congress promised that "the utmost good faith shall always be observed towards the Indians" and declared that "their lands and property shall never be taken from them without their consent; and, in their property, rights and liberty, they shall never be invaded or disturbed."[4] However, as Sioux chief Red Cloud observed, "[whites] made us many promises, more than I can remember, but they never kept but one; they promised to take our land and they took it."[5]

Today, Indian communities are defined by the native peoples who live in them, not just by contiguous blocks of land. Present-day Indians reside everywhere. Some live in cities and small towns, in tightly-knit communities, such as the Mississippi Choctaw who migrated to Tennessee during the Great Depression or the Wampanoag Indians who occupy 160 acres of tribal land on Martha's Vineyard Island. Others live on vast reservations in the West, such as the Navajo whose reservation sprawls across 17.5 million acres in New Mexico, Utah, Colorado, and Arizona.

Some tribes have reconstituted themselves and now are federally recognized. Among these are the Tunica-Biloxi in Louisiana, who own just 160 acres of their original lands as measured in square leagues by French explorers three centuries ago. And because so much Indian title to land has been lost, especially for the eastern tribes, sacred sites and shrines may be hundreds of miles from where tribal peoples live; the Zuni Indians of New Mexico and the Hopi of Arizona, for example, feel responsible for ancient shrines that lie far from the present boundaries of their pueblos. Thus, as Weldon Johnson of the Colorado River Indian Tribes explained, "our starting point in our cultural resources program is that we never did give up ownership of cultural resources off the reservation."[6] Peter Jemison of the Seneca stated that "my tribe has lived for 300 years away from the land base where I now work," adding that "the [Seneca] Nation brings children to the site and I tell them, 'from the time you left home two and a half hours ago, you never left your original territory.' "[7] The Stockbridge-Munsee Band of Mohicans have lived in Wisconsin, but their roots are in Massachusetts. After a pilgrimage back to Stockbridge, Steven James David wrote, "While [there], the moments that I will never forget are the tobacco offering we did at our ancient burial grounds and climbing Monument Mountain. When we finally reached the top, we were out of breath and my chest filled both with pride and sorrow. Pride because my ancestors chose a most beautiful place to call home and sorrow because they weren't able to keep it, and we weren't able to keep all of the rich culture that was ours."[8]

For native peoples, centuries of oppression have not been forgotten. In California during the gold rush, miners hunted and killed Indians and forced others into a form of slavery. In later decades, the killing stopped, as did forced servitude, but the theft of tribal lands continued. In Nevada, the Western Shoshone Tribe still insists on tribal boundaries set by the 1863 Treaty of Ruby Valley, which the government does not honor. And at Fort Washakie, Wyoming, the Eastern Shoshone

1992
The Year of the Anti-Celebration

1992
IMPORTANT DATES

≈ JUNE 26 ≈
(Anniversary of the Pine Ridge shoot-out)
INTERNATIONAL SOLIDARITY WITH Leonard Peltier Day

≈ JULY 6 ≈
(Anniversary of the Big Mountain deadline)
•••INTERNATIONAL•••
Big Mountain Day

≈ OCT. 12 ≈
International Anti-Celebration of Columbus— Solidarity with 500 YEARS of Indians Resistance.

For more information write:
Support For Native Sovereignty
post office box 2104
Seattle, Washington 98101

THE INVASION NEVER ENDED!!!

FREE LEONARD PELTIER!
FREE EDDIE HATCHER!
FREE RED KNIFE!

SUPPORT INDIAN LAND STRUGGLES!

BIG MOUNTAIN, WESTERN SHOSHONE, MOHAWKS, LUBICONS, PEIGANS, Lil'WAT, BLACKHILLS, BLACKFEET

COLUMBUS DIDN'T DISCOVER AMERICA.
He INVADED it.
1492-1992

Bayou La Rose
— support poster —
P.O. Box 5464
Tacoma, Wa.
98415-5464

1992—"The Year of the Anti-Celebration: Columbus Didn't Discover America—He Invaded It," a graphic art poster from the Northwest depicting local tribal sentiments about the 500-year anniversary of Christopher Columbus's arrival in the New World. Native peoples celebrated their survival, not his arrival. Negative anti-Columbus sentiments have now found positive expression in tribal preservation and museum programs and in respect for Indian elders. Poster by Bayou La Rose, Tacoma, Washington, 1992.

Chief Washakie of the Wind River Shoshone in Wyoming stands with missionary women who seek his support for the idea of sending Shoshone children to school. Reluctantly, the chief agreed to their proposal, but he knew that it would result in the loss of many tribal traditions and that children would be separated from their families. Courtesy, American Heritage Center, University of Wyoming.

The former Episcopal Mission Boarding School on the Wind River Reservation near Fort Washakie, Wyoming, is boarded up and in need of repair. For some Indians, attending boarding school was a satisfying, enriching experience, but for others, it brought despair and deep loneliness as old ways were forgotten and new ways were forced on unwilling children. Photo by author, September 1998.

remember that in the nineteenth century, their reservation of forty-four million acres shrank to twelve million in just five years.

Land is but one dimension of the dilemma facing native peoples today, for, as Alvin Josephy wrote, "White teachers and missionaries, in particular, deriding or ignoring the Indians' past have robbed Indians of their inheritance, destroying their pride in themselves and undermining their sense of identity."[9] Until the 1930s, scholars, teachers, and non-native Indian experts insisted that Indians would assimilate into the American mainstream, but they did not. Despite forced attempts at cultural assimilation from the 1870s well into the 1950s, Native

Americans, Native Alaskans, and Native Hawaiians still have separate and distinct cultural identities. Moreover, Indian people have been subjected to an American educational system that forced them to cut their hair and deny their language and oral traditions; it also separated families by compelling children to attend boarding schools far from their homelands. On returning, many young men and women were total strangers to their grandparents; they could not even speak to their elders because they had forgotten much of their native language.

Thousands of American Indians died from the onslaught of European diseases, and though tribes attempted to maintain their sense of community and traditions in subsequent generations, U.S. federal government policy as late as 1952 urged the "termination" of tribal peoples and their relocation into American urban centers.[10] Many Indian nations are still reeling from these government-sponsored actions. Apesanahkwat, the former tribal chairman of the Menominee Indian Tribe of Wisconsin, wrote, "Through the periods of ceding aboriginal lands, relocation, termination of tribal status, restoration and now treaty abrogations, the Menominee Tribe has lost much of its cultural heritage and identity." He added, "The possibility of losing Menominee culture and values completely, looms heavily in the minds and hearts of the Menominee people."[11]

In *Native American Tribalism*, D'Arcy McNickle aptly noted that "until the third decade of the present century Indian policy was rooted in the assumption that the Indians would disappear. Authorities responsible for policy continued to refer to a diminishing population long after the growth had turned upward." He also pointed out that because the federal government mistakenly assumed Indians represented a vanishing race, "nothing was invested in the development of tribal and individual resources."[12]

In today's society, the need for tribal preservation and the maintenance of tradition are essential if Native American customs and beliefs are to be passed on to the younger generation. Yet, given all that Indians have lost, the challenge is formidable—a point made clear by numerous native spokespeople. Representatives of the Pyramid Lake Paiute Tribe from California, for instance, observed that it is "hard to recreate the lost culture." The goal for the Mashantucket Pequot of Massachusetts is "to reconstruct from the vast fragmented pieces the threads of our shattered history."[13] And writing for the Coyote Valley Tribal Council in Redwood Valley, California, Priscilla Hunter explained, "In Mendocino County where the Coyote Valley Reservation is located, our people have experienced a century and a half of oppression so severe that much of our cultural heritage is all but destroyed. What knowledge is left of our ceremonies, traditional arts, foods, and medicines, historic properties and our language, is in critical need of being documented, preserved, and passed on to our children so that they may understand who they are, where they come from, and what makes them unique." She added, "By instilling a sense of cultural pride in our young people we can give them the strength they will need to become productive and healthy adults."[14]

Though some tribes are flourishing, many Native Americans face ongoing problems with alcoholism, disease, unemployment, and infant mortality. High levels of accidents, obesity, diabetes, hypertension, and early death on reservations have been well documented; indeed, the average age of an Indian male at death is only fifty, compared to seventy-six for the average American white male.

Patricia Parker, of the National Park Service, has argued that "preservation of heritage is seen as a key to fighting such contemporary problems as alcoholism and drug abuse, which flourish where society is in stress." She added, "Preservation can help to restore structure and pride to tribal society, providing direction from the past that is vital to the future."[15] Mental and physical health is intimately linked to self-identity, and a sense of pride in the past is a bulwark against the uncertainties of the future. "The problems that the youth are having in most cases are related to a cultural vacuum [as is] the high degree of alcoholism," stated Parris Butler from Fort Mohave.[16] Native peoples must learn their history and traditions to gain a stronger tribal identity and to cope better with a dominant, competitive, capitalist culture so different from the ancient cooperative ways of Indian life. Preserving sacred sites is part of that process.

One aspect of tribal preservation involves safeguarding physical landmarks and living traditions, and across the United States, sacred and special rocks with ancient carved petroglyphs or pictographs have been protected (although vandalism at Indian sites persists). Another aspect involves returning artifacts and information taken by white scholars decades ago. Many accounts of Indian rituals and thousands of artifacts and objects have been collected and stored in museums, universities, and archives located far from tribal peoples, but now, because of reverse anthropology and reverse archaeology, those cultural treasures are going home. Instead of taking from tribes, archaeologists and anthropologists are giving back. For example, sound recordings of Indian chants and dances once housed in the Library of Congress's American Folklife Center have been returned to tribes, along with field notes from the original collectors. Tribal members and Indian children can learn a good deal about themselves by listening to songs sung by their great-great-grandfathers.

In addition, archaeologists now help tribes establish their own preservation offices, and anthropologists and linguists assist tribes in starting language programs. Producing phonetic tribal dictionaries is a major accomplishment of the language certification committees that are hurrying to preserve tribal languages before the last of the native speakers pass on. For many Native Americans, language preservation is far more important than saving buildings or structures because the spoken word and oral tradition embody the full history of the tribe in stories

Alice C. Fletcher with Meepe and Martha, two women who pitched and kept the tent for the allotting agents in the field. Fletcher served as special agent to the Winnebago from 1887 to 1889 and inadvertently helped to weaken their culture by encouraging tribal members to take private property from communal Indian landholdings, rather than leaving their land in tribal trust status. Under the Dawes Act, passed by Congress in 1887, Indians lost 65 percent of the land they once owned because so much tribal land became private property and was then acquired by whites for back taxes or very few dollars per acre. Courtesy, Smithsonian National Anthropological Archives, no. 4439.

Frances Densmore with Mountain Chief, a Blackfoot Indian, who interprets in sign language a song being played on a phonograph, ca. 1916. Densmore captured on wax cylinders hundreds of Indian songs from numerous tribes, including the Sioux, Blackfeet, Seminole, and Lac Du Flambeau. Staff members at the American Folklife Center have returned those songs to the tribes on cassette tapes and records, and young Native Americans are now learning the traditional songs to play with their drum groups. Courtesy, Smithsonian National Anthropological Archives, no. 55,300.

John P. Harrington, Bureau of American Ethnology linguist, making records of language and songs with Margarita Campos (seated) and (standing, left to right) Alfred Robinson, interpreter, and James Perry, Washington, D.C., 1924. Courtesy, Smithsonian National Anthropological Archives, no. 4305-A.

and legends and because only a handful of the elderly can still converse easily in native dialects.

Although some knowledge is sacred and not meant to be shared with people outside the tribe, tribal preservation also requires exchanging information with nonnatives and noting locations, taking photographs, creating maps, setting up museum displays, and talking to elders. For many native peoples, these are new skills to be learned as they seek hegemony over their own cultural history, protection of their religious objects from theft, and preservation of their sacred sites.

This book explains tribal attitudes toward the preservation of culture and discusses federal legislation such as the Antiquities Act (1906); the National Historic Preservation Act (NHPA, 1966), with its recent amendments (1992); the American Indian Religious Freedom Act (AIRFA, 1978); the Archaeological Resources Protection Act (ARPA, 1979, and amended in 1989); the Native American Graves Protection and Repatriation Act (NAGPRA, 1990); and President William Clinton's

Executive Order No. 13007 of May 1996 protecting Native American sacred sites located on public lands.

Chapter 1 looks at "bones of contention" and the successful crusade of tribal peoples to have the human remains of their ancestors returned for proper burial. In 1868 during the Plains Indian Wars, a directive from the Army Medical College specifically requested that battlefield "specimens" be sent to Washington, D.C., which led to the decapitation of Indian corpses by U.S. Army soldiers. At the height of the nineteenth-century preoccupation with race and racial classification, museums around the world competed to gather native artifact collections and native bones. Now, at last, some of those human remains are returning to their proper homes so that spirits and relatives can rest in peace. The Native American commentaries that conclude this chapter vividly illustrate why this is important, though the controversy with physical anthropologists continues. Provisions of the Native American Graves Protection and Repatriation Act will soon be tested in federal court.

Chapter 2 focuses on museums and the curation of sacred objects, examining the ways in which native peoples seek repatriation to their own tribal museums of sacred objects such as the centuries-old Omaha Shaman Pole and the White Buffalo Skin. Commentaries in this chapter include an analysis of a sacred Pawnee medicine bundle unopened since a high plains massacre in 1873, as well as an Apache Gaan Dancer's mask not yet returned to its tribe of origin.

Chapter 3 describes landscapes sacred to native peoples and explains the need to protect special mountains, buttes, canyons, springs, and waterfalls. Many Indian sacred sites are powerful places, and visitors are encouraged to approach them respectfully. Younger tribal members who accept the responsibility of protecting such sacred landscapes undergo a lengthy initiation into rituals and traditions and serve a long apprenticeship with elders. Chapter commentaries include Hopi, Navajo, and Zuni statements on preservation philosophy and the sacredness of sites. The chapter concludes with a nonnative archaeologist's vivid description of working with Wyoming tribes.

Chapter 4 discusses tribal preservation offices, whose staff members work to preserve sacred and cultural sites and perform a host of other duties. Because tribes build relationships with individuals instead of institutions, establishing trust in handling sensitive data is a critical issue. In addition, provocative questions must be addressed regarding how to identify and protect sacred sites on public lands while also retaining the confidentiality of the sites' locations. This chapter's case studies on sacred site protection include descriptions of the Bighorn Medicine Wheel National Historic Landmark, Bear Butte in South Dakota, the misnamed Devils Tower National Monument, and others.

Chapter 5 concludes the book with a discussion on living tribal cultures and the empowerment of native peoples as they develop successful strategies to carry tribal preservation into the future. They are doing this with innovative yet traditional programs, such as building dugout canoes on the Northwest Coast or establishing tribal buffalo herds on the Great Plains. Indians must also wrestle with the difficult issue of who is and who is not a tribal member and what to do about "wanna-be" Indians or nonnatives who misuse sacred locations and debase Indian religion by creating artificial vision quest sites or conducting inauthentic sweat lodge ceremonies. Sadly, some Native Americans themselves also improperly sponsor ceremonies without having the authority or training to do so. Such ceremonies are especially irritating to elders if nonnatives are allowed to participate for a sizable cash fee.

Major controversies persist among tribes long exposed to Christian missionaries and Christianity as to the relevance and utility of returning to ancient traditions. As ethnohistorian Clyde Ellis wrote, "Contention and discussion about these things doesn't fall along a strictly white/ Indian fault line." The Kiowa have disagreed over reinstituting the Sun Dance, and the Omaha Tribe had an internal debate about whether (and how) to accept the return of the Sacred Pole from the Peabody Museum.[17] Ellis cautioned that a renaissance of old traditions results in complicated issues "inside Indian communities" and stressed that we need "to resist flattening the details of cultural encounter and negotiation."[18] Because such cultural compression will inevitably occur within a book of this scope, I have included case studies that offer specific examples of repatriation and sacred site protection. Though there are references to sacred sites in the eastern United States, most of the examples and case studies are from the West, where "Indian Country" remains more intact than it does east of the Mississippi River.

In the introduction to *Vision Quest*, Vine Deloria Jr. observed that "a significant percentage of tribal enrollments today are mixed bloods, and as intermarriage outside the tribe increases, the computer can now project the day when the Indian genetic heritage will have vanished, leaving in its place a large population in which it is possible to trace Indian ancestry but only as a remote factor in the creation of families and individuals." He added that today, as in past centuries, "the tribal traditions, not the genetics, [hold] people together."[19]

Tribal preservation is an affirmation of living traditions. It is about maintaining the old ways and remaining connected to Indian identity and the power of place. While researching and writing this book, I was invited to join a Ute family for the Northern Ute Sun Dance at Fort Duchesne, Utah. Each year, the plains and mountain tribes build the Sun Dance lodge anew under the direction of a Sun Dance chief, replicating an ancient ceremony. What is important to tribal members is not just the structure of the lodge or the sacred center pole but also the ritual of renewal. During this ceremony, dedicated men dance barechested, moving back and forth to an incessant, rhythmic drumbeat. They blow eaglebone whistles adorned with eagle plumes that vibrate with shrill sounds, and they send prayers upward to the Creator. The

Northern Ute Sun Dancers vow to help the community by personally sacrificing themselves through fasts, prayers, and the rigor of sustained dancing, without food or water, for up to four days in the heat of mid-July. They dance from Friday at sundown to midday on Monday, with occasional rests but always without sustenance or liquids of any kind.

After a long night of dancing, all was quiet before dawn. Standing at the entrance to the Sun Dance lodge, the Ute elders and family members and I waited for the first rays of light to top the eastern rim of the Uintah Mountains, welcoming the sun and blessing the Creator for another bountiful day.

Because the intensity of the dancers' devotion inspired my research and my writing, I respectfully offer this book as my small contribution toward preserving tribal traditions.

1

Bones of Contention
The Repatriation of Native American Human Remains

The Surgeon General is anxious that our collection of Indian crania,
already quite large, should be made as complete as possible.
—MADISON MILLS, surgeon, U.S. Army, January 13, 1868

White bones are reburied, tribal bones are studied in racist institutions.
. . . The tribal dead become the academic chattel, the aboriginal
bone slaves to advance archaeological technicism and the
political power of institutional science.
—GERALD VIZENOR, *Crossbloods*, 1976

Of all the cultural resource issues affecting Indian tribes today, none
is more complicated than the return and reburial of human
remains. Some tribes seek to rebury all their ancestors on tribal lands.
Others are not concerned with having bones reburied but are keenly
interested in claiming unidentified remains found on public land for
various reasons, including the assertion of expanded territorial boundaries, the settlement of land claims disputes, and as a means to achieve
tribal recognition. This chapter explores the history of the collection of
Native American skeletons and explains the unintended effects of
recent legislation that was passed to help return Indian remains to tribal
hands.

During the nineteenth century, no Indian society was left unmo-
lested in the race to systematically collect and classify human remains
from all American aboriginal cultures. The same nineteenth-century
mind-set that regarded tribal peoples as "savages" saw their human
remains as worthy of scientific inquiry (but not respect). As Indians
were being killed on battlefields and forced onto reservations, native
bones were collected, examined, and then placed in long-term permanent storage in hundreds of private collections or in the U.S. Army
Medical College in Washington, D.C.

In 1988, the American Association of Museums reported to the
Senate Select Committee on Indian Affairs that 163 museums held 43,306
Native American skeletal remains.[1] The Smithsonian Institution alone

had 18,600 American Indian and Alaskan native remains and thousands of burial artifacts. Indian activist Susan Shown Harjo explained that Indians were "further dehumanized by being exhibited alongside mastodons and dinosaurs and other extinct creatures."[2] For most of America's native peoples, no issue has touched a more sensitive chord than these disrespectful nineteenth-century collecting practices. For that reason, the repatriation of human remains to their tribes of origin for reburial is one of the most important cultural resource issues today.

Many Indians seek to rescue their ancestors' remains from what they believe to have been dubious and prolonged scientific research. As Curtis M. Hinsley noted, "The painful and immensely complex matter of repatriation of bones and burial goods has become an issue extending beyond proprietorship per se; indeed, the debate is ultimately not over control of bones at all, but over control of narrative: the stories of peoples who went before and how those peoples (and their descendants) are to be currently represented and treated." "The heart of the matter," he added, "as always, lies in the negotiation between power and respect."[3]

As early as 1972, anthropologists and Indian people cooperated in the reburial of Narrangansett remains.[4] In the late 1980s, major protests by Native Americans and the national exposure of commercial grave-robbing incidents, such as the devastation of Slack Farm in Kentucky, brought repatriation to the forefront of public discourse. In 1989, sympathy and understanding for native issues prompted Congress to pass the National Museum of the American Indian (NMAI) Act to create an Indian museum in the last space available on the mall in Washington, D.C. The NMAI Act helped solidify a constituency that pushed for a broad national law to redress a century of Indian grave robbing.

After years of intense wrangling and dissension among college professors, archaeologists, museum directors, and native tribes, Congress passed the Native American Graves Protection and Repatriation Act (NAGPRA) in 1990. This act required all museums and facilities receiving federal funds to inventory human remains and associated burial goods in their collections and to notify modern tribal descendants about the institutions' findings by November 1995.[5] The burden of notification was placed on the museums, and native peoples were allowed to choose which materials, if any, they wished to consider for repatriation. The bill represented a major victory for native peoples: it is a significant piece of human rights legislation that permits the living to reassert control over their own dead.

At issue has been not just the interests of science versus the interests of descendants but also, as many Indians see it, "the rights of the dead themselves, toward whom the living bear responsibility."[6] Cultural resources consultant Thomas King explained, "The living are responsible for the dead, and the dead—often seen not as being really 'dead' but as transformed, and still powerful—must be treated with respect."[7] In testimony prepared for the U.S. Senate, University of Colorado anthropologist Deward Walker stated: "Everywhere in Native North America one encounters a great religious importance attached to the dead who are believed to have a continuing influence on the lives of their descendants and other survivors." He continued: "Given proper rituals and proper respect, [the dead] are believed to provide assistance in curing illnesses, in determining the future, in guaranteeing the outcome of risky events, and in other general ways helping make the lives of the living more secure."[8]

Scientific theories of the nineteenth century supported notions of nonwhite inferiority and denied Indians their religious beliefs and their humanity. Robert Bieder noted that in the second and third decades of the nineteenth century, "critics pointed out that neither Africans nor Indians could ever advance beyond their allegedly low mental states and must either be kept in slavery or exterminated (or allowed to pass into extinction) in order to make room for progress."[9] Providing scientific "proof" of nonwhite inferiority became an international undertaking that involved linking the "science" of craniology with "the politics of colonial exploitation."[10]

Racial Hierarchies

Contemporaneous with the idea of a rigid racial hierarchy was the belief that each race had a uniquely shaped skull. In 1823, Samuel Morton, the founder of physical anthropology in America, began to teach at the Philadelphia Hospital and Pennsylvania College, where he actively solicited skulls to add to his collections. The appropriation of human specimens enabled Morton to publish his *Crania Americana* in 1839, which supposedly validated racial prejudice and determined that Caucasians had a brain capacity of 87 cubic inches whereas American Indian skulls, as judged by 147 samples, had a capacity of only 82 cubic inches.[11]

Collecting skulls continued as a hobby of gentlemen. For example, clergyman Orson S. Fowler managed a large skull library in New York City. He and others of his time advocated the ideas advanced by Austrian Joseph Gall and German Johann G. Spurzheim, who believed that cranial capacity and brain size determined intelligence: the most intelligent or civilized race—that of white men—must therefore have the largest brains. By measuring the volume of cranial capacity in skulls, Fowler, building on the work of Samuel Morton, believed he could scientifically prove the superiority of the white race. The supposed link between skull size, brain capacity, intelligence, and race led to the wholesale looting of thousands of Indian burials and a brisk "scientific" trade in human remains from the 1830s to the 1930s.

Though all sorts of human remains and cadavers were used in early medical schools, including the bodies of paupers and poor whites, collectors developed a preference for Native American skeletal material because it was easily obtainable without the moral taint and illegality associated with stealing from Caucasian graves. Indian skulls had a dollar value, and amateur scientists or philosophers collected them and other relics much as one would collect butterflies. It is no accident that vast collections of skeletal remains, grave goods, and Indian artifacts came to repose in the Smithsonian Institution's National Museum of Natural History (NMNH), along with elephant tusks, ostrich eggs, and reptile skins. The robbing of Indian graves became a fashionable gentleman's avocation in the pursuit of knowledge. Enthusiasts exchanged letters, field notes, and even skulls.[12]

Collecting Skeletons for the U.S. Army

The acquisition of Indian skulls for scientific study eventually became institutionalized. On May 21, 1862, Surgeon General William A. Hammond established the Army Medical Museum. He ordered all medical officers "diligently to collect, and to forward to the office of the Surgeon General, all specimens of morbid anatomy, surgical or medical, which may be regarded as valuable. . . . These objects should be accompanied by short explanatory notes." As an added inducement, the surgeon general stated, "Each specimen in the collection will have appended the name of the medical officer by whom it was prepared."[13] Two years later, when Col. John M. Chivington and his drunken troops killed Cheyenne Indians in the infamous dawn massacre at Sand Creek, Colorado, the troops also cut off their victims' heads for shipment to Washington, D.C.[14]

In January 1865, Harvard University zoologist Louis Agassiz reminded Secretary of War Edwin Stanton that he had promised to let him "have the bodies of some Indians; if any should die at this time . . . all that would be necessary . . . would be to forward the body express in a box. . . . In case the weather was not very cold . . . direct the surgeon in charge to inject through the carotids a solution of arsenate of soda." Agassiz added, "I should like one or two handsome fellows entire and the heads of two or three more."[15]

Three years later, on January 13, 1868, an additional request went out from the U.S. Army "urging upon the medical officers . . . the importance of collecting for the Army Medical Museum specimens of Indian crania and of Indian weapons and utensils, so far as they may be able to procure them."[16] Personal letters had been mailed to most of the army medical officers "stationed in the Indian country," but Madison Mills appealed to "Acting Assistant Surgeons who would doubtless collect such things if they knew they were desired." He explained that "the Surgeon General is anxious that our collection of Indian crania, already quite large, should be made as complete as possible."[17] The Army Medical College believed that "making this task obligatory might make it distasteful," but to facilitate voluntary collecting, Mills noted that "when the collection of these things involves a pecuniary outlay that cannot be met otherwise, the Surgeon General sanctions a disbursement from the Museum Fund to reimburse such outlay—to a judicious extent."[18]

Thus, in the same year that army representatives sought to negoti-
ate the significant Fort Laramie Treaty of 1868, another branch of the
military actively encouraged the robbing of Indian graves. A military
secretary sent handwritten copies of the surgeon general's letter to the
Department of the Missouri at Fort Leavenworth, Kansas; to the
Department of the Platte at Omaha, Nebraska; to the Department of
Dakota at Fort Snelling, Minnesota; and to the Department of New
Mexico at Santa Fe. At some frontier posts, collecting Indian skulls
became a cottage industry, and the Plains Indian Wars included battlefield decapitations.

Collectors also looted ancient and prehistoric burials. Warren K.
Moorehead shipped hundreds of Indian remains to Chicago for the 1893
World's Columbian Exposition, an unabashed celebration of the triumph
of American civilization. Many of these bones and artifacts became the
property of the Field Museum of Natural History. Nineteenth-century
competition for collections pitted the Peabody Museum of Harvard
University against the Smithsonian Institution, and several institutions
contended for control of burial mounds. The sharpest competition erupted
between the Field Museum and New York City's American Museum of
Natural History over access to Northwest Coast skeletons and artifacts,
which had become highly profitable for collectors—skulls were fetching
$5 each and complete skeletons $20 apiece.[19]

Franz Boas, the father of cultural anthropology and an advocate of
cultural relativity, apparently did not see the contradiction between his
high regard for native Northwest cultures and his disregard for their
beliefs about the dead. To help pay for his fieldwork, he sought to collect
and sell Indian skulls. After admitting that "it is most unpleasant work
to steal bones from a grave," he went on to state, "but what is the use,
someone has to do it."[20] Boas wrote to the Smithsonian to explore their
willingness to buy skulls. When word came back in the affirmative, he
collected 100 complete skeletons and 200 crania and kept acquiring human remains until he had 179 samples from Northwest Coast Salish and
Kwakiutl Tribes. These eventually came to reside at the Field Museum. He sold another large collection in Berlin. Turf wars ensued as
museums staked their claims to American geographic regions and
Indian cultures whose human remains and artifacts became scientific
"trophies."[21]

In 1891, the Peabody Museum at Harvard University hired Boas to
organize the Northwest Coast exhibit for the World's Columbian Exposition in Chicago, where he came into direct competition with George
A. Dorsey, the curator of anthropology at the Field Museum. Traveling
by train to the Northwest, Dorsey stopped off in Browning, Montana, to
raid remains of the Blackfeet, who had suffered and died on Ghost Ridge
during the starvation winter of 1883–1884. Almost one-fourth of the
Blackfeet Tribe weakened and died in the bitter cold that winter, and
Dorsey came along seven years later to loot the shallow graves, seeking

specimens for shipment to Chicago. Thirty-five skeletons eventually arrived at the Field Museum.[22]

In 1896, Arctic explorer Robert E. Peary took living specimens to New York City's American Museum of Natural History for scientific measurements performed by Aleš Hardlička, a colleague of Boas's. According to Douglas Preston, when four of the six Eskimos from Greenland developed tuberculosis and died, this was considered "a splendid, unparalleled opportunity to add postmortem data to their Eskimo file." In fact, "Hardlička directed that all four be macerated, boiled, and reduced to skeletons at the College of Physicians and Surgeons of Columbia University." As a final gesture, "he then installed the skeletons in the museum's collections where he could study them at leisure."[23]

Two years later, in 1898, the Army Medical Museum donated over 2,000 crania, and most of the skulls and skeletons remained in storage in the National Museum of Natural History of the Smithsonian Institution. Looting continued unabated. Between 1931 and 1936, Aleš Hardlička of the Smithsonian's Department of Anthropology traveled to the Larsen Bay Village of Kodiak Island, Alaska, and, aided by a white cannery worker and other field staff, exhumed and carried away 800 dead bodies and over 1,000 burial offerings.[24]

As with most such "collections," the bones were kept in storage and were not open to public view. But while scientists beginning the field of physical anthropology studied human remains in laboratory settings, skeletons also became tourist attractions. Scientists sought to confirm ideas about race and intelligence using Indian skeletons; tourists just wanted to gawk. Across the United States, ancient Indian burial sites fell into the hands of petty promoters who saw the rise of automobile tourism in the 1920s and the morbid fascination with death as means to make a dollar.

Displaying Ancient Skeletons for Tourists

During the 1930s in Wickliffe, Kentucky, near the confluence of the Ohio and Mississippi Rivers, amateur archaeologists excavated an ancient prehistoric burial ground of the Mississippian people and operated it as one of the largest and best-known open burial displays in the nation. Promoter Fain King labeled the site "King Mounds" and popularized it as an "ancient buried city," complete with "tombs, temples, altars, jewels, dwellings, and tools."[25] The deceased had been carefully interred, but beginning in the 1930s, lurid advertising, sensationalist interpretation, and disdain for archaeological or museum expertise characterized King Mounds, which featured over 150 Indian skeletons exposed atop earth daises under a tin roof, with grave goods scattered about. Fain King charged admission to ogling tourists and in turn sold them purloined Indian artifacts.[26]

A similar tourist site near Salina, Kansas, displayed the shellacked bones of Pawnee Indians who had died 600 years earlier. Four miles

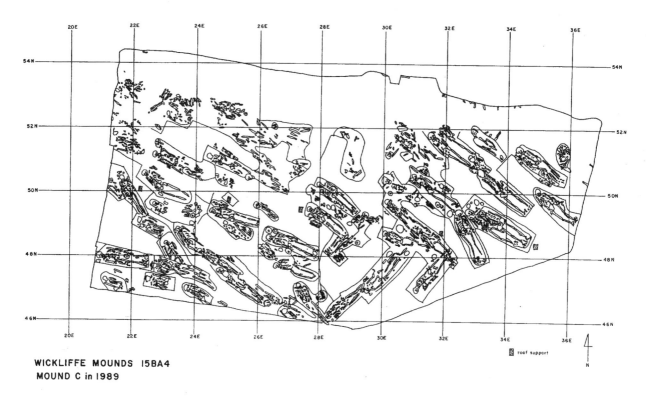

WICKLIFFE MOUNDS 15BA4
MOUND C in 1989

outside of Salina, the Price brothers' "Indian Burial Pits" could be viewed for $3.50 per person. The bones had been dug up in 1936 by an amateur archaeologist. "We took care of the bones," proprietor Howard Price said. "Every year we varnished them so they wouldn't deteriorate."[27] Amateurs in the Mimbres Valley of New Mexico also "dug" Indian ruins in the 1930s and had "skeleton picnics" in their frantic pursuit of pre-historic ceramic pottery. As they searched for Mimbres classic black-on-white burial bowls, these pothunters routinely discarded Indian bones and scattered them across the landscape.[28]

In Illinois, the state park system lent its imprimatur to public displays of Indian human remains by making Dickson Mounds a state park, regularly visited by 80,000 tourists and school groups who came to stare at exposed Indian dead.[29] Excavated in 1927 near Lewistown, Illinois, the mounds featured the open burial site of 237 people who had occupied the Illinois River valley between 800 and 1,000 years earlier. Purchased by the state in 1945, Dickson Mounds Museum became a popular tourist attraction.

But by the late 1980s, the question of the rights of science and physical anthropology versus the rights of the dead and their descendants became a critical issue, pitting the discipline of physical anthropology against the deep religious convictions of Native Americans. In the face of Indian demands for repatriation, museum boards of directors and curators of anthropology argued that museums had a "proprietary right" to maintain the items in their collections. Local citizens also

Native Americans prefer that photographs of their ancestral dead not be published or exhibited. Line drawings, however, are permissible. This is a drawing of ancient Mississippian human remains previously exposed at the Wickliffe Mounds Research Center of Murray State University in Kentucky. The remains are no longer displayed. Courtesy, Kit Wesler, director, Wickliffe Mounds.

defended their right to visit exposed Indian burials.[30] For Native Americans, legal redress came slowly.

Lawsuits and Resolutions to Protect Their Ancestors

Beginning with the 1888 lawsuit filed by the Cowichan Tribe in the Northwest against James Hutton, who had been "collecting" for Franz Boas, Indians decried the desecration, looting, and robbery of their ancestors.[31] But native protests remained scattered and ineffective throughout the first half of the twentieth century and the years of forced Americanization, during which Indian agents and missionaries insisted that tribal members join the mainstream culture. Later came the urban resettlement of Indians after World War II and tribal "termination," or the ending of official tribal status for specifically targeted Indian groups that were rich in natural resources. With the impact of the tribal sovereignty movement and Indian self-determination in the 1970s, the issue of caring for human remains gathered momentum. By the mid-1980s, American Indians, Alaska natives, and Native Hawaiians sought the return of their ancestral remains through lawsuits and eloquent pleas to legislators and museum board members.

In June 1986, the Skokomish Tribe of Shelton, Washington, passed Resolution No. 86-37, which stated that "the necessary time for holding these human remains for scientific inquiry has expired" and "the practice of keeping Native American skeletons for further study is in conflict with our tribe's cultural and moral beliefs, and is in total disregard to the rights, dignity, and respect that all human beings in the United States of America enjoy under the Constitution."[32] The tribal council demanded the immediate return of Skokomish-Twana Indian remains by the Smithsonian Institution. Other tribes, including the Pawnee Indians of Oklahoma and Kodiak Island natives from Alaska, also asked for the return of their ancestors' remains.

On May 29, 1987, the Larsen Bay Tribal Council in Alaska passed a resolution seeking the return of human remains because "we honor and respect our ancestors and their traditional ways, which enrich our personal and spiritual lives today as they will strengthen the lives of our children and our children's children in years to come." The resolution stated: "The skeletal remains, burial objects, and artifacts held by the Smithsonian Institution belong to us, the Native people of Larsen Bay and Uyak Bay, who have the traditional right and spiritual responsibility to reinter our ancestors' remains, burial objects, and other artifacts."[33] Legal expenses for the Quikertarmiut would exceed $100,000 before the case was closed, but as Gordon Pullar explained, "the repatriation issue was closely related to efforts to promote a strong identity and self-esteem among youth through cultural revitalization on Kodiak Island." Scientists and villagers had "a fundamental difference in world views," he observed. "Indigenous people and western science have very different ways of seeing time, family, and the universe." Ancient skeletal remains

MORE "WHISPERS FROM THE PRAIRIE"

LET MY
ANCESTORS GO...

©'89 JOURNAL-STAR PRINTING CO.

LINCOLN JOURNAL 1-24

One of the significant legal contests that established precedence for the Native American Graves Protection and Repatriation Act of 1990 occurred in Nebraska when Pawnee demanded their ancestors be reinterred, against the wishes of the Nebraska State Historical Society. After the society refused to honor tribal traditions, public opinion rallied on behalf of the tribe, and the cultural conflict has since been resolved. Courtesy, Paul Fell for the *Nebraska Journal-Star*; original in the possession of Walter Echo-Hawk, Native American Rights Foundation, Boulder, Colorado.

are "resources" for scientists, but they are relatives for living tribal peoples. Pullar expressed an important element of native belief when he wrote, "We must respect our ancestors as they are still with us."[34]

Controversy and the Smithsonian

In 1987, in the middle of this controversy, Secretary of the Smithsonian Institution Robert McCormick Adams asked the U.S. Senate to support a National Museum of the American Indian authorization bill, which would create a national Indian museum. But he said he was not willing to repatriate the human remains of "individuals who cannot be directly identified."[35] Attorney Walter Echo-Hawk of the Native American Rights Foundation in Boulder, Colorado, favored a new Indian museum but complained of "the deplorable fact that the Smithsonian is America's largest Indian graveyard in possession of almost 19,000 dead Indian bodies."[36] In Senate testimony, Echo-Hawk said, "It is therefore critical, as a matter of moral consistency, that the founding principles of the proposed museum, as well as its enabling legislation, cause the Museum to be built as 'a living memorial' to the Nation's First Citizens—and not be built upon a foundation of tens of thousands of dead bodies and over the sensibilities of the nearest living next of kin."[37]

Secretary Adams admitted that skeletons in the Smithsonian's collection had been acquired under unscrupulous circumstances: "Some officers were excessive in their zeal to collect, robbing fresh graves or forwarding battlefield finds and the remains of Indians who died while Army prisoners."[38] Yet, as an archaeologist himself, he argued for "the claims of science" and stated that the Smithsonian's collection existed

In the Southwest, pothunters locate remote prehistoric Indian villages on public lands and indiscriminately dig for valuable ceramics and casually discard human remains. This vandalized site in the Burro Mountains near Silver City, New Mexico, became the focus of a federal Archaeological Resources Protection Act case against the vandal, while a cultural resources team from the U.S. Forest Service, the Bureau of Land Management, and the National Park Service tried to glean as much information as possible in a salvage operation before backfilling the site. Photo by author, 1989.

"to enable scientists to learn about human adaptations and biology by studying living and past populations."[39] It is revealing to note that although native peoples represent less than 1 percent of today's American population and were an equally small demographic percentage a century ago, they represented 54.4 percent of the Smithsonian's collection of 34,000 human specimens; blacks represented 5.1 percent of the collections and whites 20 percent. Clearly, collecting specimens of Indian human anatomy was a racial and racist preference far in excess of any statistical Indian representation in the American population.

In 1988, the year after Adams's testimony, the Oglala Sioux Tribe requested the return of their honored dead, including three known individuals: Smoke, Black Feet, and Two Face. Severt Young Bear, an Oglala Sioux, explained that "Lakota view the spirit of a person as being entirely different from the Christian view. In Lakota, after death we take care of the spirit." He added, "If you disturb that spirit it starts wandering. The spirit of my grandfather Smoke is still walking back and forth from his [burial] hill to Washington."[40]

Thanks to the legal clout of the Native American Rights Fund, the state of Kansas and the Kansas State Historical Society agreed to close the "Indian Burial Pit" near Salina by virtue of a February 1989 agreement known as the Treaty of Smoky Hill. Additional arguments for repatriation came with the publication of Douglas Preston's article

"Skeletons in Our Museums' Closets" in the February 1989 issue of *Harper's Magazine*. Preston wrote, "To many Native Americans, the collecting of their ancestors' bones and bodies by museums is a source of pain and humiliation—the last stage of a conquest that had already robbed them of their lands and destroyed their way of life."[41]

Protecting Unmarked Graves

In March 1989, *National Geographic* published "Who Owns Our Past?" accompanied by stark photographs of wholesale commercial looting and grave robbing at the Slack Farm site in Kentucky, where 800 to 1,200 prehistoric bodies had been dug up over a two-year period in the mid-1980s for a $10,000 treasure hunters' fee.[42] If skulls could not be sold for candleholders or ashtrays, the looters smashed them. Despite these outrages, the grave robbers could only be charged with a misdemeanor offense because Kentucky lacked a burial statute protecting unmarked graves on private property. However, public opinion began to shift, and in May 1989, the Native American Rights Fund successfully represented the Winnebago and Pawnee Tribes in securing passage of the Unmarked Burial Sites and Skeletal Remains Protection Act in Nebraska.[43] At that time, over twenty states already had burial protection statutes for unmarked graves.[44] Local pothunters, a term used for thieves who dig up Indian graves in search of burial goods, expressed their antagonism to the law.

The author of the Colorado burial bill received an unmarked package at his legislative office containing a box of bones, a skull, and a complete, 1,000-year-old Anasazi skeleton wrapped in a Cortez, Colorado, newspaper; an attached typed note read, "This is none of your business."[45] In New Mexico, pothunters, knowing the new state law would take effect at midnight on a given day, worked around the clock with a small bulldozer to excavate the Croteau site in the Mimbres Valley.

NAGPRA protects burials on public lands, but each state must pass its own laws to protect unmarked burials on private land. Weeks before passage of the New Mexico Burial Bill, which protects unmarked graves, pothunters bulldozed an ancient Mimbres village site in the Mimbres Valley, adjacent to the Gila National Forest. Using a bulldozer to uncover Indian burials and rare pottery seems ludicrous, but pothunters worked on the Croteau site until midnight of the day before the law went into effect. Photo by author, 1989.

In their haste, the looters destroyed bones, bowls, and burial artifacts dug from the site, a Mimbres Indian village adjoining the Gila National Forest.[46]

Returning Human Remains

By the late 1980s, a few universities and museums acquiesced to public pressure, realizing it was past time to relinquish their collections of human remains. The Museum of New Mexico in Santa Fe drafted its own repatriation policy for the return of tribal human remains and grave goods, as did the Arizona State Museum in Tucson. In 1989, Stanford University agreed to return 550 Indian bodies to the Ohlone-Costanoan Tribe of California for reburial because the remains came from the tribe's historic areas.[47] When one anthropologist argued that "the proper owner of these remains is the scientific community," Rayna Green of the Smithsonian's National Museum of American History countered that most Indian remains "have no scientific value [because] a mere fraction of remains has ever been studied, period."[48] She explained, "These are human remains, not study specimens. There should not be endless research to benefit scholars without a compelling reason."[49] Most skeletal remains are now studied for biochemical and genetic analysis to trace the evolution of diseases and changes in diet, but they are then reburied.[50]

In Minnesota, the state legislature appropriated $90,000 over three years to study skeletons at a cost of $500 to $1,000 each prior to the University of Minnesota's relinquishing of 150 human remains to the Devil's Lake Sioux. Another 1,000 remains excavated from diverse Indian burial mounds were also studied and reburied.[51] In 1989, Seattle University returned 150 boxes of bones to Indian tribes in Washington State, and Omaha Indians received artifacts and human remains both from the University of Nebraska at Lincoln and from Harvard University's Peabody Museum.[52]

Then, in August 1989 at a special meeting between Indian tribes and Smithsonian representatives, including Secretary Robert Adams, an agreement was reached for the return of human remains and burial artifacts from the Smithsonian itself, provided they could be linked with "reasonable certainty" to present-day tribes.[53] By that date, twenty-two states had passed laws against disturbing unmarked Indian grave sites. In November 1989, President George Bush signed into law the National Museum of the American Indian Act, which established a new Indian museum as part of the Smithsonian Institution complex and mandated that the Smithsonian return human remains and associated and unassociated funerary objects to culturally affiliated Indian tribes.[54] Tribal members considered the Smithsonian concession a major victory for Indian rights, including the right of the dead to remain buried. Under Secretary Adams's direction, the Smithsonian organized a repatriation office to begin the long and complicated task of returning human remains and grave goods.[55]

Civil Rights for the Dead

Finally, in October 1990, President Bush signed into law the Native American Graves Protection and Repatriation Act, providing sanctity for unmarked graves on public land and the return of human remains and associated grave goods to their tribes of origin from any museum receiving federal funds.[56] A century after the theft of Blackfeet bones, Curly Bear Wagner, then cultural coordinator for the Blackfeet Tribe, and John "Buster" Yellow Kidney, a spiritual leader of the tribe, traveled to the Field Museum in Chicago to arrange for their ancestors' reburial. In 1991, Yellow Kidney commented that "returning remains to their rightful place has stirred a hot bed of political controversy both on and off the reservation," adding that "tribes are experiencing infighting and squabbling among themselves."[57] Some tribal members want human remains to return home so that the dead can rest in peace. Others fear that the dead may harass the living or that human remains might have been mixed up and the wrong bones might be returned. Tribal members do not want to accidentally bury on tribal soil the bones of their historic enemies.

Curly Bear Wagner stated firmly, "We believe the return will have a huge bearing on the future of our people. We feel their spirit is still roaming around. Elders feel this is the reason why the drugs and alcohol and all this misbehaving is going on." He concluded, "There are people who aren't at rest yet."[58] Earlier, the Blackfeet had sought the return of human remains from the Smithsonian Institution. Scientific research on the skeletal remains had proven to be an asset because positive genetic links could be made between living Blackfeet and human remains in the collection. An excellent example of cooperation between the Smithsonian and Indians involved the return to the Blackfeet of fifteen skulls stolen in 1892 and sent to the Army Medical College. Secretary Adams noted that the skulls had been collected "in an inappropriate manner," but he also added that the Blackfeet wanted positive identifications because "in 1892 there were open hostilities between themselves and many of their Indian neighbors, and to bury Blackfeet remains next to those of enemies would result in an undesirable mixing of spirits."[59] The identified remains have since been returned and reburied in Montana, and a monument has been erected on the Blackfeet Reservation.

To the surprise of some, scientists have found that Indians are also interested in their ancestry and prehistoric past. In such cases, excavated or discovered human remains can be removed for scientific study and analyzed, provided that no destructive techniques are used on the bones, and then they can be returned for reburial within a reasonable time of a year or two. Indians generally do not oppose legitimate scientific research; they oppose the unnecessary warehousing of their dead. One case study of a successful scientific investigation that concluded with a reburial involved an 8,000-year-old man.

The 8,000-Year-Old Shaman

In 1992, the bones of an 8,000-year-old shaman, or medicine man, were found by cavers in the White River National Forest of Colorado. The body lay in a mountain cave some 10,000 feet above sea level. Distinguished archaeologist Patty Jo Watson from Washington University in St. Louis, Missouri, helped to study this remarkable find, and Bill Kight, U.S. Forest Service (USFS) archaeologist, and Kenny Frost, then the Ute Indian liaison for the White River National Forest, coordinated the removal and reburial.

Detailed analysis and radiocarbon dating confirmed that the man was between thirty-five and forty when he died after squeezing through a low, narrow passage into the high mountain cave. Casts, X rays, and photographs of the remains were taken for further scientific research. Then, after a special cave gate was installed for security, the research team respectfully returned the bones to the cave in a cedar box.[60] Southern Ute Indian Kenny Frost blessed the remains and personally took them back to the site where they had been found. In a special repatriation ceremony he conducted at the cave entrance, Frost smudged all the participants with the sweet scent of burning sage as a blessing to put the shaman's spirit to rest and to keep the living safe from harm. Nature also cooperated. Though it was summer, snow fell and cleansed the site.[61]

In 1989, an even older skeleton, one of the oldest nearly complete skeletons ever found in North America, was uncovered in a gravel pit at Buhl, Idaho. The bones were protected thanks to Idaho's 1984 Graves Protection Act, which required that the state archaeologist be notified of the find. Members of the Shoshone-Bannock Tribal Council agreed to a physical description and radiocarbon analysis, and although carbon dating took three years, tests finally determined the female skeleton was 10,765 years old. Significant to scientists because of its age, the skeleton, nicknamed "Buhla," was also important to local Indian elders. Because of the lengthy period in which the bones were out of the ground (three years), tribal elders claimed that recent deaths on the reservation had been caused by the woman's roving spirit. The tribal council required that the remains be reburied immediately in a spot known only to Indians.[62] Scientists regretted the reburial, but they had not developed a comfortable, trusting relationship with the Shoshone-Bannock and therefore had little choice but to acquiesce to the Indians' wishes.[63]

Science Versus Indian Beliefs

Anthropology Professor Emeritus Clement Meighan of the University of California at Los Angeles (UCLA) complained that Shoshone Indians had reburied "one of the two or three major finds in the New World." Because the skeleton "was around 5,000-years-old before the pyramids of Egypt were built," he argued that "repatriation is a loaded and improper term because it implies that you're giving something back to people who own it. They don't own it, and never did."[64] Meighan also contended that "fifty years from now, people will look back on this situation and wonder how we could have been so short-sighted as to consign a research area to the jurisdiction of political and religious restrictions." He added, "Condemnation will come to those who gave away for destruction irreplaceable museum materials, many of which had been cherished for over a hundred years and had been acquired and maintained at great cost."[65]

Meighan represents a small group of archaeologists opposed to any and all reburials. Most mainstream anthropologists now seek accommodation with Indian tribes through collaborative efforts. In his essay "Do the Right Thing," Randall H. McGuire concluded, "We can no longer practice archaeology without consulting and involving the people that we study. . . . Their demands for repatriation show us that they do have interests in the past, that these interests are different from our own, and that these interests are now supported by the force of law."[66] For all these reasons, reburial can be a highly emotional issue, providing catharsis for historically tragic events. As Walter Echo-Hawk of the Native American Rights Foundation put it, "All we're asking for is a little common decency. . . . We're not asking for anything but to bury our dead."[67]

Returning to the Earth

One excellent example of this paradigm shift in anthropological practice is the repatriation of the human remains of 1,000 individuals to Kodiak Island, off the coast of Alaska. On October 5, 1991—half a century after scientist Aleš Hardlička had excavated those remains for the Smithsonian—a human chain of Kodiak Islanders and friends lifted boxes containing the remains into a common grave. Village residents, guests, and children participated in the reburial, as did three priests of the Russian Orthodox Church, which has served as the primary religion for Kodiak Islanders for the past 200 years. Like other Alaskan natives, Gordon Pullar experienced a "sense of relief," and he has optimistically predicted that in the future, "far from stifling research, a scientific system that recognizes both the western and indigenous world views will produce new and exciting information that will benefit all of humankind."[68]

Two years later, on October 16, 1993, the Northern Cheyenne reburied seventeen skeletal remains of ancestors who had fled north from Indian Territory in Oklahoma under Chief Dull Knife. The 1993 reburial by the four warrior societies, the Crazy Dogs, the Elkhorn Scrapers, the Kit Foxes, and the Bowstrings, was an emotional event attended by 200 people and led by James Black Wolf. Into a box containing the skull of a girl who died between the ages of nine and eleven, a grateful Cheyenne woman placed pink beaded earrings as a gift from the living to the dead.[69]

The Southern Cheyenne had a similar experience as they buried human remains collected by the U.S. Army after the Sand Creek Massacre of 1864. On July 10, 1993, eighteen ancestors were buried in the Concho, Oklahoma, cemetery after more than 125 years in the Army Medical Museum and the Smithsonian's Museum of Natural History. Earlier in Washington, D.C., Southern Cheyenne leaders Moses Starr Jr., Nathan Hart, and Lucien Twins had placed human remains in blankets packed with cedar chips and spoken the words *Naevahoo' ohtseme*, which in Cheyenne means, "We are going back home."[70]

The Blackfeet, Southern Cheyenne, and Northern Cheyenne repatriation stories are only a few of the successful efforts of the Smithsonian Institution's National Museum of Natural History's Repatriation Office, which returned 1,491 individuals from the Physical Anthropology Division between 1984 and May 1995. Case officers handle formal repatriation requests and schedule meetings with tribal officials and interested parties. Human remains have gone home to the Sisseton-Wahpeton Sioux, the Southern Arapaho, the Shoshone-Bannock, the Makah, the Warm Springs Confederated Tribes, and the Pawnee. The Archaeology Division of NMNH has also returned materials, most noticeably to Larsen Bay at Kodiak Island, and the Ethnology Division has returned objects to the Zia and Zuni Pueblos.[71]

Uncovering skeletal material is an issue for land developers, as well, for they, too, must be sensitive to repatriation requests. In Hawai'i, developers removed over 1,100 ancient burials for a beachfront Ritz Carlton Hotel in 1988. This act galvanized Native Hawaiians and prompted them to create Hui Malama I Na Kupuna 'O Hawai'i Nei, an organization whose name means "group caring for the ancestors of Hawai'i." As Edward Halealoha Ayau explained, "The bones of our ancestors nourished the ground from which our food grows, which, in turn, nourishes our bodies. Secure in the knowledge that our ancestors are where they belong, in Hawaiian earth, free from harm, our spirits are nourished as well." He added, "When speaking of one's ancestors, it is appropriate to recite one's *mo'ok u auhau* (genealogy). By reciting the names of my ancestors, I am reminded that but for their existence, I simply would not be. I am humbled by this reminder and duty bound to care for those who came before me."[72] Pressure from Native Hawaiians resulted in the state's purchase of the grave site, and the bones have now been reburied within a bottomless cement vault "intended to protect our ancestors' return to the earth goddess Haumea."[73]

Some tribes and native peoples are uninterested in the repatriation of human remains and fear the consequences if skeletal material is returned. In fact, there is no consensus on reburial issues among the more than 550 federally registered tribes in the United States. The Eastern Shoshone on the Wind River Reservation in Wyoming, for example, do not want their ancestors repatriated because they doubt that the museum provenience (record keeping) of the bones is accurate.[74] The

California Chumash are not interested in assuming responsibility for reburial, and neither are the Zuni of New Mexico, who feel that in leaving their home area, ancestral bones lost their cultural identity. In addition, the Navajo have not yet repatriated human remains, though that may change.

Difficulties in Implementing NAGPRA

After more than a century of exploitation, a national consensus on granting tribal people hegemony over their dead has emerged. Across the nation, the return of human remains has added to a renewed spirit of cautious optimism among Indian peoples. Human remains on public display have been removed or closed from view at Mesa Verde National Park in Colorado, the Allen County Museum in Ohio, the Wickliffe Mounds in Kentucky, and the Dickson Mounds Museum and State Park in Illinois.[75] But the successes of the Native American Graves Protection and Repatriation Act of 1990 and the Smithsonian's Repatriation Office have not been without their consequences.

Indians have been overwhelmed with paperwork from museums, and few tribes have adequate staff or facilities to process the immense flow of formal letters and computer-generated inventories, which may weigh several pounds. Tribes question who should answer the inquiries they are receiving as well as which tribal members should actually seek repatriation of associated funerary remains and sacred objects. Deep divisions have developed within tribes over who has the authority to speak on repatriation issues, and tribal cultural committees have found themselves embroiled in squabbles among Indian bands split between two or more reservations. Native American families argue over ancient artifacts and worry about the repercussions of bringing home human remains and the belongings of the dead.

According to Native American consultant Kenny Frost, those who have been the most troubled are the medicine men and women responsible for assessing human remains. "One of my friends at the Standing Rock Reservation in South Dakota has been handling human remains. Those medicine men are being separated by tribal members and being treated as if they are spirits," Frost reported. "They are not being accepted as a living person on this side but rather as a person from the spirit world. They are shunned by their own people." Medicine men and women who take human remains home for reburial must themselves undergo cleansing ceremonies, and some want to stop handling human remains altogether. As Frost observed, it is an "emotional drain, particularly in handling the crania of small children and women with evidence of bullet holes and trauma to the head."[76] For all tribes, the psychological effects of revisiting a bitter frontier past can trouble everyone.

An equally thorny issue involves Indian tribes not seeking repatriation of skeletal remains in museums but instead claiming skeletons found on public land as their descendants, thus pressing for an extension of land claims. Though these Indians are unwilling to have scientific DNA studies conducted to see if the human remains really are their genetic forebears, they argue that, because of cultural affiliation and oral traditions about their tribal origins, human remains found on public lands are their ancestors and tribal land claims should therefore be re-opened. This issue is especially acute in the Southwest, where tribal rivalries continue among the Navajo, Hopi, Zuni, Ute, and Pueblo peoples. The dead are being used as pawns in land claim cases and political disputes.[77]

In Colorado, when human remains are found on public land, four-teen different tribes who at one time or another hunted or gathered within the present boundaries of the state must be notified. The legal complexities of complying with NAGPRA are enormous and include respectful repatriation and reburial even for Indian remains for which there are no known descendants. Federal regulations have also been written concerning the disposition of human remains from prehistoric or historic tribes that no longer exist.[78]

As for science, physical anthropology, and archaeology, a century after the wholesale looting of Indian graves, a quiet truce has been nego-tiated. The dialogue has begun on how to conduct scientific investiga-tions. According to Kenny Frost, "If scientists approach Indian tribes in regards to testing human remains in a manner that will benefit mankind, then tribes are somewhat willing to agree to testing if the benefits are there and the remains are returned for repatriation at a later date." He also mentioned that scientists can have longer than a year to do their studies if they "work diligently on the remains and show cause why the remains should be kept for additional study."[79]

Kennewick Man and the Umatilla

Much of this accommodation has come about because of the Native American Graves Protection and Repatriation Act, but the act is now being challenged in federal court in a case involving Kennewick Man, a prehistoric skeleton found in 1996 along the Columbia River in Kennewick, Washington. The U.S. Army Corps of Engineers, which controls the river basin, determined that the bones (which were shown by carbon dating to be 9,000 years old) should be returned under NAGPRA. The Umatilla Indians, leading a coalition of five tribes and bands in the Columbia River basin, claimed the skeleton and quickly sought to rebury it in an undisclosed place.

However, early forensic reports found that Kennewick Man has few Indian traits. The first examiners thought he was a Caucasian despite the fact that an Archaic Cascade projectile point was embedded and broken off in his pelvis. Physical anthropologist Grover Krantz, a pro-fessor at Washington State University, concluded that "this skeleton cannot be racially or culturally associated with any existing American Indian group." He went on to contend, "The Native [American Graves

Protection and] Repatriation Act has no more applicability to this skeleton than it would if an early Chinese expedition had left one of its members here."[80]

Prominent physical anthropologists are now suing in federal court for the right to examine the bones. NAGPRA will be tested, as will the idea that the earliest inhabitants of the New World may have arrived in several migrations, with Native Americans coming later. The U.S. Army Corps of Engineers stored the remains in a vault at the Pacific Northwest National Laboratory in Richland, Washington, and according to Douglas Preston, "they are now at the center of a legal controversy that will likely determine the course of American archaeology."[81] For native peoples, the issue of "who was here first" is a deep moral and religious question that is not easily resolved. Meanwhile, under a judge's ruling, further study of Kennewick Man has taken place at the Burke Museum of the University of Washington in Seattle, where research may redefine racial typologies as we have known them for a century and a half.

Whatever happens legally with Kennewick Man, NAGPRA has been successful in repatriating human remains back to tribes, and a basic human right, the right of the dead to stay buried, has been generally agreed on. The long-term storage of Native American human remains that began in the nineteenth century is over. A century ago, scientists thought there was much to learn about Native Americans and other indigenous peoples as "vanishing races." A century later, there is even more to learn from living tribal peoples. This chapter concludes with commentaries by Native Americans and a Native Alaskan who express some of the personal difficulties they have encountered while reburying their dead.

Return to Mother Earth

Our children must learn that we honor those who have returned to Mother Earth. We must put our ancestors to rest. We must let them go on their journey. Should we dig up Custer and see what he ate? No, we would be put in jail. Now my religious leaders are afraid to put their things out in the mountains. Nonnatives need to leave these things alone because they are placed there for their good, too. We don't want to be studied any more. We have been studied enough.

—REX SALVADOR, second lieutenant governor
Acoma Pueblo, Acoma, New Mexico[82]

The Spirits

Our Indian people have different types of spirits—the land, the birds, the sky. The spirits can latch on to you. Our medicine men, some of them were evil. They destroyed men and marriages. My grandfather would take the hair of someone and destroy their lives. There's not a whole lot of good in the past. We get along better today.

My father was a medicine man who took care of burials. If someone was being haunted he took care of that and dusted graves with rose bushes. When the missionaries came we gave up our songs and our traditions. My 104-year-old aunt told me about giving medicine bundles to priests and missionaries. Some of the bundles were not very good. She said I should not want them back. They could damage the lives of the grandkids. Don't bring back my grandfather's medicine bundle she said. When you use medicine to damage people you inherit all their sins and then you must work hard to be cleansed—if you can.

This is how we feel. In our area there are a lot of people buried with shiny, polished grinding stones. And these were buried with women and it was their most important possession. And it should be buried for all time.

Sometimes when you go into an area as an Indian you feel the presence of others. I was in a canyon with my adopted father and we could feel the presence of the dead buried along the rim under rocks, because in the old days we had no shovels. It's really a gift that you have to feel these things. You need not worry about being haunted—just walk with respect.

I have done reburials for forty years. I have reburied hundreds of our ancestors. I am grateful to have been called on. I am grateful to assist because I feel our ancestors' presence through the Great Spirit. We always left food at the grave because the spirits will come nibble at the food or if it washes away in the rain that is the way it is meant to be.

—ANDREW JOSEPH, repatriation manager
Colville Reservation, Colville, Washington

Ancient Acoma

We are one of nineteen pueblos and our home at Acoma is ancient. We are still there today. We are faced with a common destiny to define who we are and to respect each other's ways. We have seen all the laws come down. The laws that define how I am to be an Indian and how I am to relate to the land. Now there is a law about how I am to relate to my ancestors. We have received 400 letters on NAGPRA but very few human remains directly relate to Acoma. Now the challenge of the Native American Graves Protection and Repatriation Act is to explain how we are culturally affiliated with objects and remains. This is very difficult. The law had good intentions to right the wrongs of the past, but this law is creating difficulties for us.

As a modern tribal people we listen to what scientists say, but we know where we came from and we have always been willing to tell about ourselves. Science, especially archaeologists, will now have to involve Indian peoples and look at our ancient myths. We insist that human remains not be stored in museums or kept in boxes. They should go back close to where they came from. This is quite a challenge—to explain to scientists why we reject further research on our people and our beliefs of the spirit world. We do not have a ceremony for reburial. How do we ask forgiveness? How do we apologize for the bones of our mother's people having been removed from the earth?

There has to be mutual cooperation as we move forward with NAGPRA. There must be cooperation with time and money. If we can get the understanding not to remove our native people without our involvement, we will have gained ground. There will be times when removal will have to happen. All that we ask is that we be involved together.

At Acoma we are really opposed to the science of archaeology. When human remains have to be disturbed we must be involved. Today at the Zuni Archaeology Program or with the Hopis we hear about doing tests to prove cultural affiliation, but it has to be done with mutual cooperation. We must learn together. Human remains were reburied in Rainbow House at Bandelier National Monument in New Mexico. It rained because the spirits were happy to be back in the ground.

> —PETUUCHE GILBERT, tribal councilman and realty officer
> Acoma Pueblo, Acoma, New Mexico

Naevahoo'ohtseme—"We Are Going Back Home": Repatriating a Young Cheyenne Girl Killed at the Sand Creek Massacre

One of the successful repatriations we have conducted was to return 18 human remains from the National Museum of Natural History of the Smithsonian Institution. The remains had been collected during that period from 1860 to 1880, mostly in Kansas and Colorado. After battles were fought, apparently the army medical personnel, under orders of General Otis, collected these remains and shipped them to the army medical museum. They were later transferred to the National Museum of Natural History.

We were one of the first tribes in Oklahoma to successfully conduct repatriation. Every time that the Cheyenne societies, namely the Elk Scraper, the Bowstring, the Dog Soldiers and the Kit Fox society plus the chiefs, met, the tepee was always set up and people were invited to come—especially members of the societies and those who were chiefs and their families, and there was always a meal served and then, after the meal, the societies and the chiefs went into the tepee to discuss the repatriation.

It was initially difficult to talk about the remains of our ancestors, because of the 18 remains at the Smithsonian, five of those were victims of the Sand Creek Massacre. And of the five, one was a ten-to-thirteen-year-old female; an adolescent girl was killed and we made special plans for her. The society suggested that we appoint four women to be in the delegation that went to the Smithsonian to prepare the remains, and they were charged to specifically be the ones to handle the remains of this female.

The issue of reburial came up, but I explained to them that all of these remains of the victims had never been buried. Their deaths occurred during a massacre or during a battle, and they were laying in a field when they were collected by the army medical personnel so there had been no burial service. Upon that knowledge then, the societies and the chiefs went ahead and planned for a special ceremony to be conducted

Sets of Cheyenne human remains from the Sand Creek Massacre are wrapped in blankets and packed with cedar chips in cedar boxes by three leaders of the Southern Cheyenne— (left to right) Moses Starr Jr., Nathan Hart, and Lucien Twins. The handmade boxes then made the journey to Oklahoma for tribal burial. Photo by Laurie Minor-Penland, National Museum of the American Indian.

at the National Museum and that was accomplished on the first of July in 1993.

By the 10th of July, we had a burial ceremony at the Concho Cemetery, which is located near our tribal headquarters. It was selected because the remains would be fairly close to us and they'd be guarded or at least relatively safe. The traditionalists selected representatives from their group along with those four women and included among the men were priests of the Arrow Ceremony and the Sun Dance Ceremony. They went along and were the ones who were responsible for conducting the ceremonies and the various rituals in preparing the remains of our ancestors. My job was simply to raise funds to help with expenses and I did that.

I raised enough funds for everyone to fly. The Smithsonian was able to purchase about four airplane tickets plus a couple of hotel rooms. For the rest of the group of about fourteen we'd have to find funds for traveling and for lodging, which we did. We also asked for contributions, in addition to funds, of small Pendleton blankets that would be used to wrap the skulls, and then we collected funds to have small boxes or small coffins made of cedar. This was what was prescribed by the societies—that cedar wood would be used.

I have a friend in Pennsylvania. I contacted him to see if he might find a cabinetmaker who could construct those boxes for us in Lancaster County, not far from Washington, D.C., and this friend agreed that he would find someone and would help transport all the boxes, the eighteen boxes, to the National Museum of Natural History. He did find a cabinet maker named Immanuel Fisher. He's an Amish craftsman. I actually went to visit him to make the contract. He had selected some wood, some cedar wood, at least three different types, and I selected one of them. He also had some various finishes. I selected them and gave him the dimensions of the boxes, which had been given to me by the National Museum of Natural History and we shook hands and that was our contract. This was their way and it was also their way of preparing for the burial of their people.

On the day of the repatriation ceremonies, there were many traditions that our people used. First of all, we had to wait until a choir announced our coming. The Cooper Room of the National Museum of Natural History building had been selected by both Dr. Killion [director of the Repatriation Office of the NMNH] and me. Tables were set up there and the 18 human remains were placed there along with the boxes underneath the tables. The boxes were then marked with the accession numbers of each of the skulls, so that we would know where each of the human remains were, especially the young thirteen-year-old female.

The cryer then called the general calls that they announce four times. They cry toward the southeast, southwest, northwest and northeast. They wait a few minutes before they begin again for their second round and the third round and then after the fourth round we went into the Cooper Room. The remains had been prepared that evening by the museum personnel. They were transported to the room, and I had asked the staff to cover the remains with white sheets. They were covered so when the people gathered, when our people gathered around the tables and it was time to start the ceremony, then appropriate rituals were conducted.

Dr. Killion and I removed the sheets, and it was a very difficult moment for our people to see these remains, but they relied on priests to conduct the appropriate ceremonies using medicine, and we then proceeded to prepare each of those remains. We took the boxes out from underneath the tables and placed them beside the skull and then someone would hold the Pendleton blankets, and then they would be carefully wrapped. Before they were placed into the box there were some cedar shavings that were poured into the bottom and then the remains were carefully placed into the boxes. But before all that occurred, one of our

The exact location of the Sand Creek Massacre in eastern Colorado has recently been determined, thanks to a new National Park Service research project funded by a congressional bill that Sen. Ben Nighthorse Campbell sponsored. Photo of the Sand Creek area courtesy of Hal Gould, Camera Obscura Gallery, Denver, Colorado.

priests went around the entire room beginning with remain number one to remain number eighteen and painted each of the skulls with red paint from our sacred mountain, Bear Butte. And, he conducted rituals at each point, at each station where the remains were. Following that, as each tribal member was called to assist in actually handling the remains, they were brushed off with cedar so that they could touch the remains of our ancestors who were then wrapped in a blanket. Once they were placed into the box, the void spaces were filled with the cedar and the lid was put on.

That continued routinely until we got to box number 13, which was the adolescent female victim's number in addition to the accession number that was already on the box. She was victim number 13 among the 18, and it was very difficult for the women. There was open weeping. It was a traumatic experience. My daughter, Connie, was one of those four women, and she had been asked to be the one to actually handle the remains of this adolescent female victim. She was so moved that when she picked up the remain to place it into the box, she actually brought it to herself and hugged it, because as my daughter told the story later, when in the confusion of the attack on the village at Sand Creek, no one had been there to hold the young girl. Then the other three women also participated in preparing her, and once the lid to her box was placed we proceeded on. Richard West, who is the Director of the National Museum of the American Indian, made his appearance.

He was taken aside and was empowered, I use that word, he was empowered by one of our priests to help with the ceremony. He was given one of the other Sand Creek victims, and he assisted then with the Cheyenne human remains, because he is Cheyenne. Later on I visited with him and he said that was an experience that he'll never forget.

We had also invited the Northern Cheyenne to be represented and Mr. Steve Brady and Mr. Alfred Strange were there. Each of them were also given the remains of Sand Creek victims, and I also handled one of the remains so that everyone, every Cheyenne person who was there, had the task of handling the remains and placing them into the boxes. When we finished the priests had to go outside to conduct the closing ritual. After that we were done, and we had the staff of the repatriation office then pack the boxes into various cartons, and as it turned out, I think we had about four large cartons that we picked up the following day.

We had rented a truck, a moving truck, and they were loaded on the truck, and the deaccession papers were signed by our tribal government officials, and then the truck was driven to Oklahoma by our traditional people [who were] the representatives of the four societies that I mentioned earlier. And, in their prescriptions, they made four stops along the route to conduct rituals, and one of the [rituals] was to sit down and light a pipe and smoke together. They repeated this four times, and my younger son was traveling with them.

He and I actually sealed the boxes with screws while the remaining group was outside conducting a ceremony on the lawn of the National Museum. We sealed those boxes with tools and they were never to be

Native Americans, particularly Cheyenne Indians, want the Sand Creek site acquired by the National Park Service and interpreted as a site of shame. In this group portrait at Sand Creek are (left to right) Joe Big Medicine, Sun Dance priest, from Longdale, Oklahoma; Laird Comet-sevah, traditional chief, Southern Cheyenne, and president of the Sand Creek Descendants Association, from Clinton, Oklahoma; George Black Owl, Southern Cheyenne artist, from Clinton, Oklahoma; Colleen Comet-sevah, genealogist, of the Sand Creek Descendants Association; Arly Rhodes, director, Cheyenne-Arapaho Senior Center, from Clinton, Oklahoma; and the son of Joe Big Medicine—Little Joe. Courtesy, Hal Gould, Camera Obscura Gallery, Denver, Colorado.

opened again. He traveled with the caravan and got an opportunity to conduct one of those rituals, because that's how our people learn these traditions, these rituals. They are instructed. An elder who is qualified, generally a priest in this case, assisted him and told him exactly what to do during the whole ritual. He had observed two of them already so he basically knew, but then on the third one when he was asked to perform the ritual, he was given some instruction, and so that's how he learned.

When we got to Oklahoma, the remains were temporarily stored at the Oklahoma Historical Society, and then later on July 10th they were picked up and transported to the Concho Cemetery where we had graves dug in a circle. We marked on paper exactly where each of the remains would go so that we'd know where the Sand Creek victims are buried. We know where the victim was killed at [a frontier fort], the victim killed on the Saline River, the victim killed on the Republican River, we know exactly where they are, and especially that female adolescent.

What was really moving about the female adolescent was that there were many families who had responded to her especially. Some of them made some goods for her to take, as they expressed it, on her journey. One of them made a special case of brain-tanned skin. It was a bag, and in that bag were some sinew and beads and some small pieces of brain-tanned skin. Another family brought a shawl. Others brought things like a necklace or a bracelet for her, and these were then placed on top of her coffin after her coffin was lowered by one of our Cheyenne men. And so those objects became associated funerary objects and were buried with that adolescent female victim.

We had a large crowd of people. Families with children, and I especially appreciated that they brought their children so that they could learn about this event and especially about the Sand Creek Massacre. People would pause at grave number 13, and just openly weep, because in our oral tradition stories, we know what happened to her. We know that she was deliberately shot—that's backed up by U.S. Congressional testimony from an inquiry held following the massacre.

One of the things that I appreciated was that the ceremonies would have been used a century ago had these people been given proper burials. In the beginning in the 1860s and into the 1880s, they wouldn't have had elements of the Christian religion. It was planned that way. I didn't have to mention it. The societies understood and planned it such that all the ceremonies would be traditional and they were. I think the traditionalists assumed a very important responsibility and allowed the people to see what could be done by the traditionalists when they would get together for a task such as this. They met several times and it brought the people together, and brought a sense of reliance upon these traditional leaders, and that was the good part about it, along with the use of our traditions. None of the decisions that were ever made was made outside the tepee. It was always inside the tepee, and every decision was by consensus.

—LAWRENCE HART, executive director
Cheyenne Cultural Center, Clinton, Oklahoma

A Smallpox Cemetery in Sitka, Alaska:
Voices From the Tlingit Ancestors

Ten years ago there was a housing project that came into our village and the contractors were building new homes for our citizens and part of the homes were being built on our cemetery. The contractor went up there and dug up the ground, and they destroyed our whole graveyard and destroyed the headstones and the cremation mounds from an 1830 smallpox epidemic that came through our village. All our children and elders were wiped out so they were all cremated up there. That site was completely destroyed by this housing contractor.

Bones and skulls were all over the place and when I came on the scene and saw what was there, it really affected me very deeply, and with the help of some of the other residents we gathered up all of the remains that we could and put them in boxes and took them up to the church and stored them in the basement of the church. As far as I was concerned that was the end of my duty there.

But after that, the following evening, I started getting nightmares. After weeks of nightmares and becoming accident prone and a lack of sleep I ended up having to return those remains myself. Then I went up to the site and found about seven acres of a very neglected cemetery. It was overgrown so I started clearing all the brush. It took us all summer to clear about seven acres of cemetery and we were really very surprised at what we found. We thought there was only a few graves in there, but it turned out there was about sixteen hundred graves. All the headstones and grave markers were destroyed over the years from vandalism and neglect. After we cleared it out, we discovered that there were a lot of graves that were robbed and some that were sunken and right around the whole perimeter were all these skulls and bones and desecrated graves. I had to do something.

I spent the next two years re-intering remains from that cemetery, and I put them all underneath the trees. I ended up isolating myself for two years because I became a very angry person. I resented what had happened to my ancestors and I was very bitter about it. So I isolated myself to the point where I quit participating among the living. I just spent all my time in the cemetery filling in sunken graves, up-righting headstones, re-intering remains and clearing all the brush and making the place look better. I spent all that time those first few years in just total isolation. I got sick. I got pneumonia and I almost died.

My elders were watching me. They were very concerned about my health and very supportive of my work. So they came up and they asked if I would be willing to be trained as a spokesperson for my tribe as a storyteller, and that they would train me to speak on behalf of our people to share what I experienced with the remains. So they sent me to Juneau, Alaska where we formed this theatre company, and we were all hand-picked to be storytellers. It was a very rewarding experience for me, because it helped bring me back to the living.

—ROBERT SAM, Tlingit storyteller
Sitka, Alaska

Photo of a whalebone-and-sod house, ca. 1900, from an abandoned village on an island on the farthest western point in the Chuckchi Sea, Alaska. Perhaps the structure was abandoned because of disease. The entrance to the house, which would have been home to a large extended family, is on the right. For most native peoples, abandoned home sites are sacred places. Photo by Jet Lowe, Historic American Building Survey, 1991.

Staff members of the Ak-Chin Him Dak Ecomuseum in Arizona with director Marilyn Peters, second from left. The staffers are standing in front of a reconstructed desert dwelling. Photo by author, January 1997.

After decades of having their sacred and historical materials curated and exhibited elsewhere, Native Americans are demanding control over how their histories are to be interpreted. On the San Carlos Reservation in Arizona, Dale Miles, the first tribal historian, directs the San Carlos Apache Cultural Center for the Western Apache and collects oral histories. He poses in front of a reconstructed Apache brush house. Photo by author, January 1997.

Native Americans and Museums
Curation and Repatriation of Sacred and Tribal Objects

> The National Museum of the American Indian is not only about the preservation of physical objects, of things. It is also about the preservation of cultures, of ways of being. Native communities throughout the Hemisphere have persisted, against almost overwhelming odds, to this very day. And their cultural viability, including, as it always has, response, adaptation, and innovation grounded in a timeless tradition, not only continues to exist but is experiencing a profound renaissance.
>
> —W. RICHARD WEST, founding director,
> National Museum of the American Indian

Across the country, Indian museums thrive as tribes preserve and protect their cultures by interpreting tribal histories to their own peoples and to a growing number of tourists interested in Native American culture and tradition. Over 150 tribal museums and cultural centers now exist, with both simple and elaborate exhibits, public programs, educational programs for children, and collections of prehistoric and historic materials. On the Apache Reservation at San Carlos, Arizona, the museum features an introduction to Apache lifeways and artifacts such as saddles, bridles, and rifles from the days of Geronimo and other Apache warriors and scouts. At Ak-Chin Him Dak, an ecomuseum in central Arizona, the tribe curates its own prehistoric lithic materials and actively engages in ongoing oral history projects. In Idaho, the Shoshone-Bannock Museum utilizes both historic and contemporary photographs to tell the tribe's story. But the flagship of tribal museums will be the National Museum of the American Indian on the mall in Washington, D.C.

Other buildings of the National Museum of the American Indian are located on the upper west side of Manhattan, far from the sources of many of its artifacts, and they contain over a million items. The old Heye Foundation structure on Broadway at 155th Street has housed one of the largest collections of North American tribal objects in the world. Begun at the end of the nineteenth century by industrialist George Gustave Heye, the Heye Collection is distinguished not by its quality or its careful provenience, for both are lacking in the collection, but by the sheer volume of prehistoric and historic materials collected by scouts and buyers who roamed from Inuit villages on the Arctic Circle to tribal encampments on the tip of Tierra del Fuego.[1]

Wampum belts, battle axes, bows, arrows, shields, beaded dresses and beaded moccasins, masks, rattles, and ceramics of all kinds characterize Heye's vast private collection. In 1989, Congress reorganized the Heye Foundation Museum of the American Indian as the National Museum of the American Indian. By acquiring the Heye Collection with a $150 million authorization, Congress established the fifteenth museum of the Smithsonian Institution and the first national museum dedicated to the living cultures of the native peoples of the Western Hemisphere. The museum's founding director, W. Richard West Jr., a member of the Cheyenne-Arapaho Tribe, has stated, "The new museum seeks to represent and interpret Indian cultures as the contemporary living people that they are—from roots in a glorious past to a difficult but vital present."[2]

Across the United States, Native Americans are asserting hegemony over their own cultural values and insisting on curatorial change in the nation's museums. A bellwether of that change was found in the stone building on Manhattan's upper west side in Washington Heights, which is now the Research Branch of the NMAI; the public visits exhibits at the Old Customs House. Thousands of objects had been displayed at the original Heye Center in the Bronx, including a magnificent Ghost Dance shirt, a Paiute shaman's rattle made from the head and claw of a bald eagle, and a Medicine Society bonnet attributed to the Oglala chief Crazy Horse, but ceremonial calumets, medicine bundles, and peace pipes had been removed from display. An empty exhibit case on the first floor in the hall of North American ethnology contained pins and labels but no artifacts.

Under the heading "Medicine Bags & Bundles" a caption explained that the National Museum of the American Indian had contacted tribal leaders "to discover what are the appropriate and sensitive methods for storing, displaying and interpreting objects in its collections."[3] Trips by museum staff to tribal leaders began in the fall of 1990 and included visits to the Prairie Band of the Potawatomi in Kickapoo, Iowa, the Sac and Fox Tribes in Kansas, and the Hannaville Potawatomi of Michigan.

When museum staff conferred with tribal leaders, they learned that bundles and contents of medicine bags "possess life forces of their own" and that the public display of medicine bags is "disrespectful and possibly harmful to people who come near them." Because all bundles have a specific purpose known only to their owners and possibly other members of the tribe, when the bags and bundles are not used for their original purpose, they must always be stored "reverently."[4] Such reverence increased with passage of the Native American Graves Protection and Repatriation Act in 1990.[5]

The act specifically required all museums and institutions receiving federal funds, including national and state parks and historical societies, to inventory their Native American collections within five years and to identify funerary objects, sacred objects, and objects of cultural patrimony with specific ceremonial or religious significance for tribes. Sacred objects were defined as "specific ceremonial objects which are needed by traditional Native American religious leaders for the practice of traditional Native American religions by their present day adherents." Museums were asked to make a "good-faith effort" to inventory and identify their holdings of sacred objects, associated funerary objects, and human remains, sending inventories and descriptions to the tribal leaders who had cultural authority over the final disposition and exhibition of the artifacts. The Peabody Museum of Harvard University allocated one million dollars to begin this inventory process by replacing their mainframe computer and hiring eight additional staff members.[6]

Some tribes prefer that major cultural institutions continue the curation of artifacts or human remains while transferring actual ownership and legal title back to the tribes. Others actively seek the repatriation or return of special objects; the long-standing Zuni claim for the return of

Zuni War Gods reverently placed in a Zuni shrine, 1897. The return of these gods to the Zuni Tribe in New Mexico is one of the ongoing repatriation success stories for Native Americans. Museums, courts of law, private collectors, and federal law enforcement officials have all come to realize that Zuni War Gods are communal tribal property and not to be displayed, traded, or sold. The War Gods represent continuing religious traditions and are considered vital to Zuni spiritual health. Young Zuni athletes even visit the remote shrines before participating in athletic events off tribal lands. Photo by F. H. Maude. Courtesy, Southwest Museum, Los Angeles, California.

Return of the Omaha Sacred Pole in the courtyard of the Peabody Museum, June 1988. The Omaha Sacred Pole is central to the spiritual life of the Omaha Tribe. Elaborate Plains Indian buffalo ceremonies centered around such poles, which were adorned with special feathers or scalps as this one is. Revered for centuries as a symbol of the Omaha, the pole was returned to the tribe prior to passage of the Native American Graves Protection and Repatriation Act. The use of a sacred shaman's pole to ensure successful buffalo hunts may represent an unbroken cultural tradition from ca. 6,000 B.C. to the end of the nineteenth century. The cultural and religious importance for peoples dependent on bison makes this pole a sacred object of un-paralleled value. Courtesy, Peabody Museum, Harvard University, Cam-bridge, Massachusetts, no. N31958.

all their wooden War Gods to sacred tribal caves and shelters in New Mexico is one such example. There, the hand-carved figures gradually age and deteriorate, thus reaffirming both the cyclical nature of all Zuni-made objects and the power of the spirit world. Keeping the War Gods in acid-free boxes in climate-controlled vaults violates their sacred purpose.[7]

Many tribes also believe in the residual power of sacred artifacts. At the NMAI in New York City, an empty exhibit case testified to the belief of Potawatomi elders that medicine bundles should have been buried with their owners. Consequently, the museum returned the bundles and medicine bags "to their communities so that the people could bury or burn them." Sacred powers inherent in the bundles are not to be dealt with lightly and may not have diminished over centuries. Martha Kreipe de Montaño, from the Prairie Band of Potawatomi and manager of the NMAI Information Center, discussed medicine bundles: "We were advised that some of the communally owned bundles could be danger-ous, and that only war veterans could handle them without personal risk. It was widely felt that the public display of all these materials is inappropriate." Therefore, on October 19, 1990, a Native American war veteran removed all Potawatomi, Kickapoo, Iowa, and Sac and Fox bundles from public exhibition at the National Museum of the American Indian. Staff members then stored the items "in an appropri-ately respectful way as dictated by the elders of these communities."[8]

Museums across the United States must now carefully consider the curation and exhibition of prehistoric and historic Native American artifacts, especially those of dubious provenience. As early as 1906, wide-spread trafficking in grave goods and wholesale looting in the Southwest prompted passage of the federal Antiquities Law, which Congress strengthened in 1979 with the Archaeological Resources Protection Act (ARPA). However, a thriving black market in Indian artifacts continued, and in 1989, new ARPA provisions increased fines and penalties. Unfortunately, the black market is still booming because many non-Indians simply do not consider Native American burials sacred.

Margaret Kimball Brown, director of the archaeologically unique Cahokia Mounds Historic Site in Illinois, is experienced in evaluating prehistoric sacred sites and objects. Just across the Mississippi River from St. Louis, Cahokia represents the height of the Mississippian mound-builder culture and has been proclaimed a World Heritage Site. Brown explained, "Most of our problems in dealing with the issues of sacred materials and human remains spring from our lack of understanding of Indian cultures [and] Indian spirituality. That it is pervasive through all actions rather than a separate element called religion, has blinded our perceptions of the meaning of sacred."[9] Because Native Americans did not mark graves in the same way that Anglos did, amateur collectors who unearth Indian grave goods such as pottery and jewelry believe they have recovered abandoned property. This "finders keepers" philosophy negates centuries of tribal tradition and respect for the dead.

The Navajo did not disturb dozens of cliff dwellings left by earlier peoples, perched high on south-facing cliffs; instead, they respected the ghosts of the ancient ones, whom they named the Anasazi. Destruction of those ancient Puebloan sites and their subsequent looting only came with white exploration and settlement in the nineteenth and early twentieth centuries. Today, many artifacts and grave goods, buried for centuries in the dust of abandoned southwestern villages, are in museums and private collections in the United States and around the world. A prime example of this unrestrained looting is the irreplaceable loss of much of the eleventh-century ceramics representative of the Mimbres people of the Mogollon culture from southwest New Mexico.

The Ancient Mimbres People

Having lived in apparent peace and harmony for 300 to 400 years, the Mimbres people reached their cultural height between A.D. 900 and 1150, when villagers produced exquisite black-on-white pottery decorated with ingenious animal and human motifs. The Mimbreños were a people of mystery because they had no distinctive architectural traditions and left no direct descendants.[10]

What this people did leave, however, was an outstanding tradition of black-on-white pottery. They used magical symbols and extraordinarily sophisticated geometric designs to produce perhaps the finest prehistoric ceramic pottery in the United States. The designs on their beautiful bowls and jars give us a vivid, timeless perspective on the Mimbres culture, with realistic images of animals, insects, birds, deer, antelope, mythic creatures, and paintings of the Mimbreños themselves. Women

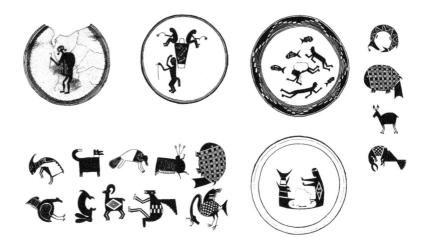

Most of the pottery designs are from mortuary ware at the Western New Mexico University Museum in Silver City, New Mexico.

A priceless ceramic bowl damaged by the FBI. Valuable pieces of Mimbres pottery were stolen from one southwest New Mexico pothunting couple and resold in Phoenix and San Francisco. The FBI recovered most of the collection in San Francisco but then shipped the irreplaceable prehistoric ceramics back to New Mexico in single-strength cardboard boxes. As a result, eighteen of twenty-six bowls were smashed like this one. The author was in the Grant County, New Mexico, sheriff's office when deputies opened the boxes. Photo by author, 1988.

Unharmed by the FBI, this magnificent Three Cranes Bowl represents the height of Mimbres ceramic art. The painting is exquisite, and the hatchmark lines are excellent, with no lines that touch and no errors anywhere in the design. A very wide and thin bowl, it rang like a fine crystal goblet when tapped with a finger. Having recovered the bowl from thieves, the elderly pothunting couple who had dug it from a Mimbres grave quickly sold it on the black market before anyone else could steal it. Photo by author, 1988.

potters depicted their people coming from the belly of the earth, gambling for arrows, hunting, fishing, wrestling, making love, and giving birth. Within the span of 150 years, in a burst of inexplicable creativity, the Mimbreños mastered perspective in a way that would not find its equivalent in Europe until the Renaissance. Approximately 5,000 Mimbres bowls are thought to be in existence today; all come from graves.

The Mimbres buried their dead in the floor of their houses. The deceased's knees and elbows were flexed, and one of these magnificent black-on-white pots was placed on the head. Because the person had died and would be reborn in the next life, the pot, too, was killed by making a small hole in the bottom. The ritualistically killed bowl was then placed on the head of the deceased so that the human spirit and the spirit of the pot would be joined in the next world.[11]

The semiarid climate and the relative isolation of southwest New Mexico protected Mimbres villages and the sacred burials until the first decade of the twentieth century, when looting began. Local pothunters would spend their weekends probing for Indian burials and even bring their families on "skeleton picnics." In addition, because outlines of the ancient villages were visible from the air, military crews training for World War II near Deming, New Mexico, routinely bombed these sites. By 1987, when the General Accounting Office (GAO) of Congress issued a report titled *Cultural Resources: Problems Protecting and Preserving Federal Archaeological Resources*, the GAO estimated that over 75 percent of the ancient Mimbres sites had been destroyed because Mimbres bowls were selling for up to $75,000 on the black market.[12]

This rare pottery is scattered in American museums such as the Smithsonian Institution, the Peabody Museum at Harvard University, the Metropolitan Museum in New York, the Logan Museum of Beloit College in Wisconsin, the University of Minnesota Museum, the Museum of New Mexico, and others. According to National Park Service (NPS) federal regulations about exhibiting grave goods, these bowls should not be displayed, but they are nevertheless exhibited frequently. Their exotic designs make them some of the most coveted prehistoric ceramics in a museum's collections. In Europe, Mimbres grave goods can be found at the National Museum of Denmark, the University Museum of Archaeology and Ethnology at Cambridge in England, the Musée de l'Homme in Paris, the Statens Etnografiska Museum in Stockholm, the Ethnographic Museum in Budapest, and the Museum für Völkerkunde in Leipzig, Germany.[13]

Unfortunately, these sacred burial bowls may never be returned to their places of origin because many efforts at repatriation from international collections have failed. However, before foreign nations can be expected to return Native American artifacts, the United States must first pass legislation banning its own international sale and export of sacred objects. Such legislation has not been forthcoming, and both Germans and Japanese speculate and trade in sacred Indian materials.

When two Navajo and one Hopi mask came up for sale at a Sotheby's auction in New York City, the auction firm insisted on proceeding despite vehement protests from tribal members. Elizabeth Sackler, a wealthy socialite, bought the masks for $40,000, explaining she would return them because "period examples of Native American ritual objects should not be for trade, purchase or collecting . . . people shouldn't be paying enormous amounts of money for such objects for their personal enjoyment."[14]

For similar reasons, the National Museum of the American Indian urges an increasing dialogue and involvement between Native Americans and white museum curators and directors. Because of such a dialogue, the Sacred Pipe of the Sioux, *ptehincala hu cannupa*, has been removed from display. A label placed in the exhibit case above where the pipe once stood announces, "When a pipe bowl and stem are joined a consecration occurs and the pipe becomes an instrument of divine communication." Therefore, pipe bowls and stems are traditionally stored separately when not in use. Plans have been made at NMAI to ensure that "pipes which have long been exhibited with their bowls and stems joined will be separated and purified and removed from display." Gary Galante, assistant curator of North American ethnology, explained that the museum had begun discussions with Arvol Looking Horse, a Minneconjou (or *Mnikowoju*) who is the keeper of the Sacred Pipe. In a cultural tradition without parallel among white Americans, Arvol Looking Horse is the nineteenth generation of his family to keep the Sacred Pipe originally given to the *Mnikowoju* by the White Buffalo Woman.[15]

Other objects pulled from exhibition at the National Museum of the American Indian included four Zuni masks, an Iowa tribal tomahawk with a unique design, and an ancient blade crafted from native copper. The Bear Cult Knife worn by members of the Bear Society from Montana's Blackfeet Tribe has also been removed. With a handle made from the jawbone of a bear and a sheath of buffalo hide, this ritualistic knife has

Indian masks used in sacred ceremonies are subject to repatriation under the 1990 Native American Graves Protection and Repatriation Act; however, some sacred items are still traded and sold on the open market. Navajo masks like this one were purchased in 1990 at a Sotheby's auction by philanthropist Elizabeth Sackler, who then created the American Indian Religious Object Repatriation Foundation in New York City. Courtesy, Navajo Nation Historic Preservation Department.

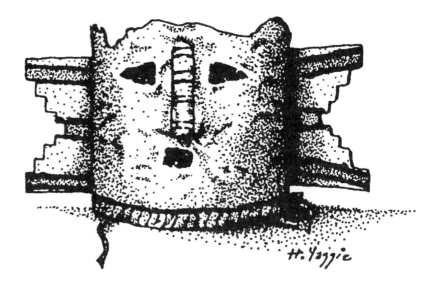

been labeled by curators as "extremely sacred"; they have also verified that it has been "used in initiation ceremonies as well as in warfare."[16]

As the museum world begins to consider its own ethnocentrism and as the hegemony of whites over the curation and interpretation of native objects lessens, a new kind of museum may emerge. Ivan Karp and Steven D. Lavine have argued that "the museum is a uniquely Western institution": "exotic objects displayed in museums are there only because of the history of Western imperialism and colonial appropriation, and the only story such objects can tell is the history of their status as trophies of imperial conquest."[17]

Previous exhibitions of Native American materials at the National Museum of Natural History of the Smithsonian Institution demonstrated the treatment of Indian artifacts as "trophies." Exhibits interpreted Indians as a warlike and proud but vanishing race in the curatorial equivalent of Jean-Jacques Rousseau's "noble savage." Visitors found Indian exhibits in proximity to snakes, whales, and saber-tooth tigers. The insensitivity of locating exhibits about living tribal peoples adjacent to the bones of million-year-old reptiles has not been lost on Indian activists. Cultural symbolism remains important, and poet Susan Shown Harjo has argued, "If we can get Indians out of the halls with the dinosaurs and elephants, we may really do something to change federal policy."[18] Indeed, museum policies are already changing. Removal of sensitive objects from display at the National Museum of the American Indian represents a significant shift in curatorial practice and increasing respect for tribal and native cultures.

Using Indian Consultants

Part of this transformation is taking place in Washington, D.C. Other changes are occurring with the use of Indian consultants by traditional museums and archaeological sites and the establishment of successful tribal museums on reservations. In the nation's capital, the Smithsonian Institution, under the direction of Secretary Robert McCormick Adams, reversed its previous position against repatriating human remains and artifacts. Forced by legislative fiat to change its policies, the Smithsonian reevaluated all aspects of the curation of Native American artifacts and now actively seeks the help and support of tribal peoples and Alaskan natives. As Secretary Adams made clear in testimony before the U.S. Senate, "Native Americans today are increasingly asserting their right for [their] heritage to be reclaimed and protected as a national responsibility." "They do so," he continued, "not as dwindling numbers of survivors whose communities are on the verge of disappearance, but as vital, growing components of the diverse, multiethnic society in which we as a nation take pride."[19]

In addition to the new National Museum of the American Indian, the American Indian Program at the National Museum of American History has been expanded to offer curatorial training for Indian curators and museum professionals. At the National Museum of Natural History, Native American public programs include select artisans and craftspeople who demonstrate their crafts before live audiences visiting the museum. Don Tenoso, a Hunkpapa Lakota Sioux dollmaker, became the first artist-in-residence. Before an eager and fascinated public, he crafted faceless Sioux-style dolls or toys and displayed his personal interpretations of an Aztec Jaguar-Warrior, a Zuni Buffalo Dancer (ca. 1875), and a Lakota-style Coyote Storyteller stick puppet.

The use of Native American consultants by museum professionals at state or national historic sites continues to increase along with sensitivity to Indian curation issues. Evelyn Voelker, a Comanche, directs the American Indian Center of Mid-America in St. Louis and has advised both the Cahokia Mounds Site in Illinois and the Missouri Historical Society in St. Louis. From her institution, Voelker also accepted human remains for reburial. Through a purification ceremony using smoking cedar, she cleansed the remains, the staff who had handled them, and the building where the remains had rested. As she waved a beaded eagle feather to gently waft cedar incense over the remains, she observed, "If people say they respect the American Indian culture, they can't ignore the beliefs of that culture."[20]

In the Northwest, the Makah Tribe built the Makah Cultural Center on Washington's Olympic Peninsula near the site of a thousand-year-old mud slide that buried a tribal village and preserved it untouched.[21] On the Columbia River plateau near Pendleton, Oregon, the Umatilla, Cayuse, and Walla Walla Indians have opened the Tamastslikt Cultural Institute, which features dramatic museum exhibits and their version of the social impacts resulting from zealous Christian missionaries, settlers on the Oregon Trail, and mandatory boarding school attendance at the turn of the twentieth century.

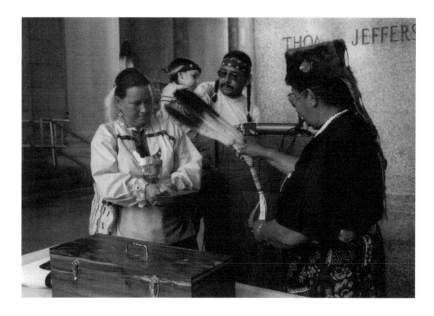

Native American repatriation ceremony, June 1990, Missouri Historical Society, St. Louis, Missouri. Evelyn Voelker, right, fans cedar smoke over a box containing the remains of Native Americans. Lynn Kussman holds the tray of cedar as Richard Bear and his son, Jacob, watch. Photo by Marilyn Zimmerman. Courtesy, Missouri Historical Society.

In the southeastern United States, tribal museum activities include setting up a conservation lab on the Tunica-Biloxi Reservation near Alexandria, Louisiana, to repair seventeenth-century historic ferrous artifacts returned from the Peabody Museum at Harvard University. The tribe hired expert conservators to teach young Indians proper techniques to conserve and curate sacred objects, relics, and cultural material from other tribes. The unique conservation facility was a specially outfitted and climate-controlled tractor trailer.[22]

Ongoing repatriation to tribes includes the return of a historic Revolutionary War–era Bible to the Stockbridge-Munsee Tribe in northern Wisconsin. Chief Red Cloud's Sharps carbine model 1851 rifle from the Sam Davis Historic Home in Smyrna, Tennessee, went home to Bernard Red Cloud of the Oglala Sioux Indian Tribe in Pine Ridge, South Dakota. The Heye Foundation also divested itself of eleven wampum belts repatriated to the Six Nations Iroquois Confederacy on Grand River in Canada.[23]

What has happened to cultural items that have been returned? Most of them remain in the care of tribal elders or are secure in tribal museums, but rumors persist that some sacred objects have been resold on the black market for even higher prices, though such allegations have been impossible to verify. The fact that native peoples continue to be unemployed or underemployed, with few opportunities to earn a decent living on or near tribal lands, persists as a depressing reality. But reselling repatriated objects to collectors would be a heinous crime, indeed. Tribal thieves would face severe consequences.

Sensitive Curation and Pesticide Applications

Rare objects that have been returned must be properly curated and stored. Gordon Yellowman of the Cheyenne-Arapaho Tribes discussed some of the sensitive curation issues for Great Plains objects; he pointed out, for example, that male and female objects should not be stored together and that care must be taken when moving objects because some should be stood up and all need sunlight. Dilemmas occur over the repatriation of war trophies such as scalps or fingerbone necklaces, for although one tribe may possess a trophy of this type, the scalp or fingers may have come from an enemy. Should that item be repatriated? If so, to which tribe should it go? As this scenario suggests, one negative aspect of the NAGPRA legislation has been that it can bring division into a tribe and create discord between tribes and their former rivals. Yellowhair also cautioned that a sacred object can have an impact on all who handle it.[24]

Another serious problem brought to light by NAGPRA is the historic curatorial treatment of rare feathered objects such as eagle-feather headdresses, prayer feathers, and bustles. Decades ago, nonnative curators, thinking only of preserving the objects, sprayed them with insecticide or arsenic compounds to eliminate insect infestations, but now that

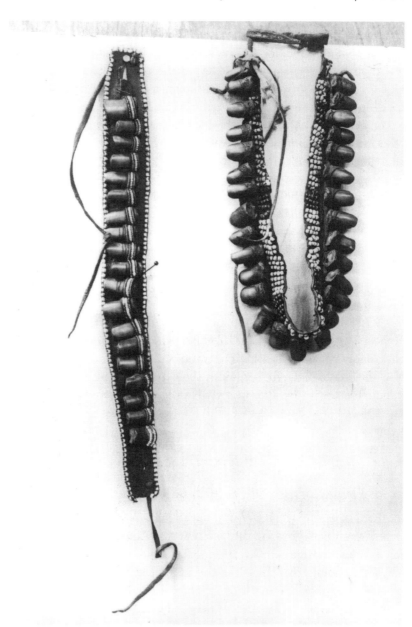

Nineteenth-century fingerbone neck-lace war trophies represent a repatri-ation enigma under provisions of the Native American Graves Protection and Repatriation Act: Warriors tortured their enemies and then removed their fingers. Who would claim grisly artifacts made from these bones? To what cultural group should they be repatriated? Courtesy, National Museum of Natural History, Smithsonian Institution, no. 246-C.

those sacred objects are returning to their tribes of origin to be used in rituals and ceremonies, what will happen to the health of spiritual lead-ers who will wear or handle these items? New conservation methods must be developed for tribal leaders who use sacred objects for initia-tions and ceremonies before "ritually retiring" them to caves or secret storage areas.

NAGPRA and Cultural Items

NAGPRA may not work effectively for the return of cultural goods and cultural patrimony because of the vague wording in the federal law. For example, if a state historical society refuses to return a cultural good (such as a chief's headdress) to a tribe, does the law need to be amended to clarify congressional intent regarding the return of cultural materials, as distinct from burial goods and sacred religious objects? If a tribe makes a request for repatriation, why not honor that request as a matter of goodwill and reciprocity, regardless of whether the item fits within NAGPRA categories—just as Curator David Bailey of the Museum of Western Colorado did when he returned an elegant beaded vest and a buckskin dress decorated with elk teeth to Northern Ute families.

Bailey discussed the need to return family heirlooms to the Ute: "We never put ourselves in their place and that's a mistake. Everybody benefits when we return items and receive valuable information back." "Other curators seem to believe their job is to fill their museum's storerooms and lock the door," he said, "but I would rather have a dialogue and exchange with living Indians to gain their respect and insight into our collections."[25] By returning the vest and dress, the Museum of Western Colorado received new beaded items as a gift from the tribal chairman, as well as stories and information. Thomas Livesay, director of the Museum of New Mexico, concurs with Bailey's position, and he reported that his institution's repatriation policy has brought it much closer to New Mexico's tribes; in fact, tribal members have gone through the museum's storerooms and told the staff about many of the objects there. Thus, the museum and the tribe have not had to deal with the formal, adversarial relationship that is sometimes brought about by implementation of the Native American Graves Protection and Repatriation Act.

Tribal Success Stories

Tribal museums are thriving, and collections are going home to the over 150 tribal museum and cultural centers in the United States, including the massive, five-story, $193 million Mashantucket Pequot Museum in the hills of rural Connecticut.[26] With few actual artifacts to exhibit, this tribal museum, the largest ever built, features a two-acre indoor diorama and a presentation of Pequot history going back 11,000 years but focusing on the Pequot Massacre of 1637, when Puritans burned their village and killed at least 400. The 85,000-square-foot main gallery contains eleven permanent exhibits, incorporating life-size dioramas modeled from living Pequots as well as interactive programs and artifacts from ethnographic and archaeological collections owned by the museum.[27]

In New York, the removal from public display of pipes, knives, and medicine pouches at the National Museum of the American Indian's Bronx facility represents only the beginning of a heightened awareness about the rights of tribal peoples to their own cultural heritage. The advent of tribal museums, which are both repositories and community centers, provides Native Americans with a positive sense of historical identity and an opportunity to look toward the future by sharing the past with the next generation. As one Indian staff member explained, when exhibits become redefined and artifact collections are returned, the larger American society will continue to learn of Native American traditions—but "on our terms, in our time, by our people."[28]

To explain ongoing native concerns about sacred objects, commentaries by tribal members and nonnative museum curators conclude this chapter. The common thread throughout their commentaries is respect for tribal beliefs, including the concept of sacred medicine bundles as portable altars.

Modern Native American museum exhibits often display the handiwork of local elders, such as the Shoshone beadwork of Helene Oldman and Millie Guinia from Crowheart, Wyoming. Photo by author, June 1997.

The Loss of Sacred Blackfeet Medicine Bundles, Related by George Kipp, Blackfeet Reservation, Browning, Montana

The largest collection of sacred Blackfeet medicine bundles in existence was acquired over decades by the family of Robert Scriver, whose father was an Indian trader at Browning, Montana. While Congress debated the Native American Graves Protection and Repatriation Act, Scriver secretly sold the collection to the Glenbow Museum of Alberta, Canada. Blackfeet cultural leader and language specialist George Kipp described the devastating loss of those bundles and the shock of having a trusted friend betray the tribe by selling its priceless heritage outside the United States.

Private collectors saw a lot of value [in] these religious and cultural artifacts. . . . At some point in time, when you are in an area where you're suffering from 90 to 95 percent unemployment and [you are] looking for the necessary food for the next meal and you have something of value, instead of letting your children starve you will sell that item.

In the Blackfeet way the rights [to open and use a sacred medicine bundle] are the prime thing of importance, and the object is secondary, but we find out now you need both the rights and the objects to perform these type of ceremonies. The United States government, through their agents, established quite a market [for] our items, and once that market was established we started rapidly seeing these items disappear, along with the deterioration of [our] whole society, culture, and social system. Now we're trying to regain our identity and our way of life, but we're having a very difficult time doing that without the artifacts—the ceremonial bundles that are placed all over the United States and Germany and Japan. So we're finding it very difficult to regain what we are, who we are.

Scriver was reared and raised here with the Indians. He was accepted. He became an artist and he saw a value in Indian artifacts and ceremonial objects. To make himself renowned in the Western art world, he entered into the culture of the Blackfeet. He gained acceptance and trust. He obtained a medicine pipe bundle from the Little Dog family, went to the traditional ceremonies of the transfer and all the items that were given to him were given to him in trust, because he was an [important] man in the Indian world.

Pipe men have a certain social status. Consequently to the Western art world [because of our trust in him] he was also held in renown. He got to experience and touch and feel the actual cultural items. He made a living out of Western art, and a lot of it was duplication of Blackfeet objects. He wrote a couple of books, so he was well accepted.

All this time he was collecting items, and some of the items he purchased for I think $3,500, $5,000, $1,500, something like that. It was very minimal, but he ended up selling them for $125,000. A bear knife that was stolen from an old lady ended up in his hands and he sold that for $10,000.

There is renewed interest. There are a lot of younger people looking for these certain items that he sold so that they can start taking care of them in a traditional manner, but they're no longer available. . . . Those items were the prime backbone for us to assure ourselves that we would be Blackfeet in the future. We need them back.[29]

Curating a Sacred Pawnee Family Medicine Bundle, Related by Diane Good, Kansas State Historical Society

In the summer of 1873, after planting their corn crop, 350 Pawnee Indians left their earthen villages along the Republican River on their annual buffalo hunt into western Nebraska. They traveled peacefully, though pioneers had already begun to take up land and establish homesteads. After a successful hunt, the Pawnee stopped in a small canyon to prepare and process their buffalo meat, unaware that over 1,000 armed Sioux were also in the area. White

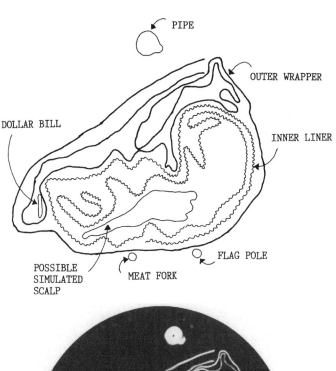

Honoring tribal traditions by not opening the Pawnee Sacred Bundle, Kansas State Historical Society staff members had the bundle scanned through a medical imaging process to determine effective means of curation and to gain some idea of what was inside. Courtesy, Kansas State Historical Society, Topeka, Kansas.

buffalo hunters warned the Pawnee, but Sky Chief of the Kitkehaki Band did not believe the report of so many hostile Sioux. On the morning of August 5, 1873, the Sioux attacked in one of the last major intertribal battles on the Great Plains. From that day forward, the canyon has been known as Massacre Canyon.

With Sioux shooting down at the Pawnee from both rims of the low canyon, chaos reigned. Desperate Indians abandoned horses heavily laden with meat and buffalo robes. Pawnee women and children tried to flee as warriors attempted a hasty defense. Seventy Pawnee died in the massacre, and white settlers came to take the meat and buffalo robes without bothering to bury the dead. In 1930, Congress authorized the construction of a granite monument to mark the Indian tragedy—one of the few instances in which federal funds were used to identify a local historical site.

One of the survival stories involves a young girl and a sacred medicine bundle. Anthropologist and education specialist Diane Good of the Kansas State

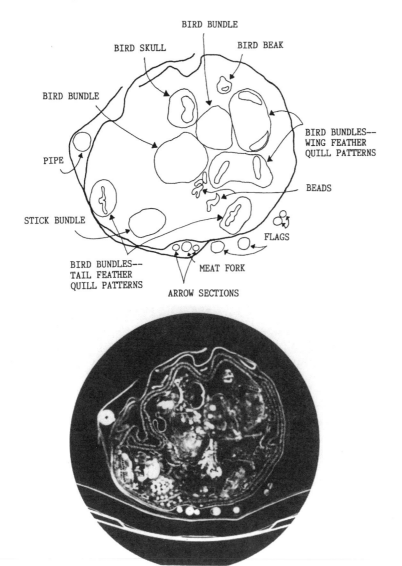

Historical Society cleaned the family medicine bundle and described in detail what it was like to work with a sacred object.

Objects themselves are interesting, but it's the stories behind them that really bring life to the whole situation. The story that we got with the bundle was that it had been in a Pawnee family for a hundred years. We don't know exactly when it was created. The family story that came with the bundle was that it had been at Massacre Canyon, and had belonged to a warrior who was there with his wife and family. As they were being attacked, in order to save his daughter, who was between 6 and 8 years of age, he cut the packs off the packhorse and tied his daughter to it. He tied the bundle to her back and put a [presidential] peace medal around her neck, which was all the medicine that he had available, all the power that he had with him, and he put all of his power onto that little girl and told her to take care of the bundle and that the bundle would take care of her. And then he whipped the horse and it ran from the canyon.

The story that was told us was told in those words—so the words themselves were almost as important as the object, and this appealed to me, being the mother of children of about that age and understanding from a parent's perspective what that meant. Knowing that the father knew he was going to die, because it was his job to fight to the death . . . but he also knew he had a chance to save his daughter, and he put a lot of faith and trust in the power that that bundle held. To me the bundle had a power and an energy that had been built into it as it was created. It became [a symbol] not only for the girl but for her family, as she grew up and had children and then grandchildren.

The other thing that was intriguing to me was that it came to us as a family bundle, yet the Pawnee don't have family bundles; they have individual bundles and they have village bundles. They don't have family bundles. And so what was a family bundle? It was clearly identified for us by the Pawnee owner as a family bundle, and I began to see that through time it had become a family heirloom.

This bundle really had two symbol sets attached to it. One was the symbol of the power, the medicine that it contained that it was originally created to have, and the second was the symbol of family that was tied so tightly to this bundle, which had been maintained according to Pawnee custom but had not been opened because the ceremony that was necessary to safely open the bundle had been lost with the warrior in Massacre Canyon. It was perpetuated and maintained as a sacred item but could not be used for its original purpose. So it took on a second sort of sacred meaning as an identity for the family, but it eventually became a liability to them because of the unknowns of what was in it. They felt that there would be people who would break into the house and steal it and possibly endanger the family in the process of stealing it, which was one of the reasons that it was donated to us.

I knew that whatever I did [as a curator] had to be reversible and defendable. I had to do the right thing for the right reasons. I also chose to look at this bundle as if it were a person with its own spiritual energy, and in a sense working with it, cleaning it, looking at it, studying it, I almost began to know it as its own personality. I tend to believe that things that are created with that kind of purpose have their own spiritual power anyway.

[The donor originally] did not want her name associated with the bundle, because she said too many people in the tribe said that harm would come to the tribe and to her because she gave this to a museum. She said it was her mother's dying wish that the Pawnee Indian Village Museum [be given the bundle, for it] was the appropriate place to safely care for this bundle [and in the museum] it wouldn't endanger anyone. They were concerned about keeping it in the family home for fear someone would break in and murder them in the process of trying to steal it. [The donor] was concerned about the bundle's safety. But she was also concerned about her own.

I can see where the woman was caught in a real turmoil because she had been raised by Pawnee cultural law [which] says the bundle is to be passed down from mother to daughter and to be properly cared for. The original owner of the bundle and the ceremonies that went with it were lost, so it's like having a locked box with no key. You can't get into it. You can't use it. It's there. You have to maintain it, but you can't do anything with it, and at the same time, it presents a danger because of the unknown of what's in it. People want it.

a mother's dying wish

She had to dispose of it in an appropriate manner, and she asked her daughters if any)) of them were interested in it, but none of them wanted to take the responsibility. Her son who was interested in it was not eligible by Pawnee law to receive it, because it is the property of a woman, handed down from mother to daughter. Even though her son wanted it, she didn't feel that she could give it to him because it would violate the law surrounding the bundle. It was her mother's dying wish that it be given to the Pawnee Indian Village, because that was a sacred place to her and to her family.

As we talked to the family, they were comfortable with us taking it, bringing it back to our facility to get the dust off it and determining how best to care for it—get it photographed, documented as much as we could, and with them it was alright if we opened it. They didn't care because when they gave it to us they broke all ties with it, at least in their own minds at that time. We've realized that because we did not choose to open it they've maintained ties to it as well.

But Mrs. Horsechief [the donor] told us that her 21-year-old grandson had died as a result of that bundle. He died within weeks after she donated that bundle to us. He was killed in a car wreck, and she was convinced and helped in that belief by several tribal members who told her it was because of her decision to give us the bundle that her grandson had died. So she really felt that she had sacrificed her grandson for that decision to give it to the white people—to take it out of Pawnee culture.

Even though she felt it was going to a Pawnee sacred place, it was still being removed from her family. She had violated the rules. I think we all feel that way when we knowingly violate a rule. We tend to look around and see what our punishment is, and we sometimes take things that are not at all associated and link them in our own minds as justification. I'm quite sure that's what was happening here. I'm convinced that the boy's death had nothing to do with the bundle, but she is just as convinced, or was at the time, that there was a connection.

When Mrs. Horsechief donated the bundle to the Kansas State Historical Society, it was one of the few nineteenth-century Indian medicine bundles that had remained unopened and was now in a museum's collections. Anthropologists struggled with the ethical question of whether they should violate the bundle by opening it and perhaps damage its contents and the buffalo hide straps that secured it or whether they should respect tribal traditions and leave the bundle unopened. To their lasting credit, staff members at the Kansas State Historical Society did not open the bundle. They left it sealed, but they did carefully clean the ancient leather and then x-ray and CT-scan the bundle to learn more about its contents and how it should be curated.

When we accept things for collection, we accept them with the idea that they're to be preserved for as long as possible, which is a real challenge when you're trying to preserve an object that was not intended to be preserved forever. It was made out of materials that were intended to disintegrate. It was intended that the bundle be buried with the warrior, because it was an individual bundle, not a village bundle. But this was a very powerful warrior, judging from what we've been able to see [by X rays] into the inside of the bundle.

The outer covering is buffalo hide that has probably been brain-tanned as near as we can determine without specific tests, which would be destructive to the object. The X rays suggest an interior lining of a woven grass mat and the objects themselves include bird bones, metal bells, glass beads, and other natural material.

It was sacred. The practical aspect of opening it would have destroyed it. We could not have opened it and put it back together again for a number of reasons, not the least of which was that the leather ties that held it had become brittle, and they would have broken in the process. But simply to open a bundle intermixes and moves things, and we had no idea if they had a special location. We did know from research that the heads of the birds were all facing the same direction, and that was related to the direction that the bundle faced ceremonially—whether it faced north or south, depending on the season. Had we opened the bundle all of that would have changed, and we would have destroyed the context of that bundle, and probably destroyed the bundle as well, but to me it wasn't just the bundle that was sacred. It was the whole arrangement of things within it as well as the mystery.

maintaining the mystery

The item was sacred and the knowledge of what was in it was limited to certain people; the male owner had knowledge of what was in it, maybe some of the males that he associated with and some of the other warriors had knowledge of what was in it. The women, theoretically, did not, although I suspect the warrior's wife probably had a pretty good idea, because generally the women would have been left to put everything back after the ceremony, so I doubt that it was a total secret to her. Sadie was the young girl who came out of the canyon, and I'm sure Sadie had no idea what was in the bundle. After her parents died, that was a mystery, and to me, preserving that mystery was as important as preserving the item itself. We did X rays which left us with more questions than answers, which is fine. I feel like we maintained the mystery, while we answered some questions that helped us to interpret it.

It served as a portable altar. During a ceremony, it would have been untied and opened and the tools within it would have been used in a variety of ceremonies. What was contained within it was like a combination of safe deposit box, insurance policies, and family bible. It had a record of where they had come from and insurance that they would get to where they were going. Items that were within it maintained the story even though the items themselves might not have been recognizable to people outside of the family. There were objects within that bundle that would help the family remember who they were and where they'd come from, to perpetuate the family and keep them on the right path.

The bundle would be considered alive in Pawnee cultural tradition. It was alive when it was being used. It was given birth at the time it was created, and I'm not sure at what point the bundle actually dies. Probably not until the warrior dies and the bundle is buried with him. Even then, there is a question as to whether the bundle actually dies at that point. A bundle would go through cycles of being used and then not being used. One component of the bundle was a perfect ear of corn—symbolizing mother corn, which was the mainstay of the Pawnee diet.

Every time they harvested in the fall, they would take a perfect ear of corn and put it into the bundle. The corn would have been encased in buffalo intestine, as if it were shrink-wrapped, and that would be in the bundle from the harvest until spring. Then the corn would be taken out and ritually used to plant the next corn crop. It was a ritual way of taking the energy of last year's corn harvest and putting it back into the ground for another successful year, so the bundle would have been without an ear of corn through most of the summer. It could be compared to a person asleep. They're still alive, but they're not consciously interacting with the world. The massacre took place in August, and the corn might not have been harvested at that point, and so it's possible that the corn was simply never replaced in the bundle, because it had not yet been harvested. So the bundle is asleep.

"I feel that it is living," said Vance Horsechief, who believes that the Pawnee know about the bundle in ways that "it was only meant for us to know." The sleeping bundle now rests in an airtight case suspended from the ceiling above an excavated prehistoric Pawnee lodge at Pawnee Indian Village Museum in northern Kansas, almost on the Nebraska border. Appropriately lit by small spotlights, the two-foot-long bundle is on the western side of the ancient lodge, in the place of religious importance—six feet atop the faint outline of a bison skull that would also have served as an altar for prayers and offerings to the Great Creator. Unopened, the bundle's sacredness remains intact. It is a sacred item in a sacred place, residing quietly in an ancient village.[30]

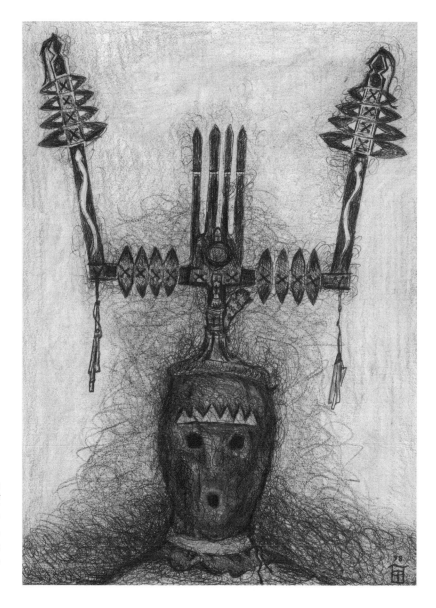

The historic Apache Gaan Dancer's mask curated at the Museum of Western Colorado awaits repatriation to the Mescalero Apache. Artist's rendition by Greg Phillipy; original art in the collection of the author.

Returning an Apache Gaan Dancer's Mask,
Related by David Bailey, Curator,
Museum of Western Colorado

The Gaan Dancer headdress in our museum is a very sacred item. I went to an Apache dance at the Native American Lifeways Festival in Montrose, Colorado, and they were wearing one similar to it so I approached them about the headdress before NAGPRA became law. The dancers talked a little, and they mentioned to the crowd about how sacred the masks are and what power they have. The masks are very powerful and in a sense dangerous if you do not know how to control the power that's within them.

This is an older Gaan Dancer's headdress. It's a black leather mask with a twisted cottonwood root that fits over the top of your head. Even people who don't know anything about sacred objects, when they see this mask, they have a reverence and also a fear. I remember the most poignant thing that happened when we first got the mask out, when we were doing our periodic inventories of the Native American collection. Several staff people were there and they stepped back, instinctively, not because of any particular reason. But all of them took a step back and I myself, as curator, felt uncomfortable handling it.

We had a Ute medicine man come in, because we have an open door policy for Native Americans interested in looking at the collections. One Southern Ute came in and he went into our collections area and then stopped from going around a corner. He said, "I can't go around that corner." And I said, "Well, why?" And he said, "Because some of our people are there." He'd never been in the museum before, and I thought, well, that was a strange occurrence, because indeed thousand-year-old Fremont human remains were stored on shelves—around the corner.

Larry Cesspooch, a Northern Ute, came up and did a ceremony here in the museum to cleanse the artifacts and then to cleanse me, because as curator I have to handle a lot of things. He wanted to make sure I was safe. He said his sense was that the spirits of the objects in our collections were confused, and he had to assure them that things were alright.

The Apache mask was donated in the late 1970s, and at that time a lot of sacred objects had gotten away from tribes for one reason or another, and I think this may have been one of those that somehow got out of the family. The museum's collection policy was more eclectic then, and the staff realized the scarcity of authentic Native American artifacts. In a way it was a good thing we did preserve it, because almost thirty years later now we can return it. NAGPRA has a good side effect of creating trust between museums and Native American cultures, because in the early days curators would try to get anything they could to round out their collections. And in the rounding out process, they weren't considering the consequences of taking objects away from families or clans.

This particular Gaan Dancer's mask is used in the most sacred Apache dance ceremony by the Mescalero crown dancers, and the mask can't be handled by women. The dance is a spiritual representation of the spirit world, so it's really sacred. Because of NAGPRA and because it was the right thing to do, we sent photographs of the mask to all the Apache tribes, and they knew it by the description and the photographs, which verified that this mask had previously been used in a ceremony. It had already acquired a sacredness to it, because it had been used in that connection between the real world and the spirit world.

The mask may date to the turn of the century. We do know it's an earlier version of the ones they use now. Instead of a modern wood frame and a cloth mask, this mask is leather. The paints vary, and it has a lot of patina on it. It looks like it's been around for quite awhile. Even the feathers that are attached to the crown of the mask seem fairly old.

This is a very special mask made even more important because one of the Apache museums burned down, so a lot of their sacred items have been destroyed by fire. The Apache museums committee works by con-sensus, and by knowing the paint and the design on sacred objects they know what should be returned and to which tribe. In this case, the mask goes to the Mescalero Apaches. They'd asked that it be personally deliv-ered so that we could attend their dance and understand the significance of it, and I think that is a great gesture because when you return it, you come to understand the significance of the sacred object from their side.

We'll come back from the meeting having learned a lot about the Apaches, and we're curious about their interaction with the Utes, too. We want to ask questions about some of the legends concerning the ancient people before the Utes. So the mask will be returned. You try to handle it in a very careful manner. This headdress with the black leather mask and the cottonwood root represents the lightning beings and in that aspect something happened to me.

lightning strikes near the curator

I'm home and I walk out in my backyard to see an afternoon storm. The storm seems a long way off, and I'm walking towards my shed and there's this noise and everything goes pure white. The next thing I know, I'm on the ground, getting up, and a sixty-foot tree over in the next yard is split down the center—a sycamore tree, which is a pretty stout tree. When the lightning hit I was knocked to the ground and couldn't hear for about 20 minutes.

Interestingly enough, the neighbors cut out the center trunk and the tree is still alive. It's split down to the base of the trunk, which is about 12 feet off the ground, but it's alive, and I am reminded of the Gaan Dancers and the association with the spirit world. I've been told that Indians believe if you're hit by lightning, then it's probably a sign that you're cursed by the power object that you've handled, but if it hits nearby, you're empowered. Probably my empowerment is to return the mask to the group where it belongs. I hope we can return it, especially since we had the Northern Ute tribal member do the cleansing ceremony. He felt like the spirits were lost and this is one we can get back home.[31]

Crow Tribe Family Heirlooms in Museums, Related by Janine Pease Windy Boy, President, Little Big Horn College, Crow Agency, Montana

One of my great-grandfathers died in the 1930s, and he was buried and only three weeks later our family members found his war shirt that he was wearing upon burial—in a museum. It seems that now that wouldn't happen, but actually things are happening as we speak. There is a trader who has been living in our community waiting for the right moment to acquire a very important medicine bundle that has to do with our sacred tobacco society. The young woman that is caring for it is someone who has been in and out of work. She has had a lot of family losses because she's a woman who's about forty and that is when you start losing your parents. He's just like a vulture waiting for her to have too many crises in her life and be [forced] to sell this medicine bundle for three or four thousand dollars.

Museums have an assumption that objects are not living, that they're just so much inanimate matter, but objects are a vital part of our culture. They have a nature to them and they have a spirit to them. Let's say you have a medicine bundle that has rocks in it. To one person they're simply rocks. They're so much matter. They're so much mineral, and they could be stepped on or they could be thrown across the river with no sentiment involved. But for us these rocks have a vital character. And it's not just a rock that is separated or alienated from the people; it is a rock that we know that we have been familiar with, that we understand and interact with and in some respects even have dialogue with.

Museumologists will say unless you have humidity control or you have security and perhaps a number of conditions, you don't have the right to repatriate sacred objects. But there are many things that are being preserved in contemporary Indian society. They're under the utmost care, under daily care of their stewards or the owners whom those objects live with. So [these objects] are perfectly preserved and cared for and have survived for centuries or certainly lifetimes in wonderful repair, and if they need repair, we have the artists who probably made them in the first place. We don't have certified museums and we don't have lots of money, but we care deeply for these objects. Why would we want to repatriate them if we wanted to destroy them?

The ones who wish to repatriate wish also to involve these objects in ceremonies. It requires a very special understanding of the place held by the object in community functions. There are some ceremonies that cannot happen unless certain medicine bundles are present and their power and their personage is a part of the community that undertakes the ceremony. Now I'm not a member of [those societies], but I understand that you don't have the ceremony unless that bundle is also present among the persons there, and it's thought of as a person, as a life. Now if the bundle is gone, then the function of that society is broken and the value that society brought, the relationships that it made among the people, the songs, the stories, the history, the cohesiveness of that group of people, the family nature of that society is broken, and that is a human tragedy.

A lot of stuff was swindled, and we've been so impoverished that in order to actually put food on our table my grandpa sold baby cradles that were in our family for absolutely years just in order to feed us. My father was a little boy at the time. And we know now that [those cradles were] sold to the Denver Art Museum, which doesn't understand that we don't have a baby cradle anymore and that my kid didn't get to be in the same baby cradle as all the rest of the babies in our family. They don't understand that. They don't understand my feelings as a mother not to see him beautifully put in that baby cradle. They look at the cradle as a piece of art, something that should be observed for its aesthetic beauty, its design qualities. For me, it's all those things, but it is also my connection to the fact that my father was in that baby cradle and I would also like to have had my son in that cradle.[32]

3

Sacred Places and Sacred Landscapes

It is difficult to verbalize in another language, for another culture, exactly what makes a place sacred, but I'll do what I can. There are spirits that dwell in certain places that may be beneficial to a fast and helpful in other ways to the individual and to The People when one fasts and prays there. Other things that make a place sacred are what our grandfathers and their grandfathers before us have put there, or how the Great Spirit has shaped the rocks, or the ancientness of the grandfather trees, or the power of the plants. Our brothers, the animals know these places and come to these places.

—HAWK LITTLE JOHN, Cherokee

When we hear the voice of our ancestors speak of the struggle of Native Americans to retain their homeland, clearly we understand that it was not only a struggle for land, but a religious battle to retain its sacred character.

—GARY NILES KIMBLE, Gros Ventre

For traditional native peoples, the landscape includes not only the physical world of rocks, trees, mountains, and plains but also the spirit world. Indigenous Native American worship depends on a detailed and particular sense of place that goes back in language and in stories for centuries, whereas Protestant Christianity has been evangelical, transportable, Bible-based, and not rooted to a particular landscape. Europeans abandoned their cemeteries and cathedrals as they set sail for America. They crossed the water and then crossed the continent and reconstituted their religious communities by building new churches. In contrast, Native Americans felt obligated to protect and defend the graves of their ancestors and the sacred locations where the Great Spirit resides and communicates with them—locations such as Mount Graham in Arizona, Bear Butte and Harney Peak in South Dakota, and Big Sheep Mountain in Colorado. Centuries spent living in the Great Basin or on the Great Plains brought about a deep love and understanding of the landscape, and Indians believed themselves inseparable from the land and sky. They found the Great Creator, and he spoke to them in special places, just as God spoke to Abraham, Moses, and others in the Old Testament.

In the nineteenth and twentieth centuries, many American Indians joined Catholic and Protestant churches, but a small number retained ancient indigenous religious beliefs and became known as "traditionals" in their own communities. In seeking and guarding access to sacred sites, American Indians need a guarantee of religious freedom for their ceremonies, festivals, medicinal plant gathering, and pilgrimages, which differ from Christian traditions. Because most Americans have not understood the uniqueness of Indian religions, they have violated the free exercise of it. We need, instead, to understand landscapes in the context of traditional Native American religion and the powerful, enduring presence of sacred geography.[1]

In his book *God Is Red,* native writer and activist Vine Deloria explained that Indians "have many more sacred places than do non-Indians . . . because of our considerably longer tenure on this continent." Moreover, he said, these sites are "sanctified each time ceremonies are held and prayers offered."[2] Anthropologist Deward Walker wrote that "sacred sites are places of communication with the spirits, portals where people enter the sacred . . . where spiritual power can be accessed and even attained."[3] Deloria noted that these "are places of overwhelming holiness where the Higher Powers, on their own initiative, have revealed Themselves to human beings. . . . This tradition tells us that there are places of unquestionable, inherent sacredness on this earth, sites that are holy in and of themselves."[4]

Although the word *sacred* may have multiple meanings, for most native people, it connotes respect, whether applied to a song, a dance, or a landscape. Sacred qualities may change over time. "The meanings of terms such as *sacred* and *religious,*" wrote anthropologist Luke Lassiter, "are contested, situational and multifaceted within their community contexts."[5] In describing the Gourd Dance in Oklahoma, a Kiowa tribal member explained, "When we say it's 'sacred' it means we respect it. We have to take care of it, to pass it on to our children."[6] Thus, Native Americans have a strong sense of stewardship in regard to their sacred places.

Many sacred sites, such as Bear Butte and the Black Hills in South Dakota, Wallowa Lake in Oregon, and Mount Adams in Washington, are "monumental geological features that have sacred meaning—mountains, waterfalls, or unusual geologic formations."[7] Deloria described them as special places that "regenerate people and fill them with spiritual powers."[8] He said, "People have been commanded to perform ceremonies at these holy places so that the earth and all its forms of life might survive and prosper. . . . They must perform certain ceremonies at specific times and places in order that the sun may continue to shine, the earth prosper, and the stars remain in the heavens."[9]

For most tribes, a sacred place is one where the Great Creator or spirits, both good and evil, communicate with the living. Most Anglo

Americans consecrate a church as a sacred place, and it remains sacred as long as a congregation meets there. But when congregations outgrow a building, they may well sell it and purchase a new space to make holy. By contrast, what is important for traditional Indian religious believers is not the sacred space of a church or cathedral but rather a location made holy by the Great Creator, by ancient and enduring myth, by repeated rituals such as sun dances, or by the presence of spirits who dwell in deep canyons, on mountaintops, or in hidden caves. An entire landscape may be sacred because Indians migrated from place to place in search of food, on seasonal rounds that took them into the high country in the summer and to lower elevations in the winter. Sacred sites remain integral to tribal histories, religions, and identities.

Indians honor oral traditions linked to specific sites. One such site is Ribbon Falls in the bottom of the Grand Canyon, where the Zuni believe they emerged from the center of the earth as a people. Similarly, Native Hawaiians have a special reverence for Haleakala and other volcanoes. A sacred site is always sacred, and human burials or village sites remain hallowed ground. If shamans carved rock-art panels to evoke spirits in southern Utah or at the bottom of Echo Park in Dinosaur National Monument in Colorado, then those places are special today and should not be disturbed. They are sacred sites where the living communicate with the dead or with the powerful animal spirits of deer, elk, and mountain lions that the rock artist came to see in his or her visions.

Continuity Over Time

Repetition and tradition, unbroken continuity over time—these elements define traditional Indian spirituality, whether expressed by a young man seeking a vision at a remote vision quest site, by a tribe such as the Shoshone or the Ute at their annual sun dances, or by Miwok leaders on a pilgrimage to collect plants for religious purposes as they visit sacred shrines in California. Indian religions—not religions in the sense of rules and dogma but rather highly individualistic approaches to honoring the Creator—are intricately bound to a tight web of place and an intimate, subtle, and even secret understanding of landscape.

Klara Bonsack Kelley and Harris Francis, in their book *Navajo Sacred Places*, wrote about the 17.5 million acres of the Navajo Nation. They explained that the stories about Changing Woman, First Man, Salt Woman, and Monster Slayer function as tribal histories of the Navajo's Athabaskan migration southward from the Arctic before their arrival in Arizona and New Mexico in the early seventeenth century. Kelley and Francis said, "The stories that go with these places, and with the mortals and immortals who have come together there, are a large part of Navajo chronicles of the origin and evolution of the Navajo world, people, and customs."[10] The landscape at Shiprock, at Monument Valley, and at collapsed volcanoes along the banks of the Little Colorado River "provides a material anchor for those stories and thereby stores them [as] a physical link between people of the present and their past."[11] Navajo specialist Leland Wyman explained further: "Place is of the utmost importance to the Navajo. . . . The geographical details of long journeys of the protagonists of the myths almost literally bound the Navajo country: at least they state its landmarks," which include four sacred mountains that have "an inner form, a sexual identity . . . and stories that explain their creation."[12]

Indeed, for traditional tribal peoples, spirits exist and can help or hurt the living. For the Shoshone, those spirits may be the elfin *NunumBi*.[13] Different tribes have other names for spirits, but in every case, the spirit world is intimately linked to place. As the Warm Springs Pow-Wow announcer known as "Eight-Ball" put it, "The rocks are the bones of our ancestors and the dirt is the flesh of our ancestors."[14] But as scholar Robert McPherson lamented, "Treating the sacred places on a mountain in sacrilegious ways, including mining, road construction, logging, ranching, and recreation, causes the holy beings to flee and their power to be lost."[15]

So how can progress and development be reconciled with sacred site protection? What kinds of compromise are possible to protect sacred sites and to preserve a sacred landscape? Can development occur simultaneously with cultural resource protection? How are significant issues of the free exercise of religion for native peoples addressed? To answer these questions, Native American sacred sites must first be defined by type so that they can be identified (although in this book, I do not describe specific locations in order to protect sites from vandalism or misuse). The following typology emerged based on my research and discussion with traditional tribal cultural leaders.[16]

Religious Sites Associated With Oral Tradition and Origin Stories

The first category of sacred sites is religious sites associated with ancient myths and oral traditions that figure prominently in emergence and migration stories. To use nomenclature from the National Register of Historic Places, these sites are "traditional cultural properties" that have deep meaning for tribal identity.[17] Examples include the huge stone monoliths in Navajo Tribal Park called "Big Hands" and the symbolic barrels with spouts essential in legend for storing and providing rain for the Navajo. Rainbow Bridge near Navajo Mountain has sacred qualities for the Navajo because the arch comprises two beings, a male and female, and "from their union come the rain, people, rainbows, clouds, and moisture that originates here and spreads over the reservation."[18] On the 17.5 million acres of the Navajo Nation, sacred places may be associated with the origin stories of clans, the origins of ceremonies, the origin of specific customs, and the general Navajo creation story. Other southwestern tribes, such as the Zuni, Hopi, and Walapai, also have specific places linked to their clan migrations and creation stories.

The Hawaiian Islands have many ancient trails and trail systems. One of the most intact is known as the Hopili Trail or the King's Highway, which follows the Maui coastline. Smoother, rounded lava rocks have been placed within the path as stepping-stones. On the coast, Ohala Heiau, a sacred temple platform, faces the ocean just above the well-worn trail. Photos by author, March 1999.

Each tribe has its own story of emergence and migration. For the Kiowa, as N. Scott Momaday wrote, "the great adventure . . . was a going forth into the heart of the continent. They began a long migration from the headwaters of the Yellowstone River eastward to the Black Hills and south to the Wichita Mountains." He continued, "Along the way they acquired horses, the religion of the Plains, a love and possession of the open land . . . in the course of that long migration they had come of age as a people. They had conceived a good idea of themselves; they had dared to imagine and determine who they were."[19] Part of that journey took the Kiowa to Devils Tower, Wyoming, which became the first national monument in the United States, set aside in 1906 by President Theodore Roosevelt. Over twenty tribes incorporate stories about Devils Tower in their oral traditions, although Native Americans believe that the site should be renamed by its Indian name, Bear Lodge.[20]

Bull Lake, near the Continental Divide in Wyoming, is also sacred because of associated stories. Shoshone medicine men required their apprentices to spend a night there alone because the lake is believed to contain the ghost of a white buffalo chased to the very bottom by a

hunter. Young apprentice medicine men had to sleep all night in the Wind River Mountains there, enduring "the winds on the icy waters [which] create a roaring sound effect resembling the bellow of a bull."[21]

Trails and Pilgrimage Routes

A second category of religious sites encompasses trails and pilgrimage routes through sacred landscapes, such as the trail to Zuni Heaven or the Ute Trail. Cairns as trail markers were particularly important for migratory peoples who remembered them as places to pause and meditate, as Nez Perce guides did while traveling along the Lolo Trail with Meriwether Lewis and William Clark in 1806.[22] Indians also reverently added to the cairns, with each passing traveler saying a prayer and adding

Stone cairns high on the Columbia Plateau above the Columbia River mark the aboriginal land of the Yakama Tribe. Sacred cairns served as kinship markers, and by tradition, family members added a stone to the monument each time they passed it. The tall markers, many of them five to six feet high, also served as fishing boundary markers, indicating which tribal bands could fish east or west of the line of cairns. Photos by author, July 1992.

another rock to the pile to secure personal good luck and show respect for his or her ancestors.

Along the Columbia River in Washington, tall cairns of basalt represent kinship and family lineage for the Yakama, as well as fishing boundaries for different bands of Plateau Indians.[23] Native peoples believe that cairns contain the essence of the builder and must be approached with care. In the Arctic, cairns, or *inuksuit*, become vital landmarks in the windswept snow and ice, and for weary, isolated travelers, they offer comforting proof that ancestors passed through the area generations earlier.[24]

Pilgrims may also make ritual or ceremonial crossings along pilgrimage routes. According to Patricia Parker, "The Karuk Indians of northwestern

The Smoking Place in the Bitterroot Mountains of Idaho has long been sacred to the Nez Perce. On their return trip over the mountains in 1806, Lewis and Clark and the Corps of Discovery, accompanied by three Nez Perce guides, stopped on this ridgetop on the Lolo Trail for a Sacred Pipe ceremony. Both leaders sought to hurry on, anxious to get through mountains that expedition member Sgt. Patrick Gass described as "the turribulest I ever saw." But the Nez Perce refused and insisted that the group stop, smoke, and offer gratitude to the Creator and give thanks for their safe passage.

Captain Clark did not understand the religious significance of the ceremony, the large cairn of rocks, or the altar there, nor did he appreciate the meaning The Smoking Place held for his guides. He wanted to hurry east; the Indians wanted to pause and contemplate their natural world. He felt trapped in the mountains; the guides felt right at home.

California continue to carry on world renewal rites, ancient ceremonies featuring elaborate dances, songs and other ritual activities, along a stretch of the Klamath River that is now the site of a highway, a Forest Service Ranger Station, a number of residences, and a timber cutting operation." She wrote, "Specific locations important in aspects of the ceremony remain intact, and accommodation has been reached between the Karuk and other users of the land," even to the point that the California Department of Transportation has "erected 'Ritual Crossing' signs at locations where the Karuk religious practitioners cross the highway." The state transportation department has "built shallow depressions into the roadway which are filled with sand in advance of the ceremony, so

On June 27, 1806, Captain Clark wrote, "We halted by the request of the Guides a fiew minits on an ellevated point and smoke a pipe on this eminance the nativs have raised a conic mound of Stons of 6 or 8 feet high and erected a pine pole of 15 feet long. From this place we had an extencive view of these Stupendeous Mountains principally covered with snow like that on which we stood; we were entirely serounded by those mountains from which to one unacquainted with them it would have Seemed impossible ever to have escaped, in short without the assistance of our guides . . . after haveing smoked the pipe and contemplating this Scene Sufficient to have dampened the Sperits of any excpt such hardy travellers as we have become, we continued our march" (Bernard de Voto, ed., *The Journals of Lewis and Clark* [Boston: Houghton Mifflin, 1997], p. 411).

The large cairn is gone now, but a smaller one remains, and a fifteen-foot forked tree juts above the ridgeline. As it has for hundreds of years, the sacred Smoking Place inspires awe and contemplation. Photos by author, August 1999.

the feet of the practitioners need not be profaned by contact with man-made macadam."[25]

pilgrimage to zuni heaven

In 1540, Francisco Vasquez de Coronado encountered his first Native Americans in the high deserts of New Mexico. They were Zuni priests on a solemn, ceremonial pilgrimage. Half a millennium later, those sacred pilgrimages continue. As Richard Hart reported, "Every four years, between forty and sixty Zunis set out on a strenuous religious pilgrimage that takes four days and covers more than 110 miles. [They] represent all of the tribal members as they make offerings, say prayers, gather sacred paint pigments, and eventually reach *Kolhu/wala:wa*, where

Gathering sacred plants and materials, including feathers, is important for tribal ceremonies. Here, a young Navajo displays a sacred eagle feather that he has beaded into a prayer feather as a gift for a medicine man. Photo by author, March 1982.

Kenny Frost, a Southern Ute, holds
sacred tobacco gathered in the White
River National Forest in Colorado.
Photo by author, August 1997.

their religious activities and prayers are aimed at bringing peace, order,
and prosperity not only to the Zunis but also to the entire world."[26] The
Zuni trail itself is sacred, with every geologic and natural feature having
special meaning. For years, the Zuni have gone through complex and
expensive litigation to regain title to their lands and to guarantee
easements so that they can continue their pilgrimage uninterrupted.

Traditional Gathering Areas

A third category of religious sites includes gathering places for fish,
wildlife, sacred plants, and materials to quarry, such as mineral deposits
to secure sources for face and body paint. Crucial to religious ceremonies, Great Plains paint mines were neutral territory, and warring tribes

Indian Burial Rock, El Paso County, Colorado. This misnamed local site was not a rock on which Plains Indians were buried but rather a sacred altar; beads and other prayer offerings were left at its base. The rock is flanked by two small buttes where eagles live, and the site has a commanding view of the Front Range of the Rockies to the west, essential for spotting buffalo herds or enemies on horseback. Photo by author, July 1976.

could gather red, yellow, and black clay in peace without attacking one another. Sacred paint sources include the paint mines near Calhan, Colorado, and in Wyoming at Sunrise and Rawlins. A Colorado cave contains every clay color needed in Ute religious ceremonies. The Ute knew of the cave in oral tradition and had remembered it for decades before the Bureau of Land Management (BLM) contacted tribal leaders about its exact location. Now, the BLM officially protects the cave and discourages visitation by non-Indians.

Navajo gather hematite and special dirt and sand for sandpaintings used in healing ceremonies. Most southwestern tribes also have sacred places where men gather salt. There are sacred gathering areas for clans to acquire special roots and herbs, as well as family-use sites. There are gathering areas for willows to be made into baskets or wild tea for medicinal purposes, and there are places to retrieve special water from sacred springs or snowmelt from high elevations. For their *jish*, or medicine bundles, Navajo medicine men may also collect projectile points and pieces of petrified wood; as Rena Martin, former director of the Traditional Cultural Program for the Navajo Nation, explained, "Things are never just taken. There are always thank-yous given and prayers offered."[27]

Pipestone National Monument in southern Minnesota is one of the most important sites for gathering sacred religious materials because, for centuries, American Indians quarried the soft, red catlinite stone there to carve calumets, or pipe bowls. To unite a pipe bowl with a pipe stem is to begin holy communion by praying to the Great Spirit, with smoke offered in six directions, including all four cardinal directions, down for the earth, and up for the sky. The Sioux have jealously guarded this site for years, and to this day, the National Park Service must arbitrate disputes among different tribes over the quarrying, distribution, and sale of the red catlinite.[28]

Because native peoples use plants in religious ceremonies, traditional gathering areas for sacred sage, sweetgrass, and other herbs must be protected. Tribal sacred sites include these traditional cultural property areas where, for generations, tribes have gathered food—whether it be salmon among the Plateau Indians, bitterroot among the Shoshone, camas roots among the Nez Perce, or huckleberries among the confederated tribes of Warm Springs and the Yakama Nation. These sites retain their sacredness because they bring the people together each year at harvest time to gather plants for the first feasts and to initiate young girls as women and young men as hunters or fishermen. Indians in the Northwest are acutely conscious not only of their reservation lands but also of lands ceded by treaties that guaranteed natives the perpetual right to hunt and fish in their "usual and accustomed places." Tribal members exercise those rights every year.

Gathering roots and berries in the old way keeps the people physically strong and knitted together by social tradition. The sites of these activities reaffirm cultural and tribal identity, and when they are lost, the tragedy is real. The Yakama, Warm Springs, and Colville Indian Bands experienced such a loss when concrete dams on the Columbia River irrevocably altered the sacred landscape at Celilo Falls and decimated the runs of coho, chinook, and sockeye salmon that they had

Young men and women of many tribes withdrew into seclusion at vision quest sites to fast and pray as they waited for a sign from their spirit helpers. This vision quest site is in the high country of western Colorado. Southern Ute Kenny Frost contemplates the site before he makes an offering. Photo by author, August 1995.

In the spring of 1833, professional artist Karl Bodmer and his wealthy patron Prince Maximilian of Wied-Neuwied traveled north up the Missouri River on the steamboat *Yellow Stone*. Transferring to keelboats they continued up the Missouri deep into Blackfoot territory where Bodmer drew these authentic illustrations of northern Great Plains Indian altars and shrines. Artwork courtesy of Tish Mumford, New Harmony, Indiana.

fished for millennia. For that reason, tribes in Washington and Oregon vow to use every law at their disposal to protect remaining sacred sites and to guarantee their nineteenth-century treaty rights.

Offering Areas—Altars and Shrines

Native peoples also make offerings privately or within ceremonial cycles when they gather sacred materials. At certain times of the year, American Indians offer prayer sticks and special foods to the Creator to keep the people in harmony, to heal the sick, and to provide general balance and prosperity. Offerings are also left for powerful animals, such as bears and buffaloes. Archaeologists sometimes consider such offering sites prehistoric in terms of age and assume that they are no longer used, but native peoples consider such time distinctions irrelevant. Altars are never abandoned; they represent active conduits to the spirit world.

Vision Quest and Other Individual-Use Sites

A fifth category of religious sites encompasses locations used by single individuals, such as vision quest sites. These sites are often composed of stones piled eighteen to twenty-four inches high placed in a horseshoe or circular shape. The young man or woman seeking a vision enters the earth or stone enclosure, remaining without food or water until the arrival of an animal or bird spirit, which then becomes the source of his or her personal power or medicine. Indians have built most vision quest sites on high precipices with panoramic 360° views; these "are among the most common forms of sacred geography in North America," according to Deward Walker.[29] Small sweat lodges used by individuals or wooden tree platforms used by medicine men or women for meditation and healing exist in deep canyons or on mountain ridges.

Vision quest sites can be found at remote locations throughout the Rocky Mountains, and Indians who visit them today often leave offerings

Some 700 feet long and 300 feet wide, the ancient Hawaiian *heiau* of Pi'Ilanihale on Maui is the largest pre-Christian sacred site in the islands. Once used for human sacrifices, it is now a National Historic Landmark. During its construction, 50,000 people brought lava rocks to form the temple platform. *Ili*, small round rocks for the top and base, came from a riverbed five miles away and were passed along by a chain of human hands. The site may date from the eleventh century; the rocks are 1.5 million years old. Located at Kahuna Garden, one of the five gardens that make up the National Tropical Botanical Garden, Pi'Ilanihale Heiau took 128,000 man-days to build. The site was overgrown throughout the 1970s, with 25 percent of the top gone and 75 percent of the upper wall in need of mending, but a five-man crew of native Hawaiian stonemasons completed the project, which was expected to take three years, in just eight and a half months. The job was like putting together a giant, three-dimensional jigsaw puzzle— of heavy stones. The crew moved ten tons of rock by hand, and not a single rock is out of place today. Here, Francis Sinenci, one of the expert masons, is about to present a *lei*, or flower-wreath offering, to a special river-polished sacred stone that was inserted into the volcanic rock walls long ago. Photos by author, March 1999.

Authentic Hawaiian offerings include special water-polished stones placed atop Ohala Heiau (*top*), along the King's Highway on Maui, and exotic orchids laid along a rocky beach, also on the Maui coast (*middle*). Leaf-wrapped stones left at sacred sites are inauthentic, a nuisance, and a travesty (*bottom*). As Sara Collins of the Hawaiian State Historic Preservation Office explained, "Leaf-wrapped stones are popularly called *ho'okupu* although they are really nothing of the kind. A *ho'okupu* is an offering or gift made in a ceremonial context, usually to a high-ranking chief or a deity. Needless to say, a rock would hardly ever be an appropriate offering or gift to such exalted beings. Somehow, people (including tourists who have been wrongly instructed to do so) have gotten the idea that it's appropriate and a sign of respect to leave leaf-wrapped rocks at Hawaiian historic sites. The leaf wrapping is often ti (coryline terminalis) leaves. The *ho'okupu* clutter up a site and, at worst, hasten a site's deterioration because people pull the rocks they use right out of the existing structure" (E-mail to author, August 27, 1999). Photos by author, March 1999.

Kukaniloko—the birthstones where, beginning in ancient times, royal Hawaiian women went to give birth beneath large palm trees—is a revered sacred site on Oahu. Commoners stood at a respectful distance to watch the births and to ensure proper heirs for the royal lineage, while the women in labor leaned against the deeply weathered rocks to support their thighs. A male child born at Kukaniloko in the presence of chiefs himself became a chief. As at many sacred sites, offerings of toys, coins, fishhooks, charms, and fruit continue to be left there. This traditional cultural place, now surrounded by pineapple plantations, has been in use for over 800 years. Photos by author, March 1999.

A modern, one-man sweat lodge framework (*left*) was built with fresh-cut willow branches at the Flathead Culture Summer Camp in western Montana. Photo by Carl Fleischauer, 1979. Courtesy, American Folklife Center.

In Canyon de Chelly National Monument, Arizona, Navajo traditional cultural places and sacred areas include a large historic forked stick male hogan (*bottom*). Photo by author, spring 1981.

Native Americans believe that ancient villages are sacred because the
spirits of their ancestors may linger
there, as at the White House Ruins in
Canyon de Chelly National Monument, on the Navajo Reservation in
Arizona. Photo by author, 1981.

of sacred sage, tobacco, or water to placate the spirits. An Indian might
reuse the site for a modern vision quest or leave it undisturbed; in either
case, a seeker of visions has made it a sacred place.

Group Ceremonial Sites—Sweat Lodges, Dances, and Sings

Ceremonial dance sites, such as Sun Dance, Bear Dance, or other
dance sites, are also sacred places, and their usage may date back decades
or centuries. Plains Indians erect the Sun Dance lodge at the same spot
in a lengthy ritual that includes a virtuous woman selecting the forked
aspen or willow tree for the central lodge support. Under the direction
of the Sun Dance chief, dancers and helpers raise the twelve roof poles
of the lodge, which always faces east toward the rising sun. By the afternoon of the second day, assistants cover the outer perimeter of the lodge
with fresh willow branches to give the dancers shade as they rest
between dances.

Once the dance is completed, the prayers offered, and the people
healed, the dancers leave the lodge by midafternoon of the last day.
Erecting a permanent Sun Dance structure is not the traditional
Shoshone, Ute, or Arapaho way, for they believe the lodge loses its
religious purpose after the dancers leave; thus, the space is no longer
hallowed. With the dancers' sacrifice over, the cosmic spell has been
broken. What endures is the process, the community ritual, and the

repetition of the dance, with each group of committed dancers sacrificing themselves at the same sacred place. Ten months out of the year, no one visits the sites.[30]

Just as with the routes taken by the Shalako spirits at Zuni or the Deer Dancers at Taos Pueblo plaza, what is sacred is the reconstruction of tradition through meditation and performance. Keeping the Sun Dance structure intact in the tradition of Christian churches would be contrary to Indian beliefs. Moreover, building the lodge anew brings people together. The wooden frames of large, group sweat lodges are also sacred, whether they are the stout cedar poles of Navajo sweat lodges in the bottom of Canyon de Chelly National Monument in Arizona or the framework of thin willow pole lodges found in the Montana mountains.[31]

Ancient ceremonial sites include Serpent Mound National Monument in Ohio and Pueblo Bonito at Chaco Canyon in New Mexico's

This ceremonial rock art, from the Pony Hills site near Deming, New Mexico, depicts a Mimbres storyteller sitting with his arms outstretched in front of a fire. His hair is tied in the distinctive Chongo style still popular among the Navajo. Behind him is a recently killed desert bighorn ram. Photo by author, 1989.

This large panel of various ceremonial carvings from the Pony Hills site raises numerous interpretive questions about the variety of Mogollon culture figures and their meanings. Photo by author, 1988.

Chaco Culture National Historic Park. Men's societies in the Southwest still use kivas to initiate young boys, and on the high mesas, at places such as the village of Walpi on First Mesa at Hopi, ancient plazas still reverberate with dance steps of the Katsina dancers.

Ancestral Habitation Sites

Another category of sacred sites to be respected and protected includes ancient Puebloan ruins and tepee rings, where Plains people once set up large seasonal encampments. The brush shelters, or wickiups, of the Great Basin tribes or the Ute in Colorado would also qualify as sacred village sites. Zuni tribal leaders closed the ancient site of Hawikuh to visitors; it is now protected by the Zuni Preservation Department.

Petroglyphs and Pictographs—Ceremonial Rock Art

Many petroglyphs, pictographs, and pictograms qualify as sacred. The Eastern Shoshone believe that petroglyphs represent messages from the spirit world and that only properly trained shamans can decipher them. Ceremonial rock art often illustrates origin and creation stories and can be found on mountaintops, on boulders in the bottom of drainages, and along pilgrimage routes—any place where the rock surface can be incised down to the desert patina under ledges protected from weathering.

The Spanish priests Fray Francisco Atanasio Dominguez and Fray Sylvestre Vélez de Escalante, traveling north from Santa Fe, New Mexico, in 1776, encountered a variety of Fremont-era and Ute rock art south of present-day Rangely, Colorado, in a canyon they named Canyon Pintado ("Painted Canyon") because of the colored drawings. In their journals, they specifically noted the famed *kokopelli*, or flute player, represented in stylized form throughout the Southwest.[32] Much rock-art symbolism has been analyzed and described, and distinct motifs vary among cultural and geographic regions.[33] Petrogylphs and colored pictograms also represent living tribal traditions, and some examples of historic rock art may help to validate tribal claims to ceded lands.[34]

Individual Burials and Massacre Sites

As with all cultures, human remains are sacred to tribal peoples, and with the passage of the Native American Graves Protection and Repatriation Act of 1990, unmarked graves found on public lands now come under federal protection. Although some tribes find every individual burial sacred, for the Navajo in the Southwest, burials are to be protected but are also places to avoid out of respect.[35]

In addition to Indian burials, another sacred category includes massacre sites and mass burials, such as the Marias River Massacre site in Montana, Sand Creek in eastern Colorado, Washita River in Oklahoma, the Camp Grant Massacre in Arizona, and Wounded Knee at Pine Ridge, South Dakota.[36] These sites of shame, where armed military forces attacked sleeping Indian villages, rarely receive protection or interpretation.

Expressing respect for their dead, native peoples maintain spirit houses built atop graves in the Alaskan village of Eklutna. All the graves face east so that the dead may rise when the world is reborn. Photos by author, August 1992.

Without question, the sites are sacred to Native Americans, who feel an obligation to tell the living about past atrocities. As Patricia Limerick has written in *Sweet Medicine*, "Americans ought to know what acts of violence brought them their right to own land, build homes, use resources and travel freely in North America. Americans ought to know what happened on the ground they stand on."[37]

Observatories and Calendar Sites

Massive stones atop Fajada Butte at Chaco Culture National Historic Park in New Mexico functioned as a solar and lunar calendar, designed by ancestral Puebloan peoples to mark the passage of time and seasons. Throughout the Southwest, stone alignments and concentric circles on rock art indicate solstice markers. For the Fremont people who once lived near Rangely, Colorado, a ridgetop observatory may have helped determine their very limited agricultural season at high elevations on the northern boundary of the Colorado Plateau. In southern Colorado, Chimney Rock near the Southern Ute Reservation is high in elevation and would have been used as a solstice marker. In the South, the misnamed Old Stone Fort near Manchester, Tennessee, represents a sacred earthen enclosure, with an earth entrance built to the east to admit maximum sunlight on June 21, the longest day of the year.

One of the most powerful sites in North America is the Medicine Wheel in northern Wyoming, which is aligned to both the summer solstice and the rise of the summer stars Aldebaran, Rigel, and Sirius, though the wheel has been periodically altered over the centuries. The Medicine Wheel must be considered as an entire religious complex that includes vision quest sites, sacred trails, and even stone cairns in the shape of an arrow pointing to the site from over forty miles away across the Big Horn Basin. According to Fred Chapman, Native American liaison with the Wyoming State Historic Preservation Office, the Medicine Wheel represents an "archetypal form of religious architecture."[38]

In his book *Wisdom Sits in Places*, an extraordinary analysis of Apache place-names and their relation to clan histories, anthropologist Keith Basso eschewed the word *sacred* and stressed that in Indian religion, "matters are much more complex and . . . outsiders seldom do justice to the subtlety or sophistication of native systems of thought." He explained that the Western Apache language "contains three distinct words for marking kinds of 'sacredness,' and that at least three Apache terms could be translated (all of them imprecisely) as meaning 'spiritual' or 'holy.' "[39] Basso was reluctant to use the word *sacred* in identifying Western Apache locations, but his ethnographic work mapped 496 Apache places with specific names within a forty-mile radius of Cibeque, Arizona. When the Apache say names, such as Scattered Boulders Standing Erect or Circular Clearing With Slender Cottonwood Trees, they repeat the words of their ancestors because those names give a picture of a place as it once existed. Place-names rooted in the ancestral past remind modern Apache of who they are, what they have been, and even who they should be in a strict moral sense because many of the names encapsulate stories of deeds from long ago.

Basso eloquently argued that sensing or knowing a place is a basic form of cultural activity and that naming places "can deepen and enlarge awareness of the present" because the principal themes of Apache place-naming "are the endless quest for survival, the crucial importance of community and kin, and the beneficial consequences, practical and otherwise, of adhering to moral norms."[40] He explained that the original Apache name of Phoenix, Arizona, once meant "A Great Expanse of Cottonwood Trees" and that Apache names have been used with accuracy in lawsuits to help identify valuable historic water sources now lost.

If the term *sacred* has multiple meanings for tribal peoples, at least it is generally understood by non-Indians who do not easily comprehend how Native Americans value their lands and landscapes. Perhaps with the use of the term, despite its ambiguity, Indian sites can be better protected. Certainly, Presidential Executive Order No. 13007 on Indian Sacred Sites (May 1996) provided new protections to special areas and helped to accommodate American Indians and Alaska natives in the free exercise of their religions. As Deward Walker has noted, "Clearly sacred geography is a universal and essential feature of the practice of American Indian religions."[41]

After centuries of religious oppression and denial of Indian religious freedoms, it is time to respect tribal traditions and to understand how tribes work within the matrix of state and federal laws to protect their ancient sacred sites. The next chapter discusses tribal historic preservation programs and the ways in which native peoples establish cultural offices and enforce relevant laws and regulations.

Former Hopi vice chairman Vernon Masayesva stated, "If an Indian says a rock contains the spirit of God, courts and judges must not dismiss this as a romantic description. Keep in mind, to a Catholic consecrated bread is no longer bread but the very physical body of Christ." "No court would challenge the Catholic belief in that regard," Masayesva asserted, "and no court should challenge as romantic overstatement that places or things contain the spirit of God either."[42] This chapter concludes with commentaries on sacred places and tribal preservation by the Hopi, Navajo, and Zuni, with additional insight by a nonnative archaeologist whose work with tribes is both profoundly satisfying and frequently disorienting as he tries to straddle two different worldviews.

The Hopi View of Land Use, by Ferrell Secakuku

All land should be respected and all land used only for survival, whether it be physical, spiritual or mental. Our religion does not teach us to subdue the earth. Our religion teaches us to take care of the earth in a spiritual way as stewards of the land.

Hopis do not view cultural resources such as ruins, as abandoned or as artifacts of the past. To a Hopi, these villages were left as is when the people were given a sign to move on. These homes, kivas, storehouses, and everything else that makes a community, were left exactly as they were because it is our belief the Hopi will someday return. Our people are still there. Today the Hopi designate these ruins as a symbol of their sovereign flag. Potsherds are left in abundance, usually broken into small pieces with the trademarks showing. These are the footprints of the occupants. Hopis believe that ruins should remain untouched because when anything is taken it breaks down the value of holding the village in place.

Hopi prophecy recognizes these cultural resources as part of today's living cultures. They indeed should be protected for the future of our people. Most of the time, the way white men view protections, interpretation and education seems not to be the Hopi way. For Hopis, protection is based upon the honor system, upon respect and trust. Sometimes Hopis feel that the things they believe—honor, respect, and trust—are not compatible with other societies but we continue to think it should be the Hopi way.

The Hopi way of measuring the value of cultural resources and other so-called artifacts is not in terms of money. Rather it is their importance for life today and their future destiny. The future of the Hopi is a great burden to them because we believe we must live a life of spiritual meditation and humbleness in order to take this corrupt world, which will get worse, into the better world. Yes, we believe in the fifth world and our spiritual integrity must be strong to keep our ruined villages alive. Our houses, kivas, and our shrines must be kept warm and active. We rely on our spiritual ancestors who passed this way and are still there to receive the messages.[43]

Voices of the Diné, by the Navajo Historic Preservation Department

Diné tradition teaches that all things occur in a circular pattern and progress clockwise. Much like our tradition, the historic preservation and archaeology departments teach preservation of cultural heritage within four realms of action and interaction beginning with ourselves; our tribal government and educational institutions; our community; and finally, external entities. We maintain our heritage within the boundaries of the four sacred mountains, and use plants and minerals to remind us of our path.

Ha'a'aah (east): One always starts in the east, which is white in color and represents the morning. We are taught to take time out for ourselves to pray and reflect. To teach preservation ethics, we must first prepare ourselves through traditional and formal education. Tradition teaches that Sis Najini (Mount Blanca), in southwestern Colorado, is the sacred mountain of the east. White shell is the precious gem associated with the east; it represents discipline and our physical being. Corn is the plant associated with this direction; we are made from corn and it enables us to grow.

Shádi'ááh (south): Once we have prepared ourselves, our days are spent learning, working, and abiding by unwritten and written tribal laws. We work with our tribal government by making decisions that affect our precious cultural resources and by teaching preservation ethics to our people. The sacred mountain of the south, *Tzoodzil* (Mount Taylor), is in northwestern New Mexico. Blue is the color given to our working day and is symbolized by the gem turquoise. This precious stone represents knowledge, wealth, and well-being, and enables us to think clearly. Beans are also associated with this direction as they provide nourishment for our day's work.

E'e'aah (west): When the sun travels to the west, we return home to the warmth of our communities; the color yellow represents the family hearth. It is here we find additional strength and gain knowledge from our elders and clans, and in return, we teach our families and community about preservation. We also help local traditional people, who are stewards of sacred places, to preserve these places. *Dook'o'oosłííd* (San Francisco Peak), in northeastern Arizona, is the sacred mountain of the west. The abalone shell is the precious stone of the west; it encourages our bodies to stay healthy, from birth into old age. Squash is the plant of the west because it represents water; water is essential to life and thus, the continuity of the family.

Náhookos (north): The north represents the night and is black in color. It embodies the time for rest, rejuvenation, and old age. Sensing danger from without, being aware of our surroundings, and being prepared to work with outside entities are all ideas our traditional teachings tell us about the north. Thus, it is natural that our interactions with external entities lie in this direction. *Dibé Nitsaa* (La Plata Peak) is the sacred mountain of the north, and black jet, representing protection from outside influences, is the gem associated with this direction. As we smoke tobacco, we reflect on our day's journey and bring ourselves back into harmony; this is important because being in harmony is an essential concept of Diné philosophy. There are many ways we work with outside entities to protect our heritage, and to maintain our traditions outside the control of tribal laws and community trust.

The Zuni and the Grand Canyon, by Zuni Leaders

The Zunis first emerged out of Mother Earth's fourth womb at a sacred place deep within the Grand Canyon. Zuni religious leaders explained that the Zunis came out of *Chimik'yana'kya dey'a* in a group which included those peoples now known as the Havasupai and Hualapai. The Hopis emerged at the same time but at a different location. The Zunis, or A:shiwi as we call ourselves, came into the first light of Sun

Several tribes throughout the Southwest, including the Havasupai, Hualapai, Hopi, Zuni, and Navajo, claim
sacred sites in the Grand Canyon.
Photo by author, November 1997.

Father at a beautiful spot near Ribbon Falls. Naturally the first things
that happened to us and the first things that we saw became prominent
in our prayers, ceremonies and religion. The point from which the first
ray of sunlight reached us over a spot on the canyon rim; the plants that
grew along the stream that flows from Ribbon Falls to the Colorado
River; the birds and animals that we saw as we traveled out into the
world; the brilliantly-colored minerals in the rock walls of the canyon;
all of these things are recounted sacred in our prayers, and have a central
place in our ceremonial religious activities and way of life.

After emerging into what non-Indians now call the Grand Canyon,
we began a long search for *Idiwana'a*, the "Middle Place," a place where
equilibrium and stability could be achieved, and where we could sustain
ourselves for the foreseeable future. Many stops were made journeying
up the Colorado River. Villages were built, and wherever a village was
built shrines were built and offerings were made. When ancestral Zunis
died, they were buried near these villages with accompanying ceremonies and blessings.

At certain places during the later migration along the Little Colorado, the *Kokko*, our supernatural beings, delivered sacred information
to the Zunis. Many of these villages and sacred places are remembered in
our prayers and in the religious narratives that tell the story of our
migration to *Idiwana'a*, the "Middle Place."

Still searching for the "Middle Place," the A:shiwi continued up
what is now known as the Little Colorado River, stopping and settling
at villages periodically, before moving on in their search. At the junction of the Little Colorado and the Zuni River the migrating A:shiwi
had important interaction with the *Kokko*, and supernatural beings. This
spot came to be the place where all Zunis go after death, and is known in
Zuni as *Kolhu/wala:wa*, or "Zuni Heaven."

Eventually the Zunis located the "Middle Place" near the headwaters of the Zuni River and settled there. The current village of Zuni is

located at that "Middle Place" and we have been living there ever since, for many hundreds of years. The point of emergence, the place where Zunis go after death, and the village of the living Zunis, these three places and all their ancient villages and shrines in between them are all tied together by the sacred flowing waters of the Zuni River, the Little Colorado River and the Colorado River. The water of these rivers is of central importance to Zunis' prayers and offerings. The history of the A:shiwi is not only told in the prayers and religious narratives maintained by Zuni religious societies today, but in the ancestral ruins, graves, shrines, trails, and sacred places left along these rivers and their tributaries from the time when Zuni was undertaking its great migration.

Zuni religious activity is oriented towards bringing rain, prosperity and stability to Zuni and to the rest of the world. Periodic visits and pilgrimages to locations along the Zuni migration route are necessary in order to carry out the duties of the various Zuni religious societies. At these sacred locations, Zunis say prayers and make offerings. Zuni religious leaders also collect samples of plants, pigments and water, and take those samples back to Zuni where they are used in religious ceremonies. Many ceremonial activities cannot be undertaken without these samples, which must be collected at the precise locations mentioned in the ancient Zuni prayers.

It has been thousands of years since Zunis first emerged into the world in the Grand Canyon; long, long before Europeans ever set foot upon this continent, or on Zuni territory. Zunis, consequently, have been making pilgrimages to shrines and sacred places on the Zuni River and in the Grand Canyon for many centuries.

Zunis do not make the same distinctions concerning "living" and "non-living" that many non-Indians make. To Zunis, the earth is alive. The walls of the Grand Canyon, the rocks, the minerals and pigments there, and the water that flows between the walls of the canyon are all alive. Like any other living being, the earth can be harmed, injured and hurt when it is cut, gouged, or in other ways mistreated. So, we believe that the Grand Canyon itself is alive and sacred. The minerals used for pigments, the native plants and animals mentioned in our prayers and religious narratives, and the water of the river and its tributaries are sacred to us and should be protected.[44]

Working With Wyoming Tribes, by Fred Chapman

Fred Chapman is the senior archaeologist and Native American liaison for the Wyoming State Historic Preservation Office in Cheyenne. He works effectively with tribes, but, as he explained in this piece, the work can be exhausting.

I work with about sixteen or seventeen Native Americans depending upon what day of the month it is. Some of them are closer to me than others. They will divulge information that as an anthropologist and archaeologist I think needs to be recorded. However, I generally ask

Native Americans [when] they give me a particular piece of information if it's okay for me to write it down, and almost invariably they say, "No, it's not. We don't want anybody to know but you; this is just for you."

Well, I have an impulse as a former academic archaeologist and a current applied archaeologist to commit this to some kind of report, to something I can distribute and hopefully enlighten others, but I have chosen not to do so because if I was to divulge this information, which I've been told is restricted, this would set back what I'm trying to do [by] ten or fifteen years. Who knows what it would do? I can't justify a short-term asset that might prove to be a liability over the long term.

Often I'll be told certain details about Sun Dance ceremonies or certain details about how one goes about conducting or participating in a sweat ceremony or a fasting vision quest ceremony, and most of the information Native Americans consider discretionary is of a spiritual nature. They are unwilling to have this written down because it is contrary to their tribal beliefs. It is traditionally transferred from generation to generation by mouth. You have people who function as tribal historians in an oral sense; there might be one, or usually there are several, who each maintain a certain segment of the tribal memory. You simply don't write that down; the only way you can communicate that is orally.

There are some tribes that seem to be more forthcoming and more willing to let you write about the information that they divulge, but on the average most Native American tribes I deal with are very uncomfortable [about] having spiritual information committed to a written medium.

When you deal with Native American elders, traditional people, traditional practitioners of their respective tribal religions, you've got to play by their rules. So the kind of thing that happens is you might be at a meeting with some Native Americans and you're all in the same hotel or motel and part of the business, what I'm there for, is to ask them some things about particular projects that come up in our office, like a natural gas pipeline.

They don't have any defined schedule like I do. The Shoshone that I deal with talk about spiritual issues in the Section 106 context [of the National Historic Preservation Act], but they talk about spiritual issues late at night. They don't talk about it during the day; they talk about it at 2:00 in the morning. So you're in their motel room talking to them about this stuff at 2:00 in the morning, and you're awfully tired and you're used to an 8-to-5 day, but that's irrelevant because they don't do business during office hours.

Sometimes if you're talking about something that Native Americans regard as particularly sensitive spiritually, you'll have to go through a cleansing ceremony. That's part of the game. That's part of the rules. That's how they do business. Sometimes you'll have to do a sweat afterwards to cleanse yourself properly, because you've been talking about burials—just talking about burials, understand—not touching them, but just talking about them. And the sweat can be a rigorous, physical experience.

I was consulting with some Shoshone around Devils Tower a couple of years ago, and for them to do business at Devils Tower, which is a very sacred place to many Native American tribes in this region, I had to engage in a pipe ceremony at different locations all around Devils Tower. It took hours and then they wanted me to stay and have a vision with them, and I explained that I was so tired I was in no condition to have a vision. This is how they do business though, and it places me as a white man of European descent on an edge, on a knife edge, between the two cultures, my culture and theirs. It's very disorienting, and I find I can't do it for very long. Just a few days of close contact with Native Americans doing spiritual things, and I have to get away from it.[45]

4

From the Sweetgrass Hills to Bear's Lodge
Preservation of Tribal Sacred Places

> Resource preservation, especially of cultural resources, is one way
> indigenous people respond to threats to their traditional lifeways.
> Increasing numbers of nations and tribes of American Indians (or Native
> Americans) commit themselves to exercising *cultural sovereignty*. The
> Hualapai Tribe exemplifies this approach.
>
> —Loretta Jackson and Robert H. Stevens,
> Hualapai Tribe Office of Cultural Resources

> The native philosophy to which I have been exposed in my community
> is one that conveys responsibility upon my generation to serve our
> ancestors, who love us dearly, and to provide a good place on earth for
> future generations, who are depending on us to pass these values on to
> them. The role of caretaker is extended by tribal leaders and
> representatives to archaeological sites, burial grounds, and sacred places,
> and it is our responsibility to protect and care for these places
> during our time in this world.
>
> —Leonard A. Forsman, Suquamish Indian Tribe

Quietly but inexorably, Native Americans have become intimately involved in the preservation of their historic and sacred sites. Years of cultural repression have not deterred them, and a new generation adamantly seeks to preserve the traditions and special places of their ancestors. Such an emphasis on sacred places and landscapes will ultimately affect historic preservation in the United States because one of the most exciting aspects of preservation today is the way native peoples seek to protect archaeological and historic sites and cultural resources on the approximately ninety million acres owned by over 550 federally recognized tribes, including Alaskan villages. Whether at the restored cemetery at Eklutna Village north of Anchorage, Alaska, or at remote shrines on the Zuni Reservation near Zuni, New Mexico, a wide variety of activities and strategies are being employed by native peoples to preserve and protect their irreplaceable heritage. In Wisconsin, the Lac Du Flambeau Band of Lake Superior Chippewa Indians has opened a museum and cultural center, appointed a tribal preservation officer, and begun the process of listing several historic sites on the National Register of Historic Places. On Martha's Vineyard Island off the coast of Massachusetts, young Wampanoag Indians study their heritage while practicing with the Noepe Cliff Dancers and Singers. Revitalization has begun, but the legal framework for protecting Indian culture and cultural sites remains tenuous.

The concept of sacred landscapes may exist in geography, history, and philosophy, but it must also exist in law if native peoples are to have freedom of religion. The first federal law to protect Indian sites was the Antiquities Act of 1906, which established national monuments and attempted to stop looting on public lands, but it did not address the traditions of living Indians. The legislation described ancestral remains as "resources" to be used and studied by archaeologists with federal antiquities permits. At the turn of the twentieth century, wealthy Boston Brahmins fascinated with the Southwest helped draft and support the antiquities law at a time when American Indians were considered a "vanishing race" whose only hope was integration and assimilation. The law protected prehistoric sites from foreign collectors eager for Indian grave goods, but it did nothing for living communities of native peoples, and it legally separated them from stewardship of their ancestral past.

Law professor Rebecca Tsosie, a Pascua Yaqui Indian, explained, "The Antiquities Act of 1906 . . . defined dead Indians interred on federal lands as 'archaeological resources,' as 'objects of historic or scientific interest,' and thus treated these deceased persons as 'federal property' (16 U.S.C. §§431–433). Thus under federal law it was entirely permissible to disinter Indian bodies—provided that the necessary permits were secured—and deposit the bodies in permanent museum collections."[1]

Sixty years later, in 1966, the National Historic Preservation Act (NHPA) created state historic preservation offices to oversee identification and documentation of American historic sites for the National Register of Historic Places, under the purview of the National Park Service and the keeper of the register. The federal statute included the provision for a Section 106 review process, which requires consultation to mitigate damage to archaeological and historic sites whenever federal funds are being used for an undertaking or project such as highway expansion or bridge building or any ground-disturbing action across federal lands, such as the placement of a power transmission line or natural gas line.

Designation on the National Register of Historic Places required a Euroamerican historical perspective for categories listed as A—related to events "that have made a significant contribution to the broad patterns of our history"; B—"associated with the lives of persons significant in our past"; C—related to significant architecture "of a type, period or method of construction [that] represents the work of a master, or possesses high artistic values"; or D—archaeological sites. In the National

Register process, history was viewed as a linear, progressive pageant in which significant people led significant events and built impressive houses.

Over time, social history research affected the register process, and historians came to acknowledge the contributions of women, African Americans, other ethnic groups, and whites who lived in vernacular housing rather than great mansions. Urban neighborhoods, factory complexes, and rural farm buildings became eligible as historic sites under criteria of local significance, but archaeologists and historians continued to ignore tribal perspectives, in part because nonnative preservationists did not understand tribal traditions.

Indian elders refer to tribal historic sites in oral traditions that may never have been described in writing. Tribal "histories" can involve emigration and migration stories, accounts of warriors meeting gods and spirits, or individuals' encounters with animals who spoke to them and guided them to particular places. Tribal versions of "significant events" may involve ancestors meeting spirits or migrating across vast landscapes, and "significant people" may include spirits and gods. Tribal histories are not conventional, not written down, and not focused on chronological events. Elders set tribal stories in place, not in time, and for native peoples, the concepts of prehistory and history can be arbitrary, irrelevant distinctions. For the National Register of Historic Places, tribal oral histories, so different from nonnative chronologies of historic Indian people and events, were not considered meaningful, and most Indian heritage sites listed on the National Register are archaeological sites. Very few of those listings have involved consultation with living tribal peoples.

Failure of the American Indian Religious Freedom Act

The National Environmental Policy Act (NEPA), passed in 1969, requires the preparation of environmental impact statements, but only recently have impacts on cultural sites been included. Sacred sites should have been protected under the 1978 American Indian Religious Freedom Act (AIRFA), but Congress construed the law too broadly, and it did not hold up in federal court. A famous California case, *Lyng v. Northwest Indian Cemetery Protective Association*, involved access to sacred sites high in the Chimney Rock area of California's Six Rivers National Forest. In 1988, the Supreme Court decided that the "practice of religion" would not have been denied to Indians by putting a road through a remote stretch of forest, despite strong protest from California tribes. The high court agreed that the federal government could use its land any way it desired, much to the detriment of Indian religious practitioners. Even though contractors never completed the road, the legal precedent now exists at the Supreme Court level to deny the validity of Indian claims to sacred sites.[2] At the same time, however, the opinion also helps Native Americans by acknowledging that federal agencies have the power—and the responsibility—to maintain Indian religions by accommodating access for practitioners to sacred sites on public land.

With the vote on AIRFA, Congress recognized Indian religious beliefs but made no real effort to protect those beliefs and practices. Legislators passed a useless law. And as attorney Steven C. Moore observed, despite the intentions of AIRFA, federal agencies "have exhibited outright resistance and hostility to efforts by Native people to protect sacred sites on public lands."[3]

Such laws did not protect sacred sites such as Chimney Rock or Rainbow Arch along the Colorado River in Utah. In *Badoni v. Higginson*, Navajo religious leaders sued federal officials to limit access to Rainbow Arch after completion of the Glen Canyon Dam in 1977 by the Bureau of Reclamation because tourist boats could easily access the site, which had previously required an arduous journey over a dry, slickrock desert landscape. Licensed concessionaires ran tourist boats and sold alcohol to the disgust of Navajo elders, but the case failed in court, and AIRFA did not uphold Navajo religious beliefs.

Though historic preservation law initially failed to protect Indian sacred sites, archaeological sites on federal lands received more attention. By 1979, because of the international black market, looting and vandalism of Indian sites and graves had escalated. As a result, Congress passed the Archaeological Resources Protection Act (ARPA), which legislators amended in 1989 to provide stiffer penalties and felony convictions for the desecration of sites. Still, archaeologists did not consult native peoples about the bones of their ancestors, nor did they ask about the disposition of grave offerings left with the deceased. Despite 1980 amendments to the National Historic Preservation Act that required federal agencies to inventory all significant cultural resources on federal land and nominate them to the National Register, archaeologists and historians rarely spoke with native peoples about the preservation of tribal sites.

Dowa Yalanne Mesa is a traditional cultural property that is sacred to the Zuni because villagers hid and defended themselves there between 1680 and 1693, during the Pueblo Revolt and the reconquest of New Mexico. Photo by author, November 1997.

In Glacier National Park in Montana, on land historically belonging to the Blackfeet, numerous sacred sites abound, including Running Eagle Falls. Legend states that a young Blackfoot woman went to this site for her vision quest and gained the power to become a brave female warrior who would rescue other Blackfeet warriors during numerous raids against their traditional enemies. Photo by author, July 1992.

Defining Traditional Cultural Properties

A major breakthrough occurred in 1990 when anthropologists Patricia Parker and Thomas King wrote *National Register Bulletin #38*, "Guidelines for Evaluating and Documenting Traditional Cultural Properties," which explained Indian sacred site issues to non-Indians and provided a framework for identifying and evaluating the significance of such sites for National Register listing. The bulletin defined a "traditional cultural property" as a property "that is eligible for inclusion in the National Register because of its association with cultural practices or beliefs of a living community that (a) are rooted in that community's history, and (b) are important in maintaining the continuing cultural identity of the community." However, as the authors admitted, "properties having traditional cultural values are often hard to identify. A traditional ceremonial location may look like merely a mountaintop, a lake, or a stretch of river. . . . As a result, such places may not necessarily come to light through the conduct of archaeological, historical, or architectural surveys."[4]

Many tribes do not accept the phrase *traditional cultural property* and prefer to speak of *traditional cultural places*. Yet the idea behind *National Register Bulletin #38* is sound and reflects an appreciation for Indian religious ideas and concepts of natural landforms as having deep meaning for tribal peoples who know such places through their origin stories, clan migrations, annual ceremonies, and traditions. Frequently, rock outcroppings and natural geographic features have their own Indian names, and detailed stories are attached to those names. A mountain, canyon, cliff, or bluff may function as a mnemonic device, and in remembering the name and retelling the related story, tribal elders pass on vital cultural moral values and essential histories. In comparison, most historic preservation in the United States focuses on houses,

Corrals long in use by Navajo herds-
men may be protected as traditional
cultural properties because of nearby
sacred rock outcroppings or secret
springs. Photo by author, spring 1981.

Traditional cultural places include
this earth-roofed hogan and brush
arbor in Canyon de Chelly on the
Navajo Reservation. Photo by author,
spring 1981.

commercial buildings, fences, streetscapes, factories, bridges, and other
aspects of the built environment. For tribal peoples, structures are
secondary to sacred places.

Land shaped by the Creator and imbued with meaning by generations of tribal elders and storytellers resonates for contemporary native
peoples. As Choctaw member Gary White Deer explained, "To Native
America, burials are sacrosanct, certain geographies are counted as holy
places, and the earth itself is a living entity."[5] For the first time in the
historic preservation process, the ability to describe traditional cultural
properties as valuable to tribes now opens the door for Indian participation. Some native peoples have established traditional cultural property
sections within their own historic preservation departments. The
Navajo Nation, for example, has established a policy concerning the

importance of traditional cultural properties for tribal cultural continuity. Types of Navajo traditional cultural properties include (but are not limited to) "sites that may have been blessed and where ceremonies may have occurred such as those with hogans, houses, sweathouses, game corrals (*needzii´*), eagle traps and so forth; other sites where ceremonies and rituals occurred . . . trail shrines; rock art; and both marked and unmarked graves."[6]

Navajo traditional cultural places include "places for gathering contents of sacred bundles . . . prayer-offering places; places associated with the general Navajo origin stories; places associated with origin stories of particular ceremonials; places associated with the origin of a clan; places associated with the origin of a Navajo custom; places identified as the home of a Holy Being such as Wind, Lightning, Big Snake; locations of echoes (Talking Rocks, which convey human words to the Holy People); natural discoloration of rock that has some kind of supernatural power; places where an apparition or other supernatural event occurred; and places that have played a part in the life-cycle rituals of individuals (such as the spot where a newborn baby's umbilical cord is placed)."[7] Other tribes share the Navajo reverence for landscape. Among the Northern Cheyenne from Montana, to ensure a deep attachment to their land, mothers place birth bundles "in the trees to ensure that children will always know their home."[8] Those trees would then, over time, become traditional cultural properties.

The 1990 publication of *National Register Bulletin #38* helped define sacred sites and provided a framework for their identification, description, and protection. Also in 1990, Congress passed major human rights

This historic Shoshone war lodge is similar to Crow Indian war lodges still found in the backcountry of Yellowstone National Park. Courtesy, the Wyoming State Historic Preservation Office.

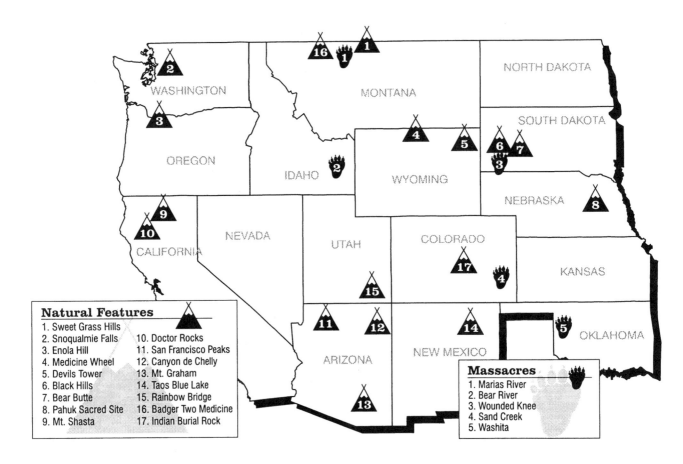

Natural Features

1. Sweet Grass Hills
2. Snoqualmie Falls
3. Enola Hill
4. Medicine Wheel
5. Devils Tower
6. Black Hills
7. Bear Butte
8. Pahuk Sacred Site
9. Mt. Shasta
10. Doctor Rocks
11. San Francisco Peaks
12. Canyon de Chelly
13. Mt. Graham
14. Taos Blue Lake
15. Rainbow Bridge
16. Badger Two Medicine
17. Indian Burial Rock

Massacres

1. Marias River
2. Bear River
3. Wounded Knee
4. Sand Creek
5. Washita

Selected Native American sacred sites in the West. Map research by author.

Ancient cliff dwellings need protection, and so do fragile wickiups—wooden tepeelike structures from the nineteenth century that are found on ceded lands or lands given up by treaties. Although tribal peoples may have ceded certain rights, they seek cultural sovereignty over land they once owned, and they want their ancestors' dwelling places to be protected. A freestanding Ute wickiup is still intact on public land in western Colorado. Photo from the author's collection.

For the Hawai'i State Historic Preservation Office, Nathan Napoka helps to identify, document, and protect native cultural sites. Among them are the ruins of the 1845 summer house of King Kamehameha III and Queen Kalama on the island of Oahu. Kaniakapupu, in Nuuanu Valley, is still very special to native Hawaiians. Recent archaeological work has revealed over 100 features or human-made changes on the landscape within close proximity to the house, including this stone wall marking the boundary perimeter of the king's residence. Many chiefs feasted at Kaniakapupu, and over 10,000 people attended one luau there in 1847. Photos by author, March 1999.

legislation protecting unmarked Indian burials on public lands. Because most tribes feel strongly about the sanctity of burials, Indians applaud the Native American Graves Protection and Repatriation Act, which firmly establishes tribal rights to grave offerings and to the bones of ancestors.

In 1992, Congress passed amendments to the 1966 National Historic Preservation Act, which (under Section 304) acknowledged that tribes have the right not to disclose sensitive information about sacred sites. The amendments also created the option of establishing tribal preservation offices separate from those of the state, and they gave tribes legal authority over administering sacred sites on their own reservation lands. Fifteen tribal preservation offices now meet specific statutory requirements in states as diverse as Arizona, California, Louisiana, Minnesota, Montana, Rhode Island, Washington, and Wisconsin.

Tribal sovereignty has been a hotly contested issue ever since Chief Justice John Marshall in 1831 defined tribes as "domestic dependent nations" inherently sovereign in their own right.[9] The 1992 amendments, ironically coming 500 years after Christopher Columbus's voyage, gave tribes, Alaskan natives, and Native Hawaiians more latitude in making decisions about their cultural properties. Future sovereignty issues will invariably focus on cultural protections.

The Keepers of the Treasures

The Keepers of the Treasures, a national native preservation organization with regional chapters, has been initiated. Ellen Hays of Sitka, Alaska, recommended the group's name because it more accurately reflects native concepts of conserving tradition than the term *historic preservation*, which has little meaning for native peoples. The articles of incorporation of Keepers of the Treasures define the organization's goals: "to support and assist preservation, maintenance and revitalization of past and present cultural lifeways unique to American Indians, Alaska Natives, and Native Hawaiians" and to encourage and assist in "the protection of historic and cultural properties," including "the nomination and listing of such properties on the National Register of Historic Places." The Keepers of the Treasures helps Native Americans promote tribal preservation with funding, training, and policy consultation.[10]

An important dialogue has begun. Tribal consultations on preservation issues have dramatically reshaped the field of historic preservation. For western states with large federal landholdings and sizable Indian reservations, tribal insistence on Section 106 consultation, to mitigate the adverse effects of development funded with federal dollars or authorized and permitted by federal agencies, is becoming commonplace. This fundamental shift in emphasis reflects not only a rebirth of pride in Indian heritage and identity but also a mandate for federal agencies, state governments, and private developers to abide by both the letter and the spirit of federal and state legislation.

Stages in the National Register Process

When a physical landmark or landform under federal jurisdiction may need to be protected as a sacred place or traditional cultural property, archaeologists and tribal preservationists utilize options available under the National Historic Preservation Act. According to Section 106 of the act, any undertaking such as building a road or installing a power line requires an archaeological and historical review of the property to be affected. If the property contains one or more sacred sites, several groups, including the state historic preservation office (SHPO),

The high dams on the Columbia River have reduced wild salmon species almost to the point of extinction. Columbia Plateau tribes have fished the river for millennia, and they continue to do so today, just as they once did at Celilo Falls, which was flooded in 1957. Downstream of the dam at the Dalles, Oregon, Native Americans build and maintain fishing nets and platforms and continue the centuries-old tradition of subsistence fishing in a spiritual manner in order to maintain their treaty rights to hunt and fish in "usual and accustomed places." Wesley Spino, a "rock runner" of the Wasco Band from Warm Springs, Oregon, fishes for salmon in the traditional way to help maintain fishing rights through continuous use of the site. He uses a dip net, with a safety line around his shoulder. Photos by author, June 1997.

Wesley Spino (left) and a friend at their fishing camp along the Columbia River, near an abandoned Indian Shaker Church at the Dalles, Oregon. Photo by author, June 1997.

must work cooperatively. Under 36 CFR Part 800 of the NHPA, in agreement with the SHPO, the federal agency can seek a "consensus determination" that the property in question possesses significant importance and cultural values to be protected. Under a different part of the code, 36 CFR Part 60, the federal agency may seek a "determination of eligibility" for heightened protection of the sacred place, still with a minimum of paperwork. Full-scale identification, evaluation, documentation, and tribal consultation must be completed before final and authoritative listing on the National Register of Historic Places, and that includes the consent of the tribes and the keeper of the register, who works for the National Park Service in Washington, D.C.

Because many Indian sacred sites in the American West are found on private land and because private property owners can legally object to having their property listed on the National Register, state and federal historic preservation staff members often do not complete the National Register process in favor of a negotiated "consensus determination" or a "determination of eligibility." A more thorough review of National Register eligibility and formal listing on the National Register may occur in the future as tribes revive their nineteenth-century treaty rights and demand cultural sovereignty over land they own and land they lost.

Tribal Treaty Rights

Because tribes are sovereign nations with treaties negotiated and signed by the U.S. Senate, tribal attorneys and tribal councils study and evaluate those treaties to reaffirm treaty rights. The authors of the nineteenth-century treaties did not anticipate the National Historic Preservation Act and other laws protecting cultural sites, but the treaties enumerate Indian rights to hunt and fish and gather food "in usual and accustomed places" on ceded lands that the Indians gave up in agreeing to be placed on reservations. Though an Indian reservation in the West may cover a million acres, tribes insist on having cultural oversight of their entire aboriginal domain, which could encompass thousands of square miles and ten times their current land base. Moreover, today's native descendants expect their treaty rights on ceded lands to be protected. They view hunting, fishing, and the gathering of roots, berries, sweetgrass, and sage not as sport and recreation but as vital seasonal activities that are essential for cultural continuity and the maintenance of family, clan, and tribal ties.

Indians also challenge the thrust of the preservation movement to centralize cultural resource information, so they establish their own cultural committees, cultural preservation officers, tribal archives, tribal museums, and historic preservation programs. The Zuni fund an archive that contains dozens of historic photographs of Zuni Pueblo, and they built the A: Shiwi A:wan Museum and Heritage Center, which is "an eco-museum in harmony with the cultural and environmental values of the Zuni People."[11] Elders on the Zuni Cultural Resources Advisory Team have broad cultural and religious backgrounds and work with the Zuni Historic Preservation Department to make site visits to locales both on tribal reservation lands and on lands used for centuries but no longer included within present tribal boundaries.

Hopi tribal preservation incorporates a concern for prehistoric sites no longer on Hopi land, such as the ancient village of Wupatki, which is now a national monument near Flagstaff, Arizona. Over the centuries, Hopi pilgrims traveled on a direct pilgrimage route from the Hopi villages to the sacred San Francisco Peaks. Sacred shrines in the area are still visited by the Hopi, who consider Wupatki a sacred site. Photo by author, November 1997.

For the Navajo, the Hataalii Advisory Council of sixteen traditional chanters or medicine men and women offers guidance on traditional concerns and has been "instrumental in the revision of tribal policies" and keeping information at the local level.[12] Rather than send highly sensitive information to Washington, D.C., Indians maintain preservation data on their own reservations, and they insist on privacy in the Section 106 consultation process. After centuries of loss, Indian tribes and Alaskan villages seek to reverse the flow of cultural objects to museums and the transfer of cultural resource data to outside scholars. Hopi preservation officer Leigh Kuwanwisiwma expressed his belief that no research on his people should be published without tribal permission and stated that "part of my job is to educate the Hopi people" about not being misused by outsiders. He sadly noted, "We have become victims of our own hospitality."[13] Native peoples seek not only tribal sovereignty in an economic and legal sense but also cultural sovereignty, and they treat cultural information about their ceremonies, their beliefs, their dances, and their songs as tribal intellectual property.

Preservation for native peoples in America is about values and traditions and only remotely about architecture. Tribal preservation involves a deep-seated sense of place and a relationship to the landscape that reflects cultural patterns that are hundreds, if not thousands, of years old. Tribal preservation embodies a totally different worldview from that of Euroamerica: it considers spirituality an essential element of cultural protection, and it stretches disciplinary boundaries among the fields of history, archaeology, ethnography, anthropology, planning, and architecture.

Archaeologists claim that they can understand prehistoric peoples from studying habitation sites, lithic scatters, and hunting camps. Alaska Natives and American Indians contend that archaeologists should consult them, too, because they can provide personal insight into the lifeways of their ancestors even if an archaeological site is thousands of years old.

Projects contemplated by the U.S. Army Corps of Engineers in the Columbia River corridor have featured consultation with the Warm Springs Tribes and a budget request from the tribal archaeologist to do oral histories. The corps questioned the funding of oral histories and payments to Warm Springs elders to learn about a 4,000-year-old archaeological site because nonnative managers doubted whether contemporary Indians could provide useful data, given the site's ancient history. But that bureaucratic skepticism fails to appreciate the continuity of native culture and the utter resilience of tribal tradition despite decades of cultural repression—long years during which Indian agents and missionaries banned dances and ceremonies, prohibited religious practices, and condoned white teachers who ridiculed and sometimes beat Indian children for speaking their native tongues.

Active tribal preservation is a new phenomenon; for decades, customs and traditions survived only by being kept underground. Indian

Tribal members spend hundreds of hours each year consulting with archaeologists and federal land managers to ensure the protection of sacred sites located on public lands. Here (left to right), Clifford Duncan and Betsy Chapoose, of the Cultural Rights and Protections Office of the Northern Ute Tribe from Fort Duchesne, Utah, confer with Kenny Frost, a Southern Ute, about sacred sites on the White River National Forest in Colorado. Photo by author, August 1997.

For many tribes, including the Northern Ute and the Eastern Shoshone, every arrowhead in its original location may be sacred because of the prayers said by its maker as it was created. This 3,500-year-old broken point (center of photo) was found by an archaeological team in western Colorado. The team mapped, photographed, and identified the point, which Ute spiritual leader Clifford Duncan reburied. Photo by author, August 1997.

elders and traditional leaders therefore have justifiable suspicions about sharing their wealth of knowledge with outsiders and even with younger tribal members who are not yet initiated or who come from different clans. Historic boarding schools and church buildings on reservations may seem dilapidated and in poor repair in part because they represent forced assimilation and the abandonment of cultural values by an older generation of natives coerced into the mainstream of American society by governmental policies. At its heart, historic preservation should be a celebration of values and a sense of place, and for native peoples it is.

In Alaska, preservation issues also focus on retaining native languages, subsistence hunting and fishing, and continued access by Alaskan natives and Athabaskan Indians to traditional hunting grounds.[14]

Native identity is crucial. Rachel Craig, from Kotzebue, north of the Arctic Circle, is chair of the Kotzebue Elders Council, secretary of the regional council, and on the board of the Alaska Historical Society. She stated, "We grew up at a time when we were punished in school for speaking our native language. We didn't know anything about our own people. We knew about Columbus and Jefferson and Washington and all those Europeans but we did not know about us! And who could we talk to except ourselves? So we started talking to our elders." She continued, "This is what I want our kids to feel—pride in being Inupiat. They must know their own people."[15]

In Hawai'i, a state law protects *Na Iwi Kupuna*, the ancestral bones once wrapped in *kapa* cloth and bundled with a woven *lauhala*, an outer covering prepared from pandanus leaves. Native Hawaiians fear attempts by the U.S. Department of Energy to tap geothermal resources near the active volcano Kilauea, which they believe is the physical embodiment of the goddess Pele. Just as Hawaiians still leave offerings of fruit or flowers at *heiau* (temple platforms of rock where ancient Hawaiians worshipped their gods), they also revere and respect Pele and believe that Kilauea is a sacred site that should be protected under federal laws.

Tribal Protocols

Understanding cultural attitudes and tribal protocols and gaining a sensitivity to native issues take years and cannot be learned from textbooks or field manuals alone. Tribal people prefer to develop long-term relationships with individuals whom they trust. They seek face-to-face relationships and want commitment from individuals, not a federal program. Consequently, to be effective in their work, nonnative resource managers must significantly alter their own career paths to stay in one place long enough to learn and respect Indian ways.

On the Yakama Indian Reservation in Washington State, the tribal council issues archaeological permits only to individuals who have earned the trust of the cultural committee. Archaeologists applying for those permits must appear before the committee and be assessed not only on their academic degrees and previous work experience but also and more importantly on their character, honesty, personal family ties, and respect for their own elders and family traditions. According to former Cultural Resources Program director William Yallup, the committee quickly identifies those nonnative consultants interested only in financial gain and not in the preservation of the tribe's heritage. The goals of the Yakama Indian Nation Cultural Resources Program "are to protect and preserve cultural resources on the Yakama Indian Reservation and ceded areas. These resources include burials, fishing, food-gathering, cultural/historic sites and locations which are recorded and unrecorded."[16]

On the Colville Reservation in central Washington, the eleven bands of the confederated tribes manage 1.3 million acres of reservation land, but their aboriginal land base once stretched from the Cascade Mountains on the east, south to the Snake River, and north to the Idaho

Tribes insist on storing their own preservation information. Adeline Fredin (on right), of the Colville Reservation in eastern Washington, has established an award-winning tribal archive and artifact storage area. Photo by author, July 1992.

border. On those 18 million acres, the tribes also seek oversight rights on federal or state projects that might impact burial grounds, prayer sites, and areas traditionally used for hunting and fishing. Under the watchful eye of Adeline Fredin, director of history and archaeology, the Colville Tribes have an exemplary curation facility for the long-term storage of archaeological materials and historic information and photographs.

Throughout the West, Alaska, and Hawai'i, tribal preservation officers have brought elders to particular locations on tribal and ceded lands to record their memories and to learn how mountains, meadows, and valleys have been essential to tribal lifeways. Tribal cultural resource specialists gather valuable ethnographic information that would otherwise be lost. Tribal preservation also includes community evaluation of tourist impacts on tribal members, and on the Zuni Reservation in New Mexico, for instance, tribal leaders voted to cancel implementation of a Zuni-Cibola National Park and banned Anglo visitation at their sacred midwinter Shalako ceremonies.

Native Americans increasingly take positive steps to preserve ancient sites, decorative arts, craft skills, and traditional ceremonies. In Wyoming, tribal leaders host summer schools for language skills on the Wind River Indian Reservation and offer culture camps for young Arapaho children. In an ironic twist of fate, the Shoshone Tribal Cultural Center at Fort Washakie, Wyoming, promotes pride in local culture, language, and traditions in a large white structure that once housed the local Indian superintendent. He had insisted that the Shoshone assimilate into the white world; now they use his house to retain their culture and to teach Indian ways.

American Indian tribal preservation takes many forms. The Navajo Tribe operates its own tribal preservation office in Window Rock, Arizona, with twenty-six full-time staffers for the 17.5 million acres of the Navajo Nation. The Navajo Preservation Department is larger than any state historic preservation office and even larger than the Advisory Council for Historic Preservation, which has offices in Washington, D.C., and Denver.[17] Preservation issues on Navajo Nation lands include protecting sacred mesas, mountains, buttes, herb-gathering areas, brushwood corrals, cornfields, historic hogans, sweat lodges, and the small carved wooden figurines that indicate that a medicine man or woman currently uses a site as part of a curing ceremony.

Confidentiality of Sacred Sites

To the south of the Navajo Reservation, Zuni Indians have trained young members of their tribe to help identify cultural resources and historic sites on tribal lands and to perform cultural resource contract work throughout Arizona and New Mexico. Under pressure, the Bureau of Indian Affairs consulted with community members of the Fort Belknap Reservation in Montana about the potential cultural and religious impacts of reconstructing the Bear Gulch Road, which connects two gold mines. In the Badger–Two Medicine area south of Glacier National Park in Montana, seismic testing and exploratory oil wells had threatened to spoil traditional Blackfeet cultural sites.[18] Staff members from the Lewis and Clark National Forest evaluated whether the sites might be eligible for nomination to the National Register of Historic Places. Complicating the documentation of traditional use patterns, the Blackfeet were reluctant to discuss sacred sites with non-Indians, much less to identify locations for burial sites and fasting places. Eventually, the forest superintendent suspended the drilling permits, and the Blackfeet kept their sacred sites intact without divulging exact locations.

For these reasons, ethnographic research and oral histories must be used to evaluate Native American sites for which there may be few, if any, collaborative written sources. Outsiders should not consider this information as esoteric knowledge because successful Native American preservation efforts may help tribal well-being. As just one example, the Kodiak Area Native Association in Alaska received Department of Health and Human Services funds to reconstruct a ceremonial meetinghouse in which traditional ceremonies and dances would be held; that improved community health in an area that is hard hit by alcoholism. Clearly, cultural preservation can aid a community's mental health.

Native peoples seek greater access to some sites for private ceremonies, and they want to restrict access to nonnatives and prohibit development at sites such as Spirit Falls on Mount Hood in Oregon, Snoqualmie Falls in Washington, and the Crazy Mountains in Montana.[19] Whether restricting access to public lands for Indian religious purposes will withstand court challenges has yet to be determined. A few roads have been closed on federal lands to protect sacred sites; when the Bureau of Land Management closed a mining road in Colorado, a permanent gate was placed on the road, thereby making it much more difficult for looters to visit an ancient village and shaman site halfway up a canyon wall. Site protection also includes preventing additional erosion along the banks of the Colorado River in the Grand Canyon and along the Columbia River in the Northwest.

In a recent environmental impact statement, the Zuni made it clear that they want no written documentation of sites or removal of any archaeological materials and no disturbance of graves except by natural processes. Damming the Colorado River at Glen Canyon in the late 1950s has forever altered the natural ebb and flow of the river, and tribes want their remaining ancient sites protected.[20] Regis Pecos, executive director of the New Mexico Office of Indian Affairs, explained that tribal leaders choose not to go public about the location of sites "almost like a mother losing a child, only to keep her mourning private."[21] Shoshone traditional leaders in Wyoming refuse to map sacred sites, and the Zuni in New Mexico insist that their Grand Canyon shrines remain undocumented and unmapped, with no written descriptions. They may choose to work with specific trusted archaeologists and historians, but the Zuni pass information on only through oral tradition and allow no written record keeping.

Part of the reason for confidentiality is the growing attraction of Indian spirituality for nonnatives. New Age religious believers seek the power of Indian sites without proper invitation, initiation, and personal sacrifice, resulting in a "violation of the ritual order through which the purity of a sacred place is maintained."[22] "Wanna-be" Indians covet the last thing that some Native Americans say is unique to their identity—their personal and tribal relationship with the Great Creator.[23]

Only three times have sacred sites been returned to native peoples. After fifty years of explaining their position to politicians, elders from Taos Pueblo received legal title to Blue Lake from Congress in 1970. Two

118 sacred objects and sacred places

Hawaiian sacred sites may be found on remote mountaintops or in the center of busy Waikiki Beach in Honolulu, where these sacred healing stones are fenced for their protection. Photo by author, March 1999.

years later, the Yakama Indians received full ownership of Washington's Mount Adams, the most important sacred site of that tribe. And in Hawai'i, native Hawaiians have reclaimed Kaho'olawe Island from the U.S. Navy, which had requisitioned it during World War II for aerial bombing practice.

Returning Kaho'olawe Island to Native Hawaiians

The state of Hawai'i holds the 28,800 acres, or 45 square miles, of Kaho'olawe Island in trust for Native Hawaiians to establish a cultural reserve with no commercial uses. After a $280 million cleanup and a $44 million revegetation of the island, legal ownership will pass from the federal government to the state of Hawai'i and then on to Native Hawaiian groups. Much needs to be done because of the earlier intense bombing of the island, which lies across a channel from the tourist mecca of Maui. Originally, Kaho'olawe had been managed by a local chief representing a Maui district chief. Despite being hit by thousands of tons of ordnance and used as a target range from 1941 to 1968, several sacred sites remain intact, including temples, or large *heiau*, and shrines closely associated with several deities, including Kanola, the god of the ocean, the deep sea, navigation, and carving. In May 1994, the navy received a Cultural Resource Management Plan for Kaho'olawe Archaeological District.

D. P. McGregor discussed the concept of *wahi pana*, or sacred place, and the Hawaiian belief that "the various forces of nature were Gods who formed the earth and imbued it with a dynamic life force and energy."[24] Hawaiian creation myths, chants, and oral tradition revere Kaho'olawe as a *wahi pana*. The island includes the remains of a platform used for a navigational school and a house site for the *kahuna*, or instructor. There are also many *ko'a*, or fishing shrines.

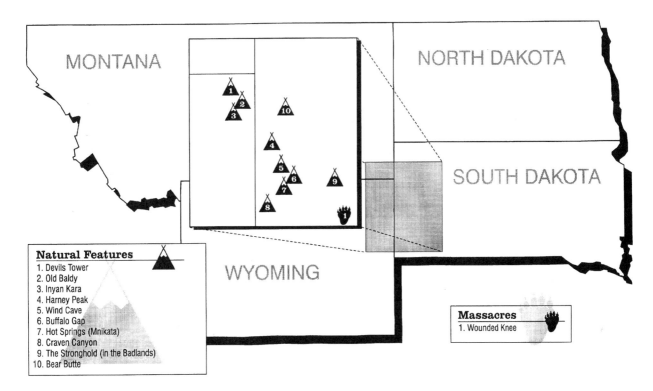

Selected Native American sacred sites in the Black Hills. Map research by Heather Fearnbach.

Under the influence of Christian missionaries, King Kamehameha II abolished traditional Hawaiian religious practices in the islands in the nineteenth century, but on Kaho'olawe, the use of sacred geography and the spiritual beliefs persisted until the U.S. military took the island over in 1941. Since 1976, the Protect Kaho'olawe'Ohana preservation group has helped to restrict public access to the island, but group members regularly visit it for religious and cultural purposes. As the example of Kaho'olawe shows, native peoples now demand that federal laws protect sites they know to be theirs by centuries of tradition and continued use.

Tribal Consultation

On May 24, 1996, President Clinton issued Executive Order No. 13007, requiring federal land managers to "accommodate access to and ceremonial use of Indian sacred sites by Indian religious practitioners and avoid adversely affecting the physical integrity of such sacred sites."[25] According to that order, "in furtherance of Federal treaties and in order to protect and preserve Indian religious practices," the Bureau of Land Management, the U.S. Forest Service, the National Park Service, and other federal agencies are "hereby ordered" to consult Indians in the management of sacred sites.[26]

This executive order represents an attempt to replace the American Indian Religious Freedom Act without rancorous legislative debate. An Implementation Report on Executive Order No. 13007 clarifies that the Department of the Interior, which has jurisdiction over millions of acres of public land, will "accommodate the right of American Indians and Alaska Natives in the free exercise of religion by ensuring access to and

The Heart of the Monster, the legendary place of creation for the Nez Perce (or Nee-Me'-Poo), is a small hill found along the Clearwater River near Kamiah, Idaho. According to tradition, Coyote fought the monster to save the animals of the world. He eventually slew the monster and cast parts of him to different areas in the Pacific Northwest, and wherever a piece of the monster fell, a tribe came forth. The Heart of the Monster is the spiritual place of origin for the Nez Perce people. The National Park Service administers and protects this sacred Nez Perce origin site as part of the Nez Perce Historic Trail. Photo by author, August 1999.

ceremonial use of Indian sacred sites"; furthermore, it will "avoid adversely affecting the physical integrity of such Sacred Sites" by consulting "with American Indians and Alaska Native tribes on a government-to-government basis."[27] Key elements of the new policy include using tribal standards to identify sites, maintaining control of information about those sites, and allowing tribes to provide only general, not specific, locations. The Interior Department realizes that "agencies must also recognize that tribal culture is dynamic, and tribal religions are practiced in the present context. Accordingly, not all Sacred Sites are necessarily historical in nature; some sites may be of recent origin."[28] Another key element of the federal-tribal consultation process is the explicit caveat that "federal agencies must maintain the confidentiality of Sacred Site information, not only because such knowledge is regarded by many as intellectual property, but also to protect against those who would exploit or abuse such knowledge or intrude upon, interrupt, or disrupt religious ceremonial activity."[29]

From reburying their ancestors and repatriating artifacts to writing preservation ordinances and rebuilding ceremonial houses, native peoples are reclaiming hegemony over their cultural practices. In the future, they will have a tremendous impact in helping other Americans develop a parallel preservation movement—one that does not focus solely on bricks and mortar and historic structures but also on landscapes, sacred places, ceremonies, pilgrimages, and respect for elders.

To explain these preservation principles, this chapter concludes with specific case studies and examples of efforts to protect sacred sites on private, state, tribal, and public lands. As more native peoples become thoroughly involved in historic preservation, existing regulations and procedures will change and evolve. All Americans will benefit as the values and traditions of the first Americans reshape the preservation movement.

San Francisco Peaks, Arizona

The highest peaks in Arizona rise to the west of the Colorado Plateau and stand as silent sentinels catching the morning sun and reflecting the last light of day near Flagstaff. Sacred to the Hopi and the Zuni, the San Francisco Peaks are also revered by the Navajo, whose traditional homeland is bounded by four mountains, with the San Francisco Peaks as the boundary mountains to the west. Solitary volcanic mountains, the peaks can be seen eighty miles away by the Hopi who live on high mesas and who for centuries have made annual pilgrimages back to the peaks to leave offerings for the Katsinas who dwell there. Former Hopi chairman Vernon Masayesva wrote that the peaks are "the shrine we look to because it is the home of ancient Katsina spirits, emissaries of life. Sometimes we felt we could touch the mountain near Flagstaff."

Sacred to local Indian tribes, the San Francisco Peaks also represent a benchmark for secular science. Here, naturalist C. Hart Merriam climbed the peaks in the 1890s and first described the concept of biological "life zones," realizing that as he went higher in elevation, he saw plants and animals similar to those one would encounter by moving north in latitude from desert to windswept rocky ground above timberline.

Threats to the peaks include expansion of mines near the mountains. Previously the U.S. Forest Service restricted Indian access for plant gathering on Hart Prairie and adjacent slopes, and tribes also object to being watched as they leave prayer offerings. Periodically, the local ski area, the Snow Bowl, also seeks to expand, and native and environmental groups block its expansion plans for reasons similar to those of the native groups blocking ski area growth at Mount Shasta in California.

Sacred to southwestern tribes, the San Francisco Peaks contain plant-gathering areas used for Hopi pilgrimages. For the Navajo, the peaks are one of the four holy mountains that bound the Navajo world. Photo by author, November 1997.

Attempting to utilize both the National Historic Preservation Act of 1966 and the American Indian Religious Freedom Act of 1978, the Hopi filed suit against the U.S. Forest Service in 1982 to prevent an expansion of the ski resort, which would physically affect ancient shrines, religious ceremonial sites, and gathering areas held sacred by their clans. The tribe lost in court. Frustrated by a judge who determined that ski area expansion and more parking spaces would have little impact on religious sites, Hopi cultural officer Leigh Kuwanwisiwma found that "there is no final, absolute protection under either act." Equally grating to the Hopi, who, according to Kuwanwisiwma, "once used to go to the mountains unhindered," is the condescending requirement for a special use permit to gather the sacred plants they have collected for millennia. The permit is required because under U.S. Forest Service rules, such plant gathering is now subject to federal jurisdiction.

Leigh Kuwanwisiwma explained, "It bothers me because I have been assigned by my clan to lead pilgrimages to the peaks. The last time I led a pilgrimage we were supposed to get a permit, but a Hopi goes where his heart tells him to—not where he is told to gather spruce branches." He added that there are numerous trails from Hopi villages to the San Francisco Peaks, and though some trails are no longer used, "ceremonial activities deified the trails that then came into disuse with better maintained roads into Flagstaff. Now when pilgrimages are made we think of the trails and offer special prayers so that the trails do not lose their significance." Pilgrims originally came to the mountains on foot and then by burro, horse, and horse-drawn wagon. Now the clans come in pickup trucks, but their purpose is the same as it has been for centuries.

Kuwanwisiwma argued that "regardless of its use or not, in our prayers and ceremonies the trails still have integrity because you always have a spiritual element. Clans have living memories and hold specific place names for ancestral sites." Offering areas are associated with the sacred peaks, and on the ancient trail from Oraibi to Wupatki National Monument, formal shrines with distinct characteristics mark the route for male Hopi travelers. Because of the prominent San Francisco Peaks, an entire sacred landscape exists across the Colorado plateau. All area tribes will continue to protect their rights of access and the religious traditions of their ancestors.[30]

Pahuk Pawnee Site, Nebraska

Just north of Cedar Bluffs in eastern Nebraska, a high sacred hill, or *pahuk* in the Pawnee language, rises on the south side of the Platte River. For the Pawnee, this site is the holiest of five such sacred places in the area, and it is especially revered as the home of the *Nahu-racs*, or supernatural animals, who helped them understand how to build their earth-sheltered homes and who taught knowledge and communicated power to Pawnee medicine men. The site was also known as *rahurahwa:ruksti:'u*, which means "Sacred Ground" or "Wonderful Ground."

As Douglas R. Parks and Waldo R. Wedel noted in "Pawnee Geography: Historical and Sacred," for the Pawnee, "animal lodge locations were the preeminent holy sites." Many tales originate at Pahuk, but unlike other Indian sacred sites on public lands, it is privately owned. Fortunately, the family who owns it respects tribal traditions and has placed covenant restrictions on the site to prevent development and to preserve the native prairie as the Pahuk Historic Natural Area.

In past centuries, the Pawnee were crucial traders because of their geographic location on the plains where the rolling high-grass prairie becomes the short-grass prairie of the Great Plains. Pawnee warriors met Coronado in central Kansas in 1541, and they traded with the Spanish during the seventeenth century and the French in the eighteenth century. Once among one of the largest and most powerful of the Plains tribes, two-thirds of the 8,000 to 10,000 Pawnee succumbed to smallpox and died during the 1850s. The Pawnee were then forced off their ancestral lands and sent to Oklahoma between 1873 and 1875.

In 1914, Melvin Gilmore, from the Nebraska State Historical Society, brought Skidi Pawnee elder Letekots Taka (White Eagle) along with interpreter Charles Knife Chief to document Pawnee history in Nebraska. They went to the Pahuk site, where Gilmore noted that White Eagle "identified the place as confidently as I would identify my boyhood home."

Writing in *Prairie Smoke: A Collection of Lore of the Prairies* (1921), ethnologist Gilmore stated, "Each of the nations and tribes of Indians had certain places within its own domain which they regarded as sacred. These places were sometimes water springs, sometimes peculiar hills, sometimes caves, sometimes rocky precipices, sometimes dark, wooded bluffs." "Within the ancient domain of the Pawnee Nation in Nebraska and northwest Kansas," he reported, "there is a cycle of five such sacred places. The chief one of these five mystic places is called Pahuk by the Pawnee," and it is known as "the place of the sacred animals." Each of the five sites represented animal lodges for different animal species, and each lodge possessed the medicine power of the animals that lived there. The animals, or *rahrurahki*, "were the terrestrial media for the celestial gods, who were the ultimate source of knowledge and power."

With the coming of white homesteaders to settle the public domain, the sacred Pahuk site became simply "township 17 north, range 7 east, section 22, Saunders County, Nebraska," and though much of the local area was plowed under for corn and other crops, the Pahuk site retained its natural integrity and has since been reseeded. Now the sacred place has hiking trails and access to the headland overlooking the Platte River. The Pawnee believed that *Ti-ra-wa*, "the one above" or the Great Spirit, had supernatural animals who were his messengers. A Pawnee father sacrificed his son to the Great Spirit, and the supernatural animals brought the boy back to life to deliver secrets and messages from *Ti-ra-wa* to the Pawnee elders who would forever pass them down.

The notion of "forever" is important to consider. Pawnee historian Roger Echo-Hawk identified "a spectrum of oral traditions with potential for shedding light on Pleistocene worldscapes," and he made innovative use of stories concerning the origins of earth lodges and how the Pawnee learned from animal helpers. Echo-Hawk said that near Fremont, Nebraska, an Indian "received instructions on building 'a new kind of house' which was to be a gift to the Skidi people," or the ancient Pawnee. The archaeological record verifies that an older form of Pawnee house had a square floor plan, but after about A.D. 1500, a circular floor plan was introduced—possibly by spirit helpers from the Pahuk site.

Physician Louis Gilbert and his wife, Geri, purchased the 150-acre Pahuk site as a retreat in 1962, intending to build a house on the headland, but once they understood the sacred nature of the place and came to know the grasses and the wooded ravines, they left the site intact and remodeled an old farmhouse instead. In 1973, the site was listed on the National Register of Historic Places, and ten years later, the Nebraska Historical Society received a perpetual preservation easement, forever ensuring that the home of the *Nahu-racs* will never be disturbed (unlike the other four Pawnee sacred sites in Nebraska, which have been altered). Public access at Pahuk is restricted, and tour groups may not use cameras or recording devices.

In 1994, Knife Chief's grandchildren and a number of Pawnee elders returned to the area to tour their sacred sites, burial grounds, hunting grounds, and earth lodge sites. Indian people went back to share their knowledge, and local Nebraskans eagerly met them and assisted with the tour. Pawnee oral traditions may be centuries or even millennia old, but with the private protection and preservation of the Pahuk site by Louis Gilbert's family, rich narratives will continue to be firmly affixed to a sacred place.[31]

View of the prehistoric and historic Ute Trail on the White River National Forest, looking east to the confluence of the Eagle and Colorado Rivers. There, the trail begins its ascent to cross the Flat Tops Mountains. Photo by author, July 1995.

Ute Trail, Colorado

Finding intact Indian trails in the United States at the end of the twentieth century is a major historical discovery, but thanks to dedicated volunteers, archaeologists, and Ute Indian spiritual leaders, one of the last pristine Indian trails left in America has been located. Fifty-seven miles long, the Ute Trail across the Flat Tops Mountains has remained largely untouched because of its remote location on the White River Plateau between the Colorado and the White Rivers.

Originally the domain of Ute Indians who fiercely defended their "Shining Mountains," this land was set aside by President Benjamin Harrison in 1891 as the second oldest forest reserve in the nation, after

Signs once marked the Ute Trail. When this photo was taken, this was the only known sign that hadn't been knocked down or stolen. Since then, Boy Scouts have installed poles marking the Ute Trail in the Flat Tops. Photograph copyright Nan Johnson.

Kenny Frost examines the view from one of several old cairns. Lichen on the formations attests to their old age, indicating they may have been created by Native Americans or sheepherders. Photograph courtesy Nan Johnson.

Kenny Frost leads a ceremony at a Vision Quest site along the Ute Trail in the Flat Tops. Eagles flew overhead during the ceremony, and there is a glow around the drum, which Frost believes indicates the presence of a spirit. Photograph courtesy Nan Johnson.

Yellowstone. The forest floor rises abruptly from irrigated river valleys into steep canyons rimmed by dark stands of Colorado blue spruce, Douglas fir, and ponderosa pine. Higher still are magnificent aspen groves. Though perhaps three-fourths of the main Ute Trail corridor has been discovered, its exact location will always remain a mystery, and there are many research riddles that will never be solved. Some sacred sites close to the trail have been identified; others will probably remain unknown and hopefully undisturbed. Few other Indian trails in the central Rocky Mountains are in such pristine condition and present such an opportunity for a partnership in preservation involving the three Ute tribes, the USFS, the BLM, and private landowners.

Understanding the trail and the migratory patterns of the Ute Indians requires stepping back in time half a millennium. The Ute, who traveled in family bands with older relatives and small children, followed the landscape and terrain contours in a way that four-wheel-drive vehicles cannot. Walking the trail today represents a unique wilderness experience because the trail widens to almost three miles and then funnels down to narrow thirty-yard passageways between ecotones, where open meadows and small aspen groves give way to thick, dark spruce. Unlike many trails within federally designated National Wilderness areas, the Ute Trail is not an overused, deeply rutted bridle path.

The trail corridor is of sufficient width and length to evoke a sense of prehistoric and historic travel, and it offers a unique passport back in time. A key component of finding and identifying the Ute Trail is to think about Indian usage of the forest, for it was excellent summer range for small bands of Ute families who came to the Flat Tops from the south, moving up the Roaring Fork River Valley and from Utah to the west from the Uintah and Piceance Creek basins. These close-knit family bands came to hunt, fish, gather berries and seeds, collect eagle feathers, and worship among the tall stands of Engelmann spruce and high mountain meadows. Ute use of the forest was part of an age-old rhythmic cycle that began about the middle of May and ended around the first of November or when early snows began to close off the high country. The Ute used the lush mountain meadows in the summer and then descended in the winter from 10,000 feet to the warmer basin and plateau country, some 5,000 feet in elevation.

Kenny Frost looks at what may have been a game blind on a flat area in the Flat Tops. Photograph courtesy Nan Johnson.

Eagle traps can be found along cliffs on the Flat Tops. Photograph courtesy Nan Johnson.

The Ute lived off the land and knew the landscape intimately. They also kept a wary eye out for Shoshone, Arapaho, Cheyenne, and even Sioux warriors who may have ventured into the Ute's high mountain domain from Wyoming and the northeast in search of food or the spoils of war (including women and children to take as hostages). Consequently, the Ute Trail usually commands a high lookout and follows the ridgelines rather than adhering to the course of streambeds.

The trail is still intact because of the historic remoteness of western Colorado and the Ute's successful attempts to deter Anglo settlement and live in peace with whites until 1879. Under the skilled leadership of Chief Ouray, who was fluent in Ute, Spanish, and English, and because of the belligerence of Chief Colorow, the Ute managed to keep white settlement out of western Colorado through a series of treaties and through friendships with whites, among them the Spanish friars Dominguez and Escalante, Kit Carson, John Wesley Powell, and a host of Colorado citizens. As late as the 1870s, Colorado remained a frontier, and the carefully negotiated Treaty of 1868 provided the Ute with over sixteen million acres on Colorado's Western Slope. Considering that throughout history, the Ute probably never numbered more than 4,000 to 5,000, their defense of their mountain homeland against other Indian tribes and white incursions is remarkable.

When prospectors discovered gold in Colorado in 1858, hordes of miners poured into Ute territory, so the federal government requested a treaty designating reservation boundaries. In the Treaty of 1868, the Ute received title to one-third of Colorado territory, and they had the right to bar any whites from entering the Western Slope and the peaks they called "The Shining Mountains." Though Ouray had negotiated a generous treaty and though he was at the height of his diplomatic powers, he told reporters, "Agreements the Indian makes with the government are like the agreement a buffalo makes with the hunter after it has been pierced by many arrows. All it can do is lie down and give in." Ouray insisted that the treaty be made "final forever."

But white settlers continued to encroach on Ute lands, and prospectors discovered gold in the rugged San Juan Mountains of southwest Colorado. Six years after the treaty guaranteeing the Ute one-third of Colorado, Chief Ouray and others signed the Brunot Treaty of 1873, in which the Ute agreed to give up the mineral-rich San Juans. In that year, teams of geographers and geologists working with F. V. Hayden begin to map the territory of Colorado from their base at the White River Agency. It was the network of Ute Indian trails that provided access for the first organized expedition of American scientists into the Colorado Rockies. The white men's survey instruments would ultimately endanger Indian landownership, though the Ute could not conceive of dividing the mountains by lines of latitude and longitude.

The surveys would continue for three seasons and would represent some of the most remarkable work ever done in the United States, with a sextant and transit triangulating straight survey lines off the highest peaks and drawing in canyons, creeks, and alluvial fans in remarkable scale and detail. The report of the Hayden Survey was published in Washington in 1877. In the following May, Nathan C. Meeker became the Indian agent at the White River Agency, and in a gesture of friendship, Chief Douglas guided Meeker to Trapper's Lake and up to Marvine Lake on the Flat Tops in June.

Five years after the first surveyors climbed onto the Flat Tops, prospectors discovered silver at Leadville, Colorado. In that same year, three miners traveled down the Eagle River to the point where it joined the Colorado River, and they crossed the river onto the Ute Reservation. After hundreds of years of quiet use by prehistoric and historic Indian families and small bands, the eastern edge of the Ute Trail was about to be extensively used by prospectors in a burst of activity. While miners and prospectors swarmed up the trail in the spring of 1879, conditions at the White River Agency continued to deteriorate as sanctimonious Nathan Meeker insisted that the horse-loving Ute give up their nomadic ways for farming. But the Ute detested the plow.

Meeker became increasingly agitated with the Ute, who wanted him replaced. After being harassed and shoved by Chief Jack, Meeker sent a desperate message for U.S. troops to ride south from the railhead at Rawlins, Wyoming. On September 25, 1879, soldiers camped on Fortification Creek, and four days later, the Milk Creek Siege began. Desperate Ute killed Agent Meeker and ten others because once the soldiers had crossed onto the reservation, the Indians considered the armed trespass an act of war.

Chief Ouray had tried to defuse the Meeker situation, but whites in Denver would have nothing but the complete removal of the Ute. In other words, an entire nation would be forced off their ancestral lands because of the depredations of a few. By 1880, a hastily written treaty in Washington, D.C., forced the White River Ute out of western Colorado and onto the Uintah Indian Reservation in northeast Utah. On September 4, 1881, Ute Reservation lands in western Colorado were thrown open to settlement and official entry by the General Land Office.

As soon as the Ute were forced to leave their beloved homeland, cattlemen rushed in from Texas and New Mexico and ran huge herds of bony longhorn and Hereford cattle on the public domain. Tempers flared between cowboys and settlers as immigrant families began to homestead the creek and river bottoms, but it was nothing like the antipathy between the cattlemen and sheepmen as vast sheep herds moved east from the Great Basin. On the high Book Cliffs above the Colorado River Valley, masked and armed cowboys routinely lassoed sheepherders, tied them to their sheep wagons, and beat them severely, then the cowboys would whoop and holler and drive the herds off the steep cliffs to their deaths in the shaley bottoms. Mormon sheepmen and Mexican and Greek immigrant herders knew that safety and valuable grass could be found in the high mountain meadows of the White River Plateau, but how could they get there without arousing the wrath of the cattlemen? How could a few herders move thousands of sheep almost sixty miles and not be seen?

The answer to the prejudice of the day and the reason the Old Ute Indian Trail can now be located a century after the Ute were banished was that on the west side of the White River National Forest, the herders found the historic Indian trail and quickly and quietly adopted it. As they moved sheep eastward up and out of the Piceance Basin, in their own way, four generations of sheepmen and thousands of bleating sheep have performed a unique service; they have protected a valuable cultural resource by following one of the basic precepts of historic preservation—continued traditional use.

Existing archaeological features include what could be the only known high-altitude mountain bison hunting blind of piled stones, from which aboriginal hunters stalked herds of a buffalo species now extinct. Over the decades, mountain bison skulls have been found on the Flat Tops, but this was the first time a hunting blind was identified from which prehistoric hunters would have prepared to hunt with spears and, later, bows. Near a high-altitude lake, the team also identified distinct patterns in the rock where stones had been moved to either side of the trail to permit easier travel with horse-pulled travois. As Ernest Ingersoll explained in his 1883 book *Knocking Round the Rockies*, "A trail is not a road; it is not even a path sometimes. As the word indicates, it is the mark left on the ground by something dragged, as lodge-poles, which the Indians fasten to the saddles of horses."

But perhaps the most interesting find on the Flat Tops, in addition to rock arrangements for sacred vision quest sites, was a series of lichen-covered stone cairns as tall as a man. Four of these cairns stand as silent sentinels on a windswept plain at an elevation of 10,000 feet. They possibly mark an intersection of trails, and though within the last hundred years sheepherders have also piled up stone cairns in different parts of the forest and added stones to older archaeological features, these cairns seem ancient.

The exact location of the Ute Trail on the Flat Tops in Colorado is not public information because U.S. Forest Service managers and the Ute Trail Research Team are preparing a draft management plan whose primary objective is to prevent degradation of the existing resource. Baseline monitoring of remote cultural sites is essential, as is extensive consultation with the three Ute Tribes—the Northern Ute, Southern Ute, and Ute Mountain Ute—to discern what amount of management participation the tribes want. As archaeologist Mike Metcalf noted, "The Utes appear to see the trail as part of a larger context which includes access to sacred sites and protection of them." He also explained that "the trail itself has less meaning than the landscape and Ute spirituality connected with traditional homelands."

On dozens of national forests, pioneer packers, bushwhackers, and settlers carved trails through the woods out of a desire to cover distance between two points. But Indians traveled differently, and to hike or ride the Ute Trail is to experience the forest through the eyes of its first inhabitants. Much remains to be done, especially with respect to Ute Indian sacred sites and the cultural values those sites represent. The National Register process has not been completed, but just as the Ute preserved and protected the Flat Tops for centuries prior to the white man's arrival, so they should now be a part of the Ute Trail planning and management process. The potential is exciting: to keep intact for generations what may be the longest high-altitude Indian trail left in the United States.[32]

Mount Graham, Arizona

The failure of the Apache to stop the construction of two telescopes high atop 10,720-foot Mount Graham in the Pinaleno Mountains of southeast Arizona represents a critical defeat for Native Americans and environmentalists and a resounding victory for the University of Arizona, expensive lobbyists, and Washington, D.C., lawyers willing to play hardball to protect their clients. A small tribe of Apache challenged the Mount Graham International Observatory and its associated Angel Mirror Laboratory, "one of the most important astrophysical projects in the world." Observatory partners included the Vatican, Germany's Max Planck Institute, Italy's Arcetri Observatory, Ohio State University, and other academic and scientific institutions.

Originally, the third and most important telescope, which has yet to be built, was ironically named "the Columbus project," but that moniker proved to be a public relations disaster, so its title became "Large Binocular Telescope," or LBT. The Apache, environmental activists, members of the American Indian Movement, and even radical Earth First!ers all fought to defend Mount Graham, but despite ecosabotage and the theft of scientific equipment from the University of Arizona, the project continued. As Bron Taylor has written, "The Mount Graham controversy provides what may prove to be an archetypal example of conflicts over American sacred space tangled with environmental disputes."

The Apache lost by providing too little cultural information too late about the mountain known to them as "Big-Seated Mountain," or *Dzil Nchaa Si An*. Indians claimed that the mountain is one of four sacred Apache mountains, that it contains the burial sites of medicine men and the homes of spiritual beings (including Gaan Dancers), and that it is a sacred pilgrimage site for the collection of plants and medicines. "There are songs about Mount Graham that are an important part of our religious practice," stated Apache medicine man Franklin Stanley. "There are herbs and sources of water on Mount Graham that are sacred to us. Some of the plants on Mount Graham that we use are found nowhere else." He explained, "The mountain is part of spiritual knowledge that is revealed to us. Our prayers go through the mountain, through and to the top of the mountain. Mount Graham is one of the most sacred mountains. The mountain is holy. It was holy before any people came, and in the mountain lives a greater spirit." Eighteen varieties of plants and animals are found there that live nowhere else.

Equally adamant about protecting Mount Graham, Ola Cassadore Davis, chair of the Apache Survival Coalition, said, "Most of what was once ours has been taken from us. The telescopes will destroy what little we Apaches have left." Anthropologist Keith Basso concurred: "For the Apache people of San Carlos, Mount Graham is a lasting friend and a powerful ally, a holy place of the highest order that helps them survive as an ongoing people."

The writings and journal notes of early Apache ethnographers were used in court depositions by both sides, but in the end, not enough had been published on the sacredness of Mount Graham, and a federal judge felt he did not have adequate documentary evidence to prove historic Indian religious use of the mountaintop, despite various depositions. Mount Graham represents the failure of the American Indian Religious Freedom Act and the National Historic Preservation Act to protect traditional cultural properties of indigenous peoples. Though the issue of siting telescopes high atop the mountain began in the early 1980s, the U.S. Forest Service and the Coronado National Forest never treated the mountaintop as eligible for the National Register of Historic Places and did not adequately consult with the Apache. Legal chicanery included riders on a congressional bill passed in 1988 to require the U.S. Forest Service to approve the project by ignoring provisions of the National Environmental Policy Act (1970) and the Endangered Species Act (1973), despite the impact of telescope construction on critical habitat for the endangered red squirrel.

Biologists have argued that "the project would permanently fragment and destroy one of the most unique boreal forests in North America." Mount Graham, located 75 miles northeast of Tucson, is an ecological island in a sea of Sonoran Desert, and "this very small, extremely fragile 400-acre subalpine forest is a relict forest ecosystem of primal biological and evolutionary significance" because it is "the southernmost boreal forest in North America," composed of spruce and fir. Scientists for the Preservation of Mount Graham is an organization of 350 members. Astronomers, however, did not agree with the biologists, and the star-gazers successfully argued that only Mount Graham would work as the perfect site for their long-range telescopes.

A formidable environmental alliance to stop the telescopes included Defenders of Wildlife, Earth Island Institute, Greenpeace, National Audubon Society, National Wildlife Federation, the Sierra Club, and the Wilderness Society. Other opposition came from the National Council of Churches, the Unitarian Universalist Association of Congregations,

and tribal groups (including the Apache Survival Coalition and Apaches
for Cultural Preservation). Commentators argued that environmentalists sought Indian alliances only after earlier attempts to stop the construction on environmental grounds failed.

A U.S. district court judge in Phoenix ruled that the U.S. Forest
Service had "put forth an extensive effort over a six-year period" to
gather public comments. In the end, on appeal in federal district court,
a judge threw out Indian claims because he said they had come too late
to be represented in the legal dispute. The judge ruled that because of
the doctrine of *laches,* or an undue lapse of time in enforcing a right of
action and negligence in failing to act more promptly, Native Americans were too late to respond to the legal issues at hand. Complicating
the matter was the fact that the legal brief had been filed by the Apache
Survival Coalition, which is not a federally recognized tribe. The judge
concluded the Apache Survival Coalition's constitutional arguments were
"without merit." The White Mountain Apache Tribe at San Carlos issued tribal resolutions opposing the telescopes but declined to be a party
in the lawsuit.

A slow tribal response from the White Mountain Apache to federal
letter writing was construed as disinterest. But frequently, tribal politics
force a long response time, which is often misunderstood by federal agencies whose staff members do not realize that the wishes and beliefs of
traditional medicine men and women healers may not be shared by the
tribal business council or that there may be conflicting positions held by
different clans. Internal tribal rivalry also occurred. The San Carlos
Tribal Council repudiated the Apache Survival Coalition's attempts to
speak for the tribe, and University of Arizona attorneys questioned the
status of those who had incorporated as the Apache Survival Coalition.

In a June 1991 letter to the U.S. Forest Service, the San Carlos
Apache Tribal Council demanded that construction of the telescopes be
stopped because of Mount Graham's "vital importance for maintaining
the integrity of our Apache culture and tradition." The letter continued, "Mount Graham is essential to the continued practice of physical
and spiritual healing by Apache medicine men and medicine women
and to their apprenticeship as competent traditional religious specialists." The council argued that "any permanent modification of the present
form of this mountain constitutes a display of profound disrespect for a
cherished feature of the Apache's original homeland as well as a serious
violation of Apache traditional religious beliefs." Along with the Zuni,
for whom Mount Graham is also a sacred site, the San Carlos Tribal
Council called for an assessment of the mountain under Section 106 of
the National Historic Preservation Act, but construction permits had
already been approved.

A failure of communication occurred, and neither the provisions of
the National Environmental Policy Act, which should have been in-
voked because of rare squirrels found atop Mount Graham, or the Na-

tional Historic Preservation Act, which should have honored ancient Apache sacred sites, rock alignments, and medicine gathering areas, could stop the international juggernaut and the sophisticated Washington, D.C., lawyers who argued on behalf of the University of Arizona that "the Forest Service's compliance with NHPA has been documented in hundreds of documents comprising more than one thousand pages."

University attorneys also argued that the sacredness of Mount Graham had been compromised over the years by the construction of nearly 100 summer homes and a bible camp. Heavy logging had been permitted until the 1970s, and only 600 acres of untouched ancient forest remains. An "antenna farm" had been placed on Mount Graham, and the entire mountain is used extensively in the summer as valley residents come to higher altitudes to escape oppressive heat.

Apache silence about their religious traditions did not help in this legal battle. Because Native Americans had previously not objected to change on the mountain and had not discussed or described their sacred sites, federal officials assumed no important sites existed, and they acted accordingly. The USFS sent letters to the tribal council after locating two rock cairns and a shrine on the mountain, but they received no written response.

The Coronado National Forest supervisor then approved the telescope project without entering into a true dialogue with Native Americans or engaging in meaningful consultation. On August 12, 1985, the University of Arizona sent unregistered letters to elected leaders of nineteen surrounding tribes. The university also sent a draft environmental impact statement in 1986, but tribes did not respond to the letters or the impact statement. The university made few efforts to involve Native Americans in critical cultural resource planning; however, political pressure against the project mounted, and the Smithsonian Institution, Harvard University, the University of Chicago, and the University of Texas all dropped out as scientific partners.

Issues escalated in 1993 when Earth First! designated Mount Graham as the location for their annual ribald rendezvous, despite the sacredness of the site. Environmental radicals came to Mount Graham out of sympathy with the Apache, but they camped too close to sacred ground, argued with Indians about the use of alcohol, sang songs, held fire circles, cried in each other's arms, and generally proved ineffective despite joining the Apache for an eighteen-mile run up the mountain to promote solidarity. Earth First!ers demonstrated before the construction gate near the telescopes, and other radicals occupied the office of the University of Arizona's president in the school's administration building.

The University of Arizona and other institutions involved with the telescopes do not deny the Apache their religious beliefs. Instead, the problem is the familiar dilemma of restricting access to sacred sites on public land. James Welch, historic preservation officer for the Fort Apache Reservation, argued that non-Apache "experts" should not de-

cide issues of cultural significance for the Apache and that native oral
traditions must be recognized on a par with academic findings.

Despite sympathy from the press toward the protesters, the university remained adamant that the first two telescopes would be built and
dedicated in September 1993 on 8.6 congressionally designated acres.
With completion of the third telescope, the $200 million Mount Gra-
ham International Observatory would become the world's largest optical
telescope. A small, $3 million telescope has been built and operated by
the University of Arizona and the Vatican, and the second telescope is
operated by Germany's Max Planck Institute. The battle over the much
larger LBT, or Large Binocular Telescope, to be erected at a cost of $60
million, continues. Religious scholar Bron Taylor has suggested that
Vatican involvement and support of the project may not be anti-Indian
but rather that astronomers view outer space as "the ultimate sacred
space . . . partly because it is the place where divine mysteries are still
being revealed . . . through the miracle of astronomical technology."
Indians feel otherwise and want the respect that federal laws and regulations should provide them.[33]

Bighorn Medicine Wheel, Wyoming

Located atop Medicine Mountain at 9,642 feet in the Bighorn National Forest of Wyoming, the Medicine Wheel is one of the most intriguing combinations of archaeological features and sacred sites west of
the Mississippi River. Situated above timberline, Medicine Mountain
represents over 10,000 years of Native American culture in a spectacular
setting that generates its own weather and spiritual power. A National
Historic Landmark since 1970, the Medicine Wheel attracted the attention of anthropologists and historians early in the twentieth century,
and it is one of dozens of wheels scattered across the northern Great
Plains and southern Canada; eighty feet in diameter, it is the largest in
the United States.

Northern Cheyenne elder William Tall Bull explained that the Medicine Wheel "is an altar for the mountain," and the Historic Preservation
Plan developed in 1996 to manage the wheel represents one of the best
case studies in sacred site access, compromise, and preservation protection. The preservation plan's purpose "is to ensure that the Medicine
Wheel and Medicine Mountain are managed in a manner that protects
the integrity of the site as a sacred site and a nationally important traditional cultural property."

The medicine wheel complex of cairns, spokes, tepee rings, lithic
scatters, buried archaeological sites, system of ancient travois trails, and
rock clusters is revered by mountain and Plains tribes, including the
Northern Arapaho, Eastern Shoshone, Northern Cheyenne, and Crow
Indians. A stone tool quarry close by may be thousands of years old.
Classic U-shaped vision quest enclosures are at the site, in addition to
small stone circles. Possibly constructed 1,500 years ago, the wheel has

been utilized, built, rebuilt, and formed over centuries and is still an actively used religious site both for local tribes and native peoples from all over the nation who come on pilgrimages and leave offerings of cloth, sage, sweetgrass, beads, and bundles. Approximately 245 feet in circumference, with a central cairn, the wheel includes twenty-eight spokes that radiate to the outer rim of the circle. Around the rim are six smaller cairns, four of which face the center; one faces north and the other east. At one time, the smaller cairns may have been covered with skins placed atop wooden posts. The central cairn is the largest and measures twelve feet by seven feet.

Who built the cairn and why remains a mystery, though Crow Indians insist it was built "before the light came" and "by people without iron," possibly the Shoshonean band of Sheepeaters who lived at high elevations and hunted mountain sheep. A piece of wood found in the wheel has been dated to A.D. 1760, a trade bead dates to the early 1800s, and other radiocarbon dates vary from 420 to 6,650 years ago. A projectile point has been found nearby that dates to 9,000 years before the present, and trails leave the wheel from all directions as they go up and over the Bighorn Mountains toward the Great Plains to the east or the Yellowstone Country to the west. The Medicine Wheel may be an ancient astronomical observatory, with cairns placed at specific locations to mark rising stars during the summer solstice. Other scholars suggest the structure resembles the Sun Dance Lodge or Medicine Lodge so important to Plains Indian religious traditions. The Crow believe that spokes of the wheel are also similar to the placement of poles for tepees and that the wheel was built to demonstrate how to correctly construct homes.

A contemporary Cheyenne cultural leader explained, "The tribes traditionally went and still go to the sacred mountain. The people sought the high mountain for prayer. They sought spiritual harmony with the powerful spirits there. Many offerings have always been left on this mountain. The center cairn, once occupied by a large buffalo skull, was a place to make prayer offerings. Vision questors would have offered prayers of thanks for plant and animal life that had, and would, sustain them in the future. Prayers of thanks were offered for all of creation. Prayers are made for families and for loved ones who are ill. Atonements are made for any offense to Mother Earth. When asking for guidance, prayers for wisdom and strength are always part of this ritual. All of this is done so that spiritual harmony will be our constant companion throughout the year."

Young men go to the wheel for vision quests today as they have done for centuries, and many chiefs and prominent Indians have fasted there. A Crow story relates the vision quest of Red Plume, a Crow chief of the early nineteenth century who found spiritual medicine at the wheel during four days there without food or water. Red Plume was visited by little people who inhabited the wheel. They took him into the earth where they lived, and he learned that the red eagle would be his

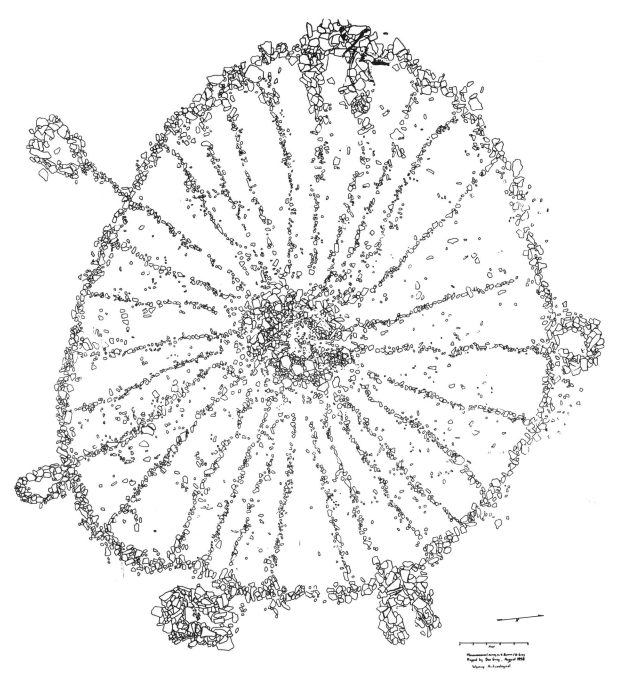

spirit guardian, so he always wore the small feather from the back of the eagle, above its longer tail feathers—hence the name Red Plume. As he lay dying, he told his people that his spirit would live at the wheel and that they could talk with him there.

John Hill from Crow Agency, Montana, said, "The Medicine Wheel is very dear to the American Plains Indian tribes; in fact, the Medicine Wheel itself is the root of the Plains Indian religion." Enemy tribes would approach the wheel at certain times of the year and would "come up to the foot of the hill and lay down their arms and prepare their

Line drawing of the Bighorn Medicine Wheel, mapped by Don Grey in August 1958. Courtesy, Wyoming State Historic Preservation Office.

The Crow Indian "Cut Ear" stands near the center of the Medicine Wheel in this photo by H. H. Thompson. In this view to the northwest, note the large number of stones surrounding the wheel. Dated ca. 1916, this is one of the earliest known photos of the site. Courtesy, Wyoming State Historic Preservation Office.

A photo of the Medicine Wheel dating from the mid-1930s shows that the loose stones have been collected and made into a perimeter wall. Over time, the wheel continues to evolve. Courtesy, American Heritage Center, University of Wyoming.

One of the most sacred Indian sites in North America, the Bighorn Medicine Wheel on Medicine Mountain, Wyoming, regularly receives Native American pilgrims from many tribes, as it has done for centuries. To protect the wheel, local residents erected a chain-link fence around the circumference, and Indians now leave offerings on the fence. Beginning in 1992, the U.S. Forest Service hired a part-time summer interpreter to guard offerings left at the site and to prevent vandalism. Photo by author, July 1992.

candidates for the fasting program or their vision quest programs and others would prepare those candidates for the pilgrimage up the hill to the Medicine Wheel itself and they would meet up there, these enemy, these warring tribes."

John Hill explained that the Medicine Wheel "is a religious shrine, it is a prayer site, it's a spiritual site [similar to] holy places throughout the world—the Vatican in Rome, the Temple in Salt Lake City, other places across the seas. It is not the church that is powerful; it's the spirit transmitted through the church, and here we have a site that we observe and recognize as a spiritual prayer site."

For tribes, the Medicine Wheel is an ongoing religious site of paramount importance, but for most of the twentieth century, the U.S. Forest Service, which manages Medicine Mountain, misunderstood the site and thought of it only as an interesting archaeological site with no contemporary significance. Forest Service personnel insisted on managing the site within the ideological framework of "multiple use" for a variety of timber, grazing, and other interests. A district ranger for the Bighorn National Forest once stated at a public meeting, "That pile of rocks could be bulldozed over the side of the mountain" for all he cared, as long as the Forest Service complied with certain regulations. Religious values at the site were ignored, and local nonnative residents insisted they had never seen Indians near the Medicine Wheel and that it was not important to nearby tribes.

But as the Wyoming State Historic Preservation Office noted, "To contemporary Native Americans, the Medicine Wheel and the surrounding terrain constitute a uniquely important and sacred landscape that figures prominently in tribal oral and ceremonial traditions. To Indian people, the rock alignments and cairns that comprise the Medicine Wheel represent religious architecture rather than inanimate archaeological data." Quietly over the years, Indians had secretly used the wheel for

Modern view of the Medicine Wheel to the east, showing the radar tower atop Medicine Mountain. Note that the perimeter stone wall no longer existed when this photo was taken in 1994. Courtesy, Wyoming State Historic Preservation Office.

Within the wheel itself, vision quest sites are used by medicine men and their pupils when access is closed to nonnative visitors. Fresh sage left as an offering within the U-shaped rock cairn indicates that this part of the wheel was recently used for a vision quest. Photo by author, July 1992.

vision quests and made special pilgrimages to the mountain in the nineteenth and early twentieth centuries despite the fact that white Indian agents on reservations prohibited travel for traditional religious purposes. Native Americans are reluctant to talk about sacred sites, and as *National Register Bulletin #38* revealed, "Particularly because properties of traditional cultural significance are often kept secret, it is not uncommon for them to be 'discovered' only when something threatens them—for example when a change in land-use is proposed in their vicinity."

Imagine the consternation when, in 1988, the superintendent of the Bighorn National Forest, in conjunction with businessmen in Lovell, Wyoming, sought to erect at the sacred wheel a massive metal overhead observation platform, a parking lot for 200 vehicles including recreational vehicles, road improvements, and huts for cross-country skiers and snowmobilers. Years of Indian silence came to an end. The tribes became incensed at this commercialization of their religious shrine. The Medicine Wheel Alliance targeted the Forest Service's proposal to cut timber on Medicine Mountain, and the Medicine Wheel Coalition was formed to stop the threat to the wheel because of its National Historic Landmark status. Both groups insisted that the U.S. Forest Service abide by national preservation laws, and they successfully thwarted local development of the site and demanded that the Bighorn National Forest staff consider other alternatives.

The U.S. Forest Service prepared an environmental assessment and, to their surprise, received over 800 letters; 95 percent of the letter writers "wanted nothing done at the site except to protect it for Native American spiritual use," stated Mary Randolph, who was the Bighorn Forest's public affairs officer. She remembered, "No one was quite sure how to deal with this. At forestry school, they don't teach you religion or spirituality, or how to manage a sacred site. Meetings between state and federal agencies and Native American organizations involved were not going well. Meetings between the parties were antagonistic, unproductive and usually ended with less and less trust." Eventually, as the nonnative land managers came to understand Indian spirituality and began to act as interested individuals instead of federal bureaucrats, discussion began.

Seven parties consulted on the Wheel, including the Medicine Wheel Coalition, the Medicine Wheel Alliance, the Advisory Council for Historic Preservation, the Wyoming State Historic Preservation Office, the Federal Aviation Administration (FAA), Big Horn County Commissioners, and the U.S. Forest Service. The FAA got involved because a little over one mile east of the wheel is a radar dome that tracks airplanes crossing the northern Rockies. Issues focused on development and access. Native Americans agreed that tourists could continue to visit the site but said that it should be closed for traditional cultural use for religious ceremonies. Development should be minimal, and the site should be treated with respect. In 1995, 16,275 visitors came to the site, including 840 Native Americans.

Final completion of the Medicine Wheel Historic Preservation Plan in 1996 represents one of the best models of cooperation among tribes and federal agencies, although the agreement took years to work out because relationships between Indians and land managers were originally hostile. Before the eventual compromise was reached, several USFS employees had been transferred or resigned because of heated pressure and public debates. Forest Service managers and Big Horn County Commissioners also threatened preservationists. According to Alan Stanfill of the Advisory Council for Historic Preservation, "More than once, the Forest Supervisor met with State and Council officials in unsuccessful attempts to have staff members of the SHPO and Advisory Council dismissed from the negotiations and their jobs. Newspaper articles quoting the commissioners and the Forest Service appeared regularly and invariably contained personal insults, accusations of impropriety, misinformation, and political posturing to promote public and political sympathy." Defending Indian sacred sites is never easy in the West, especially when locals favor development dollars over First Amendment religious freedoms.

Controversy began with the ill-conceived plan to publicize the wheel and to install a massive observation tower that tourists could climb. In order to reduce vandalism to the prehistoric spokes and stone alignments, the wheel was already encased in a chain-link fence with barbed wire jutting out at the top. Crow Indian John Hill explained that in 1991, a Pennsylvania family picked up a rock at the wheel during their vacation and took it home with them, only to experience much bad luck and numerous accidents in the next several months. Hill related that, in desperation, "the family wrapped up their rock very neatly, very nice like a Christmas present, and they sent it back to the Postmaster of Crow Agency" with a plea to have the rock returned.

Hill continued: "So that was in December and the Medicine Wheel is the hardest to get to at that time of year with snowdrifts sometimes as high as fifteen feet. So we took it up the 12th of July, took the rock up there and went through what we call a cleansing ceremony for the rock itself, used sweetgrass, sweet cedar, sweet sage, Indian tobacco, not from North Carolina, but native Indian tobacco from right here, and we used medicine root and smudged the rock." Hill and a friend restored the rock to the Medicine Wheel and simultaneously restored the health and safety of the family who had taken it.

As for the wheel itself, Alan Stanfill explained that the sacred qualities of this special place "still exist because people cared enough about it to become involved in deliberations over its future. The destruction of the Wheel was as likely as its protection. The reason that some assurance of its protection resulted from the consultation effort is because enough people put enough pressure on the decision makers to make it too painful to decide otherwise."

A key facet of the Historic Preservation Plan requires all new Forest Service staffers to meet with concerned tribal members and be briefed on the significance of the wheel before they take on their new responsibilities. In this way, the acrimony and misunderstandings of the past will not be repeated, and Native Americans will be part of the training process to ensure that new USFS personnel understand the mysteries of the wheel and its deep and abiding religious importance; thereafter, "when leadership changes in the agency occur, management direction will not." The plan "is meant to be an on-going living document which adapts to the needs of the site and the people who use and treasure it."

In the final preservation plan, the Wyoming State Historic Preservation Office stated, "The Medicine Wheel, and the surrounding ethnographic, historic, and archaeological localities comprise a set of uniquely significant cultural resources that merit the greatest possible protection under the law. The Native American traditional use areas and other sites that occupy Medicine Mountain express a profound spiritual heritage, as well as anthropological values, that are connected by the common thread of centuries of use by Native Americans. It is one of the very few historic reserves in the United States where the prehistoric past and ethnographic present are unequivocably linked." As the preservation plan indicated, "Ceremonial activities are ongoing today, resulting in the continued creation, renewal, or modification of these sites."

This is the dynamic nature of ongoing religion. Multiple uses such as grazing, camping, timber management, and commercial pursuits will now be excluded from the area near the wheel. Mary Randolph stated that the Medicine Wheel Preservation Plan "has become a model for management of sacred sites across the country and for many federal agencies." Though working on the plan was difficult, she added that "for many of us it represents the highlight of our careers in federal government."

According to the National Register nomination, "The Medicine Wheel clearly represents a continuity of Native spiritual symbolism that extends into an unknown and distant past and is now recognized among virtually all contemporary Plains tribes." Indian religion is highly individualistic, and the nomination said, "Each different practitioner acts within a deep and complex spiritual tradition, but within that tradition he acts as his own direct connection [with the Creator] when the Spirit moves him," and thus Indians may realign stones or set up new stone features at an ancient site, as Bill Tall Bull did. Though religious practices among tribes differ, common sacred site requirements include land that "must be largely undisturbed, the plants and animals and rocks and waters must be accessible, there must be opportunities for solitude, and free movement and access to the Mountain must be available." This is essential because "there must not be such intensive intrusion into the natural landscape that the spirits inhabiting the landscape are forced to leave. All this requires a National Historic Landmark of some size."

The Wyoming State Historic Preservation Office is now in the process of expanding the boundaries for the Medicine Wheel National Historic Landmark to fully accommodate associated trails, shrines, cairns, petroglyph sites, and other religious features not fully understood when the wheel itself was discovered by settlers and scientists a century ago. Adjacent sites include staging areas for religious activities, such as sweat lodges in the lower valleys. Local people over the years had helped to protect the wheel and suggested it be fenced to deter vandalism. Now the Medicine Wheel is both protected and properly interpreted as a sacred place, and tribes will be contacted to help provide on-site interpreters. Visitors must walk a mile and a half to the site, and for a minimum of twelve days between July 1 and November 1, the site is subject to a voluntary closure to allow Native Americans privacy to conduct ancient ceremonies and initiations. Otherwise, visitation is encouraged, provided the site is approached in a respectful manner. At the wheel, Indians also gather plants, herbs, and other materials for ceremonial, religious, or traditional cultural purposes. At 10,000 feet in elevation, the viewshed of the Medicine Wheel is an important value of the sacred site, and currently, the Federal Aviation Agency's Long Range Radar Facility is a jarring visual factor on the landscape directly to the east of the wheel. As the satellite global positioning technology system (GPS) becomes perfected, it is hoped the dome will be removed within the next twenty years.

To stand on Medicine Mountain at dawn on a summer morning is to sense the power of the peak and the sacred spokes of the wheel. When the fog slowly lifts, one may feel spirits there among the stones and offerings carefully hung on the fence and placed in vision quest sites by those seeking knowledge. When the Framers of the Constitution drafted the First Amendment to protect religious freedom, the Medicine Wheel was already centuries old. To be there at dawn is to know the power of a sacred place.[34]

Bear Butte, South Dakota

Designated as a National Historic Landmark in 1965, Bear Butte, South Dakota, is the most sacred site to the Lakota people, who know it as a powerful butte on the northern Great Plains and a historic site for vision quests. Bear Butte commands an open view in all directions, especially south to the Black Hills. To gather the people to Bear Butte for councils, runners would go out with sacred pipes to bring in different bands. Historian Stephen Ambrose wrote that the scattered Sioux bands "often gathered at the foot of the butte" for an annual summer convention "to exchange news and gossip, to trade for goods, and to carry out various religious rituals."

As a young boy entering manhood, the great Sioux holy man and warrior chief of the Oglala, Crazy Horse, underwent a purification ceremony, or *Inipi*, with his father on Bear Butte in the fall of 1857 after a summer council that brought together between 5,000 and 7,500 Sioux, including Teton Dakota, Oglala, Miniconjou, Sans Arc, Blackfeet, Two Kettle, and Hunkpapa. As the council ended, fifteen-year-old Curly helped his father build a sweat lodge at Bear Butte. The boy learned about his future duties and the need to help the hungry and to be brave. During the sweat ceremony, he told his father of an earlier vision in which he had seen a warrior painted with lightning streaks on his cheek, a single pebble behind one ear. The warrior wore a single eagle feather and rode a fast horse. His father interpreted the earlier vision and said his son would become a great warrior, but cautioned that he must always go into battle dressed as the warrior from his vision. Then the father gave his son his own name, Crazy Horse. In June 1871, the young man returned to the top of Bear Butte for another *Hanblecheyapi*, or vision quest, in which he foresaw much warfare between Indians and whites.

Three years later, in July 1874, as the nation suffered in the grip of a financial depression and thousands of laborers sought work, George Armstrong Custer violated the 1868 Fort Laramie Treaty and advanced into the Black Hills looking for gold. He found it, and reporters clamored that gold nuggets were there for the taking in the roots of the long prairie grasses. On August 15, 1874, Custer and his men camped at the foot of Bear Butte, unaware that they slept near Crazy Horse's birthplace, but Custer would soon learn more of Crazy Horse. That winter,

Crazy Horse had a vision atop Bear Butte, which Native Americans still use for vision quests and sacred retreats. In the nineteenth century, hundreds of Lakota camped near Bear Butte in different seasons of the year. Courtesy, South Dakota Tourism Office, Pierre, South Dakota.

the U.S. government demanded the Sioux sell the mineral-rich Black Hills and move back to their agencies and reservations by January 31, 1876. Indian runners carrying this provocative ultimatum issued in the depth of a Great Plains winter found the warriors Crazy Horse and Black Twin camped at the foot of Bear Butte. The men refused to come to the agencies, and they would not surrender their homelands. As the snow melted, the U.S. Army began to move against them, and by summer, war had begun.

At the Little Big Horn in June 1876, Sioux swarmed over the Seventh Cavalry and left Custer's men stripped and dead in the hot June sun. Though it was a great victory for Indian peoples, by the winter of 1876, tribes and bands split up as the U.S. Army relentlessly pursued them. His people starving because hide hunters had slaughtered thousands of buffalo, Crazy Horse finally agreed to surrender at the Red Cloud Agency. When he was murdered in a guardhouse scuffle on September 5,

1877, at Fort Robinson, Nebraska, his parents took his remains north on a travois. They may have buried him somewhere near Bear Butte because he had been born there at the base of Rapid Creek.

Pine-covered Bear Butte, located six miles northeast of Sturgis, South Dakota, keeps watch over the northern and western Black Hills. As Winona LaDuke described, "The Black Hills are an oasis in the Great Plains, a source of water and life to the whole region. They lie at the center of North America, and they are a spiritual center for the Lakota Nation; for as long as the old people can remember, there have been prayers and songs to *Paha Sapa*, our life blood."

Unlike other sacred Indian sites on federal public land, Bear Butte became a South Dakota state park in 1961, and it receives thousands of nonnative tourists each year, who come for recreation and not for religious purposes. They use one trail while the Northern Cheyenne use another route to access a very sacred place, where they hold special ceremonies using sweetgrass. Nominated to the National Register of Historic Places in 1973, the butte has been designated a National Natural Landmark and is on a National Recreation Trail.

Rising above adjacent prairie grasses, the 4,426-foot sacred butte hosts ceremonial events and Sun Dances for Northern Cheyenne, Lakota, and other tribes, as well as year-round spiritual activity such as vision quests, prayers, and sweat lodges. Tribes concerned about development on or near Bear Butte include the Northern Cheyenne, Rosebud Sioux, Oglala Sioux, Standing Rock Sioux, Devils Lake Sioux, and the Omaha of Nebraska. For the Northern Cheyenne, who are adjacent landowners on both the northeast and southeast sides, Bear Butte is extremely important because the Cheyenne lawgiver, Sweet Medicine, received the four sacred arrows or medicine bundle from spirits who lived in a cave on the butte.

"The Lakota originated in the Black Hills and the sacred instructions given to us by the Creator were given to us on Bear Butte," stated Larry Red Shirt. "This makes Bear Butte the central and most sacred mountain to the Lakota people. The sacred [white buffalo] calf pipe is the most sacred object with which to pray in the Lakota religion. Bear Butte is the most sacred place to pray with that pipe." He added, "Bear Butte and the sacred calf pipe hold the secret to the past, present, and future of the Lakota people in this life cycle." Lakota revere Bear Butte as their most sacred altar and the place where they can contact the Great Spirit, or *Wakan Tanka*, who gave them seven sacred elements— land, air, water, rocks, animals, plants, and fire. All of these are found at Bear Butte.

"The four colors of soil found merging on the butte mark it as a place of spiritual communion," wrote geographer Kari Forbes-Boyte. "The air is pure and clean, and the site contains particular rocks that can be used in ceremonies." She noted that sacred plants also grow there, and though they can be found elsewhere, they have even more power because they come from sacred ground. A few special plants can only be found at Bear Butte.

Despite these traditional tribal values, the South Dakota State Park Service has built campgrounds, parking lots, a visitor center, paved roads, and public hiking trails for easy access to the site. Though a ceremonial area has been designated, in a 1982 lawsuit (*Fools Crow v. Gullet*), U.S. District Court Judge Andrew Bogue stated that Indians could not receive "full, unrestricted, and uninterrupted religious use of Bear Butte" because in so doing, "the State might be establishing religion by protecting Native Americans' religious practices at the Butte." Testimony during the lawsuit confirmed the significance of Bear Butte to medicine men whose totem of power is the bear. A witness explained, "Bear Butte is especially important and sacred for the medicine men who use herbs and roots and other forms of plant life to cure diseases and who have to go to Bear Butte regularly to renew their power to cure diseases and sickness." The U.S. district court recognized that Native Americans "have been deprived of the ability to conduct ceremonies at the required time of the year," but the lawsuit against the state failed. The judge did not accept testimony about the importance of Bear Butte to tribal religion, and he ignored Indian concerns about nonnative visitation, which has escalated.

Officials from the South Dakota State Game, Fish and Parks Department have attempted to establish a formal, written policy to monitor visitor use of the mountain, but Native Americans have challenged the state's authority to do so. The state has also asked for written recommendations, but tribes would prefer managing the sacred site themselves—for healing instead of recreation. Oglala Lakota elder Oliver Red Cloud, a member of the Gray Eagle Society, demanded that the *wasicus*, or whites, be kept away from the mountain and quit interfering with Indian religion. "The *wasicus* should leave us alone and let us have what we have left, our religion," he stated.

Just as the tribal business council at Taos Pueblo has sought to protect sacred Blue Lake by purchasing land near it to restrict non-native access, northern tribes have also bought land near Bear Butte to host their own ceremonies and to serve as a meeting place prior to approaching the butte. A wildfire in August 1996 may have served to purify the butte or cleanse it. Leonard Elkshoulder, member and spokesperson of the Northern Cheyenne Chiefs Society, stated, "There are people that go there, wannabe medicine men. They take anybody over there without a good reason to go up there and fast. Historically, I heard that pilgrimage to the mountain is a rare occasion." He explained, "Our feeling is that the fire is kind of a cleansing of the mountain," particularly because trails go all the way to the top and many nonnatives take those trails. Indian tradition would restrict access to those individuals who have attained the proper spiritual power and humility.

Non-Indian New Age religious seekers have used Bear Butte without proper instruction and have stolen Native American tobacco ties, prayer feathers, and flags of the six sacred colors that have been left as offerings despite signs at the visitor center prohibiting such theft. New Agers have left crystals, barged into Indian events, and conducted bogus sweats, vision quests, and pipe ceremonies. State park officials have expressed their desire to provide for "consecrated use" of the butte while stressing that "at the same time we've got an obligation to the general public."

Possible management solutions include strict regulation of access to the butte and "designated sacred areas" that would be reserved only for enrolled tribal members receiving prior authorization from spiritual leaders of the Arapaho, Arikara, Cheyenne, Crow, Dakota, Hidatsa, Kiowa, Lakota, Mandan, or Nakota, all of whom revere Bear Butte as a sacred site. Participants at a meeting of the Lakota Nation Summit V in Kyle, South Dakota, also suggested that the state employ one or more tribal members as full-time cultural advisers who could also "sensitize park staff to concerns of traditional Indian people," but no Lakota people have yet been hired as site interpreters. Limiting access to certain areas of Bear Butte to native people might be possible, but Indians from many tribes go to the site on pilgrimages, and strict access for only local tribes would not work. Currently, Native Americans are allowed to gather sage to be used with vision quests, and religious users pay no entrance fees.

Like other sacred sites, Bear Butte is spiritually alive. Young men and women go there for vision quests, and their fasting and visions provide strength for their families and their tribes. But like other sites on public land, Bear Butte does not now provide Native Americans the privacy they need for religious activities. Geographer Kari Forbes-Boyte interviewed many native people and "sensed a great sadness and hopelessness among the Lakotas about what has happened at Bear Butte." She recommended greater communication between Indian communities and land managers, who must become sensitized to native concerns because "transmitting sacred knowledge to outsiders may be considered sacrilegious; therefore information about sensitive sites should be sought only on a need-to-know basis."

Hence, the conundrum: land managers need to know sacred information to better manage sacred sites, but that information must remain confidential, and in the larger American culture, restricting access to tribal peoples and keeping their intellectual property secret go against the grain of the dominant society. Meanwhile, wanna-be Indians and New Agers remain infatuated with Native American religion without respecting it.

The bear sleeps, and Indians wait. From the top of Bear Butte stretch the Black Hills, or *Paha Sapa*, far to the west. Crazy Horse admonished his followers never to sell the land on which the people walk, and the Sioux have not. A recent fire burned the butte, but as the elders believe, it may have cleansed it, too.[35]

Sweetgrass Hills, Montana

The Sweetgrass Hills of northern Montana are volcanic buttes of biologically diverse island mountain ranges rising more than 3,000 feet above the surrounding plains to a height of 7,000 feet. They are just south of the Canadian border, near Whitlash, Montana. The name Sweetgrass Hills is a mistranslation of the Piegan for Sweetpine Mountains. The area is rich in sacred sites and overlays a major aquifer vital to hundreds of farmers and local residents. Once Blackfeet Indian land ceded in 1888 and now owned by ranchers and the BLM, the hills became a focal point for development and preservation in the early 1990s. An unlikely coalition of Blackfeet Indians, miners, ranchers, and local environmentalists sought to prevent issuance of a permit for an exploratory plan to estimate gold deposits. Congressman Pat Williams wrote the Secretary of the Interior, "I must tell you that in my years of working with Montanans on the protection of critical wildlands, I have never found such strong unanimity in opposition to development."

The BLM sought to issue a permit for gold exploration under its policy on the multiple use of federal resources, but the site has deep meaning for local ranchers and is sacred to northern tribes, including the Blackfeet, Gros Ventre, Kootenai, Chippewa Cree, Salish, and Assiniboine. Mining might also have taken large quantities of water from beneath the land and would possibly have lowered the water table for local users.

In "Sweetgrass Saga," published in *Preservation*, Jane Brown Gillette wrote that Curly Bear Wagner, former cultural director of the Blackfeet Tribe in Browning, Montana, was told by his tribe to go to Great Falls, Montana, and protest the BLM's decision to permit gold mining in the hills, but he did not know what to say. " 'So I went and I talked with my senior elder, and he said, "Curly Bear, here: Take this sweet pine, and on

The Sweetgrass Hills in north-central Montana, along the Alberta, Canada, border, rise to 3,000 feet above the surrounding dry prairie and serve as an essential watershed to farms and ranches. The hills are home to a herd of elk and other wildlife, including moose. They are continuously used for traditional religious practices by Native American Plains peoples, such as the Blackfeet. Illustration by Marcy Marchello for the Sweetgrass Hills Protective Association, Chester, Montana, 1989.

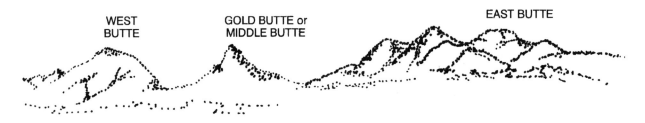

WEST
BUTTE

GOLD BUTTE or
MIDDLE BUTTE

EAST BUTTE

Illustration by Marcy Marchello for the Sweetgrass Hills Protective Association, Chester, Montana, 1989.

your way to Great Falls, you're driving, about halfway between Great Falls and Browning, you turn off and you get out of your car and you face to the east and you burn the sweet pine. You smudge yourself with it all over, and you ask for help from the Great Spirit. Ask Him for help, and by the time you get to Great Falls, you'll have the knowledge of what to say." Curly Bear relates, 'So I did this. I stopped and I smudged and I got in my car and I drove on and I got to the Bureau of Land Management office in Great Falls and I walked in and there were a lot of government officials sitting at this table. And I said, "I'm here to represent the Blackfeet tribe, and we the Blackfeet people appeal your decision." That was all I had to say, and they folded up their books, and I came on home and we gave it to our lawyers.' "

Bureau of Land Management staffers came to realize that virtually no one in Montana was interested in gold mining on a commercial scale in the Sweetgrass Hills. In 1993, the hills were listed as one of the "Eleven Most Endangered Historic Sites in the Nation" by the National Trust for Historic Preservation. For various tribes and especially the Blackfeet, the Sweetgrass Hills are essential as the location for origin stories and as significant sites for vision quests, with numerous rock cairns and eagle-catching pits among the buttes. "Curly Bear noted, 'The Sweetgrass Hills are a Blackfeet Cultural Treasure. The Hills hold a historical, cultural, religious, and spiritual significance that is an integral part of traditional Blackfeet life.' He explained, 'Blackfeet people have resided near the Sweetgrass Hills for many centuries. During that time we have developed a spiritual relationship with the Hills and their plants, rocks, trees and animals that is profound to our culture. As they have been for thousands of years, the Sweetgrass Hills continue to be a place for vision quests, fasting, offerings and other traditional Blackfeet activities that are impossible to translate into the non-Native language but are the essence of who we are as a people.' "

Indians view the hills as a living entity that has been used as a sacred place for perhaps as long as 12,000 years. The oral traditions of the Blackfeet, Chippewa Cree, Gros Ventre, Salish, Kootenai, and Assiniboine demonstrate that the hills continue to be an area of spiritual retreat where ceremonies are conducted. "Curly Bear explained, 'The Hills, in their natural form, as home to many plants and animals, are part of our traditional economy and spirituality. No one part of the Hills is more important than another. The Sweetgrass Hills, in their entirety, are sacred.' " In the draft nomination of the hills to the National Register of Historic Places, the Montana State Historic Preservation Office wrote, "Rising above the surrounding plains and conspicuously visible from the neighboring country, they appear distinctive and prominent in their prairie setting. It is the Hills themselves, organic and primal, which comprise the essence of this cultural landscape. Within this landscape, the cultural remains form the tie between the Hills as a sacred, living place and the native people."

For Indians, the buttes also represent tepees and spiritual powers, and there are written as well as verbal accounts of their sacred meaning. George Horse Capture edited *The Seven Visions of Bull Lodge*. Bull Lodge (1802–1886) was the last medicine man of the White Clay People or Gros Ventre to be keeper of the feathered pipe. He had his final two sacred fasts on Middle Butte and West Butte. Percy Bullchild, in his book *The Sun Came Down: The History of the World as My Blackfeet Elders Told It*, described in detail a four-day fast and vision quest beginning at East Butte in the Sweetgrass Hills.

In *Grassland*, Richard Manning wrote about ongoing vision quests in the Sweetgrass Hills, beginning in the intense heat of a sweat lodge. "This sweating and crying, though, is only a beginning. It is purification, and expiation of one's sins. It prepares one for a vision." He explained, "The Blackfeet and most other natives hold that human beings are a deprived lot, that a wretchedness of spirit is the price of our cleverness. We have forgotten the order of creation: First there was spirit, then there was sun. Sun was and is the creator that first brought forth the animals." Because humans came after the animals, we need their wisdom and guidance. Manning stated, "The ritual of the vision quest is a seeking of that guidance, a time when one goes atop a mountain to fast and wait for a vision relayed by an animal. For vision, one goes only to those mountains with a sweeping view of the rising sun and the surrounding plains." A sacred place like the Sweetgrass Hills is perfect for such vision quests, as it has been for centuries.

The three buttes of the Sweetgrass Hills are Middle Butte (or Gold Butte), which is largely privately owned, and East Butte and West Butte. In August 1992, Canadian campers found artifacts that totally validated Native American claims to the area as a sacred place. Deep in a cave, the hikers discovered two 500-year-old ceremonial gorgets, or chest ornaments, made of seashells from the southern Atlantic coast, which must have been traded north during prehistoric times across a vast network of trails, before the arrival of horses. The valuable shell ornaments represent spirit offerings.

BLM's Montana state archaeologist Gary Smith wrote, "The shells are probably whelk, but we're not sure whether they were originally taken in the Atlantic Coast, the Gulf Coast or the Pacific Ocean." He explained that the design template for the shell gorgets "certainly was from the Southeast area, but we do not know whether they were actually made there." Perhaps long-distance traders brought the shells north from

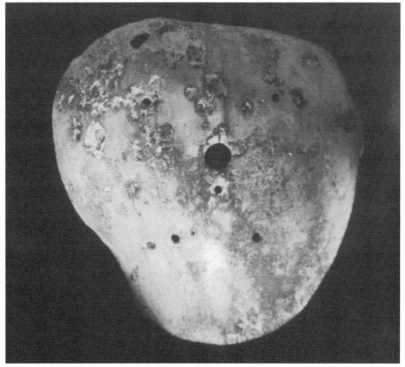

These seashell gorgets, found in the Sweetgrass Hills near the Canadian border, are ancient trade items and spirit offerings. They were carried to the area by native peoples who traveled thousands of miles on foot into the northern Great Plains, centuries before the arrival of modern horses. Courtesy, Montana State Office, Bureau of Land Management.

the coast only to be fabricated by artisans on the northwest plains. The ornaments are powerful, ancient symbols left in a cave in the Sweetgrass Hills as offerings to spirits.

Today, the sweetgrass itself has value to numerous tribes who reverently pick the grass, braid it, and trade it far from the northern plains, just as their ancestors once traded shells from distant shores. Curly Bear noted, "The grass that is gathered in the Hills for ceremonial purposes is unique and irreplaceable." Adjacent sacred sites include an area known as "Writing on the Stone" in Alberta, Canada, the Devil's Chimney Cave Site on East Butte, which is important to the Chippewa-Cree, as well as nearby Chief Mountain in Glacier National Park, sacred to the Blackfeet.

Protecting the Sweetgrass Hills meant inventorying and describing them and defining their legal boundaries as a "National Historic District" eligible for the National Register as a "Traditional Cultural Property." Early on, the Confederated Salish and Kootenai Tribes explained to the BLM that "traditional Indian religions are of a highly unique nature. Unlike Western religions which are written and based upon theological doctrine, Indian religions are unwritten; for this reason it is critical that this inventory include information obtained by Tribal informants with appropriate safeguards taken to protect the privacy interests of those interviewed."

The Montana State Historic Preservation Office had to determine legal boundary parameters for the Sweetgrass Hills. Though the area of the hills covers thousands of acres and includes numerous stone circle or tepee ring sites in Toole and Liberty Counties, among the least common sites on the flat lands are the rock structures used as vision quest enclosures and talus pits. Although rare across the entire landscape, at elevations between 4,300 and 6,900 feet, twenty-five stone structures dominate and provide "unusually dense clusters of vision quest structures along the high ridges of all three buttes of the Hills," representing "continued ritual use extending from ancient times to the present day." Indians found it difficult to draw a boundary around the Sweetgrass Hills, but they continually referred to traveling "up into the Hills" for activities and ceremonies.

Because the tepee rings had been found at lower elevations and the vision quest enclosures were higher, Chere Jiusto and David Schwab of the Montana State Historic Preservation Office identified "a clear break between the point where tepee ring sites taper off in elevation, and where pits and stone structures begin to occur," thus determining that the legal boundaries of the protected area should be "the break between domestic campsites and special use sites as a culturally significant indicator reflecting the cultural practices of native people in the area."

Saving the Sweetgrass Hills is one of the major accomplishments of preservation in the West. Alan Stanfill of the Advisory Council on Historic Preservation argued that "the Hills were held to be valuable by diverse groups for compatible reasons," and now they are protected. Indians have been willing to accept grazing and farming but not the scouring of the earth, as today's open-pit gold mining requires. No decision was made on the exploration plan, and the minerals were segregated and withdrawn from mineral entry. The threat of mining the Sweetgrass Hills has now been postponed by the Bureau of Land Management, which has withdrawn 19,000 acres of the area from mineral entry, and no mining claims can be processed; however, eight private claims in the hills are currently being contested. Under the 1872 Mining Law, the claimant still has a legal right to explore for minerals.

Because of the water resources and threatened plant species, the BLM has designated the hills as an "Area of Critical Environmental Concern" (ACEC), which is similar to a wilderness study designation. Perhaps in time the private claims can be bought out or traded in a land exchange so that the BLM can consolidate its holdings in the Sweetgrass Hills and leave these ecological islands alone and protected as a sacred place where *Hierochloea odorata*, or sweetgrass, will always wave in the wind.[36]

Mount Shasta, California

Visible from much of northeastern California, 14,162-foot volcanic Mount Shasta glitters white with snow half of the year and is considered sacred to northern California Indians, including the Shasta, Modoc, Pitt River, Hupa, Karuk, and Wintu. Several tribes interested in protecting Mount Shasta are not federally recognized because they are so few in number and have only a tiny land base as compared to their aboriginal territory of hundreds of square miles. Mount Shasta was an important feature in the mythology of all groups whose territories bordered the mountain, and today's use of the mountain is rooted in traditional practices and values.

The Wintu have maintained the closest ties to the mountain and believe, along with the Pitt River Indians, that Mount Shasta is the home of the "little people," who reside inside the peak. A powerful Pitt River spirit called Mis Misa is said to live inside the mountain and has served to keep the universe in balance. Some tribes bury their dead toward the mountain because it points the way to the spirit world, and when the Wintu dance and pray, they always face Mount Shasta. Pitt River Indians believe that spirits of the deceased fly on the backs of eagles to the top of the mountain, using it as a way station before leaving for the Milky Way. Floyd Buckskin, head man of the Ajumawi Band of Pitt Rivers, explained, "Yet Achoo (Mount Shasta) being the Home of the Creator, we his creation are given a responsibility to take care of these things until his return, which . . . we carried out until the interruption of these responsibilities by the government of the United States of America during the late eighteen hundreds. During the ensuing one hundred fifty years, our inherent sovereign rights have been trampled on . . . while we as a people watched the destruction of vast areas of our homeland take place." He added, "Mount Shasta stands as an island, a remnant of that natural creation."

Mount Shasta is a site sacred to the Wintu, Pit River, Modoc, and Karuk Tribes of California. Photo by author, July 1997.

Mount Shasta also has spiritual meaning for non-Indians, and its beauty and scenic power have been noted by explorers and travelers since the mid-nineteenth century. James Mason Hutchings wrote in 1857, "Mount Shasta—This is one of those glorious and awe-inspiring scenes which greet the traveler's eye and fill his mind with wondering admiration. One almost wishes to kneel in worship as he gazes at the magnificent, snow-covered head and pine girded base of this 'monarch of mountains.' " In 1914, George Wharton James described it as well: "An altar it surely is, for it lifts up men's hearts to the sun-lit sky, to the serenity of the stars, to the pure blue of the atmosphere, to the majesty and strength, the nourishment and beauty it contains."

The Save Mount Shasta Foundation has argued that "Sacred Mountains hold a significant place in cultures all over the world, and among the mountains of America, perhaps no mountain has received as widespread recognition as a sacred mountain as has Mount Shasta. The number of recent books on sacred mountains and sites, and the beneficial value of such places on humanity's spiritual, emotional and physical health, as well as the growing awareness of the sacredness of the Earth and of places where this quality is particularly evident, indicate that the significance of Mount Shasta can only grow into the future."

Although some Indian tribes find New Age religious worshipers a hindrance and a nuisance, on the slopes of Mount Shasta religious pilgrimages may be quite eclectic, involving natives, nonnatives, and even Buddhists visiting California. The nonnative groups have joined with Indians and environmentalists for the mountain's protection. Interested parties include not only Native Americans from six tribes but also the Brotherhood of the White Temple, the Radiant School of Seekers and Servers, the Gathering of the Ways, the Zen Monastery of Shasta Abbey, and the I AM Foundation. They represent a significant group of nonnative American cultural and spiritual users who are convinced that the mountain is a source of cosmic energy. The Save Mount Shasta Citizens Group suggested that Mount Shasta has "global importance as a 'node,' 'beacon,' or 'geomantic acupuncture point' indicating an energetic exchange function affecting the whole planetary body," thus ranking it "among the major natural shrines worldwide."

Indian tribes and the Save Mount Shasta Citizens Group wanted Mount Shasta in its entirety listed on the National Register of Historic Places as a "National Register Multiple Property," which would include Panther Meadows, a small subalpine meadow that is a spiritual quest and ceremonial site, and the top of the peak above 8,000 feet as a "Native American Cosmological District" sacred as the seat of Indian gods. There are twenty-three associated sites, including Coonrod Flat on Pilgrim Creek where Wintu camp, visit, and entertain as part of a four-day spiritual preparation prior to ascending to upper Panther Meadow Spring. Other associated sites include Gray Butte and Bunny Flat. Based on ethnographical reports, the keeper of the register designated the entire 150,000-acre mountain as eligible for the National Register, only to raise a firestorm of protest from local non-Indian Californians.

Debate has swirled around exactly how much of Mount Shasta is sacred in the context of legal boundaries necessary for designation on the National Register of Historic Places. Development of a ski area has sparked the debate and pitted tribes with centuries of occupation and use against developers and local residents who became so angry over the size of the APE (an acronym for Area of Projected Effect, referring to impacts from the proposed ski area) that local residents, catalyzed by a real estate broker, formed ENOUGH, or Enraged Natives Opposing Underhanded Government Hanky-Panky.

In 1957, the Shasta Ski Bowl opened, but it closed in 1978 because of a poor location that featured frequent "white-outs" of wind and snow, blizzards, and avalanche dangers. A new ski area proposed in 1985 would have cost $20 million, covered 1,690 acres, included three lodges and seven chairlifts, and handled 5,000 skiers a day on 400 acres of ski runs. The project was postponed in 1991 by an environmental coalition, and federal courts determined that the Forest Service must review the entire area prior to approving any permits or expansions for new or existing ski areas. Only minimal archaeological sites were found, but local Indians indicated continuous ceremonial use "back to the first landings of Spaniards on the California coast." Wintu spiritual leader Florence Jones, in her mid-eighties, still conducts ceremonies and teaches tribal culture on the mountain, as did her great-great-grandfather, who lived there. An important ceremony is held at Panther Meadow because of the healing power of its spring, which forms the headwaters of the McCloud River that flows through historic Wintu tribal lands.

The 1994 designation of the entire mountain as a sacred site pleased the Indians and New Age religious users but infuriated nonnative locals

and a California congressman, who vowed to change the National Historic Preservation Act to prohibit the listing of any property that did
not include historic human structures. The Mount Shasta listing included Forest Service lands and 1,000 parcels of private land, for a total
of 150,000 acres. Placement on the National Register drew 2,500 letters, most of which were opposed to the multiple properties district that
has since been cut to a forty-acre site at Panther Meadows and a 19,000-
acre "Native American Cosmological District" within a preexisting
38,000-acre wilderness area from timberline to the summit. Only the
top of the mountain has been totally preserved. These new boundaries
reflect the original proposal by the California State Historic Preservation Office and the Shasta-Trinity National Forest, though other types
of cultural properties are not included and have not yet been evaluated
for their archaeological or ethnographic importance.

Gloria Gomes, secretary of the Wintu Tribe of Shasta County, pointed
out that "Mount Shasta is the most sacred area to our people. Our creator lives there, and that's where our spiritual leader receives her power."
To just preserve the mountain's summit dissatisfies local tribes as well as
Gomes, who said, "Declaring only the top of the mountain significant is
like considering only the steeple of the church. Why not respect the
whole church?"[37]

Taos Blue Lake, New Mexico

High in the mountains above Taos, New Mexico, at nearly 14,000
feet above sea level, a lake rests between granite stones and tall spruce
trees. Sacred to the Taos people who have lived at their pueblo since at
least A.D. 1300, Blue Lake and its watershed symbolize cultural continuity for the tribe and the source of all their health and spiritual well-
being. It is from this sacred lake that the tribe emerged, making the lake
the source of their origin as a people. Taken by the U.S. Forest Service
as public land and incorporated into the Carson National Forest in 1906,
the Blue Lake area stood as a symbol of the denial of Native American
religious freedom. As novelist Frank Waters explained, "The quest for
Blue Lake brought Indian religion to the forefront of national consciousness. And it was crucial to the Indians' success that they convince the
general public that religion lay behind their claim."

The Taos Pueblo's cacique, or religious leader, worked for over sixty
years to have legal title to the sacred turquoise lake, *Ba Whyea*, restored
to the pueblo. The cacique was responsible for the tribe's spiritual life,
and he knew all the rituals and mythic stories, which begin with tribal
emergence from their sacred lake. According to religious leaders, Blue
Lake and the surrounding area are "an ancient place of worship. It is
where our ancestors dwell, the source of our life giving water and the
heart of Taos Pueblo religion and life."

Anthropologist Alfonso Ortiz wrote about "the continuing failure
of so many historians to understand and to deal with the importance of

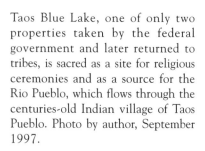
Taos Blue Lake, one of only two properties taken by the federal government and later returned to tribes, is sacred as a site for religious ceremonies and as a source for the Rio Pueblo, which flows through the centuries-old Indian village of Taos Pueblo. Photo by author, September 1997.

place to Indian people, the sense of belonging to and being at one with the land." Ortiz referred to the powerful statement Taos Pueblo issued in 1968 as leaders sought to regain full legal title to the Blue Lake watershed that had been theirs in perpetuity long before the coming of the Spanish. The Pueblo's proclamation stated, "Our tribal government is responsible to this land and to the people. We have lived upon this land from days beyond history's records, far past any living memory deep into the time of legend. The story of my people and the story of this place are one single story. No man can think of us without also thinking of this place. We are always joined together."

The Spanish arrived in the Southwest with Coronado's conquistadors in 1540, in search of the "Seven Cities of Cibola," or fabled cities of gold. They thought they had found one of them at Taos, and the Spanish began a civic administration and enforced Catholicism, which the Indians shook off with the Pueblo Revolt of 1680. Conceived in Taos and uniting all the pueblos, the Pueblo Revolt drove the Spanish back to Mexico until the entrada of 1693, when they returned. Taos remained the center of open rebellion. No other Indian resistance effort in the United States met with such success in recovering lost territory, and through it all, the Taos Indians kept to their own customs and shrines and were patient because of Blue Lake, their most sacred site.

Spanish rulers recognized Indian rights to territory used and occupied by local tribes. In 1821, Mexico assumed sovereignty over the Southwest and confirmed Indian rights to occupied territory under the Treaty of Cordova and the Mexican Declaration of Independence. The war between Mexico and the United States ended in 1848, and the Treaty of Guadalupe Hidalgo guaranteed protection of all property rights previously recognized by Spanish and Mexican law. Taos Pueblo Indians continued their religious rites unhindered. With August as the climax of the ceremonial year, young boys finished their instruction in the kivas. Each year, the August Ceremony took place at Blue Lake, and tribal members of all ages made their annual twenty-five-mile pilgrimage to its deep blue waters, which flow through the pueblo as Blue Lake Creek or Rio Pueblo de Taos.

On September 30, 1856, the Senate confirmed the Taos Pueblo Grant of 17,390 acres, but with the advent of railroad lines, white settlers came into the area, and cattle ranchers put pressure on grazing areas. Lumbermen coveted trees in the Taos Blue Lake watershed. Believing that a U.S. Forest Service designation would help protect their property, especially from rampant overgrazing, Taos Pueblo leaders acquiesced to the U.S. government's incorporation of the Blue Lake area into the Carson National Forest in 1906, but the agency's multiple-use mandate of forest resources soon distressed pueblo leaders, who regretted the inclusion. Serious disagreements arose between local Indians and Forest Service personnel, who demanded visitation permits and treated Native Americans condescendingly. Taos people increasingly felt like they were trespassing on their own sacred lands, but, in fact, it was nonnatives who had trespassed and squatted on pueblo land.

In an effort to clear disputed land titles, Congress passed the Pueblo Lands Act in 1924 and created the Pueblo Lands Board, which began work in Taos in 1926 to resolve disputes and to provide financial compensation. Twenty years after the transfer of Blue Lake to the Carson National Forest, Taos Pueblo leaders magnanimously offered to waive compensation for over 200 land claims stolen by non-Indians if only the pueblo could acquire title to Blue Lake. In a cruel hoax, Taos Indians received neither money for lost land nor their precious sacred site.

Mabel Dodge, who married Tony Lujan, a Taos Pueblo member, wrote about her visit to the lake in the early 1920s: "As we top the last bleak, shale-covered edge we see below us Blue Lake. Bottomless, peacock blue, smooth as glass, it lies there like an uncut, shining jewel. Symmetrical pine trees, in thick succession, slope down to its shores in a rapid descent on three sides." She added, "This Blue Lake is the most mysterious thing I have ever seen in nature, having an unknowable, impenetrable life of its own, and a definite emanation that rises from it. Here is the source of most of the valley life."

She described sweetgrass growing near the lake, which the pueblos use, and she said, "It has never been surprising to me that the Indians call Blue Lake a sacred lake, and worship it. Indeed, at first I felt we should not camp upon its shore, but after I found out how they conduct the camp there I knew it was all right and fitting that one should sleep beside it and try to draw what one could for oneself from its strong being." The next day, after riding back down the mountain trail to her home in Taos, she reflected, "Most of us are used only to the awesome holiness of churches and lofty arches, cathedrals where, with stained glass and brooding silences, priests try to emulate the religious atmosphere that is to be found in the living earth in some of her secret places."

Tribal leader Seferino Martinez explained, "We don't have beautiful structures and we don't have gold temples in this lake, but we have a sign of a living God to whom we pray—the living trees, the evergreen and spruce, and the beautiful flowers and the beautiful rocks and the lake itself. We have this proof of sacred things we deeply love, deeply believe."

Taos Indians could visit the lake, but so could tourists, hunters, campers, lumberjacks, and cattlemen. The sacred area and the source of water for the Taos village were no longer under the pueblo's control as it had been for centuries before recorded history. Cacique Juan de Jesus Romero feared that "if our land is not returned to us, if it is turned over to the government for its use, then it is the end of Indian life. Our people will scatter as the people of other nations have scattered. It is our religion that holds us together."

Continued perseverance by Taos leaders resulted in a U.S. Senate committee recommendation in 1933 that title be restored, but the recommendation only resulted in a permit to protect Indian use rights grudgingly issued by the Department of Agriculture in 1940. Two years later, in 1942, Frank Waters published his memorable novel *The Man Who Killed the Deer*, which is about an Indian man's struggle to accept the traditional ways of the pueblo and the pueblo's struggle to have Blue Lake returned. Waters wrote about "the deep turquoise lake in the center of the world, the blue lake in whose depths gleams a tiny star." In the foreword to R. C. Gordon-McCutchan's book *The Taos Indians and the Battle for Blue Lake*, Frank Waters stated, "*The Man Who Killed the Deer*, with its wide distribution, made people aware that the whole natural landscape, the entire fifty thousand acres, contained innumerable shrines where the Indians would go to pray and hold ceremonies. It was important that the public understand that the struggle for Blue Lake concerned not just one pilgrimage or one location, like a kiva, but the whole watershed as the Pueblo's 'church.' "

With the establishment of the Indian Claims Commission in 1946 to resolve Indian land title issues in the United States, Taos Pueblo leaders felt that, at last, their case would receive a fair hearing. In 1951, their attorneys filed suit, seeking judicial support for the validity of their land claim. In 1965, the Indian Claims Commission affirmed that the Blue Lake area had been taken unjustly, but subsequent legislative bills in 1966 and 1969 died in U.S. Senate committees (though one version unanimously passed the House of Representatives). Frank Waters had written, "Life shows as the still surface of deep blue lake. But the impact of a pebble thrown causes ripples that beat upon all shores—that affect all men's lives, that travel from pueblo to pueblo, to Washington itself."

Reintroduced in 1969, the Blue Lake Bill, or House Bill 471, received the endorsement of the National Congress of American Indians

Executive Committee, which recommended passage of the law as the cornerstone of a new Indian policy of self-determination. President Richard Nixon agreed and signed H.R. 471 into law on December 15, 1970, thereby returning 48,000 acres of forestland known as the Blue Lake Wilderness Area into federal trust status for Taos Pueblo and granting an exclusive use area making the lake and adjacent mountains off-limits to anyone who was not an enrolled member of Taos Pueblo. At the symbolic signing of the bill, President Nixon said, "Long before any organized religion came to the United States, for 700 years, the Taos Pueblo Indians worshiped in this place. We restore this place of worship to them for all the years to come." As it has since time immemorial, the War Chief's Office patrols Blue Lake and associated sacred shrines and pilgrimage trails. The office is dedicated "to maintaining the area in its most natural state: protecting trees, water, fish, wildlife, soils, and land from damage."

A major legislative accomplishment without parallel in Indian history, the return of Taos Blue Lake could not have been accomplished without the steadfast support of tribal members, tribal leaders, nonnative attorneys, and sympathetic outsiders who respected Indian religious beliefs and felt that Taos Pueblo had clearly been wronged. As a Taos tribal manifesto stated, "Our religion to us is sacred and is more important to us than anything else in our life. Our happiness, our moral behavior, our unity as a people and the peace and joyfulness of our homes are all a part of our religion and are dependent on its continuation. To pass this religion, with its hidden sacred knowledge and its many forms of prayer to our children, is our supreme duty to our ancestors and to our own hearts and to the God whom we know." Frank Waters noted that the return of Blue Lake "was the first land claims case settled in favor of an Indian tribe based on the freedom of religion."

Though visitation to the Blue Lake Area is restricted to enrolled Taos Pueblo members, the ancient village is not, and Taos Pueblo welcomes tourists to enjoy "a thousand years of tradition." It is that openness to the larger society that created the necessary coalition to achieve the return of Blue Lake, and with the passage of President Clinton's Executive Act Protecting Sacred Sites on November 12, 1996, Taos Pueblo received into trust status Bear Lake, another small, high-mountain lake, and an area of 700 acres, which protects Indian access to the sacred sites.

Other land issues affecting the War Chief's Office and the Office of Natural Resource Protection include development pressures from the east side of the wilderness area, problems with hikers in the Wheeler Peak Wilderness impinging on sacred lands, and infringement from the Taos Ski Valley. The tribe is so concerned about protecting access into their sacred areas and preserving them in their entirety that they established a gambling casino on tribal lands and have used the profits to purchase adjoining ranches as they come up for sale. Taos Pueblo has also benefited from recent financial gifts to help make land purchases more affordable. The tribe bought 1,000 acres as a buffer, and with a $250,000 donation from Vera Pratt, Taos Pueblo made the "Vera Pratt Gift Purchase" of 373 acres. Now the tribe is using gaming to protect its boundaries, and it has a contract to purchase 16,000 acres for a hefty $10 million.

Vince Lujan of the Taos War Chief's Office explained that such measures are essential for "the survival of my people." The sixty-year struggle has resulted in "an enormous burden," but there was never any hesitation about the effort or the goal. By protecting Blue Lake and their sacred watershed, the people of Taos Pueblo are protecting themselves and ensuring that future generations will be firm in their identity and rooted in a special, sacred place. As Cacique Juan de Jesus Romero said, "It is our religion that holds us together."[38]

Devils Tower National Monument, Wyoming

Among many contested sacred sites in the American West, Devils Tower is at the forefront of issues involving Native American religious freedom and access to public lands. A major landmark on the northern plains, it covers 1,347 acres, rises 867 feet from its base, and has a top of 1.5 acres. It was named Devils Tower in 1875 by a scientific team escorted by Col. Richard I. Dodge, but Indians demand that the name be changed and that recreational climbing be restricted. Native Americans resent the fact that, because of its name, their sacred site has been improperly linked with evil in Christian theology, and they argue that it should be renamed Bear's Lodge, *Mato Tipila*, or Grey Horn Butte, *He Hota Paha* in Lakota. A sacred place for over twenty Great Plains tribes, the landmark has also been at the center of a sweeping legal controversy over Indian access and privacy and the right of rock climbers to use it.

Over 450,000 people visit the site each year while crossing the upper Great Plains. Devils Tower is also a pilgrimage site for Sioux and Lakota peoples on reservations in South Dakota—but for quite different reasons. Annual Sun Dances are held there, and native peoples go to reflect, to meditate, and to visit the tower for religious purposes. The tower is also a mecca for rock climbers, who find that the volcanic plug, which is the hardened core of an ancient volcano, has some of the finest crack climbing in the world as they slowly work their way over rock spires to the top, equipped with ropes, caribiners, and pitons. And here the controversy escalates, because as climbers ascend the rock calling out to each other, making noise, and hammering, they disturb Indians below, who would never condone climbing a sacred site. Annually, over 5,000 climbers go to Devils Tower to wedge themselves into the massive columns on over 200 established climbing routes.

Congressional authorization of the 1906 Antiquities Act enabled the president to set aside land of significant scenic, archaeological, or natural value as national monuments, and President Theodore Roosevelt designated Devils Tower as the first national monument because of publicity generated by a climber. Years before, in 1868, the land had also been set aside but for another reason as part of the permanent home for the Great Sioux Nation.

On visiting the tower, Kiowa author N. Scott Momaday wrote, "A dark mist lay over the Black Hills, and the land was like iron. At the top of the ridge I caught sight of Devils Tower upthrust against the gray sky as if in the birth of time the core of the earth had broken through its crust and the motion of the world was begun. There are things in nature that engender an awful quiet in the heart of man; Devils Tower is one of them."

In his book *The Way to Rainy Mountain*, Momaday related the Kiowa story of how Devils Tower came to be. He explained, "Eight children were there at play, seven sisters and their brother. Suddenly the boy was struck dumb; he trembled and began to run upon his hands and feet. His fingers became claws and his body was covered with fur. Directly there was a bear where the boy had been. The sisters were terrified; they ran, and the bear ran after them. They came to the stump of a great tree, and the tree spoke to them. It bade them climb upon it, and as they did so it began to rise into the air. The bear came to kill them, but they were just beyond its reach. It reared against the tree and scored the bark all around with its claws. The seven sisters were borne into the sky, and they became the stars of the Big Dipper." Other tribes have other tales and cultural narratives attached to the tower, but to all of them, it is a sacred, spiritual place to be revered.

In 1970, only 312 people climbed Devils Tower; today, thousands come each year. With the recent boom in outdoor activities and rock climbing, enthusiasts come from all over the United States and the world to ascend Devils Tower, much to the distaste of Indian people who ask, "How would you like climbers constantly assaulting the outside of your church or cathedral?" In a legal brief filed by the Cheyenne River Sioux Tribe as defendants in a lawsuit brought by the Bear Lodge Multiple Use Association, Native Americans explained that the tower is "vital to the health of our nation and to our self-determination as a Tribe. Those who use the butte to pray become stronger. They gain sacred knowledge from the spirits that helps us preserve our Lakota culture and way of life." The legal brief stated that those who seek knowledge at Devils Tower "become leaders. Without their knowledge and leadership, we cannot continue to determine our own destiny."

But the locals from Hulett, Wyoming (population 459), are dismayed with a voluntary climbing ban each June to permit Indians to have quiet access to the area. Local residents sued to have an airport expanded, and they have supported the cause of climbing guide Andy Petefish, who argued that the voluntary ban represents a legal "taking" of his right to use public lands to earn an income and that the so-called

Numerous tribes claim Devils Tower as a sacred site, but they prefer to call it by a variety of Indian names, including Bear's Lodge. Views of the granite volcanic plug courtesy of the National Park Service.

taking is unconstitutional. From the Indian perspective, there have been other takings, too, such as the removal of prayer bundles and cloths and the taking of their privacy. Native Americans also resent tourists photographing them or approaching them as they fast, pray, or cry. The absence of solitude and privacy is keenly felt.

Arvol Looking Horse, the nineteenth-generation keeper of the sacred White Buffalo Calf Pipe and a resident of Green Grass, South Dakota, explained in a legal affidavit that "Grey Horn Butte is a sacred site which our people need so that we can pray for world peace, preserve our traditional culture, and exercise our Lakota spirituality. This is something we can only do if we are undisturbed and in complete isolation." He noted, "When people climb on this sacred butte and hammer metal objects into it, the butte is defiled and our worship is intruded upon. It is like they pounded something into our bodies. When they climb using ropes, they come and look at us and some of the bolder non-Indian climbers even walk right up to us and disturb us as we fast there, crying and praying for guidance."

Romanus Bear Stops, a traditional spiritual leader who lives in Red Scaffold on the Cheyenne River Sioux Reservation, said, "Even when the climbers are asked not to interfere with our people when we are praying, some of them keep on climbing. This disturbs me because *Mato Tipila* occupies a central place in the Lakota world view. . . . The vision quest ceremony requires a year of preparation but the young people couldn't finish what they started because they weren't left alone; the climbers interfered." A vision quest should take four days and four nights and be a time of absolute solitude. "We must have the opportunity to conduct our traditional ceremonies without interference at our sacred sites," Bear Stops stated. "Only in this way can we receive guidance from our creator and gain cultural and spiritual knowledge at our sacred sites."

With the passage of the American Indian Religious Freedom Act in 1978, tribal religious ceremonies were held at Devils Tower, and in 1981, Indians held a forty-day encampment. In 1984, Charlotte Black Elk applied for a permit to hold a Sun Dance near the tower, and a 1986 National Park Service General Management Plan discussed the need to interpret Native American legends at the tower and begin an archaeological survey of the area. Recently, Indians have increasingly requested access to the tower to erect small sweat lodges and to have group sweats. In 1991, the U.S. Park Service began to require "site specific climbing plans" to limit damage to the tower and to address a growing conflict between traditional cultural users and climbers.

Out of the entire National Park system, Devils Tower is the only unit where climbers are in conflict with an Indian sacred site. Former Devils Tower superintendent Deborah Liggett wrote, "The tower is revered by all Americans as an embodiment of the national park idea, but this small patch of real estate in northeastern Wyoming is also the embodiment of a classic modern conflict. The conflict is not just recreation versus the sacred, but the separation of church and state." She also stated that "the butte, now known as Devils Tower, is a sacred altar to American Indians and a premier recreational climbing destination."

To accommodate both groups, the NPS agreed to permit climbing eleven months of the year but to have a voluntary ban in June. The first year of the plan's existence, the ban registered an 85 percent approval rating with both climbers and the visiting public. The voluntary ban successfully restricted climbing during the solstitial month of June, which is important for Lakota religious activities including the Sun Dance. And yet, despite the compromise, the access issue has been argued in federal court because climbers and local nonnatives were not satisfied.

Despite the local conflicts in Hulett, Wyoming, a new era of trust is emerging between Indian peoples and the National Park Service, and at long last, Indians are able to perform ceremonies and traditions on lands that they used for centuries. But will economic interests yield to traditional values at sacred sites? Can one minority group, Native Americans, have exclusive (albeit temporary) access to specific public lands?

The U.S. district court accepted native concepts of religion and the power of place. In his April 3, 1998, ruling, Judge William F. Downes upheld the National Park Service's voluntary climbing ban and stated: "This is in the nature of accommodation, not promotion, and consequently is a legitimate secular purpose. . . . The government is merely enabling Native Americans to worship in a more peaceful setting." Romanus Bear Stops said in his court testimony, "Our traditional, cultural, and spiritual use of *Mato Tipila* is vital to the health of our nation and to our self-determination as a Tribe. Those who use the Butte to pray become stronger." He added, "They gain sacred knowledge from the spirits that helps us preserve our Lakota culture and way of life. They become leaders."

The judge's federal ruling may be appealed. But for the present, an important part of Lakota sacred tradition has been preserved, and during June, Indians visit *Mato Tipila* in peace.[39]

Pipestone National Monument, Minnesota

At the ancient pipestone quarries of southern Minnesota, which are among the most significant gathering areas for tribes, Indians have labored for centuries to separate the soft, red pipestone lying beneath layers of harder quartzite. Explorers of the North American continent were struck by the profusion of pipe ceremonies among natives and the importance Indians placed on using the pipe, or calumet, while making treaties or seeking spiritual guidance or sincerity from those who smoked with them. In the 1680s, Father Hennepin wrote about pipe ceremonies, as did Lewis and Clark on their Voyage of Discovery from 1804 to 1806. But the exact origin of the highly prized pipe bowls made of red stone remained unknown to nonnatives until George Catlin visited the Minnesota quarries in 1836.

The noted artist recorded a Dakota Sioux origin story about how the quarries came to be: "At an ancient time, the Great Spirit, in the form of a large bird, stood upon the wall of rock and called all the tribes around him and breaking out a piece of the red stone, formed it into a pipe and smoked it, the smoke rolling over the whole multitude. He then told his children that this red stone was their flesh, that they were made from it, that they must all smoke to him through it, that they must use it for nothing but pipes—and as it belonged to all tribes, the ground was sacred, and no weapons must be used or brought upon it." Other tribes also believe that the Great Spirit created the quarry site but contend that buffalo unearthed the source of red stone in this treeless low valley on the rolling prairie.

Three thousand years ago, Iowa and Oto peoples quarried the soft stone and traded it across the continent—east to Ohio, west to north-central South Dakota, and south to the Kansas River. With the arrival of Europeans and horses, trade networks flourished. Use of the pipestone spread westward across the Great Plains with the buffalo-hunting tribes, who came to revere the pipestone and carried one or two handsome ceremonial pipes in specially prepared deer or buffalo skin bags. Care was taken to always separate the wooden pipe stem from the bowl; to unite them was to begin communion with the Creator in an elaborate ceremony in which the pipe bearer offered puffs of smoke to the four cardinal directions, to the earth, and to the sky. As the smoke rose, it carried the prayers of the smoker heavenward, and the pipe itself became sacred after it was blessed by a medicine man. Use of sacred pipes and tobacco has always been one of the ways Indians communicate with the Creator.

With the coming of European explorers and metal tools, pipe bowls could more easily be drilled, and trade of the distinctive red bowls extended south to Georgia, west to Montana, and north to Canada. Because pipe bowls had previously been carved from hard animal bone, Native Americans treasured the soft red catlinite bowls, for they could be carved and decorated with relative ease. For many tribes at the height of the buffalo culture in the mid-nineteenth century, a well-made pipe and pipestone bowl had a trade value equal to that of a good horse.

George Catlin's 1836 visit to southern Minnesota drew national attention to the site, and to this day, the scientific name of the red stone is catlinite. Catlin and others were particularly impressed that the quarry was "the sacred site of peace" among warring tribes. In 1843, Joseph Nicolette became the first government-sponsored explorer of the pipestone quarries, and Henry Rose Schoolcraft also wrote about them. Geologist F. V. Hayden visited the site in 1866, and in 1872, the Smithsonian Institution published a scientific report on the legendary pipestone. By 1898, John Wesley Powell, former head of the United States Bureau of Ethnography, declared the quarries "the most important single locality in aboriginal lore."

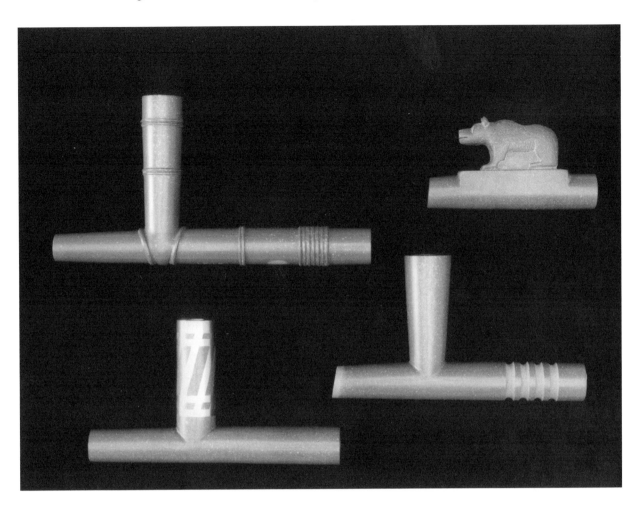

Pipe bowls carved by American Indians are part of a living cultural tradition that has been carried on for centuries; from the earliest contact period, Europeans found Native Americans smoking tobacco for ritual purposes. The primary source for the red stone from which these pipes are made is the pipestone quarry at Pipestone National Monument in southwest Minnesota. The pipes are carved from catlinite (named after the painter George Catlin), and archaeologists have found catlinite pipes spread over a large area, from Anasazi and Hohokam sites in the Southwest to the Ohio Valley. Two modern carvers—Chäska, a member of the Santee branch of the Dakota, and Heyoka (whose name means "the trickster"), a member of the Sisseton-Wahpeton Dakota—modeled these pipe bowls after traditional designs. The T-shaped pipe, also known as the Plains pipe, became common in the nineteenth century and was based on a widely distributed older pipe style. Courtesy, Gilbert Backlund.

The poet Henry Wadsworth Longfellow described the site in the first line of his epic poem *Hiawatha*, and the ancient quarries became part of the nonnative romantic image of Indians as tragic, doomed, "vanishing Americans." Because of the onset of Christian missionaries and the insistence Indian agents placed on sending children to boarding schools, the ancient tradition of quarrying pipestone and carving pipe bowls was almost lost by the first decades of the twentieth century, but a few Sioux and Ojibwe pipe-makers became caretakers of the quarry and have continued this ancient artistic tradition.

Though set aside as Yankton Sioux territory in 1858, southern Minnesota became overrun by whites by the turn of the twentieth century. In 1937, a century after Catlin's famous visit, Congress converted 232 acres to federal ownership as Pipestone National Monument. Today, Indians quarry pipestone in one of eighty-three small quarries that are dug by hand with chisels, crowbars, and sledgehammers under National Park Service permits. To free the stone buried under eight to ten feet of hard Sioux quartzite, traditional carvers work in the fall when there is little water in the quarries. Then all winter, they carve and shape the stone in one of the oldest traditional art forms in America.

Though the pipestone quarries have always been a site of peace, local groups now argue over how to allocate the quarry stone. The National Council of American Indians and some Plains tribes feel that the stone has been commercialized and the quarries desecrated because local carvers sell their work to the public and the pipes are not used solely for Indian ceremonies. In the words of Joseph Chasing Horse, a traditional Lakota leader from Rapid City, South Dakota, "This is the blood of our ancestors turned to stone. We bring offerings, tobacco and prayers with hopes that someday, this place will be protected. . . . We oppose the sale of sacred pipestone," he said, because the stone should be used only for prayer pipes. Advocates of restricting the quarries argue that no one should make a profit digging and selling the stone, and yet, local Sioux and Ojibwe carvers have been maintaining a centuries-old tradition. They provide pipes for tourists and collectors but also for modern-day pipe ceremonies and pipe smoking in sweat lodges across the nation.

Clyde Bellecourt of the American Indian Movement (AIM) opposes formation of a local church named Keepers of the Sacred Tradition of Pipemakers. That church appears to be in conflict with the Little Feather Indian Center at the quarry, which is another group representing local carvers. But despite the factionalism and disagreements over quarrying the stone, Pipestone National Monument has also hosted sweat lodges and the Gathering of the Sacred Pipes Sundance, which draws Native Americans together from across the United States. Noting that "95% of people who carry the sacred pipe have never been to Pipestone," Bellecourt dreams of a great meeting at which Native Americans bring their pipes home to the "mother stone" of the quarries. He envisions an international gathering of elders and youth that would "grab hold of the young people . . . who have adopted another culture." He feels that the sacred pipe and the quarries "can bring us together. . . . We need a spiritual base. I'm convinced the only place it can happen is in Pipestone."[40]

Ute Mountain Tribal Park, Colorado

In 1895, the Ute Mountain Ute, the smallest of the three Ute Indian bands from Colorado, received in tribal trust land in the far southwest corner of Colorado and six full townships in northwest New Mexico.

Although water, precious minerals, and fields of tillable soil are in scant supply, the Ute Mountain Ute Reservation does contain pristine Anasazi ruins from the tenth century. Today, the Ute Mountain Ute respectfully refer to the Anasazi as the Ancient Pueblo people, and the land those old ones lived on is being carefully protected by the tribe. To preserve the spectacular Cliff Palace, Spruce Tree House, and Balcony House ruins, President Theodore Roosevelt signed Mesa Verde National Park into law in 1906 but with only vague boundaries. Five years later, Congress carved 14,520 acres for Mesa Verde National Park out of Ute Mountain Ute landholdings.

Al Wetherill discovered Cliff House in the mid-1880s when he was alone and on foot, but credit for publicizing the ruins goes to his brother, Richard Wetherill, and Charlie Mason, cowboys who rediscovered Cliff House on December 18, 1888, while stopping to rest their horses. Through gently falling snow in the dim light of a winter afternoon, they looked across the canyon to see a lost Indian village built into a huge alcove of rock, with room blocks almost six stories tall. After publication of William Henry Jackson's photographs of the site, learning more about Mesa Verde and protecting the area for its archaeological value became key goals for the Colorado Federation of Women's Clubs, which was concerned about collectors looting southwestern sites to carry off artifacts for European museums. Early archaeologists heralded the discovery of Mesa Verde as a major contribution to knowledge, but the Ute Mountain Ute had always known about the site, and like other tribes, they had been respectful stewards of the ruins and had left them alone. They did not visit them and certainly did not dig in the floors of ancient houses. Mesa Verde became the first national park set aside for its cultural resources, and it has been designated a World Heritage Site by the United Nations. It has 650,000 visitors annually.

Most of Native America's ancient sites are managed by state and federal agencies, such as the National Park Service, the Bureau of Land Management, and the U.S. Forest Service, but one valuable collection of southwestern prehistoric ruins is managed by Indians and open to small, guided tours. When the Ute Mountain Ute gave up 14,520 acres for Mesa Verde National Park, they received 20,160 acres, including additional ancient cliff dwellings. At many national parks, visitors learn about ancient Indians but never encounter contemporary Native Americans. This is not the case at Ute Mountain Tribal Park.

Ute Mountain Ute come from the Weeminuche Band, and their last traditional chief, Jack House, lived in the old way, spending summers on the mesa and winters in Mancos Canyon. Recognized as the hereditary chief of the tribe, Jack House wielded firm political power until his death in 1971. Because he knew the area was sacred ground where spirits dwell, he began making plans in 1967 to set aside 125,000 acres in Mancos Canyon as Ute Mountain Park. According to author Jean Akens, "It was his desire to preserve the ruins for the future, and to share them with others," but "his was an idea opposed by many in the tribe, especially those of his own generation. There still remained a strong belief that no good could come from disturbing the spirits of the Ancient Ones. But the chief was not to be dissuaded." Beginning in 1971, archaeological crews cleaned and stabilized ruins, and archaeologists worked through 1975 recording sites, preserving materials, and analyzing information. Roads needed to be improved, and archaeological assessments had to be conducted along the roadbed.

No tribal member lives permanently in Mancos Canyon, which is a sanctuary for the dead. Chief Jack House's commitment to preservation led to bitter antagonisms among his people, who after his own death burned his hogan, chiseled and defaced his image painted on rock, and tried to ignore his edict to leave the canyon alone. Now, more than twenty-five years later, the wisdom of Chief Jack House is apparent. The Ute Mountain Tribal Park, surrounded by the golden circle of national parks and national monuments in the Southwest, is a one-of-a-kind visitor experience because tourism is both small-scale and very low-impact. The park also offers vigorous hiking and climbing, including the ascent of sixty-foot-high kiva ladders. What makes a visit to the tribal park special is the isolation of the site and the intimacy that develops among twelve to eighteen people who spend an entire day with an authorized Ute guide, learning to identify Ute and Ancestral Pueblo rock art and spot ancient wild-turkey pens above the roofs of cliff houses.

The solitude in Mancos Canyon, the long silences punctuated by winds soughing through the tops of aging ponderosa pines, and the flight of eagles and red-tailed hawks soaring upward on rising thermal drafts create a vivid sense of place. The personal discovery of remote cliff dwellings arrived at by hiking original Anasazi trails, not asphalt paths, becomes all the more surreal as afternoon thunderclouds rise ominously high against the deep-blue sky. Sheer sandstone cliffs give way to hidden villages shaded by ponderosa pines and Douglas fir that grow tall at the heads of canyons. Because the cliff dwellings are approached on foot, guests feel they are among the first nonnatives to see the ruins, as indeed they are. Visitors stoop low to enter ancient Anasazi T-shaped doorways and touch rocks and boulders etched with long grooves where Pueblo peoples straightened their arrow shafts. Visitors marvel at small Anasazi rooms with ceilings blackened by smoke from ancient fires. Tourists touch prehistoric firepits, with their distinctive stone heat shields that both trapped and reflected the wood's warmth. This is tribal tourism at its best—close up, quiet, at one with the earth and sky.

Along every trail are scattered pottery sherds left untouched. In the middle of the park, a huge, six-story kiva lies collapsed and surrounded by sherds of all sizes and descriptions. At Lion House, the largest village on the Main Ruins tour, the remains of a sunken D-shaped kiva can be viewed. Ute guides point out Anasazi fingerprints still visible in the dried clay used to form and shape room blocks. Tree branches tied together with yucca-leaf fiber above a door still have the original Anasazi knot. Items found in Mancos Canyon include spools of hand-woven thread, turkey-feather cordage, yucca-fiber pot rests, pieces of woven mats, stone tools, black-on-gray bowls, hammer stones, and small corn-cobs from the beginnings of southwestern agriculture. Local corrugated pottery ware included jars, bowls, pitchers, and a canteen with a dog effigy figure attached to it. But the Ancient Pueblo people were not isolated in Mancos Canyon. An Anasazi watchtower, once used for com-munication and celestial observations, guards the canyon's entrance, and trade items included beads, turquoise, shells from the Gulf of Mexico, jet stone, and polychrome bowls from near St. John, Arizona.

Tourists meet at the junction of Highway 160 and Highway 666, twenty miles south of Cortez, Colorado, at the tribal park visitor center, then use their own vehicles to follow a Ute Mountain Ute guide deep into Mancos Canyon. There, they visit "the other Mesa Verde," which is a quiet setting not overrun by thousands of tourists. Self-guided tours are not permitted. Near Jackson Butte, named after photographer Will-iam Henry Jackson, the tour begins with a visit to a reconstructed stone hogan built in 1976 by Ute Mountain youth, a century after Jackson traveled up Mancos Canyon. In the basement is a re-created under-ground kiva with firepit, stone reflecting shield, and six pillars for the six directions. The kiva includes a *sipapu,* or hole, for the access and egress of underground spirits; it is covered up during some ceremonies because the kiva continues to be used for healing purposes.

Of course, no visitors can pick up any artifacts, but early archaeolo-gists certainly did. Earl Morris of the University of Colorado took off the roofs of houses to photograph their interiors. He removed the hu-man remains of an Ancient Pueblo woman who had lain undisturbed for centuries at a site Morris named She House, located at the far eastern side of the park. Now, thanks to help from a Hopi elder, the ancient one has been reburied with her belongings.

The Ute Mountain Ute are patiently developing a unique and sus-tainable ecotourism approach that allows select visitors to experience the beauty of remote canyons and village sites that would have been outliers to the larger prehistoric puebloan community at Cliff House. Chief Jack House risked the ire of his people by not letting them settle in Mancos Canyon to the south of Mesa Verde and by not permitting any changes to the canyon floor or canyon rim. Now, thirty years after the chief set aside Ute Mountain Tribal Park, Ute tour guides lead all-day tours into an absolutely unspoiled canyon. Visitors sense the rhythms of Anasazi life and walk single-file beside remote clusters of Anasazi houses etched deep into canyon clefts to utilize southern exposure in the winter and maximum water runoff during spring and summer rains.

At the end of the daylong tour, the most spectacular ruin awaits. Home to the head shaman, who guided his people in the precise plant-ing of corn in the red clay soil, the Eagle's Nest ruin towers above Mancos

Adjacent to Mesa Verde National Park, Ute Mountain Tribal Park in southern Colorado provides intimate access into ancient Anasazi sites. Personalized tours with Ute guides enable visitors to climb on original trails, study rocks used to polish arrow points, step down into a replica kiva near Jackson Butte, and peer into ancient houses. An all-day tour takes visitors into a large canyon; the height of the experience is the final climb up a sixty-foot wooden kiva ladder to the rock ledge of a shaman's house, where visitors duck under an overhanging cliff to see the silent, dusty rooms. Photos by author, September 1997.

Canyon with full southern exposure and a square of white ochre painted on the shaman's house to indicate to all travelers his power and prestige. Grappling with an overwhelming sense of vertigo, visitors ascend a steep ladder to walk along the sandstone ledge of the Eagle's Nest, where a granary still stands with its original small stone door hand-tapered for a perfect fit. Ancient juniper poles jut out from the walls. From the top of the Eagle's Nest, Mancos Canyon opens out below to the east and to the west, and from that vantage point, it is apparent that anyone on foot a millennium ago could easily have been detected.

Undoubtedly, the shaman had the best view. His people would have brought him food and offerings, and he would have told them when to plant and when to harvest. Thanks to the careful stewardship of the Ute Mountain Ute and the foresight of Chief Jack House, the Ancient Pueblo people of Mancos Canyon will always be remembered and thought of with respect. Standing on the narrow ledge at Eagle's Nest, peering into those dusty rooms, our modern preoccupation with time has no apparent purpose. In Mancos Canyon, centuries have passed and will pass again with no disturbance of the landscape. The view the Anasazi beheld remains complete and unaltered, and a hand on the cool rock or the ancient wooden beams touches what the Ancient Pueblo people touched. All is silence and sunlight.[41]

5

Living Tribal Cultures

It was our custom for the old people to instruct the children. That was not like the learning of today, but it was what we needed for living in this world. I paid attention to what the old people said.

—YELLOW WOLF, Nez Perce

Closing these ceremonial dances is a tough situation because our philosophy says we welcome everyone because that is the Hopi way. We have been an open community and an open society for a long time, but we've become such a focus of attention and curiosity that we're being exploited. The hard message of these closures is to let the public know that the Hopis plea for some level of sensitivity.

—LEIGH J. KUWANWISIWMA, Hopi Cultural Preservation Office

Native Americans continue to gain pride in their tribal roots. Cultural goals include protecting sacred objects and sacred places, but there are other pressing needs, as well—health care, full employment, adequate housing, and educational opportunities on and off reservations. Although over half of all American Indians today live in urban settings or away from reservation lands, Indian culture thrives and evolves within the framework of fixed traditions and the revival of ancient ceremonies. A younger generation now recognizes elders as tradition bearers, and maintaining culture has become essential to the health of tribal peoples.

Demographically, native peoples enjoy high birthrates and a very young population compared to the rest of the United States. At Zuni, New Mexico, over half the tribal population is now under the age of thirty, making the transfer of cultural traditions and values a critical issue. What does it mean to be an Indian at the turn of the twenty-first century? And more important, what does it mean to be a Shoshone, Arapaho, Hochunk, Miwok, Zuni, or member of any other tribe with federal recognition? And what about the tribal peoples who do not have federal recognition, such as the Lumbee of North Carolina and other eastern groups?

East of the Mississippi River, for those Indians who survived the waves of pandemic diseases and the historic onslaught of colonists and later settlers, their blood became mixed with that of other peoples, and farmers took native lands long ago. Yet Indian ties and traditions remain strong. Despite hardships, culture and traditional values have been passed down among the eastern Indians who hid from President Andrew Jackson's armies in the 1830s and did not travel on the Trail of Tears.

In the East, a large number of the Indians who stayed are displaced Choctaw, Chickasaw, and the ever-present Cherokee. Many of these people are not well integrated into the American economic system, and at times, they live a marginal existence, yet they feel bound to the land of their ancestors and determined to prevent the desecration of Indian graves. They hope to rekindle ceremonies and traditions. Alienated from the larger society but needing to find work in the nonnative world, urban Indians re-create their own traditional communities and seek to become culturally self-sustaining. When asked about their presence in public meetings over issues concerning prehistoric Indian villages or sacred sites, they quietly respond, "We are here. We have always been here, and we will always be here."

In their struggle for legitimacy, landless eastern Indians seek to learn and transmit the old ways as part of their personal identity. In Tennessee, for instance, there may be 10,000 enrolled tribal members living in the state, but another 25,000 individuals consider themselves culturally affiliated with Native Americans and claim, but cannot prove, Indian heritage. Displaced themselves, contemporary Native Americans vow to prevent further displacement of Indian graves and removal of their dead. Protecting the ancestors constitutes a very real part of being Indian today.

Issues of Indian Identity

At the beginning of the twenty-first century, the issue of American Indian identity remains hotly contested. Accurate genealogical records can be very important for tribal membership. Some tribes require that their members have at least one-fourth Indian blood; others, such as the Cherokee and Chippewa, consider one-eighth Indian blood acceptable. Recently, the Osage Nation of Oklahoma decided by a 60 percent vote to broaden its membership and include anyone with ancestors on the 1906 enrollment rolls. Ironically, these are the same membership rolls that were originally used to assimilate and Americanize Indians during the land allotment process following passage of the Dawes Act of 1887. But as Jacob John Folstrom, an enrolled member of the White Earth Reservation at White Earth, Minnesota, wrote about blood quantum, or the percentage of Indian blood in people who claim Indian descent, "Is it not the emphasis on strong family ties that distinguishes the Indian Nation from other more materialistic nations? Has this not always been

Preserving tribal traditions sustains native identities, which enables Indian children to better cope with the larger, nonnative world. This young Tohono O'odham girl attended school at San Xavier, Arizona. Photo by author, March 1981.

a source of Indian pride?" He stated, "I believe it is the traditional honoring of all family members through the generations that has helped play a significant role" in Indian survival. "Lesser nations would have collapsed and disappeared."[1]

As Devon A. Mihesuah suggested, "How Indianness is defined by American Indians and non-Indians, who claim to be Indian and why, and the anxieties among multiheritage Indians are complex historical and present day issues." "Because of assimilation, acculturation, and intermarriage with non-Indians," she said, "American Indians have a variety of references to describe themselves: full-blood, traditional, mixed blood, cross-blood, half-breed, progressive, enrolled, unenrolled, re-Indianized, multiheritage, bicultural, post Indian," or they can use their tribal name.[2]

Some Native Americans drift across the country from one urban area to another in search of opportunity and jobs they cannot find at home. Thousands of Indians reside in Denver, Dallas, St. Louis, Chicago, and Nashville. Though they live far from sacred sites on tribal lands, they nevertheless feel a deep need to connect with tribal traditions, which they do at powwows, feasts, ceremonials, and giveaways. Young Indians today learn eagle dancing, girls' fancy dancing, hoop dancing, and the Grass Dance. Native attendance continues to increase at the Navajo Nation Fair at Window Rock, Arizona, the Indian Market in Santa Fe, New Mexico, the White Mountain Apache Fair and Rodeo at Ruidoso, New Mexico, the Treaty Days Pow-Wow at Fort Washakie, Wyoming, and the All-Iroquois Indian Festival at Cobleskill, New York, to name just a few Indian ceremonials. Powwows appear to unify roles in Indian life, but scholar Mark Mattern argued that they also represent "a public arena for negotiation of differences and disagreements," which "contributes to the resiliency and flexibility of Indian communities by

Native Americans who travel the powwow circuit performing traditional dances frequently go to Nashville, Tennessee, and other cities where non-Indian visitors appreciate their dances. Photos by author, October 1992.

helping manage the tension between unity and diversity."[3] Unfortunately, however, attending large, public Native American gatherings such as powwows does not end troubles at home.

Compared to a national average of 6 percent unemployment, the rate of unemployed Indians averages 38 percent, and at some reservations, the rate can be as high as 65 percent.[4] The suicide rate for fifteen- to twenty-four-year-old Native Americans is double that of any other American group, and 45 percent of Indian mothers have their first child before the age of twenty. Indians die younger than any other segment of the American population, and the alcoholism rate for Native Americans between fifteen and twenty-four years of age is seventeen times the rate for other Americans. Homicide is the second leading cause of death among Indians fourteen years and younger, and chronic unemployment combines with a high violent crime rate.[5] On the vast Navajo Reservation, which sprawls across four states, the average annual per capita income is only $6,600.

White Shamans and "Wanna-be" Indians

Clearly, tribal peoples remain in turmoil. The return to "tradition not addiction" and the need for psychic balance represent powerful incentives to seek a spiritual path via the old ways. Nonnatives' fascination with native religious ways and whites who "wanna be" Indians complicate the issue for Indians trying to learn ancient ceremonies and pass on traditions. Native peoples laughingly call these people the "wanna-be" tribe, but such spiritual seekers have a tremendous impact on sacred sites, on the work and role of shamans, and on the ability of tribes to keep and maintain their privacy.

Tribes deeply resent the use of their ancient traditions by white shamans and authors who claim to have inside knowledge of tribal traditions. "What the New Age seekers view as borrowing, some American

Indian leaders view as appropriation or downright thievery," wrote Bonnie Coffin-Glass. "The National Congress of American Indians adopted a 'declaration of war' against 'non-Indian wannabes, hucksters, cultists, commercial profiteers and self-styled New Age shamans' who exploit, abuse or misrepresent American Indians' sacred traditions and spiritual practices," she noted.[6] But misuse of religious traditions is not limited to whites. Because of a growing interest and potential cash market among middle-class seekers of spirituality, Native Americans have also misrepresented themselves.

Indian Country Today headlined lengthy articles on "The Selling of the Sun Dance" in South Dakota, where thirty whites participated in the sacred Sioux dance after each paid a hefty $5,000 fee.[7] On the Navajo Reservation, fake healers or chanters have induced families to spend excessive money on ceremonies and food preparation for a family healing event, only to find that the chanter lied. An elderly woman complained she had given $200 to a fake chanter for a Blessingway Ceremony to heal an ill family member, but the so-called medicine man's closing chant rang false, and he did not know the entire ritual. The woman sought help. "What she wanted," explained Daniel Deschinny, secretary of the Diné Spiritual and Cultural Association, "was for us to do something for her—get her money back or take action against the man who had taken her money," but no certification system exists for traditional healers for the Navajo or other tribes who have no way to police fraudulent healers. Young chanters must learn and memorize all elements of each ceremony, and they must do so without notebooks or tape recorders. Charlatans never complete the process because of the long and arduous apprenticeships. There is no legal recourse against fraudulent shamans.[8]

To prevent the theft of cultural information, the Hopi have closed their Katsina dances on First Mesa in Arizona to all visitors except for

To protect sacred places at Taos Pueblo, tourists are denied access to ancient kivas still in use for religious ceremonies and initiations. Warning signs can also be found in other areas of Taos Pueblo and at Ute Mountain Tribal Park. Photos by author, September 1997.

nonnative in-laws. The Zuni have closed their winter Shalako house blessing ceremonies to non-Indians, who previously came in tour buses, rushed to the front of host houses so that local family members could not see the Shalako dancers, and behaved as pushy, inquisitive tourists instead of gracious guests.

New Age religious believers who have rejected mainstream churches and seek Indian spirituality do so without proper initiation and without tribal permission, and they sometimes steal authentic offerings left by tribal peoples. Indian religion is private and closely held. Knowledge of sacred objects and access to sacred sites is confidential information not to be shared with outsiders or even with tribal members from different clans or medicine societies.

A legal researcher in the Hopi Cultural Preservation Office, Yvonne Hoosava, remarked that people often telephone her because they want to give their businesses or their boats a Hopi name. They want phone numbers for traditional Hopi healers, and they want to know all about the Hopi religion in a few short minutes over the telephone. She sighed and explained, "To know our culture one must grow up in it. You have to live it on a daily basis. We continue to learn every day."[9] On the Hopi Reservation, New Agers have left offerings and granules of salt, and they have strung materials up in trees. On the Coconino National Forest near Sedona, Arizona, New Agers rearrange rocks, cut boughs from trees, and make their own miniature medicine wheels, all to the chagrin of the local Forest Service employees who must repair the woods and take down the pseudoshrines.[10]

In Colorado, New Agers have damaged Ute Indian sacred sites by moving stones aligned centuries ago at high elevations in Rocky Mountain National Park.[11] An intruder on the White River National Forest near Aspen, Colorado, created a fake medicine wheel to stop expansion of a ski area. Tribal sacred sites are beset by vandals as well as misguided religious enthusiasts who seek to participate in medicine wheel ceremonies, sweat lodges, and vision quests. At Chaco Culture National Historic Park in New Mexico, a World Heritage Site, New Agers scattered the ashes of one of their friends in the main kiva at Pueblo Bonito during a "harmonic convergence." Navajo workers refused to go near the site to do any maintenance, and the National Park Service finally had to remove two inches of topsoil from the kiva before stabilization and preservation of the ruin could continue.

Some white Americans remain fascinated with Indians and Indian ways, and they co-opt Indian spirituality at every opportunity. At Grand Canyon National Park, the Hopi House Gift Shop of the Fred Harvey Company sells thumb-sized "medicine bags for luck." Each pouch contains seven medicine charms and a tag that reads, "The Native Americans believed that all things have a spirit or life force and that all these forces are interconnected. Each animal, stone, plant, has a special spiritual meaning. To use a medicine bag is to use the influences of nature to guide your earth walk." The eager tourist can purchase a small pouch for $16.99, providing instant spirituality and communion with the earth. The public remains infatuated with Indian ways but does not always respect them.

At the Hopi Cultural Preservation Office in Kykotsmovi, Arizona, Hoosava explained, "We have been taught that if you see something that you leave it alone. You do not pick it up. The term is *kyaptsi*. It means respect for all mankind, insects and animals. One of our main teachings is respect." Whereas Indians understand these implicit and explicit cultural boundaries and do not cross kiva lines or ask about the affairs of other medicine societies, nonnatives, Hoosava said, "want to know because it is secret. The more secretive it is the more they want to

Tribes have problems with white wanna-be Indians and with New Age believers who create false spiritual sites, such as this fake medicine wheel on Burnt Mountain, above Snowmass Village in Colorado. The vandal created the wheel to help stop the expansion of a ski resort, but Ute Indian Kenny Frost explained that the modern alignment of the stones in a medicine wheel shape may have been built on an ancient site, thereby destroying it. Photo copyrighted by Nan Johnson.

know. Outsiders do not understand." She has tried to explain to them on the telephone: "I tell them that your people had spirituality years ago. Go back to them. You will never learn our culture in a day or two or a week. It takes a lifetime and even then you do not know it all."[12] But frequently, the nonnatives do not listen. And meanwhile, a tour company out of Sedona, Arizona, offers "The Ways of the Ancients: Tours to Sacred Lands" by Indian guides who are "Warriors of the Sacred Path."

Consequently, the Hopi, like other tribes, express concern over their intellectual property, names, songs, dances, sacred teachings, and shrines. They insist that research protocols be followed by legitimate students and scholars.[13] Each village can decide which of the many dances to open or close, but the Snake Dances are now closed, and First Mesa is entirely off-limits for photography, audio recording, or sketching of any kind, though villagers permit walking tours. There is no fee, only a donation box. At the community center on First Mesa where the tours originate, signs proclaim "No Cameras" in six different languages.

Hopi Cultural Officer Leigh Kuwanwisiwma explained, "There are over 300 books on the Hopi and none of them have been written by a Hopi member. Much of the material is false or has been misinterpreted."[14] A prominent nonnative author on Indian topics held a Phoenix, Arizona, workshop at which he charged $150 to $250 to teach students

Most Indian people today welcome tourists—but only in certain areas of their villages and reservations. At Taos and other pueblos in northern New Mexico, tourists pay an extra fee to use their cameras and videotape recorders, and strict rules apply. Cameras may be confiscated if tourists violate sacred ceremonies or intrude on the privacy of Indian people. Photo by author, September 1997.

how to make Hopi prayer feathers. Kuwanwisiwma became incensed with the workshop, following as it did on the heels of another debacle in which Marvel comic books depicted sacred Katsina dancers as violent marauders.

Copyrighting Culture

Like the Hopi, Apache tribes seek exclusive control over their cultural property, which means "all images, texts, ceremonies, music, songs, stories, symbols, beliefs, customs, ideas, and other physical and spiritual objects and concepts" related to Apache life, including representations of Apache culture by non-Apache. In an article titled "Can Culture be Copyrighted?" Michael Brown explained that native peoples seek their fair share of any profits from "the acquisition of native crop varieties for the genetic improvement of seeds, the transformation of traditional herbal medicines into marketable drugs by pharmaceutical firms [and] the incorporation of indigenous graphic designs into commercial products." Brown called for "urgently needed public discussion about mutual respect and the fragility of Native cultures in mass societies."[15]

At Zuni, the tribe has initiated its own publishing department, and, as former publications director Anne Beckett observed, "the square peg of Zuni tradition and philosophy is trying to place itself in the round hole of Western intellectual property. Zuni tradition is predicated upon collective rights, and intellectual property is based on individual rights never conceived of by Zunis." "Conversely," she added, "Zuni traditions are collectively owned in ways never conceived of by law." The issue of trademarks and copyrights creates conflicts. Beckett, a non-Indian, said, "We are forcing them to have concepts of ownership and we are breeding dissent. This is splitting families and tribes." She cautioned, "In forcing people to adapt to Western ways we are in the process of destroying something ancient and irreplaceable." Bemoaning white infatuation with Indian ideas and perspectives, she stated, "We must temper our fascination with the need to know. We really don't need to know everything about everybody. Somewhere along the line our curiosity got lethal."[16]

Tribal intellectual property issues include the right to plant, harvest, and distribute Indian corn. Over the millennia, Pueblo peoples have grown corn, just as tribes in the Northwest have caught salmon or harvested huckleberries, but now the rare Hopi and Zuni species of drought-resistant corn in colorful colors, including blue, are coveted and used by others. One company boldly received a "certificate of plant variety protection" for "Hopi Blue Popcorn" without Hopi tribal authorization or consent. As a result, the rights of farmers, especially Hopi farmers, to sell the seed are limited.[17]

A Phoenix factory manufactures Hopi Blue Corn pancake mix, and in San Francisco, Hopi Blue Corn Flakes contain a boxtop history of the Hopi agricultural way of life and the statement "Made from the blue corn

Issues of Native American cultural property include rights to songs, ceremonies, sacred sites, and ancient gardening practices. Hopi Blue Popcorn is a U.S.-protected variety of popcorn seed that was certified or patented without permission of the Hopi Tribe. Courtesy, Leigh Kuwanwisiwma, Hopi cultural officer, Kykotsmovi, Arizona.

that the Hopi ate for strength." As Kuwanwisiwma pointed out, "Hopi society has always been an open society based on our philosophy of promoting brotherhood, sisterhood and universal community," but those shared values may not withstand the surge of interest from outsiders.[18]

Nonnatives constitute one particular set of problems, but tribes also quarrel among themselves over who can and cannot make certain kinds of art for the $.5 billion art market. Federal law specifically requires that objects sold as Indian art be made by Indians, but the legislation does not say which Indians should be the artists, so rival tribal members copy and reproduce designs or types of materials such as Katsina dolls, which represent Hopi "intellectual property."

Even more disturbing, workers in Asian countries replicate American Indian jewelry and sell fake Navajo turquoise or Zuni pincushion silver work as authentic. An island in the Philippines has even been renamed Zuni so the jewelry can be stamped "Made in Zuni," and imitation overlay on silver bracelets replicating Hopi designs comes from Taiwan and Korea. Laborers produce "American Indian" jewelry in Mexico, Taiwan, China, Pakistan, and Thailand.[19]

Despite these imitations, part of the modern Indian cultural revival includes a return to traditional arts and crafts, including basket making, ceramic pottery making, weaving, carving, mask making, and all kinds of beadwork and quillwork. Studying old designs and ancient patterns enthralls contemporary Indian artists. Though sacred objects cannot be reproduced for sale, Indian artists reproduce old traditional crafts, making new designs for an eager buying public. Some of the best of these native artists have received National Heritage Fellowships from the Folk Arts Program of the National Endowment for the Arts. In time, their art will become cultural patrimony for their own tribes. These individuals represent living treasures for all Americans.

Elder Artists as Living Treasures

Award winners include Margaret Tafoya, a Santa Clara potter renowned for her unusually large pots with a dark mirrorlike finish and a bear paw design on the neck of the vessel. "It is a good luck symbol," she said; "the bear always knows where the water is."[20] She made only hand-coiled vessels and dug her clay from deposits on Santa Clara land. Like other Indian artists, she taught her descendants to fire their wares in open fires with natural fuels and to finish their vessels with special smoothing stones.

Clyde "Kindy" Sproat has been recognized as a master of traditional Hawaiian cowboy, or *paniolo*, music, and Chesley Goseyun Wilson is an acknowledged master of the Western Apache violin made from the dried flower stalk of the agave cactus. A member of the Eagle Clan raised on the San Carlos Reservation in the White Mountains of southeastern Arizona, Wilson practices his crafts and instructs younger Apache students in the discipline of Apache Gaan dancing and singing. He said, "My fiddle only plays Apache songs."[21]

Helen Cordero explained, "For a long time pottery was silent in the pueblo [of Cochiti]," where she comes from in New Mexico. But in the late 1950s, she and her cousin began making pottery that heralded back to ancient traditions of seated female figurines. She began to make storyteller figures of her grandfather, with small clay children attached. Just as Maria Martinez of San Ildefonso Pueblo revolutionized ceramics in her village half a century earlier, Helen Cordero took an older form and created a new art style.[22]

At Haines, Alaska, Jennie Thlunaut, the last living Chilkat weaving master, told the small class of fifteen Native Alaskan weavers who apprenticed with her, "I don't want to be stingy with this. I am giving it to you, and you will carry it on." Single-handedly, she had kept the weaving tradition alive, from its Tsimshian origins to the Tlingit Chilkat blanket designs of the nineteenth century with stylized animal motifs so important for traditional potlatches and other ceremonies. Woven from mountain goat hair and the fibers of red cedar, these highly prized blankets are made for movement. As Tlingit elder Austin Hammond remarked, "The Tlingit were not writers of books. They wove their history into their garments and they wear their history on their backs." In the traditional manner, Jennie Thlunaut gave all her blankets away despite their high dollar value.[23]

From Onamie, Minnesota, Ojibwe storyteller, craftswoman, and tradition bearer Maude Kegg has written three books on the Ojibwe or Chippewa people from her store of Ojibwe legends. Born in a bark-and-cattail mat wigwam in northern Minnesota and raised by her grandmother, she produced fully beaded traditional bandolier bags, a symbol of prestige and leadership once worn by tribal leaders. Kegg also helped to construct the large diorama of Ojibwe life through the seasons at the Mille Lacs Indian Museum.

Kevin Locke, a Hunkpapa Sioux of the Standing Rock Reservation, has preserved the Plains and Woodland Indians courting flute and the courting songs, which were almost lost. He learned from an elderly uncle who only spoke Lakota, as well as from Noah Has Horns, Ben Black Bear, and William Horncloud. Also a hoop dancer, Kevin Locke has a long-standing commitment to Plains Indian art and philosophy, and he will be part of the current generation that passes on traditions to younger apprentices.

A Yurok-Hupa from the Hoopa Indian Reservation in Hoopa Valley, California, George Blake makes the regalia worn and carried in ceremonial religious dances, including elk antler purses, white deerskin dance headdresses, and otter skin Brush Dance quivers. Formerly cura-

The ongoing indigenous cultural revival is well illustrated in this modern plank community house, which measures forty-six by seventy-five feet and was built by natives in Saxman, Alaska, in 1990. The new community house includes a carving workshop in which ancient traditions can be continued. Photo by Jet Lowe, Historic American Building Survey, National Park Service, 1991.

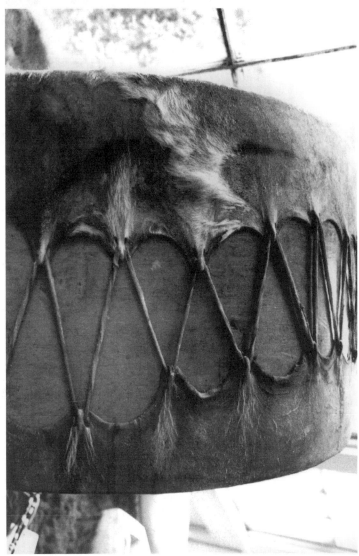

As part of the Indian revival, native peoples learn craft skills from elderly artisans. At the Shoshone Tribal Cultural Center at Fort Washakie, Wyoming, students in heritage classes were taught how to make cottonwood saddles and drums. Forthcoming classes will cover the ancient art of Shoshone basketry. Photos by author, May 1995.

tor of the Hupa Tribal Museum, he taught featherwork and the carving of antlers into Hupa purses and spoons. He said, "I wanted to do what the old people did . . . I can make elk antler purses and make them as different as I want . . . I mean, I could put elk on them, and all these other things and try to show skills an artist would, but I don't. I just like the way they were done a long time ago. And I just keep making them."[24] He has also produced the Yurok sinew-backed bow and the Hupa dugout canoe, learning skills from the last two tribal elders who knew the craft. Those men are now gone, but Blake's canoes have proven seaworthy.

The National Endowment for the Arts wrote of George Blake's contributions, "It is almost impossible now to visualize a time when, if you needed to carry something, you had to make something to carry it in; if you wanted to cook something, you had to make a pot to cook it in; or if you wanted to travel on water, you had to build a boat. That human beings can learn to solve so many problems working only with the materials of nature and the resources of the human spirit is magnificent; that they can also infuse these necessary articles with grace, elegance, and beauty is awe-inspiring." Blake learned both from elders and from meticulous library research. The NEA concluded, "George Blake has taught many lessons to his young tribal relatives in California; his example can teach the entire nation."[25]

Nick and Elena Charles are traditional Yup'ik Eskimos from the Koskokwim Delta area of southwestern Alaska. Nick is a master carver of ceremonial masks, wooden dance fans, and utilitarian items, and Elena creates women's fancy parkas and boots, birchbark and grass baskets, and traditional dolls. As a Yup'ik mask maker, Nick Charles creates masks as the embodiment of spiritual visions essential for passing on cultural knowledge. His wife has also helped to revive Yup'ik culture, and she has reintroduced Yup'ik dance and the use of carved wooden fans in deliberate dance movements. Like so many other native artisans who are local and national masters, the couple eschews personal recognition in favor of teaching others.

They are tradition bearers similar to the Kanaka'ole sisters Nalani and Pualani from Hawai'i, who are *kumu hula*, or hula masters. The sisters practice *mele*, an inseparable combination of poetry, music, and dance that reveals the deepest of Hawaiian traditional values. Daughters of the chanter and *kumu hula* Edith Kanaka'ole, they inherited Halau 'O Kekkuhi, the hula school their mother founded in 1953, which taught not only dance movements but also Hawaiian culture. Native Hawaiians consider the sisters respected elders, or *kupuna*, in their own right.[26]

Other traditional artisans include basket makers in Maine and California, but for those tribal peoples, personal hazards exist in perpetuating their art because highway workers frequently spray roadside grasses, and processing the stems, usually by pulling them through one's teeth, can be harmful. In the northern woods of Maine, brown ash trees needed for wood splints to weave baskets have declined both in quantity and quality because of acid rain. Donald Sanipass, a Micmac basket maker, stated, "Something's killing the trees. I don't know if it's acid rain or fertilizer runoff from the farms, but the tops of trees look dead and the wood quality isn't what it used to be."[27] Indian access represents another problem. "It's supposed to be a tradition that any place where there is a Brown Ash tree growing, why it's yours. You don't have to ask permission," said James Tonmah, a Maliseet basket maker. "The Indians have that right."[28] Among basket makers, the bounty of the meadows and woods is never "owned." In Maine, Native Americans consider brown ash a resource for all to use, and men who harvest the tree for bark splints must ensure a supply for the next generation. Their gathering places are sacred.

Culture Camps for Native Children

The Indian cultural revival involves not just the craftsmanship of individual artists but also culture camps for children. A few of the Pueblo tribes scoff and say, "Our traditions are alive. We don't need to send children to culture camps. They learn in the kivas." But for other tribes, culture camps mix the old and the young in intergenerational summer settings. Children and teenagers study their native language and learn how to gather berries, shoot bows and arrows, build sweat lodges, ride horses, and process wild game. The Northern Arapaho in Wyoming have culture camps, and there have been successful camps among the Salish-Kootenai near Pablo, Montana.

At Healthy Nations, or *Wolakota Yukini Wicoti*, a spiritual boot camp near Eagle Butte, South Dakota, troubled Lakota teens from broken families or with a history of drug or alcohol abuse begin each morning with prayers at dawn, and each week, they move tepees across the prairie to new sites. Greg Bourland, chairman of the Cheyenne River Sioux Tribe, said, "This camp is more than a camp. In a way it is the rebirth of

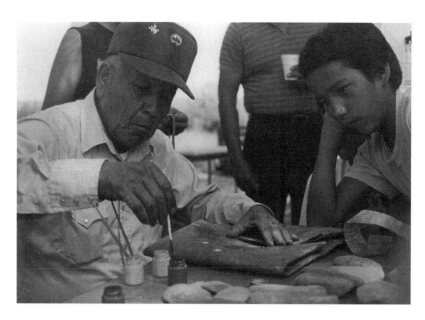

At the Northern Arapaho Language and Culture Camp on the Wind River Reservation in Wyoming, Richard Moss demonstrates painting on parfleche (rawhide that has been soaked to remove flesh and hair and then dried). Photo by Sara Wiles, Lander, Wyoming.

Students watch as drummers (left to right) Pat Iron Cloud, William C'Hair, and Steven Sun Rhodes play and sing traditional Arapaho songs. Singing "behind the drum" are the codirectors of the Arapaho Language and Culture Camp, Merle Haaas and Sandra Iron Cloud. Photo by Sara Wiles, Lander, Wyoming.

Jola Wallowme Bull displays "dollrags" that she and other students made. Photo by Sara Wiles, Lander, Wyoming.

Young culture camp participants practice their archery. Photo by Sara Wiles, Lander, Wyoming.

the Great Sioux Nation."[29] With close to 85 percent of the Cheyenne River population between the ages of twelve and thirty-five regularly bingeing on alcohol and drugs, returning to the past may be the key to the future. Similar camps include an Inupiat kayak expedition camp near Nome, Alaska, above the Arctic Circle.

Across the country, Indian nations promote temperance and spiritual revitalization. "We call it seventh-generational thinking," Bourland explained. "Seven generations ago, our ancestors loved us so much that we are still here as a people. We have to create a world not only for today, but for seven generations to come. The young people from this camp are going to be the messengers for the future," and tribal leaders are trying to revive traditions.[30] For many American Indians, that means bringing back the sacred buffalo.

Bringing Back the Buffalo

Thirty-three tribes have joined the Inter-Tribal Bison Cooperative of Rapid City, South Dakota. Former director Mark Heckert spoke of "a deep, innate abiding respect between Indian people and buffalo. It's a cultural relationship that goes into pre-history." Put simply, "if there was buffalo, they lived; if there wasn't any buffalo, they died."[31]

After the Civil War, market hunters and, later, hide hunters killed millions of buffalo, on the southern plains and then on the northern plains, which helped to spark the Plains Indian Wars. So many buffalo disappeared so fast, the Blackfeet could not believe it. By 1883, the northern herd was virtually extinct, and baffled Blackfeet thought the earth must have opened up and swallowed all the buffalo. Eleven years later, fewer than 500 wild buffalo remained in the United States, the only descendants of herds that once numbered 50 million. The 1890s were also the apogee of life for thousands of American Indians. From a population of perhaps 4–7 million in 1492, their number had dwindled to 200,000 by 1900. In fact, Native Americans living at the turn of the twentieth century knew more people who were dead than people who were alive. But just as the buffalo have come back in strength in more recent years, so have Native Americans.

Today, the Inter-Tribal Bison Cooperative represents seven tribes in Montana and other tribes from Washington, Oregon, New Mexico, Oklahoma, Colorado, Wisconsin, Nebraska, and the Dakotas. The cooperative's mission is "to restore bison to Indian tribes in a manner which is compatible with their spiritual and cultural beliefs and practices" without domesticating the animal. In the words of Fred DuBray, "Our refusal to join the overwhelming effort to domesticate buffalo and turn them into a mere commodity for exploitation sends a powerful message to the rest of the world. Our thousands-of-years-old relationship with buffalo must be recognized and understood as a critical part of the return of the *Pte Oyate* (Buffalo Nation)."[32] Buffalo are annually harvested for ceremonies and powwows and to provide meat for the elderly who need it. At Ethete, Wyoming, Northern Arapaho have hosted a "Bison Cultural Day" to study the relationship between the bison and the tribe, complete with language teachers and classes on how to make parfleche, or painted rawhide pouches used for carrying the meat. The highlight of one event featured seventy-one-year-old elder Lloyd Dewey, who demonstrated the use of obsidian and rose quartz knives and an old soft-steel blade knife with a pipestone handle, passed down from his wife's family. He butchered a one-ton animal within an hour using traditional methods.[33]

The Cheyenne River Sioux Tribe's herd of 85 animals has grown to 800, providing a harvest of sixteen two-year-old bulls per year, with 100 percent of the meat going to the tribe. Culture camp teenagers learn the old ways of butchering and how to use all the animal's parts, even the tail. Skilled elders reshape many parts of the buffalo into sacred

Richard Powaukee of Lapwai, Idaho, poses at Fort Vancouver, Washington, with an Appaloosa resplendent in traditional beadwork. For centuries, the Nee-Me'-Poo (or Nez Perce) bred these horses, but the Indian wars of the nineteenth century caused them to lose control of the breed. The Nez Perce Horse Registry has been established to create a new breed for the twenty-first century that will combine the strength, agility, and colors of the spotted Appaloosas with Akhal-Teke horses from Turkmenistan. These sturdy animals are excellent desert horses that can survive with very little water. From 12 purebred Akhal-Teke mares, colts, and stallions, Nez Perce horse breeders have created 130 horses of this new breed. The tribe will also be starting its own buffalo herd. Photo by author, May 1999.

objects, especially the skull, an essential element of the Sun Dance. The Sacred Buffalo Hat, made from the skin of a buffalo cow's head, represents female spiritual power. When the Lakota kill a buffalo, they know the animal has given them the gift of life, so they sing to release the bison's soul to the spirit world so the animal can be reborn and the life cycle continued. As Ron Goodman, a professor at Sinte Glesta University in Mission, South Dakota, explained, "We are in the process of healing spiritual wounds. The return of buffalo is a crucial part of that process."[34]

Because consumers consider free-roaming bison a healthy alternative to grain-fed beef, the bison's market value has risen dramatically. The cost of purchasing bison can be prohibitive, so tribes receive surplus bison from national parks such as Wind Cave National Park, Chickasaw National Park, and Theodore Roosevelt National Park, as well as from national wildlife refuges such as Sully's Hill National Game Preserve and Wichita Wildlife Refuge. Members of the Crow Tribe in Montana raise 1,100 head of bison, and the Arapaho on the Wind River Reservation in Wyoming have cared for a few head, but Indian cattle ranchers, fearful of brucellosis (a contagious disease that causes domestic cattle to abort), have opposed introducing more buffalo to traditional ranges along the Wind River and Owl Creek Mountains. Other tribes, such as the Devils Lake Sioux Tribe of North Dakota, know *Tatanka*, the Sioux word for buffalo, as the great provider, and they hope to replace cattle with bison on tribal lands. Among the Winnebago Tribe of Nebraska, students at local schools have developed an Adopt-a-Bison Program to learn respect for buffalo at an early age and to perceive the herd as part of the tribal family.

Saving Tribal Languages

Though bison reintroduction programs can only occur where tribes own sufficient acreage, every native group in the United States is concerned about passing culture on through language, which holds the key to tribal identities and worldviews. But most native children now grow up speaking English. The older generation, raised to think and speak in native tongues, declines in numbers yearly. At La Push, Washington, on the western edge of the Olympic Peninsula, for example, only three women still speak Quileute because when the government forced Indians onto reservations a century ago, many left home to find work and English was the language of survival off the reservation.

For several tribes, only a handful of native speakers remain, and tribal officials race to record and transcribe their elders' words in order to introduce young children to the language of their grandparents. Among the Ojibwe in northern Minnesota, only 200 of the 3,000 tribal members are native speakers, all of whom are over the age of forty-five. Marie Smith is the only remaining native speaker of Eyak, a traditional language of Indians in southern Alaska. When she passes on, the language of an entire people will pass with her. Among the Mashpee Wampanoag Tribe from Massachusetts, the native language has been lost, and the Wikchammni language from northern California will die out in the current generation.

"Less than half of the 500 languages present when Columbus stepped ashore have survived the reservation and boarding school periods. Of these less than 50 could be considered linguistically healthy today," according to Tom Webster, writing in defense of Indian bilingual education. He explained, "A human language is a window into the soul and is a deep pool of knowledge about a given culture."[35] Highly descriptive, with precise nuances for naming places, textures, weather, and events, most Indian languages utilize long, multisyllabic words, which are hard to learn if one's first language is English. Indian words can be as long as English sentences and Indian sentences can be as long as paragraphs in English because tribal speech builds on word stems to include suffixes that determine action, time, gender, location, and information about the speaker. Children easily learn languages, but many young Indian parents do not know their native tongue and cannot pass it on to their children. So what was once informally learned at home and in the natural world must now be structured into programs and community center classrooms like those of the Osage Tribe, which has only ten members left who speak fluent Osage.

Tribal sovereignty includes linguistic self-determination, yet only about 200 indigenous languages precariously survive in the United States. As Jared Diamond noted, "Linguists face a race against time similar to that faced by biologists, now aware that many of the world's plant and animal species are in danger of extinction." He said, "Each language is indissolubly tied up with a unique culture, literature (whether written or not), and worldview, all of which represents the end point of thousands of years of human inventiveness. Lose the language and you lose most of that as well."[36]

Indian culture has traditionally been passed down orally, with language serving as a storehouse of craft, culture, and religion. Elders muse that what is written is forgotten, but what is spoken is remembered, often for generations. "We need our land and we need our language," stated Dick Littlebear, a Northern Cheyenne educator. "The two are inseparable. . . . There are references to the land that can be articulated only in the Cheyenne language. I believe that once those sacred references can no longer be expressed, the Northern Cheyennes will start viewing the land much as the dominant culture views it. These vital links will no longer exist in the tribal consciousness."[37]

In trying to stop erosion of their languages, tribes have initiated language-retention programs. Language committees certify tribal members qualified to speak and teach effectively. The Pascua Yaqui, Tohono O'odham, Arapaho, Shoshone, Northern Ute, Southern Ute, the Red Lake Band of Chippewa, Zuni, and Navajo have all begun extensive language training for their young children, complete with workbooks, textbooks, and even interactive computer programs. The language policy and education code of the Red Lake Schools states, "The Chippewa language is a gift from the Creator to our people and, therefore, shall be treated with respect. Our ancient language is the foundation of our cultural and spiritual heritage without which we could not exist in the manner that our Creator intended."[38] Congress passed the Native American Language Act of 1992, agreeing in principle to support and preserve tribal tongues, but few federal funds have been made available for such efforts.

Isolated tribes have preserved native speech more easily than other tribes, but factionalism often exists over what, when, where, and by whom things should be taught. Albert Alvarez explained that for the Tohono O'odham, "I felt that was the most important thing we have, the language. As long as it's alive, it's a part of us, it's our life. [It expresses] that respect when we see mountains, when we see trees, when we see anything that grows—we don't just go and start chopping it down for our own satisfaction. When we lose that, we're just walking in the dark, trying to search our way around."[39] To lose a native tongue is to think only in English and thus miss the cultural and place connections embedded within the web of generations of experience.

At the far northwest corner of Washington State, the Makah Tribe, with 1,000 residents, instills its language and cultural stories into the lives of children, but only about twelve tribal members truly know Makah. The youngest of those speakers, Helma Ward, was seventy-four years old in 1992. The Makah actively practice tribal historic preservation. For the National Register of Historic Places, they nominate campgrounds, fishing banks, rock outcroppings, petroglyphs, and other sites, but "none of these facets of their culture can be fully understood and appreciated outside of the context of language," in the opinion of journalist Kim Keister. "Our language teaches us how to think like Makahs. To feel like Makahs. To live in Makah ways," Helma Ward said. "When we are out in a boat, we see the same things our grandparents saw if we know the language."[40]

From Tall Trees to Coastal Canoes

Just as Plains tribes bring back the buffalo, coastal Indians remake war canoes from tall cedar trees found deep in forest groves. Centuries ago, Makah traveled the Pacific coast in eight-man, thirty-two-foot dugout canoes, searching for gray and killer whales. All the coastal tribes——the Quinault and Quileute, the Chinook and Clatsop, the Klallam, Skagit, Lummi, Duwamish, and Chehali—used dugout canoes to harvest bounty from the sea, dozens of estuaries, and the Columbia River. The art of dugout canoe making was almost lost, but under the guidance of Emmett Oliver of the Quinault Nation, the tribes carefully crafted new canoes from 600-year-old cedars cut from national forests. Because of the canoe's spiritual and religious significance, Indians cut the ancient trees under provisions of the 1978 American Indian Religious Freedom Act.

Most coastal canoes had become museum artifacts, but spurred by the desire to have a special Indian event for the Washington State centennial, coastal tribes and religious leaders united to revive an ancient art and to teach young men the necessary teamwork needed to craft and then handle the great canoes. Because of antipathy toward celebrating Washington statehood, some tribes expressed opposition to the idea, but, Oliver said, "The appeal I made was restoration: 'If you believe what you had was good, why shouldn't you want to perpetuate it? As important as the canoe is to the native lore and way of life, can you tolerate that it may be lost forever?' And they saw the value of restoring something tangible of the past."[41]

The Swinomish, Upper Skagit, Nooksack, and Lummi Tribes each received two trees. Women sang and blessed the trees and explained to the cedars that they would be reborn as canoes. Just as the Plains tribes use all parts of the buffalo, for coastal peoples, the huge cedar trees provided rope, boxes, baskets, and other materials. Skilled carvers roughed out each huge tree and shaped the inside using hot rocks and steam to soften the tree. Other artists did exterior carving and special painting of animal symbols on the prows of the seaworthy vessels.

Among the Tulalip Tribe, elder Marya Moses waited in the forest for the trees to be cut. Writer Ben Smith described the scene: "As the giant tree was wedged off its balance point, it swayed slightly, stalled, and then thundered to the ground. Her arms over her head, shaking her hands, her eyes on the ground, Marya said [thanks] and then planted cedar seedlings in holes dug in the soft earth, saying, 'When we take from the earth, we must always give something back.' "[42]

The tree harvesting and canoe carving resulted in a surge of ceremonial activities, dances, feasts, and potlatches, as well as a revitalization of tribal customs, including canoe racing and the main event, the "Paddle to Seattle" across Puget Sound to make landfall and camp in a city park among supporters, friends, and relatives. Twenty tribes and forty canoes participated in the centennial race. Other associated events included salmon bakes, dances, and the singing of tribal songs.

The hand-carved, painted canoes revive old traditions, clan stories, and activities. One of the participants, Frank Brown of the Bella Bella Heiltsuk from Vancouver, British Columbia, explained, "To lose a ceremony is to lose the past; to create a ceremony is to create the future." After all the work to cut the trees, shape the canoes, practice paddling, and finally race to Seattle across Puget Sound, writer Ben Smith concluded as the day ended that "amid those canoes on the beach, there was a new spirit, but as old as the ages. The carvers, the paddlers, the elders, and the tribal members stood taller than they had for many years."[43]

Opposition to Makah Whaling

The last Makah whaling party returned in a large war canoe in 1913, but recently, the Makah received permission from the International Whaling Commission to resume whale hunts.[44] After seven decades of not killing whales, in May 1999, from a thirty-two-foot-long cedar canoe named "Hummingbird," Makah whalers on a community hunt harpooned a thirty-foot-long, three-year-old migrating female gray whale. Intense environmental protest marred their successful hunt as the whalers faced bitter opposition from organized groups such as the Sea Shepherd Conservation Society, the Sea Defense Alliance, and the Washington Peninsula Citizens for the Protection of Whales.

This opposition to Makah whaling has an ironic twist because most nonnatives link Native Americans with environmental harmony and the balance of nature. As David Waller correctly assessed, "Environmentalists are right to reach out to American Indians, and indeed original peoples throughout the world, for help in discovering less destructive ecological ideas and practices. However, we must not accept their aid and then cause their issues and their cultures to become the first casualties in our fight against environmental irresponsibility."[45] For the Makah, a return to tradition meant virulent antagonism and personal attacks.

After having been harassed by environmental groups, who had their boats confiscated by the U.S. Coast Guard, the Makah harpooned the whale as it dived under their cedar canoe. Crew member Dan Greene explained, "The energy was so strong we could almost touch it. We were along with the whale and our creator."[46] Because the International Whaling Commission requires whale kills to be as quick and merciful as possible, after harpooning, the whale hunters fired two shots at the mammal with a .50-caliber rifle and killed it in eight minutes. As the carcass filled with water, it sank and tightened up the harpoon ropes. Then the work began, for it took eight hours to tow the thirty-ton whale back to Neah Bay for a huge potlatch and historic whale feast. For an 800-person capacity crowd in the Neah Bay High School gym, the tribe served big pots of whale meat, blubber, salmon, and other fish. Clearly, the Makah lived up to the meaning of their tribal name, which translates as "generous with food." Tribal members later deposited the skeleton in the bay to be cleaned by waves and other fish before being taken out and displayed at the Makah Cultural and Research Center.

Makah elder Ruth Claplanhoo exclaimed, "These boys have been in danger to catch the whale, and I am very proud of them."[47] Tribal chairman Ben Johnson said that the right to hunt whale, guaranteed by an 1855 treaty, had been "a long hard fight" because "anytime natives do anything, they put you under a microscope. What happened [affects] all Indians in the country. It goes beyond just Makah."[48]

For Makah language teacher Maria Pascua, the successful hunt meant that theirs is "a living culture." For her students, whaling will not be "just reading about it in books."[49] Janine Bowechop, executive director of the Makah Cultural and Research Center, observed that "it's more than a hunt for food. It gives us traditional responsibilities to carry out. It binds the community in ways missing for decades."[50]

Taken off the endangered species list in 1994, gray whales now number 22,500 and regularly migrate down the Pacific coast. Moreover, returning to tradition made perfect sense to the Makah, who by law could not sell any part of the whale and whose whalers had trained physically and spiritually for months prior to the hunt. But protesters refused to understand subsistence whaling and the revival of ancient cultural traditions. Ugly letters, hate mail, bomb threats, phone calls, and vicious computer E-mail deluged the Makah Tribe, with protest letters to local papers running ten to one against the tribe's right to hunt whales. Letters to the *Seattle Post-Intelligencer* featured racist comments directed to the Makahs: "Maybe you can try just as hard at getting an education as you did training for the kill. Why don't you start a new tradition: take pride in yourselves . . . and work for a living instead of finding your courage in the death of a defenseless mammal or at the bottom of a bottle." Another letter to the editor stated, "I have a very real hatred for Native Americans now. It's embarrassing, but I would be lying if I said it wasn't the truth. What do you think will be my private thoughts deep inside my brain when a Native American drops off an application for a job with me?"[51]

Val Medicine Pipe, an interpreter at the Blackfeet Cultural Encampment near the Museum of the Plains Indian in Browning, Montana, proudly explains his cultural traditions. Photo by author, July 1992.

Other letters complained of the Makah as "a modernized welfare race," and one racist Californian wrote, "I am anxious to know where I may apply for a license to kill Indians. My forefathers helped settle the west and it was their tradition to kill every Redskin they saw. 'The only good Indian is a dead Indian' they believed. I also want to keep faith with my ancestors."[52] Despite such vitriolic attacks, Makah tribal chairman Ben Johnson stated at the victory feast, "We are here, and we are here to stay, and we are going to do what the treaty says we can do, and what we have been doing for thousands of years."[53] An elder member of the Bowechop family explained, "Today the Makah have brought the whale home. From this day forward we need to stand behind our leaders . . . to be a living culture."[54] Opposition will continue against Makah whaling, but the whaling will go on. The International Whaling Commission has agreed that the Makah may harvest five whales annually. As other native peoples seek to revive traditions, even at the cost of dissension within their own communities, opposition may grow from some nonnatives who seek to stop the ongoing cultural revival.

Preserving Tribal Traditions

As Native American populations grow, as elders pass on, as tribes continue to defend their treaty rights and sovereignty, protecting sacred objects and sacred places will become even more important. For five centuries now, Indians have fought to survive and maintain their identity amidst nonnative encroachment, theft, and misguided assimilation policies. Now, Native Americans, Native Hawaiians, and Native Alaskans can help to determine their own futures, in part by knowing their ancient cultural traditions and by preserving that which is centuries old. As tribes reassess their past, even tribal names are changing. The Winnebago have become the Hochunk, and the Papago are now the Tohono O'odham. The Flathead call themselves the Salish, the Crow are the Apsaalooka, the Northern Shoshone have become the Aqui Dika, the Blackfeet are the Pikuni, the Navajo are now the Diné, and the Nez Perce are the Nimipu.

Across the northern prairies, wind ripples the shaggy hair on the backs of buffaloes, and along the Northwest Coast, waves splash against newly carved cedar canoes. Children struggle to learn words and stories in their native tongues. Snow covers the top of Mount Shasta, and elk and moose graze the Sweetgrass Hills. The War Chief's Office in Taos guards sacred Blue Lake, and finally, after decades spent in boxes, Indian human remains have returned home. The bones are going back to the earth. For the dead, the spirit journey continues, and for the living, there is new hope.

On the Wind River Reservation in Wyoming, a recently built roadside memorial near Crowheart Butte keeps alive the ancient Indian tradition of marking special places with piles of stones. After years of frustration and forced assimilation, native peoples now seek a return to traditional ways as part of a wide-spread cultural revival. Photo by author, August 1999.

Snoqualmie Falls, located in northwestern Washington State, is sacred to Indian tribes of the Pacific Northwest, who contest the renewal of a Federal Energy Regulating Commission license at the site. Photo by author, July 1992.

Bear Butte, South Dakota, is sacred to the Lakota and to the Cheyenne, whose prophet Sweet Medicine gave them their sacred arrows and rules on how to live from this stunning high plains butte. Courtesy, South Dakota Tourism Office, Pierre, South Dakota.

Appendix A
Tribal Traditional Cultural Places

Traditional Cultural Places

A property is eligible for inclusion in the National Register because of its association with cultural practices or beliefs of a living community that (1) are rooted in that community's history and (2) are important in maintaining the continuing cultural identity of the community. Examples would include a location associated with a Native American group's traditional beliefs about its origins, its cultural history, or the nature of the world; an urban neighborhood or rural community that is the traditional home of a particular cultural group and that reflects its beliefs and practices; or a location where a community has historically performed economic, artistic, or ceremonial activities in accordance with traditional cultural practices important in maintaining its historical identity.

In the following list, NR signifies that the site is on the National Register; DOE indicates that the site has received a "determination of eligibility" but is not yet listed.

Traditional Cultural Places Listed in the National Register of Historic Places or Determined Eligible for Listing

❖ Rio Grande and Sand Bar areas of the Pueblo of Sandia, Sandoval County, New Mexico [DOE 1988]

   These Rio Grande River sandbars have been used for generations by the people of Sandia Pueblo for rituals involving immersion in the river's waters.

❖ Heikau Historic District, Del Norte County, Six Rivers National Forest, California [DOE 1981]

   This rural land area is associated with significant cultural practices of the Tolowa, Yurok, Karuk, and Hoopa Indian Tribes of the area, who have used the district for generations to make medicine and communicate with spirits.

✧ Tahquitz Canyon, Riverside County, California [NR 1972]

The site is associated with Tahquitz, a Cahulla Indian demigod who figures importantly in the tribe's traditions and is said to occupy an obsidian cave high in the canyon.

✧ Bear Butte, Meade County, South Dakota [NR 1973]

This butte is associated with the cultural beliefs of the Cheyenne Indians. The revered prophet Sweet Medicine learned how the Cheyenne should live and act at this location.

✧ Inyan Kara Mountain, Crook County, Black Hills region, South Dakota [NR 1973]

This mountain is the home of spirits significant in the traditions of the Lakota and Cheyenne.

✧ I'ito Mo'o (Montezuma's Head) and 'Oks Daha (Old Woman Sitting), Pima County, Arizona [NR 1994]

This rock formation is sacred to the Tohono O'odham people. According to their tradition, the rock outcropping is associated with the deity L'itio and his instructions to the people about living and surviving in the desert.

✧ De-No-To Cultural District, Humboldt County, Six Rivers National Forest, California [NR 1985]

This area is sacred to the Hupa people because of its place in their system of traditional cultural practices, including medicine making and ceremonial practices.

✧ Kuchamaa (Tecate Peak), San Diego County, Bureau of Land Management, California [NR 1992]

A sacred mountain associated with the Kumeyaay Indians, the mountain peak marks a significant location for the acquisition of knowledge and power by shamans and remains a site of rituals and rites important to the Indians.

✧ Tonnachau Mountain, Iras, Moen Island (Truk), Federated States of Micronesia [NR 1976]

According to Trukese traditions, this is the location where Sowukachaw, founder of the Trukese society, established a meetinghouse at the beginning of Trukese history.

✧ Coso Hot Springs, Inyo County, California [NR 1978]

This natural hot springs site is an important traditional spiritual and medicinal center. During the nineteenth century, the site also became associated with Euroamerican use as a resort, while still serving local Native American purposes.

✧ Snoqualmie Falls, King County, Washington [DOE 1992]

This dramatic natural waterfall figures in the creation myth of the Snoqualmie people and serves as an important location of powerful waterfall spirits that continue to guide the lives of the local people. Despite the impact of a hydroelectric plant at the falls, the area retains its spiritual and cultural importance to users, as well as its general physical integrity of feeling and association.

❖ Medicine Tree Site, Ravalli County, Montana [DOE 1995]

This is a place of important spiritualism for the Salish people of western Montana, where tribal members continue to carry on traditional practices important to maintaining their historic identity. There are direct associations with Coyote, an important spiritual entity in Salish culture.

❖ Chelhtenem (Lily Point), Whatcom County, Washington [DOE 1994]

This large prehistoric-historic village site and fishery area is evidenced by archaeological remains. The area also contains natural features associated with the ongoing traditional cultural and spiritual practices of the Lummi, Saanich, and Semihamoo Indians, connected with spiritual powers and salmon culture.

❖ Mus-yeh-sait-neh Village and Cultural Landscape Property, Del Norte County, California [NR 1993]

This forty-acre river terrace was the location of a prehistoric Tolowa village site; there is also a culturally altered landscape used for food procurement (fishing and gathering). Tolowa traditions maintain that the location, associated natural features, and activities offer important connections with the past that provide continuity of cultural traditions.

❖ Medicine Bluffs, Comanche County, Oklahoma [NR 1974]

A dramatic series of rock bluffs overlooking Medicine Bluff Creek form a natural crescent-shaped formation that is over a mile long. Indian tribes have long associated the formation with important spiritual powers, and historic records document traditional use by Indians during the nineteenth century.

❖ Kootenai Falls Cultural Resource District, Lincoln County, Montana [DOE 1982]

This is a location of significant archaeological remains documenting human utilization of the area for several thousand years. It is also part of the traditional use area of historic and modern-day Kootenai Indians.

❖ Cave Rock, Douglas County, Nevada [DOE 1998]

This site has important traditional cultural value to the Washoe Indian Tribe. Cave Rock (a natural rock formation) and its immediate environs represent a place of accumulated spiritual power that has played a central role in Washoe Indian traditions, beliefs, and practices since time immemorial. The site retains its importance despite physical changes related to modern highway development (tunnels) and increased recreational use.

❖ Annashisee Lisaxpuatahcheeaashisee (Medicine Wheel on the Big Horn River), Big Horn County, Montana [NR 1999]

Annashisee lisaxpuatahcheeaashisee is linked to important traditional stories (Scarface) and cultural practices associated with the Crow Indians of Montana. The site's physical features embody the distinctive characteristics of medicine wheel design in Montana, and historic ethnographic and oral histories document the continuing cultural significance of the site.

✧ Yamsay Mountain Cultural Landscape and Rocky Forks Historic District, Klamath and Lake Counties, Oregon [DOE 1998]

The two identified districts reflect places associated with spiritual, social, and cultural uses, including traditional hunting and camping sites, vision quest locations, and ceremonial sites; they also represent the overall spiritual and cultural importance of Yamsay Mountain within the cosmological world of the Klamath Indian Tribes.

✧ Medicine Lake Area Traditional Cultural Places District, Siskiyou County, California [DOE 1999]

The district represents an area of significant continuing cultural value to several northern California Indian tribes, including specifically the Modoc and Pit River peoples. Medicine Lake and the volcanic caldera in which it rests contain an interrelated series of locations and natural features associated with the spiritual beliefs and traditional practices of local Native American groups. Several isolated buttes in proximity to the Medicine Lake caldera and district (Cougar, Indian) were individually determined to be eligible based on their traditional associations with the important Medicine Lake area.

✧ Ocmulgee Old Fields, Bibb and Twiggs Counties, Georgia [DOE 1999]

The Ocmulgee Old Fields are of critical cultural and historical significance to the Muscogean peoples, who were forced to abandon the area on their forced relocation in the early nineteenth century and who still revere (and revisit) the site outside Macon as their ancestral homeland. The Old Fields site is centered around the Ocmulgee National Monument, administered by the National Park Service, and contains archaeological and natural features retaining the imprint of traditional Muscogee (Creek) culture.

✧ Spirit Mountain (Avi Kwa 'Ame), Clark County, Nevada [NR 1999]

Spirit Mountain is acknowledged by indigenous traditionalists as one of the most sacred places in the cosmological universe of the lower Colorado River Yuman-speaking tribes. The prominent natural feature is associated with events and personages of critical importance in the traditional creation stories of local Native American groups, and it continues to serve an essential role in the ongoing cultural practices and spiritual beliefs of those people.

Note: The short descriptions used in this list may not represent the full range of significant traditional values or cultural groups associated with particular sites.

Appendix B
Current Tribal Museums and Community Centers

 American Association for State and Local History
1717 Church Street
Nashville, TN 37203-2991
615/320-3203
history@aaslh.org

The American Association for State and Local History (AASLH) was founded in 1940. AASLH's mission statement is: AASLH provides leadership and support for its members who preserve and interpret state and local history in order to make the past more meaningful to all Americans.

Throughout its rich history, AASLH has remained true to its mission by offering programs, materials, service, and leadership to the field. AASLH's members differ greatly with respect to size, scope, services, and diversity. The Association's American Indian Museums Program is designed to bring much-needed assistance to a very impressive list of museums and cultural centers, as demonstrated in the directory below.

If you would like more information about membership and benefits, please contact AASLH at the address above, or visit the Association's web site at www.aaslh.org.

Directory of Native American Museums and Cultural Centers

ALABAMA

Poarch Creek Indian Heritage Center
HC 69, Box 85B
Atmore, AL 36502-8940
PHONE   205/368-9136

ALASKA

Akutan Aleut Heritage Museum
PO Box 89
Akutan, AK 99553
PHONE   907/689-2300
FAX   907/689-2301

Alutiiq Museum and Archaeological
  Repository
215 Mission Rd., Suite 101
Kodiak, AK 99615
PHONE   907/486-7004
FAX   907/486-7048
E-MAIL   Alutiiq2@ptialaska.net

Huna Heritage Foundation
9301 Glacier Hwy.
Juneau, AK 99801

Ilisagvik College Cultural Center
PO Box 749
Barrow, AK 99723
PHONE   907/852-0165
FAX   907/852-1752

Kenaitze Interpretive Site
PO Box 988
Kenai, AK 99611
PHONE   907/283-4321
FAX   907/283-4437

Ketchikan Museums
Totem Heritage Center
629 Dock St.
Ketchikan, AK 99901
PHONE   907/225-5900
FAX   907/225-5901
E-MAIL   victorial@city.ketchikan.ak.us

Nana Museum of the Arctic
PO Box 49
Kotzebue, AK 99752
PHONE   907/442-3301
FAX   907/442-2866

Nay'dini'aa Na Tribal Cultural Center
PO Box 1105
Chickaloon, AK 99674
PHONE   907/745-0707
FAX   907/745-7154

Port Graham Cultural Center
Palwik Community Center
PO Box 5510
Port Graham, AK 99603-5510
PHONE   907/284-2227
FAX   907/284-2222

Simon Paneak Memorial Museum
North Slope Borough Planning Dept.
PO Box 21085
Anaktuvuk Pass, AK 99721
PHONE   907/661-3413
FAX   907/661-3414

Southeast Alaska Indian Cultural
   Center, Inc.
106 Metlakatla St.
Sitka, AK 99835
PHONE   907/747-8061
FAX   907/747-5938
E-MAIL   seaicc@ptialaska.net

Tatitlek Museum and Cultural Center
PO Box 171
Tatitlek, AK 99677
PHONE   907/325-2311
FAX   907325-2298

Totem Heritage Center Museum
429 Dock St.
Ketchikan, AK 99901
PHONE   907/225-5900

Tribal House of the Bear
PO Box 868
Wrangell, AK 99929
PHONE   907/847-3841
FAX   907/847-2982

Yupiit Piciryarait Cultural Center
   & Museum
PO Box 219
Bethel, AK 99559-0219
PHONE   907/543-1819
FAX   907/543-1885
E-MAIL   Joan_Hamilton@avcp.org

ARIZONA

Ak-Chin Him Dak Museum
PO Box 897
Maricopa, AZ 85239
PHONE   520/568-9480
FAX   520/568-9557

Apache Cultural Center
PO Box 507, Log Cabin Rd.
Fort Apache, AZ 85926
PHONE   520/338-4625
FAX   520/338-1716

Cocopah Museum
County 15 and Avenue G
Somerton, AZ 85350
PHONE   520/627-1992
FAX   520/627-2280

Colorado River Indian Tribes Museum
Rt. 1, Box 23-B
Parker, AZ 85344
PHONE   520/669-9211, Ext. 1335
FAX   520/669-8262

Fort McDowell Mohave-Apache
   Cultural Center
PO Box 1779
Fountain Hills, AZ 85202
PHONE   602/837-5121
FAX   602/837-4896

Gila Indian Center
PO Box 457
Sacaton, AZ 85247
PHONE   602/963-3981
FAX   520/315-3968

Hatatchli Center Museum
Navajo Community College
Tsaile, AZ 86556
PHONE   602/724-3311, Ext. 205/206

Havasupai Museum
PO Box 10
Supai, AZ 86435
PHONE   520/448-2731

Hoo-Hoogam Ki Museum
Salt River Pima-Maricopa
   Cultural Center
Rt. 1, Box 216
Scottsdale, AZ 85256
PHONE   602/850-8190
FAX   602/850-8961

Hopi Cultural Center Museum
PO Box 7
Second Mesa, AZ 86043
PHONE   520/734-6650
FAX   520/734-7113

Navajo Community College Museum
Diné College
PO Box 37
Tsaile, AZ 86556
PHONE   520/724-3311
FAX   520/724-3327

Navajo Nation Museum
Hwy. 264 and Post Office Loop Rd.
PO Box 1840
Window Rock, AZ 86515
PHONE   520/871-6675
FAX   520/871-7942

Quechan Tribal Museum
PO Box 1899
Yuma, AZ 85366
PHONE   619/572-0661
FAX   619/572-2102

San Carlos Apache Tribal
   Cultural Center
PO Box 760
Peridot, AZ 85542
PHONE   520/475-2894
FAX   520/475-2894

Tohono O'odham Nation Museum
PO Box GG
Gila Bend, AZ 85337
PHONE   520/683-2913
FAX   520/683-2008

CALIFORNIA

Agua Caliente Cultural Museum
Museum of the Agua Caliente Band
   of Cahuilla
219 S. Palm Canyon Dr.
Palm Springs, CA 92262-6310
PHONE   760/323-0151
FAX   760/320-0350
E-MAIL   accmuseum@earthlink.net

Barona Band of Mission Indians
   Museum
1095 Barona Rd.
Lakeside, CA 92040-1599

Chaw Se Regional Indian Museum
14881 Pinegrove Volcano Rd.
Pine Grove, CA 95665
PHONE   209/296-7488

Cupa Cultural Museum
Pala Temecula Rd.
PO Box 445
Pala, CA 92059
PHONE   760/742-1590
FAX   760/742-4543

Hoopa Tribal Museum
PO Box 1348
Hoopa, CA 95546
PHONE   530/625-4110
FAX   530/625-1693
E-MAIL   hvtmus@pcweb.net

Kern Valley Indian Community
   Interpretive Center
PO Box 168
Kernville, CA 93238
PHONE   619/376-4240

Malki Museum, Inc.
Morongo Indian Reservation
PO Box 373
Banning, CA 92220
PHONE   714/849-7289

Oak Brook Chumash Center
3290 Long Ranch Pkwy.
Thousand Oaks, CA 91362
PHONE   805/492-5446
FAX   805/492-7996

Owens Valley Paiute-Shoshone Museum
PO Box 1281
Bishop, CA 93514
PHONE   619/873-4478

Rincon Tribal Library and Museum
PO Box 1147
Valley Center, CA 92082

Satwiwa Native American
   Culture Center
4126 Potrero Rd.
Newbury Park, CA 91320
PHONE   805/499-2837
FAX   805/499-2837

Sherman Indian Museum
9010 Magnolia Ave.
Riverside, CA 92503
PHONE   909/276-6719
FAX   909/276-6332

Sierra Mono Museum
PO Box 275
North Fork, CA 93643
PHONE   209/877-2115

Ya-Ka-Ama Museum
6215 Eastside Rd.
Forestville, CA 95436
PHONE   707/887-1541
FAX   707/887-1585

COLORADO

Southern Ute Indian Cultural Center
PO Box 737
Ignacio, CO 81137
PHONE   970/563-9583
FAX   970/563-4641

Ute Indian Museum
17253 Chipeta Rd.
Montrose, CO 81401
PHONE   970/249-3098

Ute Mountain Tribal Museum & Park
Ute Mountain Tribe
PO Box 109
Towaoc, CO 81334
PHONE   970/565-3751
FAX   970/565-7412

CONNECTICUT

Mashantucket Pequot Museum and
    Research Center
111 Pequot Tr.
Mashantucket, CT 06339-3180
PHONE   860/396-6800
FAX   860/396-6851

Tantaquidgeon Indian Museum
1819 New London Turnpike
Uncasville, CT 06382
PHONE   203/848-9145

DELAWARE

Nanticoke Indian Museum
Rt. 4, Box 107A
Millsboro, DE 19966
PHONE   302/945-7022
FAX   302/945-2930

FLORIDA

Ah-Tah-Thi- Ki Museum
HC 61, Box 21-A
Big Cypress Reservation; Seminole Tribe
    of Florida
Clewiston, FL 33440
PHONE   941/902-1113
FAX   941/902-1117
E-MAIL   museum@semtribe.com

Miccousukee Cultural Center
PO Box 40021, Tamiami Station
Miami, FL 33144
PHONE   305/223-8388
FAX   305/223-1011

Seminole Tribal Museum
5221 North Orient Rd.
Tampa, FL 33610
PHONE   813/620-3077
FAX   813/623-6862

GEORGIA

Tama Museum
Rt. 2, Box 370
Tama Tribal Town
Whigham, GA 31797
PHONE   912/762-3165
FAX   912/762-3165

IDAHO

Shoshone-Bannock Tribal Museum
PO Box 793
Fort Hall, ID 83203
PHONE   208/237-9791
FAX   208/237-0797

KANSAS

Indian Center Museum
650 N. Seneca
Wichita, KS 67203
PHONE   316/262-5221
FAX   316/262-4216

Kaw Indian Mission
500 N. Mission
Council Grove, KS 66846
PHONE   316/767-5410

LOUISIANA

Camp Coushatta Museum
PO Box 790
Elton, LA 70532
PHONE   318/584-1433
FAX   318/584-1474
E-MAIL   Leland@Coushattatribela.org

Tunica-Biloxi Regional Indian Center
    & Museum
PO Box 331
Marksville, LA 71351-0331
PHONE   318/253-8174
FAX   318/253-7111
E-MAIL   Bill_Day@Tunica.org

MAINE

Penobscot Indian Nation
6 River Rd.
Indian Island
Old Town, ME 04468
PHONE 207/827-4153
FAX 207/827-6042

Waponahki Museum and
Resource Center
PO Box 295
Pleasant Point Reservation
Perry, ME 04667
PHONE 207/853-4001
FAX 207/853-6039

MARYLAND

Piscataway Indian Museum
16816 Country Ln.
Waldorf, MD 20616
PHONE 301/372-1932

Piscataway Indian Museum
PO Box 1024
White Plains, MD 20695
PHONE 301/372-1932

MASSACHUSETTS

Mashpee Wampanoag Indian Museum
PO Box 1048
Mashpee, MA 02649
PHONE 617/477-0208
FAX 617/477-1218

MICHIGAN

Bay Mills Cultural Center
Rt. 1, Box 315-A
Brimley, MI 49715

Bay Mills Cultural Center
Bay Mills Community College
12214 W. Lakeshore Dr.
Brimley, MI 49715
PHONE 906/248-5645
FAX 906/643-3551

Museum of Ojibwa Culture
500–566 N. State
St. Ignace, MI 49781
PHONE 906/643-9161
FAX 906/643-9380
E-MAIL mmperry@up.net

Ziibiwing Cultural Society
2145 S. Summerton
Mt. Pleasant, MI 48858
PHONE 517/773-3810
FAX 517/773-0338

MINNESOTA

Mille Lacs Indian Museum
PO Box 195
Onamia, MN 56359
PHONE 320/532-3632
FAX 320/532-4625

Red Lake Nation Tribal Archives
and Library
PO Box 297
Red Lake, MN 56671
PHONE 218/679-3341, Ext. 1036
FAX 218/679-3378

MISSISSIPPI

Choctaw Museum of the
Southern Indian
Rt. 7, Box 21
PO Box 6010
Philadelphia, MS 39350
PHONE 601/650-1685
FAX 601/656-6696

MONTANA

Cheyenne Indian Museum
PO Box 216
Ashland, MT 59003
PHONE 406/784-2741
FAX 406/784-6161

Fort Peck Tribal Museum
602 Court Ave.
Poplar, MT 59255
PHONE 406/768-5155, Ext. 392
FAX 406/768-5478

Northern Cheyenne Tribal Museum
PO Box 128
Lame Deer, MT 59043

The Peoples Center
PO Box 278
Pablo, MT 59855
PHONE 406/675-0160
FAX 406/675-0260

NEVADA

Pyramid Lake Paiute Tribe Museum
PO Box 261
Nixon, NV 89424
PHONE 702/574-0195
FAX 702/574-1008

NEW MEXICO

A:Shiwi Awan Museum & Heritage
  Center
PO Box 1009
Zuni, NM 87327
PHONE   505/782-4403
FAX   505/782-4503
E-MAIL aamhc@zuni.kiz.nm.us

Mescalero Apache Cultural Center
  Museum
PO Box 227
Mescalero, NM 88340
PHONE   505/671-4494
FAX   505/671-9191

Picuris Pueblo Museum
c/o Picuris Pueblo
PO Box 127
Penasco, NM 87553
PHONE   505/587-2519
FAX   505/587-1071

Poeh Cultural Center
Pueblo of Pojoaque
Rt. 11, Box 27-E
Santa Fe, NM 87501
PHONE   505/455-3334
FAX   505/455-0174
E-MAIL www.poehcenter.com

Pueblo of Acoma
PO Box 309
Acoma, NM 87034
PHONE   505/552-6604
FAX   505/552-7204

San Ildefonso Pueblo Museum
Rt. 5, Box 315-A
Santa Fe, NM 87501
PHONE   505/455-2424

Walatowa Visitors Center
PO Box 100
Jemez Pueblo, NM 87024
PHONE   505/834-7235
FAX   505/834-7331

NEW YORK

Akwesasne Museum
RR 1, Box 14C, Rt. 37
Hogansburg, NY 13655
PHONE   518/358-2240
FAX   518/358-2649

Iroquois Indian Museum
PO Box 7, Caverns Rd.
Howes Cave, NY 12092
PHONE   518/296-8949
FAX   518/296-8955
E-MAIL info@iroquoismuseum.org
Seneca-Iroquois National Museum
794–814 Broad St.
Seneca Nation Territory
Salamanca, NY 14779
PHONE   716/945-1738
FAX   716/945-1760
E-MAIL seniroqm@localnet.com

Shako:wi Cultural Center
The Oneida Indian Nation
5 Territory Rd.
Oneida, NY 13421
PHONE   315/363-1424
FAX   315/363-1843

Shinnecock Nation Cultural Center
PO Box 5059
Shinnecock Reservation
Southampton, NY 11969
PHONE   516/283-1643
FAX   516/287-4923

Six Nations Indian Museum
HRC 1, Box 10
Onchiota, NY 12989
PHONE   518/891-2299
E-MAIL redmaple@northnet.org

NORTH CAROLINA

Museum of the Cherokee Indian
PO Box 770-A
Cherokee, NC 28719
PHONE   704/497-3481
FAX   704/497-4985

NORTH DAKOTA

Three Affiliated Tribes Museum, Inc.
PO Box 147
Newtown, ND 58763
PHONE   701/627-4477
FAX   701/627-3805

Turtle Mountain Chippewa
  Heritage Center
Box 257, #1 Hwy. 5
Belcourt, ND 58316
PHONE   701/477-6140
FAX   701/477-6836

OKLAHOMA

Ataloa Lodge Museum
Bacone College
2299 Old Bacone Rd.
Muskogee, OK 74402
PHONE 918/683-4581, Ext. 283
FAX 918/687-5913

Caddo Tribal Museum
PO Box 487
Binger, OK 73009
PHONE 405/656-2901
FAX 405/656-2892
E-MAIL Caddo@tanet.net

Cherokee Heritage Center
PO Box 515
Tahlequah, OK 74465
PHONE 918/456-6007
FAX 918/456-6165

Cheyenne Cultural Center
2250 NE Route 66
Clinton, OK 73601
PHONE 580/323-6224
FAX 580/323-6225

Chickasaw Council House Museum
PO Box 717
Tishomingo, OK 73460
PHONE 405/371-3351

Chickasaw Nation Cultural Center
PO Box 1548
Ada, OK 74820
PHONE 405/436-2603, Ext. 303
FAX 405/436-4287

Choctaw Nation Museum
HC 64, Box 3270
Tuskahoma, OK 74574-9758
PHONE 918/569-4465
FAX 918/569-4465

Citizen Band Potawatomi Tribal
   Museum
1901 S. Gordon Cooper Dr.
Shawnee, OK 74801
PHONE 405/275-3121

Creek Council House Museum
106 W. 6th
Okmulgee, OK 74447
PHONE 918/756-2324

Delaware Tribal Museum
PO Box 825
Anadarko, OK 73005
PHONE 405/247-2448

District Choctaw Chief's House
Swink Historical Preservation Associa-
   tion
PO Box 165
Swink, OK 74761
PHONE 580/873-2301
FAX 580/873-2049
E-MAIL swink1@oio.net

Five Civilized Tribes Museum
Agency Hill, Honor Heights Dr.
Muskogee, OK 74401
PHONE 918/683-3070

Fort Sill Apache Tribal Museum
Rt. 2, Box 121
Apache, OK 73006
PHONE 405/588-2298
FAX 405/588-3133

Kanza Museum
PO Box 50
Kaw City, OK 74641
PHONE 405/269-2552
FAX 405/269-2301

Kiowa Tribal Museum
PO Box 369
Carnegie, OK 73015
PHONE 580/654-2300, Ext. 217
FAX 580/654-2188

Osage Tribal Museum
PO Box 779
Pawhuska, OK 74056
PHONE 918/287-2495

Pawnee Tribal Museum
PO Box 470
Pawnee, OK 74058
PHONE 918/762-3621

Seminole Nation Museum
Box 1532, 524 Wewoka Ave.
Wewoka, OK 74884
PHONE 405/257-5580
E-MAIL semuseum@chickasaw.com

Tonkawa Tribal Museum
PO Box 95
Tonkawa, OK 74653
PHONE 405/628-2561
FAX 405/628-3378

Wichita and Affiliated Tribes
   Cultural Center
PO Box 729
Anadarko, OK 73005
PHONE 405/247-2425
FAX 405/247-2430

OREGON

Confederated Tribes of Grand Ronde
Office of Museum Development
9615 Grand Ronde Rd.
Grand Ronde, OR 97347
PHONE   503/879-2076
FAX   503/879-2126
E-MAIL lisa.watt@grandronde.org

The Museum at Warm Springs
PO Box C
2189 Hwy. 26
Warm Springs, OR 97761
PHONE   541/553-3331
FAX   541/553-3338
E-MAIL museum@madras.net

Tamastslikt Cultural Institute
Confederated Tribes of the Umatilla
   Indian Reservation
72789 Hwy. 331
Pendleton, OR 97801
PHONE   541/966-9748
FAX   541/966-9927
E-MAIL www.umatilla.nsn.us/tamust.html

PENNSYLVANIA

The American Indian Trading Post
   & Exhibit
United Indians of Delaware Valley
225 Chestnut St.
Philadelphia, PA 19106
PHONE   215/574-0902
FAX   215/574-9024

Lenni Lenape Historical Society/
   Museum of Indian Culture
2825 Fish Hatchery Rd.
Allentown, PA 18103-9801
PHONE   610/797-2121
FAX   610/797-2801
E-MAIL lenape@epix.net

RHODE ISLAND

Tomaquag Indian Memorial Museum
Summit Rd.
Arcadia Village
Exeter, RI 02822
PHONE   401/539-7213

SOUTH DAKOTA

Buechel Memorial Lakota Museum
PO Box 499
St. Francis, SD 57572
PHONE   607/747-2745

Harry V. Johnston American Indian
   Cultural Center
Cheyenne River Reservation
Box 590
Eagle Butte, SD 57625
PHONE   605/964-2542

Lakota Archives and Historical Center
Rosebud Sioux Tribe
Sinte Gleska University, Box 490
Rosebud, SD 57570

Lakota Cultural Center
Cheyenne River Sioux Reservation
PO Box 590
Eagle Butte, SD 57625
PHONE   605/964-2542
FAX   605/964-4151

Oglala Sioux Museum
Lakota College
Wounded Knee, SD 57752

Sioux Indian Museum
PO Box 1504
Rapid City, SD 57709
PHONE   605/394-2381
FAX   605/348-6182

Yankton Sioux Museum
Box 244
Marty, SD 57361
PHONE   605/384-3804

TENNESSEE

Sequoyah Birthplace Museum
PO Box 69, Citico Rd.
Vonore, TN 37885
PHONE   615/884-6246

TEXAS

Alabama-Coushatta Tribal Museum
Rt. 3, Box 640
Livingston, TX 77351
PHONE   409/563-4391

Tigua Indian Cultural Center
Tigua Indian Reservation
305 Yaya Ln.
El Paso, TX 79907
PHONE   915/859-5287
FAX   915/859-8972

Tigua Pueblo Museum
119 S. Old Pueblo Rd.
El Paso, TX 79917
PHONE   915/859-7913

VERMONT

Abenaki Cultural Center
17 Spring St.
Swanton, VT 05488
PHONE 802/868-3808

VIRGINIA

Mattaponi Indian Museum
Mattaponi Indian Reservation
Rt. 2, Box 255
West Point, VA 23181
PHONE 804/769-2194

Monacan Ancestral Museum
2009 Kenmore Rd.
Amherst, VA 24521
PHONE 804/946-5391
FAX 804/946-0390
E-MAIL Mnation538@aol.com

Monacan Ancestral Museum
PO Box 112
Monroe, VA 24574
PHONE 804/946-2531

Pamunkey Indian Village and Cultural
  Museum
Rt. 1, Box 217-AA
Pamunkey Indian Reservaion
King William, VA 23806
PHONE 804/843-4792

WASHINGTON

Colville Confederated Tribes Museum
PO Box 233, 516 Birch St.
Coulee Dam, WA 99116
PHONE 509/633-0751
FAX 509/633-2320

Lummi Museum
2626 Kwina Rd.
Bellingham, WA 98226-9298
PHONE 360/384-2262

Makah Cultural and Research Center
PO Box 160
Neah Bay, WA 98357
PHONE 360/645-2711
FAX 360/645-2656
E-MAIL mcrc@olypen.com

Puyallup Tribal Museum
2002 E. 28th St.
Tacoma, WA 98404
PHONE 206/597-6200, Ext. 308

Skokomish Tribal Museum
Tribal Center
Shelton, WA 98584
PHONE 360/426-4232
FAX 360/877-5943

Spokane Tribal Museum
Box 100
Wellpinit, WA 99040

Steilacoom Tribal Cultural Center
  and Museum
1515 Lafayette St.
PO Box 88419
Steilacoom, WA 98388
PHONE 253/584-6308
FAX 253/584-0224

Suquamish Museum
PO Box 498
Suquamish, WA 98392
PHONE 360/394-5275
FAX 360/598-6295

Wanapum Heritage Center
PO Box 878
Ephrata, WA 98823
PHONE 509/754-3541
FAX 509/754-5074
E-MAIL lseelet@gcpud.org

Yakama Nation Museum
PO Box 151
Toppenish, WA 98948
PHONE 509/865-6101
FAX 509/865-4664

WISCONSIN

Arvid E. Miller Memorial Library
  & Museum
N8510 Mo He Con Nuck Rd.
Bowler, WI 54416
PHONE 715/793-4270
FAX 715/793-1307
E-MAIL arlee_davids@yahoo.com

Forest County Potawatomi Cultural
  Center
PO Box 340
Crandon, WI 54520
PHONE 715/478-7475
FAX 715/478-7483

George W. Brown, Jr. Ojibwe Museum
  and Cultural Center
PO Box 804, 603 Peace Pipe
Lac du Flambeau, WI 54538
PHONE 715/588-3333
FAX 715/588-2355
E-MAIL museum@ojibwe.com

Menominee Logging Camp Museum
PO Box 910
Keshena, WI 54135
PHONE   715/799-3757
FAX   715/799-4525

Oneida Nation Museum
PO Box 365
Oneida, WI 54155
PHONE   920/869-2768
FAX   920/869-2959

WYOMING

Arapaho Cultural Museum
Wind River Reservation
Ethete, WY 82520

Shoshone Cultural Center
31 First St.
Fort Washakie, WY 82514
PHONE   307/332-9106

Notes

Introduction

1. Statistics on tribes from the U.S. Department of the Interior, Implementation Report on Executive Order #13007—Indian Sacred Sites, submitted May 23, 1997.
2. Patricia L. Parker, ed., *Keepers of the Treasures: Protecting Historic Properties and Cultural Traditions on Indian Lands—A Report on Tribal Preservation Funding Needs Submitted to Congress* (Washington, D.C.: National Park Service, Interagency Resources Division, Branch of Preservation Planning, May 1990), p. 7.
3. Ibid.
4. The Northwest Ordinance cited in Alvin M. Josephy Jr., *Now That the Buffalo's Gone* (Norman: University of Oklahoma Press, 1984), p. 130.
5. Chief Red Cloud quoted in *Indian Country Today*, April 20, 1994, and in Robert M. Utley, *The Indian Frontier of the American West, 1846–1890* (Albuquerque: University of New Mexico Press, 1984), p. 251.
6. Parker, *Keepers of the Treasures*, p. 21.
7. Ibid., p. 22.
8. Ibid.
9. Josephy, *Now That the Buffalo's Gone*, p. 8.
10. The federal government used *termination* as an official word to depict the end of tribal status. See Peter Nabokov, *Native American Testimony* (New York: Penguin, 1991), pp. 334–336.
11. Chief Apesanahkwat, Menominee Tribe, letter to coordinator, Tribal Historic Preservation Program, National Park Service, Washington, D.C., February 5, 1990.
12. D'Arcy McNickle, *Native American Tribalism: Indian Survivals and Renewals* (New York: Oxford University Press, 1973), p. 88.
13. Della John, tribal manager, Pyramid Lake Paiute Tribal Council, to coordinator, Tribal Historic Preservation Programs, NPS, February 12, 1990. Mashantucket Pequot Tribe, report entitled "Funding Needs for Historic Preservation on Indian Lands," February 2, 1990.
14. Priscilla Hunter, tribal administrator, Coyote Valley Tribal Council, to coordinator, Tribal Historic Preservation Programs, National Park Service, February 2, 1990.
15. Parker, *Keepers of the Treasures*, p. i.
16. Ibid., p. 10.
17. Robin Riddington and Dennis Hastings, *Blessings for a Long Time: The Sacred Pole and the Omaha Tribe* (Lincoln: University of Nebraska Press, 1997).

18. Clyde Ellis, letter to author, October 19, 1998.

19. Vine Deloria Jr., introduction to *Vision Quest: Men, Women and Sacred Sites of the Sioux Nation,* by Don Doll (New York: Crown Publishers, 1994), pp. 8–9.

Chapter 1

An earlier version of this chapter was published as "Bones of Contention: The Repatriation of Native American Human Remains," *Public Historian* 18, no. 4 (1996): 119–143, and copyrighted by the Regents of the University of California and the National Council on Public History. Permission to reprint the article here is gratefully acknowledged. I would like to thank *Public Historian*'s guest editors Ann Marie Plane and Clara Sue Kidwell for their assistance in preparing that article, and Managing Editor Lindsey Reed is to be commended for her patience. Thanks also go to the anonymous reviewers who made valuable editorial suggestions. In addition, I am grateful to the numerous Native Americans, Native Alaskans, and Native Hawaiians who have shared their anguish and their stories with me. Where possible, individual contributions are cited in the notes.

1. Edward H. Able Jr., executive director of the American Association of Museums, to the Honorable Daniel K. Inouye, Select Committee on Indian Affairs, September 12, 1988, with attachments.

2. Harjo cited in Gerald Vizenor, "Bone Courts: The Natural Rights of Tribal Bones," in Vizenor's *Crossbloods: Bone Courts, Bingo, and Other Reports* (Minneapolis: University of Minnesota Press, 1990), p. 62. For additional Harjo quotes, see Karen Swisher, "Skeletons in the Closet," *Washington Post*, October 3, 1989, p. D5.

3. Curtis M. Hinsley, *The Smithsonian and the American Indian: Making a Moral Anthropology in Victorian America* (Washington, D.C.: Smithsonian Institution Press, 1981), p. 12.

4. See William Simmons, *The Narragansett* (New York: Chelsea House, 1989).

5. The effects of NAGPRA are still uncertain, but the sheer volume of paperwork has created confusion for many tribes. In a telephone interview with the author on November 10, 1995, Gordon Pullar stated that some Alaskan villages have been inundated with over 200 letters from museums attempting to comply with NAGPRA provisions. Frequently, native villages or tribes do not have an appropriate spokesperson to handle such paperwork because most cultural issues are dealt with by committees, which always seek consensus. Appointing a single individual to respond to written requests is a difficult task, especially if grave goods or human remains are involved.

6. Thomas F. King, "Beyond Bulletin 38: Comments on the Traditional Cultural Properties Symposium." In "Traditional Cultural Properties: What You Do and How We Think," ed. Patricia L. Parker, an issue of *CRM* 16 (1993): 63.

7. Ibid. Also see H. Marcus Price, *Disputing the Dead: U.S. Law on Aboriginal Remains and Grave Goods* (Columbia: University of Missouri Press, 1991).

8. Deward E. Walker, foreword to "Pawnee Mortuary Traditions" by Roger C. Echo-Hawk, presented in Walter Echo-Hawk, Testimony Before the House Committees on Interior and Insular Affairs, Administration, and Public Works and Transportation on the National American Indian Museum Act, H.R. 2688, July 20, 1989, pp. i and ii.

9. Robert E. Bieder, *A Brief Historical Survey of the Expropriation of American Indian Remains* (Bloomington, IN: privately printed by Robert E. Bieder and Native American Rights Fund, April 1990), p. 3.

10. Ibid., p. 5.

11. Ibid., p. 10.

12. Ibid., pp. 14–15. Also see Douglas Cole, *Captured Heritage: The Scramble for Northwest Coast Artifacts* (Norman: University of Oklahoma Press, 1995), pp. 74–101.

13. William A. Hammond, surgeon general, circular letter to all frontier military posts proclaiming intention to establish the Army Medical Museum and seeking Indian "specimens," May 21, 1862. Author's copy courtesy of Tom Killion, Repatriation Office, National Museum of Natural History, Smithsonian Institution, Washington, D.C.

14. Robert Utley, the former chief historian of the National Park Service, wrote of the Sand Creek Massacre: "Men, women, children, and even infants perished in the orgy of slaughter, their bodies then scalped and barbarously mutilated"; having returned to Denver, the Colorado volunteers "paraded triumphantly through Denver's streets to the cheers of her citizens. Theater patrons applauded a display of Cheyenne scalps, some of them of women's pubic hair, strung across the stage at intermission." See Robert Utley, *The Indian Frontier of the American West, 1846–1890* (Albuquerque: University of New Mexico Press, 1984), pp. 92–93. Skulls from Sand Creek were shipped to the Army Medical College and have only recently been reburied by the Southern Cheyenne.

15. Bieder, *Expropriation of American Indian Remains*, p. 16.

16. Madison Mills, surgeon, U.S. Army, Surgeon General's Office, letter to all frontier military posts, January 13, 1868. Author's copy courtesy of Thomas Killion, Repatriation Office, National Museum of Natural History, Smithsonian Institution, Washington, D.C.

17. Ibid.

18. Ibid.

19. Bieder, *Expropriation of American Indian Remains*, p. 31. Also see Cole, *Captured Heritage*.

20. Ronald P. Rohner, *The Ethnography of Franz Boas* (Chicago: University of Chicago Press, 1969), p. 88.

21. Bieder, *Expropriation of American Indian Remains*, 31; Cole, *Captured Heritage*, pp. 114–121.

22. Loyd Smith, "Remains of 35 Blackfeet to Be Returned to Nearby Reservation," *Browning (MT) Glacier Reporter*, June 20, 1991. Also, Curly Bear Wagner, interview by author, Glacier Park Lodge, East Glacier, MT, July 26, 1992.

23. Douglas J. Preston, "Skeletons in Our Museums' Closets," *Harper's*, February 1989, p. 69. Also see Kenn Harper, *Give Me My Father's Body: The Life of Minik, the New York Eskimo* (Frobisher Bay, Northwest Territory: Blacklead Books, 1986).

24. For a complete discussion of the Larsen Bay excavations, see Tamara L. Bray and Thomas W. Killion, eds., *Reckoning With the Dead: The Larsen Bay Repatriation and the Smithsonian Institution* (Washington, D.C.: Smithsonian Institution Press, 1994).

25. Andrew Gulliford, "Bones of Contention: Wickliffe Mounds & the Evolution of Public Archaeology at a Prehistoric Mississippian Village," a report for the Museum Assessment Program, American Association of Museums, September 1991, pp. 5–6. For specific details, see Kit Wesler, "The King Project at Wickliffe Mounds: A Private Excavation in the New Deal Era," in *New Deal Era Archaeology and Current Research in Kentucky*, ed. D. Polloack and M. L. Powell (Frankfort: Kentucky Heritage Council, 1988), pp. 83–96.

26. Bryan W. Kwapil, "Coping With a Shady Past," *History News* 42, no. 2 (1987): 13–17; Kit Wesler, "The Wickliffe Mounds Cemetery: Educating the Public in a Changing Exhibit" (paper presented at the symposium "Public Education at Archaeological Parks: Doing It Every Day," Society for American Archaeology, Pittsburgh, PA, April 10, 1992). Both authors described the unsavory past at Wickliffe Mounds, but Wesler, the current director, also discussed how the site is now properly interpreted to meet NAGPRA requirements and the concerns of area Indians.

27. Montgomery Brower and Conan Putnam, "Walter Echo-Hawk Fights for His People's Right to Rest in Peace," *People* 4 (September 1984): 43. Robert Tomsho, "Indian Burial Site Becomes Big Issue in Little Salina, Kansas," *Wall Street Journal*, May 17, 1989. Richard Johnson, "Bones of Their Fathers," *Denver Post, Contemporary Magazine*, February 4, 1990. Also see Larry Fruhling, "Burial Dispute Pits Indians vs. Scientists," *Des Moines State Register*, April 16, 1989, and "Study at Indian Burial Pit," *Kansas State Historical Society Mirror* 36, no. 3 (April 1990).

28. The reference to "skeleton picnics" comes from letters written during the Great Depression by the director of Harvard University's Peabody Museum, who sought funding for the valuable work being conducted by Harriet S. and Cornelius B. Cosgrove in the Mimbres Valley. His letters to donors described local pothunters and the damage they were doing. The Cosgroves, by contrast, were amateur archaeologists in the best sense of the word. They published *The Swarts Ruin: A Typical Mimbres Site of Southwestern New Mexico*, Papers of the Peabody Museum of Anthropology and Ethnology, vol. 15, no. 1 (Cambridge, MA: Peabody Museum of Anthropology and Ethnology, 1932).

29. I have a complete file on the Dickson Mounds controversy between the years 1989 and 1991; it includes newspaper clippings from throughout Illinois and the nation. Among the sources are the *Alton (IL) Telegraph*, the *Peoria (IL) Journal Star*, the *Canton (Ohio) Daily Ledger*, the *Macomb (IL) Journal*, the *Springfield (IL) State-Journal Register*, the *Shelbyville (IL) Daily Union*, the *St. Louis Post Dispatch*, the *Chicago Sun-Times*, the *New York Times*, and *USA Today*. Publicity about the closing of the cemetery to public view prompted ten times the normal volume of visitors, or some 3,400 tourists, in just one weekend in January 1990.

30. This information comes from my files on the Dickson Mounds controversy.

31. Cole, *Captured Heritage*, p. 121.

32. Skokomish Tribe of Shelton, Washington, Resolution no. 86-37, June 4, 1986, attached to a letter to Dr. Adrienne Kaeppler, chair, Department of Anthropology, National Museum of Natural History, Smithsonian Institution, Washington, D.C., June 5, 1986.

33. Larsen Bay Tribal Council, Resolution no. 87-89, May 29, 1987, in "Larsen Bay Repatriation Letters," appendix to *Reckoning With the Dead: The Larsen Bay Repatriation and the Smithsonian Institution*, ed. Tamara L. Bray and Thomas W. Killion (Washington, D.C.: Smithsonian Institution Press, 1994), p. 187.

34. Gordon L. Pullar, "The Quikertarmiut and the Scientist: Fifty Years of Clashing World Views," in *Reckoning With the Dead: The Larsen Bay Repatriation and the Smithsonian Institution*, ed. Tamara L. Bray and Thomas W. Killion (Washington, D.C.: Smithsonian Institution Press, 1994), pp. 17, 22.

35. Robert McCormick Adams, Testimony Before the Committee on Rules and Administration and the Select Committee on Indian Affairs, November 12, 1987, p. 15.

36. Walter Echo-Hawk, Testimony Before the House Committees on Interior and Insular Affairs, Administration, and Public Works and Transportation on the National American Indian Museum Act, H.R. 2688, July 20, 1989, p. 1.

37. Ibid., p. 3.

38. Adams, Statement Before the Select Committee on Indian Affairs, p. 15. To further understand Secretary Adams's original point of view and then his changed stance in favor of Smithsonian repatriation, I interviewed him at his home in Seven Castles, near Basalt, Colorado, on August 2, 1995.

39. Adams, Statement Before the Select Committee on Indian Affairs, p. 16.

40. Preston, "Skeletons in Our Museums' Closets," p. 70.

41. Ibid.

42. H. Arden, "Who Owns Our Past?" *National Geographic* 175 (March 1989): 376–393.

43. *Unmarked Human Burial Sites and Skeletal Remains Protection Act,* 91st Legislature of Nebraska, May 31, 1989, Legislative Bill 340. For a detailed account of the conflict that led to this legislation, see the following articles in *American Indian Culture and Research Journal* 16, no. 2: Vine Deloria Jr., "Secularism, Civil Religion and the Religious Freedom of American Indians"; Robert E. Bieder, "The Collecting of Bones for Anthropological Narratives"; Larry J. Zimmerman, "Archaeology, Reburial and the Tactics of a Discipline's Self-Delusion"; Clifford E. Trafzer, "Serra's Legacy: The Desecration of American Indian Burials at Mission San Diego"; Roger C. Echo-Hawk, "Pawnee Mortuary Traditions"; James Riding In, "Six Pawnee Crania: Historical and Contemporary Issues Associated With the Massacre and Decapitation of Pawnee Indians in 1869"; Orlan Svingen, "The Pawnee of Nebraska Twice Removed"; Robert M. Peregoy, "Nebraska's Landmark Repatriation Law: A Study of Cross Cultural Conflict and Resolution"; and W. Roger Buffalohead, "Reflections on Native American Cultural Rights and Resources."

44. Tom Witty, Kansas state archaeologist, testimony on the Kansas Unmarked Burial Sites Preservation Act, House Bill no. 2144, which became law on January 1, 1990. Also see Carol L. Carnett, *A Survey of State Statutes Protecting Archaeological Resources* (Washington, D.C.: National Trust for Historic Preservation and U.S. Department of the Interior, National Park Service, Cultural Resources and Archaeological Assistance Division, August 1995).

45. Tilman Bishop, Colorado state senator, telephone conversation with author, July 10, 1992. Bishop sponsored the Colorado Burial Bill.

46. I witnessed the devastation of the Croteau site in the Mimbres Valley of New Mexico, and my photographs of the site being looted by pothunters using bulldozers have been exhibited at the Museum of New Mexico in Santa Fe.

47. Chris Raymond, "Some Scholars Upset by Stanford's Decision to Return American Indian Remains for Re-Burial by Tribe," *Chronicle of Higher Education*, July 5, 1989, p. A4.

48. Ibid., p. A5. Also see Deward E. Walker, "Anthropologists Must Allow American Indians to Bury Their Dead," *Chronicle of Higher Education*, September 12, 1990, and letters to the editor, *Chronicle of Higher Education*, October 10, 1990.

49. Rayna Green, quoted in Raymond, "Some Scholars Upset," p. A5.

50. Raymond, "Some Scholars Upset."

51. Chris Raymond, "Reburial of Indian Remains Stimulates Studies, Friction Among Scholars," *Chronicle of Higher Education*, October 3, 1990, p. A13.

52. Ibid.

53. Felicity Barringer, "Smithsonian Accord Is Likely on Return of Indian Remains," *New York Times*, August 20, 1989. For the scholarly debate, also see Douglas Ubelaker and Laurym Guttenplan-Grant, "Human Skeletal Remains—Preservation or Reburial?" in *1989 Yearbook of Physical Anthropology*, vol. 32 (New York: Alan R. Liss, 1989), pp. 249–287.

54. Public Law 101-185, November 28, 1989, 103 Stat. 1336, *An Act to Establish the National Museum of the American Indian Within the Smithsonian Institution, and for Other Purposes*, 101st Cong., 1st sess.

55. See Gillian Flynn, "Annual Report on Repatriation Office Activities at the National Museum of Natural History, June 1994 to May 1995," Repatriation Office, National Museum of Natural History, MRC 138, Washington, D.C. 20560; author's copy courtesy of Stewart Speaker in the Repatriation Office, NMNH. Stewart Speaker, telephone interview by author, November 15, 1995.

56. NAGPRA testimony included: Report of the Panel for a National Dialogue on Museum/Native American Relations, February 28, 1990; Willard L. Boyd, president of Field Museum of Natural History, Testimony Before the Senate Select Committee on Indian Affairs, U.S. Senate, May 14, 1990; and Henry J. Sockbeson, Native American Rights Fund, Testimony Before the House Interior and Insular Affairs Committee, July 17, 1990. For the impact of repatriation, see the twenty-six articles contained in "Symposium: The Native American Graves Protection and Repatriation Act of 1990 and State Repatriation-Related Legislation," *Arizona State Law Journal* 24, no. 1 (Spring 1992).

57. Smith, "Remains of 35 Blackfeet to Be Returned."

58. Ibid.

59. Adams, Statement Before the Select Committee on Indian Affairs, p. 24.

60. John Noble Wilford, "8,000-Year-Old Human Bones Are Found in Cave," *New York Times*, October 3, 1993.

61. Kenny Frost, Ute Indian liaison to the White River National Forest, and Bill Kight, heritage resource manager, White River National Forest, conversations with author, Glenwood Springs, Colorado, summer 1994. The reburial was filmed for the public television program *NOVA* in a special segment on cave archaeologist Pat Watson, from Washington University in St. Louis. Watson's team analyzed the prehistoric bones.

62. Samantha Silva, "A Famous Skeleton Returns to the Earth," *High Country News*, March 8, 1993, p. 1.

63. Ibid.

64. Ibid.

65. Clement W. Meighan, "Another View on Repatriation: Lost to the Public, Lost to History" [reply to Andrew Gulliford, "Native Americans and Museums: Curation and Repatriation of Sacred and Tribal Objects"], *Public Historian* 14, no. 3 (Summer 1992): 45.

66. Ibid., p. 182.

67. Preston, "Skeletons in Our Museums' Closets," p. 71. For an update on the repatriation of skeletal material, see Lawrence Biemiller, "A 'Bone Man' at the Smithsonian Catalogues and Repatriates the Remains of American Indians," *Chronicle of Higher Education*, February 9, 1994, p. A55. Repatriation of human remains has become an international museum issue. See "Reburying Human Remains: Making Amends for Past Wrongs," *Museums Journal* 93, no. 3 (March 1993).

68. Gordon Pullar, "The Quikertarmiut and the Scientist," p. 23. For background information on the Larsen Bay repatriation, I interviewed Pullar at the Alaska Native Heritage Conference in Anchorage, Alaska, on August 4, 1992.

69. Andrew L. Giarelli, "The Return of Cheyenne Skulls Brings a Bloody Western Story to a Close," *High Country News*, November 15, 1993, p. 5.

70. Thomas Harney and Dan Agent, "Cheyenne Ancestors Interred in Concho, Oklahoma," *Smithsonian Runner*, no. 93-5 (September–October 1993): 6. For recent scholarship on the Sand Creek Massacre, see David Fridtjof Halaas, " 'All the Camp Was Weeping': George Bent and the Sand Creek Massacre," in *Colorado Heritage* (Summer 1995): 2–17.

71. Flynn, "Annual Report on Repatriation Office Activities." Author's copy courtesy of Stewart Speaker in the Repatriation Office.

72. Edward Halealoha Ayau, "Rooted in Native Soil," in "Special Report: The Native American Graves Protection and Repatriation Act," *Federal Archaeology* (Fall–Winter 1995): 24–27. For a better understanding of Hawaiian human remains issues, I spoke with Davianna Pomaika'i McGregor, from the University of Hawai'i at Manoa, in Denver, Colorado, on October 13, 1995.

73. Author's conversation with Davianna Pomaika'i McGregor; Ayau, "Rooted in Native Soil."

74. Eastern Shoshone information comes from my extended conversations with spiritual leader Haman Wise, at Fort Washakie, Wyoming, on January 5 and 6, 1994. Zuni information is from Edmund Ladd, curator, Museum of New Mexico, Santa Fe.

75. I have photocopies of numerous newspaper articles on the Dickson Mounds Museum in Illinois and on the Allen County (Ohio) Museum controversy, including articles and letters to the editor from the *Toledo Blade*, the *Lima (Ohio) News*, the *Cincinnati Enquirer*, the *Delphos (Ohio) Daily Herald*, and the *Albuquerque Journal*. I also have numerous pieces of related correspondence, including letters from Allen County (Ohio) Museum director Raymond F. Schuck to the Piqua Sept of Ohio Shawnee Tribe, the American Indian Intertribal Association, the Cleveland Indian Center, and a number of private citizens, as well as a petition from the Indigenous People of North America & Other Concerned Citizens. After two years of debate, the 4,000-year-old Glacial Kame skeleton was removed from display.

76. Kenny Frost, telephone interview by author, Durango, CO, May 15, 1996.

77. Based on conversations with Kenny Frost, consultant; William Kight, USFS archaeologist; Hartman H. Lomawaima, associate director, Arizona State Museum at the University of Arizona; and E. Richard Hart, executive director of the Institute of the NorthAmerican West in Seattle.

78. "Draft Recommendations Regarding the Disposition of Culturally Unidentifiable Human Remains and Associated Funerary Object [sic]," circulated to federal agency and museum officials and to representatives of Indian tribes and Native Hawaiian organizations by the departmental consulting archaeologist of the National Park Service, U.S. Department of the Interior, May 16, 1995.

79. Kenny Frost, telephone conversation with author, May 15, 1996.

80. Douglas Preston, "The Lost Man," *New Yorker*, June 16, 1997, p. 72.

81. Ibid.

82. Sources for the Chapter 1 commentaries include presentations by Rex Salvador, Andrew Joseph, and Petuuche Gilbert at the annual meeting of the American Association for State and Local History, Denver, CO, October 1997, and my interviews with Lawrence Hart and Robert Sam in Denver, CO, on October 3 and 4, 1997, respectively.

Chapter 2

An earlier version of this chapter appeared as "Native Americans and Museums: Curation and Repatriation of Sacred and Tribal Objects," *Public*

Historian 14, no. 3 (Summer 1992): 23–38. Permission to reprint the article has been granted by the Regents of the University of California and the National Council on Public History.

I would like to thank two Native Americans for helping to raise my consciousness about sacred objects. Paul Lucero, from Laguna Pueblo in New Mexico, explained why prehistoric prayer sticks should be removed from a permanent exhibit, and Peter Garcia shared his pipe and explained contemporary Indian attitudes with a sparkling wit and a fine sense of humor.

1. For a critical assessment of the Northwest Coast items in the Heye Foundation Collections and some interesting insight into George Gusav Heye himself, read Cole, *Captured Heritage*. Also see Constance Bond, "An American Legacy," *Smithsonian* 20 (October 1989): 43.

2. Quote is from the brochure "National Museum of the American Indian," Smithsonian Institution, Washington, D.C., n.d. Also see Judith Weinraub, "Indian Museum Director Named," *Washington Post*, May 22, 1990, p. C1; Kara Swisher, "Indian Museum Board Picked," *Washington Post*, January 27, 1990, p. C9; and Donald Garfield, "Cultural Chronology," *Museum News* 70, no. 1 (January–February 1991): 55–56.

3. Author's notes from exhibit display viewed August 12, 1991, at the National Museum of the American Indian, New York City.

4. Ibid.

5. Public Law 101-601, *Native American Graves Protection and Repatriation Act*, 101st Cong., 2nd sess. (passed November 16, 1990). I sought clarification of the law by interviewing Geoffrey Platt, legislative adviser, American Association of Museums, in Washington, D.C., on April 29, 1991. For comments on the act, see Felicity Barringer, "Bush Weighs Signing of Law on Indian Artifacts," *New York Times* (national edition), November 4, 1990, and Rebecca Clay, "New Law Lets Tribes Ask for Return of Artifacts," *Christian Science Monitor*, January 3, 1991, p. 10.

6. Janet Hawkins, "Resting in Pieces," *Harvard Magazine* (November–December 1991): 43.

7. The Zuni demand for the return of their War Gods is an issue of long standing. See Robert Suro, "Zuni Tribe Winning Right to Restore Its War God Idols," *Denver Post*, August 19, 1990; Rebecca Clay, "Who Owns Indian Artifacts?" *Christian Science Monitor*, August 28, 1990, p. 12; "Thefts Unsettle the Zuni," *High Country News*, January 28, 1991, p. 11; and Kris Newcomer, "Museum Returns Carvings to Zunis," *Rocky Mountain News*, March 22, 1991. For an in-depth audio version of this story, listen to National Public Radio, "Giving Up the Past," *Horizons* #901122 (c), 1990, National Public Radio, 635 Massachusetts Ave. NW, Washington, D.C., 20001-3753. Also see the last chapter in Russell Chamberlin, *Loot! The Heritage of Plunder* (New York: Facts on File, 1983).

8. Author's notes from exhibit display, August 12, 1991.

9. Margaret Kimball Brown, director of the Cahokia Mounds Historic Site, letter to author, July 6, 1991.

10. See Andrew Gulliford, "Testimony on the Mimbres Culture Act of 1987," Testimony Before the U.S. Senate on March 24, 1988, Hearing Before the Subcommittee on Public Lands, National Parks and Forests of the Committee on Energy and Natural Resources, U.S. Senate, 100th Cong., 2nd sess., S 1912, published in *Senate Hearing 100-699 from the Senate Committee on Energy and Natural Resources*, "Miscellaneous New Mexico Park Related Measures," pp. 82–119, and Andrew Gulliford, "Museums and the Mimbres People: Interpreting the Mogollon Culture," in *Mogollon V: Proceedings of the Fifth Mogollon Conference*, ed. Patrick H. Beckett (Las

Cruces, NM: Coas Publishing, 1991), pp. 28–33. Standard references for the Mimbres people of the Mogollon culture include J. J. Brody, *Mimbres Painted Pottery* (Santa Fe: School of American Research, and Albuquerque: University of New Mexico Press, 1977), and J. Walter Fewkes, *The Mimbres Art and Archaeology* (Albuquerque: Avanyu Publishing, 1989). A well-illustrated volume with black-and-white prints is Victor M. Giammettei and Nanci Greer Reichert, *Art of a Vanished Race: The Mimbres Classic Black-on-White* (Silver City, NM: High-Lonesome Books, 1990).

11. Though this description of the prehistoric Mimbres' belief in an afterlife cannot be proven, a number of authors have speculated on the significance of the "kill-hole" in the pots. See Pat Carr, *Mimbres Mythology* (El Paso: Texas Western Press, 1982).

12. U.S. General Accounting Office, *Cultural Resources: Problems Protecting and Preserving Federal Archaeological Resources,* GAO-RCED-88-3 (Washington, D.C.: U.S. Government Printing Office, December 1987). Also see Arden, "Who Owns Our Past?"

13. Andrew Gulliford in "Appendix H: Institutions With Mimbres Pottery," in National Park Service, "Statement of Significance, Study of Alternatives—Mimbres Culture, New Mexico," U.S. Department of the Interior, National Park Service, Denver Service Center, NPS D-1, December 1989.

14. Rita Reif, "Buyer Vows to Return Masks to Indians," *New York Times,* May 22, 1991, p. B1.

15. John G. Neihardt, *Black Elk Speaks* (New York: Pocket Books, 1975), pp. 1–5.

16. Author's notes from exhibit display, August 12, 1991.

17. Ivan Karp and Steven D. Lavine, *Exhibiting Cultures: The Poetics and Politics of Museum Display* (Washington, D.C.: Smithsonian Institution Press, 1991), p. 16.

18. Hawkins, "Resting in Pieces," p. 43.

19. Robert McCormick Adams, Statement Before the Committee on Rules and Administration and the Select Committee on Indian Affairs, U.S. Senate, Washington, D.C., November 12, 1987, p. 4. Typescript provided by Margaret C. Gaynor, special assistant to Secretary Adams.

    For a look at the evolution of Adams's thoughts on these issues, see the following editorials: "Smithsonian Horizons: We Have an Obligation to Return the Skeletal Remains in Our Collections to Tribal Descendants," *Smithsonian* 18 (May 1987): 12; "Smithsonian Horizons: Recent Discussions With Indian Leaders Have Raised Questions About Repatriation of Skeletal Remains and Sacred Objects," *Smithsonian* 18 (November 1987): 12; "Smithsonian Horizons: Steps Are Under Way to Restore the American Indian's Cultural Patrimony, a Complex and Long-Overdue Process," *Smithsonian* 21 (October 1990): 10.

20. Evan Roth, "Success Stories," *Museum News* 70, no. 1 (January–February 1991): 45, and Tom Uhlenbrock, "Bones of Contention," *St. Louis Post-Dispatch,* April 7, 1991, pp. D1 and D8. For continuing evidence of pothunting, see John E. Ehrenhard, *Coping With Site Looting: Southeastern Perspectives* (Atlanta, GA: Interagency Archaeological Services Division, Southeast Region, National Park Service, 1990).

    Literary and popular references to pothunting and sacred objects include: Louis L'Amour, *Haunted Mesa* (New York: Bantam Books, 1987); Tony Hillerman, *A Thief of Time* (New York: Harper & Row, 1988); Hillerman, *Talking God* (New York: Harper & Row, 1989); and Oliver LaFarge, "The Little Stone Man," in *Yellow Sun/Bright Sky,* ed. David L. Caffey (Albuquerque: University of New Mexico Press, 1988), pp. 181–192.

21. On the staffing of the Makah Cultural Resource Center, Makah Indian Nation at Neah Bay, Washington, see George I. Quimby and James D. Nason, "New Staff for a New Museum," *Museum News* 55 (May–June 1977). The museum and its stunning collections were featured in Maria Parker Pascua, "Ozette," *National Geographic* 180 (October 1991): 38–53. A fictionalized account of the Makah culture is found in William H. MacLeish, "1492 America: The Land Columbus Never Saw," *Smithsonian* 22 (November 1991): 34–51.

22. For a readable overview of the Tunica-Biloxi Tribe's vast collection and its conservation needs, see Calvin Trillin, "U.S. Journal: Louisiana—The Tunica Treasure," *New Yorker,* July 27, 1981, pp. 41–51. To understand how the tribe regained legal title to their treasure, see *Leonard Charrier vs. Louise Bell, et al.*, State of Louisiana and Tunica-Biloxi Tribe, Defendants, Written Judgment, Suit Number 5,552, Twentieth Judicial District Court, Parish of West Feliciana, Louisiana, March 18, 1985. Reference works on the Tunica-Biloxi include Jeffrey P. Brain, *Tunica Treasure* (Cambridge, MA: Harvard University Peabody Museum of Archaeology and Ethnology, and the Peabody Museum of Salem, Massachusetts, 1979) and Jeffrey P. Brain, *The Tunica-Biloxi* (New York: Chelsea House Publishers, 1989), a survey for quick reading.

23. Raymond, "Some Scholars Upset"; "Historic Bible to Be Returned to Tribe," *Washington Post,* April 21, 1990, p. A7; Billy Easley, "Red Cloud's Rifle Returned to Family," *The Tennessean,* December 12, 1990, p. 3; and William N. Fenton, "Return of Eleven Wampum Belts to the Six Nations Iroquois Confederacy on Grand River, Canada," *Ethnohistory* 36, no. 4 (Fall 1989): 387. For specific references to Native American collections and tribal museums written by Native American authors, see George P. Horse Capture (Gros Ventre), "Some Observations on Establishing Tribal Museums," American Association for State and Local History, Technical Leaflet 134, published in *History News* 36 (January 1981); George P. Horse Capture, "Survival of Culture," *Museum News* 70, no. 1 (January–February 1991): 49–51; Richard Hill (Tuscarora), "Reclaiming Cultural Artifacts," *Museum News* 55 (May–June 1977): 43–46; Hartman H. Lowawaima, "Native American Collections: Legal and Ethical Concerns," *History News* 45 (May–June 1990): 6–8; and American Indian Program, *American Indian Sacred Objects, Skeletal Remains, Repatriation and Reburial: A Resource Guide, 1990* (Washington, D.C.: Smithsonian Institution, 1990).

24. Gordon Yellowman's comments in a session on NAGPRA and curation at the annual meeting of the American Association for State and Local History, Denver, CO, October 1997.

25. David Bailey, telephone conversation with author, July 17, 1999.

26. Michael Stoll, "Tribes Use New Riches to Recast History," *Christian Science Monitor,* August 11, 1998, p. 3.

27. Sources on the Pequot War include Rondale Dale Karr, " 'Why Should You Be So Furious?': The Violence of the Pequot War," *Journal of American History* 85 (December 1998): 876–905. For the new museum, see Mike Allen, "Casino Riches Build an Indian Museum With 'Everything,' " *New York Times,* August 10, 1998, p. A1, and Kay Larson, "Tribal Windfall: A Chance to Reopen History," *New York Times,* July 26, 1998, p. A1.

28. Quote from an unidentified NMAI staff member, during the author's Heye Center site visit, August 12, 1991.

29. George Kipp, interview by author, Browning, MT, June 27, 1992. Also see William E. Farr, "Troubled Bundles, Troubled Blackfeet: The Travail of Cultural and Religious Renewal," *Montana: The Magazine of Western His-*

tory 43, no. 4 (Autumn 1993): 2–17. Scriver's total disregard of Blackfeet tradition is evident in his book, *The Blackfeet: Artists of the Northern Plains—The Scriver Collection of Blackfeet Indian Artifacts and Related Objects, 1894–1990* (Kansas City, MO: Lowell Press, 1990). This book includes photographs of opened bundles, their contents rearranged by the photographer.

30. Diane Good, education specialist, Kansas State Historical Society, interview by author, Topeka, KS, June 8, 1998. Also see Paul D. Riley, "The Battle of Massacre Canyon," *Nebraska History* 54, no. 2 (1973): 221–249; Massacre Canyon National Register Nomination, vicinity of Trenton, Nebraska, July 25, 1974; Diane L. Good, *Birds, Beads & Bells: Remote Sensing of a Pawnee Sacred Bundle* (Topeka: Kansas State Historical Society, Anthropological Series no. 15, 1989); Diane L. Good, "Sacred Bundles: History Wrapped Up in Culture," *History News* 45, no. 4 (August 1990): 13–14, 27; Vance Horsechief, telephone interview by author, June 8, 1998.

31. David Bailey, interview by author, Museum of Western Colorado, Grand Junction, CO, June 26, 1998.

32. Janine Pease Windy Boy, president, Little Big Horn College, Crow Agency, MT, and MacArthur Fellowship award winner, interview by author, Little Big Horn College, Crow Agency, MT, July 23, 1992.

Chapter 3

1. For an example of Pawnee sacred geography and the Pahuk site, see Douglas R. Parks and Waldo R. Wedel, "Pawnee Geography: Historical & Sacred," *Great Plains Quarterly* 5, no. 3 (Summer 1985): 143–176.

2. Vine Deloria Jr., "Sacred Places and Moral Responsibility," in his *God Is Red: A Native View of Religion* (Golden, CO: Fulcrum Publishing, 1994), p. 272.

3. Deward Walker, "American Indian Sacred Geography," in *Indian Affairs: Special Supplement—American Indian Religious Freedom*, no. 116 (Summer 1988): vii.

4. Deloria, *God Is Red*, p. 275.

5. Luke E. Lassiter, "Southeastern Oklahoma, the Gourd Dance, and 'Charlie Brown,'" in *Contemporary Native American Cultural Issues*, ed. Duane Champagne (Walnut Creek, CA: AltaMira Press, 1999), p. 162.

6. Ibid., p. 161.

7. Walker, "Sacred Geography," p. vii. For recent information on Bear Butte, see Kari Forbes-Boyte, "Respecting Sacred Perspectives: The Lakotas, Bear Butte, and Land-Management Strategies," *Public Historian* 18, no. 4 (Fall 1996): 99–118.

8. Deloria, *God Is Red*, p. 275.

9. Ibid.

10. Klara Bonsack Kelley and Harris Francis, *Navajo Sacred Places* (Bloomington: Indiana University Press, 1994), p. 1.

11. Ibid.

12. Leland Wyman quoted in Stephen C. Jett, "Navajo Sacred Places: The Management and Interpretation of Mythic History," *Public Historian* 17, no. 2 (Spring 1995): 40. Also see Daryl R. Begay, "Navajo Preservation: The Success of the Navajo Nation Historic Preservation Department," *CRM* 14, no. 4 (1991).

13. Virginia Cole Trenholm and Maurine Carley, *The Shoshonis: Sentinels of the Rockies* (Norman: University of Oklahoma Press, 1964), p. 33.

14. Statement by "Eight-Ball" at the Shoshone-Bannock opening morning powwow, Fort Hall, Idaho, August 9, 1996.

15. Robert S. McPherson, *Sacred Land, Sacred View: Navajo Perceptions of the Four Corners Region* (Provo, UT: Brigham Young University, Charles Redd Center for Western Studies, 1992), p. 17.

16. There are several typologies of American Indian sacred sites, including guidelines by Vine Deloria and Deward Walker. See Walker's major types in Deward E. Walker, "Protection of American Indian Sacred Geography," in *Handbook of American Indian Religious Freedom*, ed. Christopher Vecsey (New York: Crossroad, 1991), p. 108. For a more esoteric, international, and philosophical approach, see James A. Swan, *Sacred Places: How the Living Earth Seeks Our Friendship* (Santa Fe: Bear), pp. 44–70.

17. Patricia Parker and Thomas King, *National Register Bulletin 38: Guidelines for Evaluating and Documenting Traditional Cultural Properties* (Washington, D.C.: U.S. Department of the Interior, National Park Service, Interagency Resources Division, 1990).

18. McPherson, *Sacred Land, Sacred View*, p. 31.

19. N. Scott Momaday, *The Way to Rainy Mountain* (Albuquerque: University of New Mexico Press, 1969), p. 4.

20. Another tribal name for Devils Tower is the Lakota Nation's name Grey Horn Butte. See "UNPO Supports Lakota Call for Peace and Unity," *Indian Country Today*, July 2–15, 1996.

21. Trenholm and Carley, *The Shoshonis*, p. 34.

22. Stephen E. Ambrose, *Undaunted Courage: Meriwether Lewis, Thomas Jefferson and the Opening of the American West* (New York: Simon & Schuster, 1996), p. 364. Bernard de Voto, ed., *The Journals of Lewis and Clark* (Boston: Houghton Mifflin, 1997). The Smoking Place or cairn site is part of the Nez Perce National Historic Trail and the Lolo Trail. See the following materials from the U.S. Department of Agriculture: *Nez Perce (Nee-Me-Poo) Trail: A Study Report* (Missoula, MT: USDA Forest Service, March 1982) and *Nez Perce (Nee-Me-Poo) Trail Decision Notice and Environmental Assessment* (Missoula, MT: USDA Forest Service, July 1985); *Nez Perce (Nee-Me-Poo) National Historic Trail Comprehensive Plan* (USDA Forest Service, July 1985, and Missoula, MT: USDA Forest Service, 1990). Also see Steven Ross Evans, *Voice of the Old Wolf: Lucullus Virgil McWhorter and the Nez Perce Indians* (Pullman: Washington State University Press, 1996), p. 36.

23. Information on the cairns came from my interview with William F. Yallup Sr., Yakama Indian Nation Cultural Resources Program, Yakama Indian Nation headquarters, Toppenish, WA, August 10, 1992. Additional cairn information on Plateau Indians can be found in Theodore Koledki, letter to John Mullan, 1859, which was included in J. Mullan, "Report on the Construction of a Military Road From Fort Walla Walla to Fort Benton, Missouri," pp. 109–112, 37th Cong., 3rd sess., ed. no. 43, S.S. #1149. Also see William Herdman Frazer, "The Sacred Altars of the Coeur d'Alene's West Shore," *Wallace (Idaho) Free Press*, November 29, 1890, and December 20, 1890.

24. Northern Canada has now become the Inuit province of Nunavut, where cairns or *inuksuit* represent many things. A recent Nunavut poster explained: "All *inuksuit* were placed upon the landscape. Whatever their age, name or purpose, they are deeply respected to this day. They attach us to our ancestors and to the land. They remind us of our origins and endurance and so will continue to inspire us in the future. Today they welcome you and other visitors from many parts of the world to Nunavut, our land." Poster in author's collection from Canada.

25. Parker and King, *National Register Bulletin 38*, p. 10.

26. Richard Hart, "Protection of *Kolhu/wala:wa* ('Zuni Heaven'): Litigation and Legislation," in *Zuni and the Courts: A Struggle for Sovereign Land*

Rights, ed. Richard E. Hart (Lawrence: University of Kansas Press, 1995), p. 199. Also see Richard Hart, "The Trail to Zuni Heaven" (paper presented at "Law for the Elephant, Law for the Beaver," Transboundary Conference on the Legal History of the West and North-West of North America, University of Victoria, British Columbia, February 23, 1991).

27. Rena Martin, interview by author, in the offices of the Navajo Nation Historic Preservation Department, Window Rock, AZ, November 5, 1997.

28. See Hal K. Rothman, *Managing the Sacred and the Secular: An Administrative History of Pipestone National Monument* (Washington, D.C.: National Park Service, 1992). Avis Little Eagle, "Controversy Chips Away at Pipestone," *Indian Country Today*, July 21, 1993, p. B1. Jacqueline Wiora Sletto, "Pipestone," in *Native Peoples* 5, no. 2 (Winter 1992): 20–24. There have been numerous newspaper articles in the *Pipestone County (MN) Star*.

29. Deward Walker, "Sacred Geography," p. vii.

30. A standard reference for the Sun Dance is Joseph G. Jorgensen, *The Sun Dance Religion: Power for the Powerless* (Chicago: University of Chicago Press, 1972). Photography at Sun Dances is usually forbidden, but to commemorate the fiftieth anniversary of the Crow Indian Sun Dance, Heywood Big Day sponsored a special dance in honor of his father, who had reintroduced the dance to the tribe in 1941. See Michael Crummett, *Sun Dance* (Helena, MT: Falcon Press, 1993).

31. See Joseph Bruchac, *The Native American Sweat Lodge: History and Legends* (Freedom, CA: Crossing Press, 1993).

32. Canyon Pintado is now a historic district listed on the National Register of Historic Places and administered by the Bureau of Land Management, White River District, out of offices in Meeker, Colorado.

33. Many books and articles have been published on rock art, including three works by Polly Schaafsma: *Rock Art in New Mexico* (Santa Fe: Museum of New Mexico Press, 1992), *Rock Art in Utah* (Salt Lake City: University of Utah Press, 1993), and *Indian Rock Art of the Southwest* (Albuquerque: University of New Mexico Press, 1986). Also see Alex Patterson, *A Field Guide to Rock Art Symbols of the Greater Southwest* (Boulder: Johnson Books, 1992). Note that Native Americans are not often consulted as to rock-art interpretation and meanings.

34. One of the most interesting locations for Navajo culture and possibly a cultural hearth (or origin area) for traditions and rock-art styles is the Dinetah area of far northwest New Mexico. Quite possibly, generations of Navajo living there in pueblitos helped shape the distinctive traits of Navajo culture today.

35. Rena Martin, interview by author, Navajo Nation Historic Preservation Department offices, Window Rock, AZ, November 6, 1997.

36. For information on the Big Hole battlefield, see "Nez Perce Ranger Feels Battlefield's Ghosts," *Billings (MT) Gazette*, August 14, 1993, and Bruce Hampton, *Children of Grace: The Nez Perce War of 1877* (New York: Avon Books, 1994). On the Marias Massacre, see James Welch, *Killing Custer* (New York: Norton, 1994). For Bear River, see U.S. Department of the Interior, National Park Service, *Draft Bear River Massacre Site Special Resource Study and Environmental Assessment* (Denver: Denver Service Center, National Park Service, November 27, 1995). For Wounded Knee, see "Sioux Remember Those Slain at Wounded Knee," *Christian Science Monitor*, December 31, 1990; Patrick H. Wyss, *Cankpe Taopi, Wounded Knee Feasibility Study—Final Recommendations, 1988–1990*, vols. 1, 2, and 3 (South Dakota Historic Preservation Center, November 20, 1990); and U.S. Department of the Interior, *Draft Study of Alternatives Environmental Assessment Wounded Knee, South Dakota* (Denver: Denver Service Center

of the National Park Service, January 1993). Also see John Young, "Wounded Knee Occupied by Protesters Who Oppose Tribal Park Designation," *Indian Country Today*, March 30, 1995.

37. Patricia Limerick, "Haunted America," in Drex Brooks, ed., *Sweet Medicine: Sites of Indian Massacres, Battlefields and Treaties* (Albuquerque: University of New Mexico Press, 1995), p. 125.

38. Fred Chapman, letter to author, September 30, 1998. Also see Fred Chapman, "The Medicine Wheel: Tourism, Historic Preservation, and Native American Rights," *Wyoming Annals* 65, no. 1 (Spring 1993): 4–5.

39. Keith M. Basso, *Wisdom Sits in Places* (Albuquerque: University of New Mexico Press, 1996), p. 156.

40. Ibid., pp. 32 and 33.

41. Deward Walker, "Protection of American Indian Sacred Geography," p. 101.

42. Vernon Masayesva quoted in Association on American Indian Affairs, American Indian Religious Freedom Project, 95 Madison Ave., New York; packet received from Eric DeLony, National Park Service, December 19, 1993.

43. Ferrell Secakuku, Second Mesa, AZ, and former chairman of the Hopi Tribe. Reprinted from *Federal Archaeology Report* (Fall 1993): 9.

44. The preceding statement was written by Harry Chimoni of the Zuni Cultural Advisory Team and E. Richard Hart, Institute of the NorthAmerican West, in consultation with the other members of the Zuni Cultural Resources Advisory Team and a number of Zuni religious leaders. It was first presented publicly at the 1994 annual meeting of the Western History Association, in Albuquerque, NM, on October 22, 1994.

45. Fred Chapman, Native American liaison, Wyoming State Historic Preservation Office, interview by author, Lander, WY, June 23, 1992. Also see Fred Chapman, "Native Americans and Culture Resources Management—The View From Wyoming," *CRM* 14, no. 5 (1991): 19–21.

Chapter 4

An earlier version of this chapter was published as "Tribal Preservation: An Overview of Cultural Management," *Preservation Forum: The Journal of the National Trust for Historic Preservation* 6, no. 6 (November–December 1992): 33–43.

1. Rebecca Tsosie, "Indigenous Rights and Archaeology," in *Native Americans and Archaeologists*, ed. Nina Swidler et al. (Walnut Creek, CA: AltaMira Press, 1997), p. 68.

2. Unfortunately, the American Indian Freedom of Religion Act was not written to cover the integrity of sacred sites, landscapes, and places; see materials of the Association on American Indian Affairs, American Indian Religious Freedom Project, 95 Madison Ave., New York. Vine Deloria Jr., "Sacred Lands and Religious Freedom," in "Special Edition on Freedom of Religion: Today's Challenge," *Native American Rights Fund Legal Review* 16, no. 2 (Summer 1991): 5. Also see *Indian Affairs: Special Supplement: American Indian Religious Freedom*, no. 116 (Summer 1988); Brian Edward Brown, "Native American Religions, the First Amendment, and the Judicial Interpretation of Public Land," *Environmental History Review* 15, no. 4 (Winter 1991): 19–44; "Second Special Edition on Freedom of Religion: A Time for Justice," *Native American Rights Fund Legal Review* 18, no. 2 (Summer 1993): 1–15; and Alfonso Ortiz, ed., "American Indian Religious Freedom: First People and the First Amendment," *Cultural Survival Quarterly* 19, no. 4 (Winter 1996).

3. Steven C. Moore, "Sacred Sites and Public Lands," in *Handbook of American Indian Religious Freedom*, ed. Christopher Vecsey (New York: Crossroad, 1991), p. 81.

4. Parker and King, *National Register Bulletin 38*. Also see Patricia Parker, ed., "Traditional Cultural Properties: What You Do and How We Think," an issue of CRM 16 (1993): 1–64, and Thomas F. King, *Cultural Resource Laws & Practice: An Introductory Guide* (Walnut Creek, CA: AltaMira Press, 1998).

5. Gary White Deer, "Return of the Sacred," in *Native Americans and Archaeologists*, ed. Nina Swidler et al. (Walnut Creek, CA: AltaMira Press, 1997), p. 41.

6. *Navajo Nation Policy to Protect Traditional Cultural Properties*, Navajo Nation Historic Preservation Department, Window Rock, AZ, January 24, 1991, p. 2.

7. Navajo Nation Historic Preservation Department, annual permit package information, Navajo Nation Policy to Protect Traditional Cultural Properties, 1/24/91, available from the Navajo Nation Historic Preservation Department, Window Rock, AZ.

8. William V. Tallbull and Sherri Deaver, "Living Human Values," foreword to *Native Americans and Archaeologists*, ed. Nina Swidler et al. (Walnut Creek, CA: AltaMira Press, 1997), p. 10.

9. Charles F. Wilkinson, "Indian Tribes and the American Constitution," in *Indians in American History*, ed. Frederick E. Hoxie (Wheeling, IL: Harlan Davidson, 1988), pp. 117–136.

10. A federal budget line item now exists for tribal preservation, and it began in part because of tribal needs described in Parker, *Keepers of the Treasures*.

11. Mission statement included in the A:Shiwi A:Wan Museum and Heritage Center brochure given to the author during a museum visit to Zuni on November 7, 1997.

12. Richard Begay, "The Role of Archaeology on Indian Lands," in *Native Americans and Archaeologists*, ed. Nina Swidler et al. (Walnut Creek, CA: AltaMira Press, 1997), p. 162. Also, Richard Begay, interview by author, Window Rock, AZ, November 6, 1997.

13. Leigh Kuwanwisiwma, Hopi Cultural Preservation Office, interview by author, Kykotsmovi, AZ, November 5, 1998.

14. Kara Elizabeth Mills, "Back to the Basics: Case Studies on the History of Native Peoples' Subsistence Practices in Yellowstone and Denali National Parks" (master's thesis, Middle Tennessee State University, 1999).

15. Rachel Craig, interview by author, Anchorage, AK, August 7, 1992.

16. William Yallup, interview by author, Yakama Cultural Preservation Office, Toppenish, WA, August 10, 1992.

17. For the history of the Navajo Preservation Department, see Alan S. Downer and Alexandra Roberts, "The Navajo Experience With the Federal Historic Preservation Program," *Natural Resources & Environment* 10, no. 3 (Winter 1996): 39–42, 78–79.

18. "Blackfeet File Injunction Over Badger–Two Medicine Drilling," *Browning (MT) Glacier Reporter*, March 7, 1991, and Bert Lindler, "A Vietnam Vet Tries to Preserve the Blackfeet Culture," *High Country News*, May 20, 1991, p. 5.

19. Mount Shasta (Axo-Yet) has been the subject of various legal battles over the development of a ski resort. The U.S. Forest Service agreed to respect Indian wishes and prohibit development above a certain elevation, but a California congressman became outraged and wanted to change the National Register of Historic Places to include only buildings, not sites. See Ted Rieger, "Discontent Lingers After Decision on Mt. Shasta's

Historic Status," *Historic Preservation News* (February–March 1995): 12, and Michelle Alvarez, "Mount Shasta: A Question of Power," *News From Native California* 8, no. 3 (Winter 1994–1995): 4–7. For Enola Hill, see Bill Donahue, "Oregon's Enola Hill: 'Diseased Forest' or Sacred Site?" *High Country News*, February 25, 1990, p. 7, and Bill Taylor, "Salvage Rider Will Destroy Sacred Sites," *High Country News*, May 27, 1996. For Snoqualmie Falls, see "An Ecumenical Group Fights for an Indian Spiritual Site," *High Country News*, December 2, 1991, p. 13. For the Sweetgrass Hills, see Pat Dawson, "Gold Company Stymied in Montana's Sweet Grass Hills," *High Country News*, August 9, 1993, p. 6. The Sweetgrass Hills was on the National Trust for Historic Preservation's list of the eleven most endangered sites for 1994. See Jane Brown Gillette, "Sweetgrass Saga," *Historic Preservation* (September–October 1994): 28–33, 90–92.

20. Richard Hart, *Zuni and the Grand Canyon: A Glen Canyon Environmental Studies Report—Zuni GCES Ethnohistorical Report* (Seattle: Institute of the NorthAmerican West, July 21, 1995). For additional references to Zuni sacred sites, see Richard Hart and T. J. Ferguson, eds., *Traditional Cultural Properties of Four Tribes: The Fence Lake Mine Project*, vols. 1 and 2, prepared for the Salt River Project (Seattle: Institute of the NorthAmerican West, August 12, 1993).

21. "Protecting Sacred Sites a Job for Land Managers," *Pocatello (ID) ShoBan News*, August 8, 1996, p. 7.

22. David Chidester and Edward T. Linenthal, eds., *American Sacred Space* (Bloomington: Indiana University Press, 1995), p. 2; see especially the chapter by Robert S. Michaelsen, "Dirt in the Court Room: Indian Land Claims and American Property Rights," and pp. 119–138 in chapter 3, "Resacralizing Earth," on Mount Graham, Arizona, where Apache met Earth First!ers.

23. See the following articles by Avis Little Eagle in *Indian Country Today*: "Lakota Rituals Being Sold," July 2, 1991; "Medicine Men for Rent," July 1, 1991; "Non-Indian Sun Dancers Bring Ohio Indian Protest," July 14, 1993; "Sacred Pipe Keeper Fears Feds Will Step In," July 17, 1991; "After the Sweat: Caviar, Wine & Cheese," July 24, 1991; and "Oh Shinnah: Prophet for Profit, August 2, 1991. Also see Valerie Taliman, "Aspen Sweatlodgers Get Heat From Utes," *Indian Country Today*, May 12, 1993; Sherman Alexie, "White Men Can't Drum," *New York Times Magazine*, October 4, 1992, pp. 30–31; Jon Magnuson, "Selling Native American Soul," *Christian Century*, November 22, 1989, p. 1084; John Bethune, "New Age: Still Glowing," *Publishers Weekly*, December 16, 1988, pp. 14–31; and Avis Little Eagle, "Paid Ads Call Her 'Medicine Woman,'" *Indian Country Today*, August 14, 1991. An archaeologist has created fake sites at his Dancing Leaf Earth Lodge near Stockville, Nebraska. See Mary L. Sherk, "Dancing Leaves Still Whisper of Prairie's Ancient Past," *Denver Post*, July 7, 1996, p. 3T.

24. D. P. McGregor, "Pre-Final Report—Cultural Resource Management Plan for Kaho'olawe Archaeological District, Vol. 1, May 1994," p. 6, prepared for the Department of the Navy, Pacific Division, Naval Facilities Engineering Command, Pearl Harbor, HI 96860-7300, contract number N62742-91-0-0507.

25. William J. Clinton, The White House, May 24, 1996. Executive Order #13007—Indian Sacred Sites. Published in *The Federal Register*, May 29, 1996. Also see Avis Little Eagle, "Sacred Site Protection," *Indian Country Today*, June 4–11, 1996, p. 1.

26. Clinton, Executive Order #13007.

27. U.S. Department of the Interior, Implementation Report on Executive Order #13007—Indian Sacred Sites, submitted May 23, 1997, by Bruce Babbitt to Bruce N. Reed, assistant to the president for domestic policy, 1600 Pennsylvania Ave. NW, Washington, D.C. 20500, p. 5, U.S. Department of the Interior, 1849 C St. NW, Washington, D.C. 20240.

28. Ibid., p. 7.

29. Ibid.

30. Vernon Masayesva, "We Can Have Electricity, Jobs and Clean Air," *High Country News*, March 30, 1998, p. 16; Jameson Fink, "Hart Prairie and the Snow Bowl Conflict" (master's thesis, Northern Arizona University, Department of History, December 1997); Leigh Kuwanwisiwma, Hopi Cultural Preservation Office, interview by author, Kykotsmovi, AZ, November 4, 1997.

31. Melvin Randolph Gilmore, "The Legend of Pahuk," Nebraska State Historical Society, 1914, ms. 231 ser. 1, folder 1; Don Cunningham, "Pahuk Place," *NEBRASKAland* (June 1985): 27–31; Douglas R. Parks and Waldo R. Wedel, "Pawnee Geography: Historical and Sacred," *Great Plains Quarterly* 5, no. 3 (Summer 1985): 143–176; Shari Buchta, "Tribal Elders to Visit Sites in Nebraska," *Fremont Tribune*, June 8, 1994; Louis Gilbert, telephone interview by author, October 1996; Roger Echo-Hawk, "Forging a New Ancient History for Native America," in *Native Americans and Archaeologists*, ed. Nina Swidler et al. (Walnut Creek, CA: AltaMira Press, 1997), pp. 88–102.

32. The principal investigator for the Ute Trail Project has been Mike Metcalf of Metcalf Archaeological Consultants, Eagle, Colorado, working with Bill Kight, forest archaeologist for the White River National Forest; Ute liaison Kenny Frost; and historian Andrew Gulliford. BLM archaeologist Frank Rupp conducted preliminary reconnaissance with volunteer Frank Olson. Ute consultation has been provided by Alvin Ignacio, Leo Tapouf, and Betsy Chapoose and Clifford Duncan from the Cultural Rights and Protections Office of the Northern Ute Tribe.

    Relevant published sources include: Robert Emmitt, *The Last War Trail* (Boulder: University Press of Colorado, 2000); Marshall Sprague, *Massacre: The Tragedy at White River* (Lincoln: University of Nebraska Press, 1980); Charles S. Marsh, *People of the Shining Mountains* (Boulder: Pruett Press, 1982); Jan Petit, *Utes: The Mountain People* (Boulder: Johnson Books, 1990); P. David Smith, *Ouray: Chief of the Utes* (Ridgway, CO: Wayfinder Press, 1986); and Ernest Ingersoll, *Knocking Round the Rockies* (New York: Harper Brothers, 1883).

33. Kim A. McDonald, "Construction of Observatory on Mount Graham Would Violate Sacred Site, Indian Tribes Say," *Chronicle of Higher Education*, July 17, 1991, p. A9; City Council of Florence, Italy, "Order of the Day or Motion," June 1, 1992; Mary Anderson, "Apache Woman Fights to Preserve Sacred Site," *Indian Country Today*, January 14, 1993, p. B4; *Apache Survival Coalition v. United States*, no. 92-15635, filed April 8, 1994; Bron Taylor, "Resacralizing Earth: Pagan Environmentalism and the Restoration of Turtle Island," in *American Sacred Space*, ed. David Chidester and Edward T. Linenthal (Bloomington: Indiana University Press, 1995), pp. 119–151; John Dougherty, "The Long, Bitter Battle Over Mount Graham," *High Country News*, July 24, 1995, pp. 1, 8–15; David C. Todd, counsel for the University of Arizona, letter to Katharine Barns Soffer, Advisory Council on Historic Preservation, August 29, 1996; group letter from environmental and Apache groups to the National Science Board, National Science Foundation, August 18, 1997; news release, Apaches for Cultural Preservation, September 2, 1997; John Welch, "White Eyes'

Lies and the Battle for *Dzi Nchaa Si'an*," *American Indian Quarterly* 21, no. 1 (Winter 1997): 75–109.

34. Medicine Wheel brochure, Medicine Wheel Ranger District, Bighorn National Forest; John Hill, interview by author, Crow Agency, MT, July 22, 1992; Medicine Wheel–Medicine Mountain National Historic Preservation Plan, USDA Forest Service, Bighorn National Forest, Sheridan, WY, July 1996; Medicine Wheel Nomination, National Register of Historic Places, ca. 1995; author's visit to the site, July 1992; speech by Mary Randolph on the Medicine Wheel at the American Landscapes Symposium, American Heritage Center, University of Wyoming, September 1997; Fred Chapman, "The Bighorn Medicine Wheel, 1988–1996: Conflict and Resolution" (paper presented at the Society for American Archaeology annual meeting, Seattle, WA, April 1998), and "The Bighorn Medicine Wheel, 1988–1999," *CRM*, no. 3 (1999): 5–10.

35. Stephen Ambrose, *Crazy Horse and Custer* (New York: Anchor Books, 1975); Peter Matthiessen, *Indian Country* (New York: Penguin, 1979); John Young, "New Agers' Assault on Bear Butte Decried," *Indian Country Today*, June 29, 1994, p. A1; Carol Gleichman, South Dakota Bear Butte Water Users Association, Advisory Council for Historic Preservation, Western Office of Review, Activity Status Report, December 1, 1994, and interview by author, Denver, CO, October 7, 1997; Mario Gonzales, "The Black Hills: The Sacred Land of the Lakota and Tsistsistas," *Cultural Survival Quarterly* 19, no. 4 (Winter 1996): 63–67; Pamela Stillman, "Did Fire Purify Mato Paha?" *Indian Country Today*, September 9–16, 1996, p. A1; Kari Forbes-Boyte, "Respecting Sacred Perspectives: The Lakotas, Bear Butte, and Land-Management Strategies," *Public Historian* 18, no. 3 (Fall 1996): 99–118; Jean Roach, "Tribes Press State About Bear Butte," *Indian Country Today*, April 28–May 5, 1997, pp. C1, C3.

36. Michael T. Pablo, chairman of the Salish and Kootenai Tribal Council, letter to David L. Mari, BLM district manager, May 8, 1992; Curly Bear Wagner, interview by author, Glacier Park Lodge, East Glacier, MT, July 26, 1992; Chere Jiusto and David Schwab, letter to Antoinette Lee, National Register of Historic Places, January 21, 1993; Curly Bear Wagner, letter to David L. Mari, BLM district manager, May 14, 1993; Pat Williams, letter to Bruce Babbitt, Secretary of the Interior, June 1, 1993; Jane Brown Gillette, "Sweetgrass Saga," *Preservation Magazine* (September–October 1994): 28–33, 90–92; Statement by the Confederated Salish and Kootenai Tribes of the Flathead Nation and the Chippewa Cree Tribe of the Rocky Boy's Reservation, submitted into the Hearing Record, House Subcommittee on Energy and Mineral Resources, January 31, 1995; Richard Manning, *Grassland* (New York: Penguin Books, 1995); United States Department of the Interior, Bureau of Land Management, Lewistown, MT, District Office, "FINAL Sweetgrass Hills Amendment and Environmental Impact Statement," April 1996; J. F. Dormaar, "Sweetgrass Hills, Montana, USA," *Alberta Archaeological Review* (April 1997): 4–28; Gary Smith, BLM Montana state archaeologist, telephone conversations with and letter to author, August 19, 1999.

37. Heller, Ehrman, White & McAuliffe, letter and attachments to Robert Tyrell, forest supervisor, Shasta-Trinity National Forest, on behalf of the Save Mount Shasta Citizens Group, April 21, 1992; Carol Gleichman, Advisory Council for Historic Preservation, Western Office of Project Review, Mount Shasta Status Report, December 1, 1994; Michelle Alvarez, "Mount Shasta: A Question of Power," *News From Native California* 8, no. 3 (Winter 1994–1995): 4–7; Ted Rieger, "Discontent Lingers After Decision on Mt. Shasta's Historical Status," *Historic Preservation News* (Febru-

ary–March 1995): 12, 14; Winfield Henn, forest archaeologist, "Analysis of Effects Upon National Register Properties, Proposed Mt. Shasta Ski Area, Shasta-Trinity National Forests," December 1995, from the files of the Advisory Council for Historic Preservation, Western Office of Review, Denver, CO.

38. Mabel Dodge Lujan, *Winter in Taos* (New York: Harcourt Brace, 1935); Frank Waters, *The Man Who Killed the Deer* (New York: Pocket Books, 1975); Alfonso Ortiz, "Indian/White Relations: A View From the Other Side of the 'Frontier,'" in *Indians in American History*, ed. Frederick Hoxie (Wheeling, IL: Harlan Davidson, 1988); R. C. Gordon-McCutchan, *The Taos Indians and the Battle for Blue Lake* (Santa Fe: Red Crane Books, 1991); Commemoration Committee, "The Return of Blue Lake: 20-Year Commemoration Celebration" booklet, September 7 and 8, 1991, Taos Pueblo War Chief's Office, Taos Pueblo, NM; Taos Pueblo War Chief's Office, "Taos Pueblo Blue Lake Wilderness Area" pamphlet, 1992, Taos Pueblo War Chief's Office, Taos Pueblo, NM; Vince Lujan, Taos War Chief's Office, interview by author, Taos Pueblo, NM, September 8, 1997.

39. Devils Tower National Monument Visitor Study, Summer 1995, Report 79 (Moscow: University of Idaho, Visitor Services Project, Cooperative Park Studies Unit, April 1996); Final Climbing Management Plan/Finding of No Significant Impact, Devils Tower National Monument, National Park Service, February 1995, Devils Tower National Monument, P.O. Box 10, Devils Tower, WY 82714-0010; minutes of a February 28– March 1, 1997, meeting between twenty-two Indian representatives and the NPS at Rapid City, SD, Devils Tower National Monument, P.O. Box 10, Devils Tower, WY 82714-0100; *Defendant-Intervenors' Brief on the Merits of Bear Lodge Multiple Use Association v. Bruce Babbit, et al. and Cheyenne River Sioux Tribe*, U.S. District Court for the District of Wyoming; Devils Tower National Monument brochure, 1996, Devils Tower National Monument, P.O. Box 10, Devils Tower, WY 82714-0100; N. Scott Momaday, *The Way to Rainy Mountain* (Albuquerque: University of New Mexico Press); Hal Rothman, *America's National Monuments: The Politics of Preservation* (Lawrence: University of Kansas Press, 1989); Devils Tower panel at the American Places Symposium, American Heritage Center, University of Wyoming, September 1997, with presenters Deborah Liggett, superintendent of Devils Tower, Steven Emery, attorney general, Cheyenne River Sioux Tribe, and Mary Fladerka, Bear Lodge Multiple Use Association; Raymond Cross and Elizabeth Brenneman, "Devils Tower at the Crossroads: The National Park Service and the Preservation of Native American Cultural Resources in the 21st Century," *Public Land & Resources Law Review* 18 (1997): 6–45; Jeffrey R. Hanson and Sally Chirinos, "Ethnographic Overview and Assessment of Devils Tower National Monument, Wyoming," Cultural Resources Selections, Intermountain Region, NPS D-36, no. 9, 1997, Technical Information Center (DSC-MS), National Park Service, Denver Service Center, 12785 W. Alameda Parkway, P.O. Box 25287, Denver, CO 80225-0287; "Court Rules for Religious Freedom," *Native American Rights Fund Legal Review* 23, no. 2 (Winter–Spring 1998): 1–4.

40. Joseph Epes Brown, *The Sacred Pipe* (Norman: University of Oklahoma Press, 1953); George Catlin, *Letters and Notes on the Manners, Customs, and Condition of the North American Indians*, vol. 1 (London, 1841); Jacqueline Wiora Sletto, "Pipestone," *Native Peoples Magazine* 5, no. 2 (Winter 1992): 20–24; issues of the *Pipestone (MN) County Courier*, 1991 to 1996; Hal K. Rothman, *Managing the Sacred and the Secular: An Admin-*

istrative History of Pipestone National Monument (Washington, D.C.: U.S. Department of the Interior, National Park Service, 1992).

41. Jean Akens, *Ute Mountain Tribal Park: The Other Mesa Verde* (Moab, UT: Four Corners Publications, 1995); Fred M. Blackburn and Ray A. Williamson, *Cowboys & Cave Dwellers: Basketmaker Archaeology in Utah's Grand Gulch* (Santa Fe: School of American Research Press, 1997); Robert W. Delaney, *The Ute Mountain Utes* (Albuquerque: University of New Mexico Press, 1989); Hal Rothman, "Pothunters and Professors," in his *America's National Monuments* (Lawrence: University Press of Kansas, 1994), pp. 6–33; author's visit to Ute Mountain Tribal Park, September 9, 1997, with tour guide Bryant Lehi and introductory remarks by park director Ernest House.

Chapter 5

1. Jacob John Folstrom, letter to the editor, *Indian Country Today*, April 6, 1994, p. B6.

2. Devon A. Mihesuah, "American Indian Identities: Issues of Individual Choices and Development," in *Contemporary Native American Cultural Issues*, ed. Duane Champagne (Walnut Creek, CA: AltaMira Press, 1999), p. 13.

3. Mark Mattern, "The Powwow as a Public Arena for Negotiating Unity and Diversity in American Life," in *Contemporary Native American Cultural Issues*, ed. Duane Champagne (Walnut Creek, CA: AltaMira Press, 1999), p. 141.

4. Michelle Rushio, "State's Job Boom Stops at Reservations," *Arizona Republic*, May 14, 1997, pp. E1, E4.

5. There are many sources for statistics on Indian health, including timely reports in *Indian Country Today*. Also see *Governors' Interstate Indian Council Newsletter* on teen suicide (Summer 1992), p. 7, Wyoming Indian Affairs Council, 115 N. 5th E., Riverton, WY 8250l, and the remarks of Robert Sundance, executive director of the Los Angeles–based Indian Alcoholism Association, who wrote, "American Indians die the youngest, have the poorest educations, the worst housing . . . and the shortest life expectancy (46 years) of any group of Americans. Until we stop the drinking, we can't solve any of the social problems," as cited in *High Country News,* July 1, 1991. For life on Pine Ridge, where 60 percent of residents live below the poverty line, see Alex Tizon, "A Calling at Wounded Knee," *Seattle Times*, October 19, 1997, p. 1. Also see Philip A. May, "The Epidemiology of Alcohol Abuse Among Native Americans: The Mythical and Real Properties," in *Contemporary Native American Cultural Issues*, ed. Duane Champagne (Walnut Creek, CA: AltaMira Press, 1999), pp. 227–244.

6. Bonnie Glass-Coffin, "Anthropology, Shamanism, and the 'New Age,'" *Chronicle of Higher Education*, June 15, 1994, p. A48.

7. K. Marie Porterfield, "The Selling of the Sun Dance: Spiritual Exploitation at Heart of Pine Ridge Controversy," *Indian Country Today*, July 28–August 4, 1997, pp. 1, A6; K. Marie Porterfield, "Pine Ridge May Face Referendum Over Sun Dance," *Indian Country Today*, August 4–11, 1997, pp. 1, A2; and related articles in *Indian Country Today*, August 11–18 and August 18–25, 1997.

8. Bill Donovan, "Fake Healers Plague Navajo Nation," *High Country News*, June 10, 1996.

9. Yvonne Hoosava, interview by author, Hopi Cultural Preservation Office, Kykotsmovi, AZ, November 4, 1997.

10. Patricia Cummings, "Native Religions, New-Agers, and the Forest Service," *Inner Voice* (September–October 1992): 8–9, 14.

11. Kevin McCullen, "Vandals Disturb Sacred Indian Site," *Rocky Mountain News*, September 13, 1995, p. 6A, and Nan Johnson, " 'New Agers' Damage Ute Sites," *Glenwood Springs (CO) Glenwood Post*, September 13, 1995, pp. 1, 2A.

12. Hoosava interview, November 4, 1997.

13. Hopi Tribe, "Office of Historic and Cultural Preservation and Protection—Protocol for Research, Publications and Recordings: Motion, Visual, Sound, Multimedia and Other Mechanical Devices," n.d., Hopi Cultural Office, Kykotsmovi, AZ. Also see David Ruppert, "Buying Secrets: Federal Government Procurement of Intellectual Cultural Property," in *Intellectual Property Rights for Indigenous Peoples: A Sourcebook*, ed. Tom Greaves (Oklahoma City: Society for Applied Anthropology, 1994), pp. 111–128.

14. Leigh Kuwanwisiwma, interview by author, Hopi Cultural Preservation Office, Kykotsmovi, AZ, November 4, 1997. Also see Kurt Dongoske, Leigh Jenkins, and T. J. Ferguson, "Understanding the Past Through Hopi Oral Tradition," *Native Peoples* 6, no. 2 (Winter 1992): 24–35, and Kurt E. Dongoske, Leigh Jenkins, and T. J. Ferguson, "Issues Relating to the Use and Preservation of Hopi Sacred Sites," *Historic Preservation Forum* (March–April 1994): 12–14.

15. Michael F. Brown, "Can Culture Be Copyrighted?" *Current Anthropology* 39, no. 2 (April 1998): 193–206.

16. Anne Beckett, interview by author, A:Shiwi Heritage Center, Zuni, NM, November 7, 1997.

17. Kuwanwisiwma interview, November 4, 1997; Hopi blue popcorn logo from *Zuni Farming for Today and Tomorrow: An Occasional Newsletter of the Zuni Sustainable Agriculture Project and the Zuni Folk Varieties Project*, no. 3 (Summer–Fall 1994): 7.

18. Sandy Greer, "Intellectual Property Rights: Where Do Indians Draw the Line?" *Winds of Change* (Winter 1995): 76–81. Also see Janet McGowan, "What's in a Name? Can Native Americans Control Outsiders' Use of Their Tribal Names?" *Cultural Survival Quarterly* 18, no. 4 (Winter 1995): 11–15.

19. Vernon Quam, curator, interview by author, A:shiwi A:wan Museum and Heritage Center, Zuni, NM, November 7, 1997. Also see Zuni Tribe, "Facts on Indian Arts and Crafts," *The Shiwi Messenger* 3, no. 32 (October 31, 1997): 4.

20. Margaret Tafoya quoted in National Endowment for the Arts, Folk Arts Program, *National Heritage Fellowships Booklet* (Washington, D.C.: National Endowment for the Arts, 1984).

21. Chesley Goseyun Wilson quoted in National Endowment for the Arts, Folk Arts Program, *National Heritage Fellowships Booklet* (Washington, D.C.: National Endowment for the Arts, 1989), p. 15.

22. Helen Cordero quoted in National Endowment for the Arts, Folk Arts Program, *National Heritage Fellowships Booklet* (Washington, D.C.: National Endowment for the Arts, 1986), p. 5.

23. Jennie Thlunaut and Austin Hammond quoted in ibid., p. 14.

24. George Blake quoted in National Endowment for the Arts, Folk Arts Program, *National Heritage Fellowships Booklet* (Washington, D.C.: National Endowment for the Arts, 1991), p. 4.

25. Ibid.

26. Nalani Kanaka'ole and Pulani Kanaka'ole Kanahele quoted in National Endowment for the Arts, Folk Arts Program, *National Heritage Fellowships Booklet* (Washington, D.C.: National Endowment for the Arts, 1993), p. 8.

27. Kathleen Mundell, *Basket Trees/Basket Makers* (Augusta: Maine Arts Commission, 1992), p. 10.

28. Ibid., p. 11. For other writings on contemporary and historic basket makers, see *American Indian Basketry Magazine,* which is edited by John M. Gogol in Portland, OR, and newsletters from the California Indian Basketweavers Association, P.O. Box 2397 (317 Spring St.), Nevada City, CA 95959.

29. Maryanne Vollers, "Indian Summer," *Time,* August 26, 1996, p. 38.

30. Ibid. Spiritual leader Black Elk witnessed the massacre at Wounded Knee Creek, South Dakota, in 1890, during which the people's sacred hoop had been metaphorically broken. In his book *Black Elk Speaks,* he later prophesied that within seven generations, the Lakota Nation would be reborn. It has been seven generations since the Seventh U.S. Cavalry left over 200 men, women, and children dead in the bloody snow along Wounded Knee Creek.

31. "Group Proposes Saving Yellowstone Bison," *Indian Country Today,* September 14, 1994, p. A2. Also see the buffalo kill ceremony reported in *Indian Country Today,* November 25–December 2, 1996, and Terry Johnson, "Buffalo Gathering at Slim Buttes," *Indian Country Today,* October 27, 1993.

32. Inter-Tribal Bison Cooperative, *Annual Report* (Rapid City, SD: 1993–1994), p. 7.

33. See Sarah Leen's photo in Bryan Hodgson's article, "Buffalo: Back Home on the Range," *National Geographic* 186, no. 5 (November 1994): 64–89.

34. Amy Onderdonk, "Indians Hope Buffalo Can Revive Tribes' Fortunes," *High Country News,* May 4, 1992, p. 6. Also see Jacqueline Wiora Sletto and Bjorn Sletto, "Prairie Tribes and the Buffalo," *Native Peoples* 6, no. 2 (Winter 1993): 36–45.

35. Tom Webster, letter to the editor, *Indian Country Today,* December 7, 1994, p. A5. For the importance of Indian languages and education, see Indian Nations at Risk Task Force, *Indian Nations at Risk: An Educational Strategy for Action* (Washington, D.C.: U.S. Department of Education, October 1991).

36. Catherine Gysin, "The Lost Horizon," *Utne Reader* (May–June 1993): 21, 24. Also see Katharine Whittemore, "To Converse With Creation: Saving California Indian Languages," *Native Americas* 14, no. 3 (Fall 1997): 46–53.

37. James T. Crawford, *Hold Your Tongue: Bilingualism and the Politics of English Only* (New York: Addison Wesley, 1992), excerpted in *Chronicle of Higher Education,* September 30, 1992, p. B5.

38. Red Lake Band of Chippewa Indians, Language Policy, Education Code of the Red Lake Band of Chippewa Indians, Red Lake School District #38, northern Minnesota, n.d. Also see Osage Nation, *Osage Language Class, Beginning Section Workbook,* n.d., Osage Nation, White Hair Memorial, P.O. Box 185, Ralston, OK 74650, and Southern Ute Tribe, *Ute Reference Grammar,* 1st ed. (Ignacio, CO: Ute Press of the Southern Ute Tribe, n.d.).

39. Crawford, *Hold Your Tongue.*

40. Kim Keister, "In the Native Tongue," *Historic Preservation* 44, no. 4 (July–August 1992): 38.

41. Ben Smith, "Return of the Great Canoes," *Native Peoples* 6, no. 2 (Winter 1993): 12. Also see Brenda Peterson, "Saving the Makah Way of Life: Whales Are the Key to a Tribe's Culture but Will They Exist to Hunt or Watch?" *Seattle Times,* October 19, 1997, p. B5.

42. Smith, "Return of the Great Canoes," p. 14.

43. Ibid., p. 20. Also see Skokomish Tribe and Anne Pavel, *The Native Canoe: Gift of the Cedar People* (Olympia: Washington Centennial Commission, 1989).

44. Robert Sullivan, "Permission Granted to Kill a Whale, Now What?" *New York Times Magazine*, August 9, 1998.

45. David Waller, "Friendly Fire: When Environmentalists Dehumanize American Indians," in *Contemporary Native American Cultural Issues*, ed. Duane Champagne (Walnut Creek, CA: AltaMira Press, 1999), p. 290.

46. Dan Greene quoted in *Port Washington (WA) Peninsula Daily News*, May 23, 1999, p. A2.

47. Ruth Claplanoo quoted in *Port Washington (WA) Peninsula Daily News*, May 23, 1999, p. A2.

48. Ben Johnson quoted in *Port Washington (WA) Peninsula Daily News*, May 19, 1999, p. 1.

49. Maria Pascua quoted in *Port Washington (WA) Peninsula Daily News*, May 19, 1999, p. A2.

50. Janine Bowechop quoted in *Seattle Post-Intelligencer*, May 11, 1999, p. A4.

51. Letters to the editor, *Seattle Post-Intelligencer*, May 23, 1999, p. A16.

52. Ibid.

53. Ben Johnson quoted in *Seattle Post-Intelligencer*, May 23, 1999, p. A16.

54. George Bowechop quoted in *Seattle Post-Intelligencer*, May 23, 1999, p. 1.

Bibliography

State and Federal Laws and Executive Orders

Executive Order #13007—Indian Sacred Sites. William J. Clinton, The White House, May 24, 1996. Published in the *Federal Register*, May 29, 1996.

Kansas Unmarked Burial Sites Preservation Act. House Bill no. 2144, January 1, 1990.

Unmarked Human Burial Sites and Skeletal Remains Protection Act, State of Nebraska. Ninety-first Legislature, Legislative Bill 340, May 31, 1989.

Public Law 59-209. *Antiquities Act of 1906.*

Public Law 89-665. *National Historic Preservation Act.* Implementing regulations at 36 CFR 800 and 36 CFR 60.

Public Law 95-341. *American Indian Religious Freedom Act of 1978.*

Public Law 96-96. *Archaeological Resources Protection Act of 1979.* As amended 1989. Implementing regulations at 36 CFR 296.

Public Law 101-185. November 28, 1989, 103 Stat. 1336. *An Act to Establish the National Museum of the American Indian Within the Smithsonian Institution, and for Other Purposes.*

Public Law 101-601. *Native American Graves Protection and Repatriation Act.* Implementing regulations at 43 CFR 10.

U.S. House and Senate Congressional Testimony

Adams, Robert McCormick. Testimony Before the Committee on Rules and Administration and the Select Committee on Indian Affairs, U.S. Senate, November 12, 1987.

Boyd, Willard L., president of Field Museum of Natural History. Testimony Before the Senate Select Committee on Indian Affairs, U.S. Senate, May 14, 1990.

Confederated Salish and Kootenai Tribes of the Flathead Nation and the Chippewa Cree Tribe of the Rocky Boy's Reservation. Statement submitted into the hearing record, House Subcommittee on Energy and Mineral Resources, January 31, 1995.

Echo-Hawk, Walter, Native American Rights Fund. Testimony Before the House Committees on Interior and Insular Affairs, Administration, and Public Works and Transportation on the National American Indian Museum Act, H.R. 2688, July 20, 1989.

Gulliford, Andrew. Testimony Before the U.S. Senate, Hearing Before the Subcommittee on Public Lands, National Parks and Forests of the Committee on Energy and Natural Resources, 100th Cong., 2nd sess., S 1912, March 24, 1988.

Sockbeson, Henry J., Native American Rights Fund. Testimony Before the House Interior and Insular Affairs Committee, July 17, 1990.

Stevenson, Kate, associate director, Cultural Resource Stewardship and Partnership, National Park Service. Testimony Before the Subcommittee on National Parks, Historic Preservation and Recreation, Senate Energy and Natural Resources Committee, March 24, 1998.

Walker, Deward E. Foreword to "Pawnee Mortuary Traditions," by Roger C. Echo-hawk. Presented in Walter Echo-Hawk, Testimony Before the House Committees on Interior and Insular Affairs, Administration, and Public Works and Transportation on the National American Indian Museum Act, H.R. 2688, July 20, 1989, pp. i and ii.

Historical Correspondence and Manuscripts

Frazer, William Herdman. "The Sacred Altars of the Coeur d'Alene's West Shore." *Wallace (Idaho) Free Press*, November 29, 1890, and December 20, 1890.

Gilmore, Melvin Randolph. "The Legend of Pahuk." Nebraska State Historical Society, 1914, ms. 231, ser. 1, folder 1.

Hammond, William A., surgeon general. Circular letter to all frontier military posts proclaiming intention to establish the Army Medical Museum and seeking Indian "specimens," May 21, 1862.

Koledki, Theodore. Letter to John Mullan, 1859, in "Report on the Construction of a Military Road From Fort Walla Walla to Fort Benton, Missouri," by J. Mullan, pp. 109–112, 37th Cong., 3rd sess., ed. no. 43, S.S. #1149.

Mills, Madison, surgeon, U.S. Army, Surgeon General's Office. Letter to all frontier military posts, January 13, 1868.

Contemporary Letters and Other Correspondence

Able, Edward H., Jr., executive director of the American Association of Museums. Letter to the Honorable Daniel K. Inouye, Select Committee on Indian Affairs, September 12, 1988, with attachments.

Apesanahkwat, Chief. Letter to coordinator, Tribal Historic Preservation Program, National Park Service, February 5, 1990.

Brown, Margaret Kimball, director, Cahokia Mounds Historic Site. Letter to author, July 6, 1991.

Chapman, Fred, Native American liaison, Wyoming State Historic Preservation Office. Letters to author, October 6, 1992, and September 30, 1998.

Gibson, Stan, Okotoks, Alberta, Canada. Letters to author, May 24, 1996, and November 19, 1996.

Group letter from environmental and Apache groups to the National Science Board, National Science Foundation, August 18, 1997.

Heller, Ehrman, White & McAuliffe. Letter to Robert Tyrell, forest supervisor, Shasta-Trinity National Forest, on behalf of the Save Mount Shasta Citizens Group, April 21, 1992.

Hunter, Priscilla, tribal administrator, Coyote Valley Tribal Council. Letter to coordinator, Tribal Historic Preservation Programs, National Park Service, February 2, 1990.

Jiusto, Chere, and David Schwab. Letter to Antoinette Lee, National Register of Historic Places, January 21, 1993.

Johns, Della, tribal manager, Pyramid Lake Paiute Tribal Council. Letter to coordinator, Tribal Historic Preservation Programs, National Park Service, February 12, 1990.

Mashantucket Pequot Tribe. Report entitled "Funding Needs for Historic Preservation on Indian Lands." Letter to coordinator, Tribal Historic Preservation Programs, National Park Service, February 2, 1990.

Pablo, Michael T., chairman of the Salish and Kootenai Tribal Council. Letter to David L. Mari, BLM district manager, May 8, 1992.

Ransom, Jay Ellis. Letters to author, March 15, 1994, and September 13, 1996; various correspondence, February 17, 1993, to February 28, 1994.

Schuck, Raymond F., director of the Allen County (Ohio) Museum. Letter to Bryan Dabe, tribal council chairman, Piqua Sept of Ohio Shawnee Tribe, December 4, 1991.

Shull, Carol, keeper of the National Register of Historic Places, National Park Service. Letter to Stan Gibson, June 11, 1996.

Smith, Gary, Bureau of Land Management Montana state archaeologist. Letter to author, August 17, 1999.

Speaker, Stewart, National Museum of Natural History. Letter to author, November 6, 1995.

Todd, David C., Council for the University of Arizona. Letter to Katharine Barns Soffer, Advisory Council on Historic Preservation, August 29, 1996.

Wagner, Curly Bear. Letter to David L. Mari, district manager, Bureau of Land Management, Billings, MT, May 14, 1993.

Williams, Pat, U.S. Representative (MT). Letter to Bruce Babbitt, Secretary of the Interior, June 1, 1993.

Government Documents, Publications, and Reports

Advisory Council on Historic Preservation. *Report to the President and Congress of the United States*. Washington, D.C.: Advisory Council on Historic Preservation, 1993.

Amara, Mark S. "Gidu'Tikadu Rock Circle District." Final Report to the U.S. Fish and Wildlife Service. Permit no. 85-HART-R1-003. Portland, OR, January 1988.

Ayau, Edward Halealoha. "Rooted in Native Soil." In "Special Report: The Native American Graves Protection and Repatriation Act." *Federal Archaeology* (Fall–Winter 1995): 24–27.

Begay, Daryl R. "Navajo Preservation: The Success of the Navajo Nation Historic Preservation Department." CRM 14, no. 4 (1991): 1, 3–4.

Blake, George. National Endowment for the Arts, Folk Arts Program, *National Heritage Fellowships Booklet*. Washington, D.C.: National Endowment for the Arts, 1991, p. 4.

Carnett, Carol L. A *Survey of State Statutes Protecting Archaeological Resources*. Washington, D.C.: National Trust for Historic Preservation and U.S. Department of the Interior, National Park Service Cultural Resources and Archaeological Assistance Division, August 1995.

Chapman, Fred. "Native Americans and Cultural Resource Management—The View From Wyoming." CRM 14, no. 5 (1991): 19–21.

Chapman, William. "Another View From Hawai'i." CRM 21, no. 8 (1998).

Chapman, William, ed. "Approaches to Heritage: Hawaiian and Pacific Perspectives on Preservation." CRM 19, no. 8 (1996).

Cook, John E. "The Cultural Legacy of America's National Parklands." CRM 14, no. 5 (1991): 38–41.

Crozier, S. Neal. "Tribal Cultural Heritage Programs in Alaska." CRM 14, no. 5 (1991).

Ehrenhard, John E. *Coping With Site Looting: Southeastern Perspectives*. Atlanta, GA: Interagency Archaeological Services Division, Southeast Region, National Park Service, 1990.

Fuller, Nancy. "Ak-Chin Him Dak—A New Model for Community Heritage Management Opens to Public." CRM 14, no. 5 (1991): -36–37, 43.

Gill, Glen. *Devils Tower National Monument Visitor Study: Summer 1995*. Moscow: University of Idaho Cooperative Studies Unit, April 1996.

Gleichman, Carol, Advisory Council for Historic Preservation, Western Office of Project Review. Mount Shasta Status Report, December 1, 1994.

Gulliford, Andrew. "Appendix H: Institutions With Mimbres Pottery." In National Park Service, "Statement of Significance, Study of Alternatives—Mimbres Culture, New Mexico." U.S. Department of the Interior, National Park Service, Denver Service Center, NPS D-1, December 1989.

Hanson, Jeffrey R., and Sally Chirinos. "Ethnographic Overview and Assessment of Devils Tower National Monument, Wyoming." Cultural Resources Selections, Intermountain Region, NPS D-36, no. 9, 1997.

Henn, Winfield, Shasta Forest archaeologist. "Analysis of Effects Upon National Register Properties, Proposed Mt. Shasta Ski Area, Shasta-Trinity National Forests," December 1995.

Hughes, David T. *Perceptions of the Sacred: A Review of Selected Native American Groups and Their Relationships With Catlinite Quarries.* Wichita, KS: Anthropological Research Laboratories, Department of Anthropology, Wichita State University, 1995.

King, Thomas F. "Beyond Bulletin 38: Comments on the Traditional Cultural Properties Symposium." In "Traditional Cultural Properties: What You Do and How We Think," edited by Patricia L. Parker, an issue of CRM 16, (1993): 63.

———. "Historic Preservation Training by and for Indian Tribes." Report, 31 pp. Preservation Technology Training Publications, National Park Service, Natchitoches, Louisiana, no. 1996-11, 1996.

Loomis, Ormond H. *Cultural Conservation: The Protection of Cultural Heritage in the United States.* Washington, D.C.: American Folklife Center and the National Park Service, 1983.

McKeown, C. Timothy. "The Native American Graves Protection and Repatriation Act: Special Report." *Federal Archaeology* (Fall–Winter 1995).

Parker, Patricia, ed. "America's Tribal Cultures—A Renaissance in the 1990s." CRM 14, no. 5 (1991).

———. *Keepers of the Treasures: Protecting Historic Properties and Cultural Traditions on Indian Lands—A Report on Tribal Preservation Funding Needs Submitted to Congress.* Washington, D.C.: National Park Service, Interagency Resources Division, Branch of Preservation Planning, May 1990.

———. "Traditional Cultural Properties: What You Do and How We Think," an issue of CRM 16 (1993).

Parker, Patricia, and Thomas King. *National Register Bulletin 38: Guidelines for Evaluating and Documenting Traditional Cultural Properties.* Washington, D.C.: U.S. Department of the Interior, National Park Service, Interagency Resources Division, 1990.

Rothman, Hal K. *Managing the Sacred and the Secular: An Administrative History of Pipestone National Monument.* Washington, D.C.: National Park Service, 1992.

———. *Navajo National Monument: A Place and Its People—An Administrative History.* Southwest Cultural Resources Center, National Park Service. Professional Papers no. 40. Santa Fe, NM, 1991.

Sivert, Ellen, and Ken Sivert. *A View of the Hills: A Cultural Landscape Study of the Sweetgrass Hills Area.* Great Falls, MT, August 1989.

Todd, Lloyd D. *Medicine Wheel National Historic Landmark: Draft Environmental Impact Statement.* Lovell, WY: Bighorn National Forest, Medicine Wheel Ranger District, 1991.

U.S. Department of Agriculture. *Compilation of State, Repatriation, Reburial and Grave Protection Laws,* 2nd ed. Washington, D.C.: Natural Resources Conservation Service, Ecological Sciences Division, July 1997.

———. *Forest Service National Resource Book on American Indian and Alaska Native Relations.* FS-600, April 1997.

———. *Medicine Wheel/Medicine Mountain National Historic Preservation Plan.* USDA Forest Service, Bighorn National Forest, Sheridan, WY, July 1996.

———. *Nez Perce (Nee-Me-Poo) National Historic Trail Comprehensive Plan.* USDA Forest Service, July 1985, and Missoula, MT: USDA Forest Service, 1990.

———. *Nez Perce (Nee-Me-Poo) Trail: A Study Report.* Missoula, MT: USDA Forest Service, March 1982.

———. *Nez Perce (Nee-Me-Poo) Trail Decision Notice and Environmental Assessment.* Missoula, MT: USDA Forest Service, July 1985.

U.S. Department of Education. *Indian Nations at Risk: An Educational Strategy for Action.* Washington, D.C.: U.S. Department of Education, October 1991.

U.S. Department of the Interior. "Draft Climbing Management Plan and Environmental Assessment: Devils Tower National Monument, Wyoming," National Park Service, Rocky Mountain Region, Devils Tower, WY, 1994.

———. "Final Climbing Management Plan/Finding of No Significant Impact." National Park Service, Rocky Mountain Region, Devils Tower, WY, 1995.

———. Implementation Report on Executive Order #13007—Indian Sacred Sites, Washington, D.C., submitted to the White House May 23, 1997.

U.S. Department of the Interior, Bureau of Land Management, Lewistown, Montana, District Office. *FINAL Sweetgrass Hills Amendment and Environmental Impact Statement,* April 1996.

U.S. Department of the Interior, Departmental Consulting Archaeologist, National Park Service. "Draft Recommendations Regarding the Disposition of Culturally Unidentifiable Human Remains and Associated Funerary Object [sic]," May 16, 1995.

U.S. Department of the Interior, National Park Service. "Bear River Massacre Site—Idaho, Draft Special Resource Study and Environmental Assessment." Denver: Denver Service Center, National Park Service, October 1995.

———. "Draft Bear River Massacre Site Special Resource Study and Environmental Assessment." Denver: Denver Service Center, National Park Service, November 27, 1995.

———. "Draft Study of Alternatives Environmental Assessment Wounded Knee, South Dakota." Denver: Denver Service Center, National Park Service, January 1993.

———. "Native American Relationships Management Policy: Final Management Policy, Part III." *Federal Register,* September 22, 1987.

———. "Northern Plains Federal Interagency Traditional Native American Issues Workshop, Rapid City, South Dakota," September 29–30, 1997.

———. "The Wounded Knee Update/*Cankpe Opi Wonahun*," issue 3. Denver: Denver Service Center, National Park Service, August 1993.

U.S. Department of the Interior, Office of the Secretary. "Native American Graves Protection and Repatriation Act; Interim Rule." *Federal Register* 62, no. 11 (January 13, 1997): 21–25.

U.S. General Accounting Office. *Cultural Resources: Problems Protecting and Preserving Federal Archaeological Resources.* GAO-RCED-88-3. Washington, D.C.: U.S. Government Printing Office, December 1987.

Warren, W. "A Model Cultural Center at Pojoaque Pueblo." CRM 14, no. 5 (1991): 4–6.

Wilson, Chesley Goseyun. National Endowment for the Arts, Folk Arts Program. *National Heritage Fellowships Booklet.* Washington, D.C.: National Endowment for the Arts, 1989.

York, Robert. *Medicine Mountain Archaeology Assessment*. Sheridan, WY: Bighorn National Forest, June 1995.

State and Tribal Documents and Publications

Beck, Peggy V., Anna Lee Walters, and Nia Francisco. *The Sacred: Ways of Knowledge, Sources of Life*. Tsaile, AZ: Navajo Community College Press, 1996.

Bieder, Robert E. *A Brief Historical Survey of the Expropriation of American Indian Remains*. Bloomington, IN: privately printed by Robert E. Bieder and Native American Rights Fund, April 1990.

Flathead Culture Committee. *A Brief History of the Flathead Tribes*. Saint Ignatius, MT: Flathead Culture Committee of the Confederated Salish and Kootenai Tribes, 1983.

Francis, Harris, and Klara Kelley. "Monument to Navajos and Mescalero Apaches Incarcerated at Bosque Redondo, Fort Sumner, NM." *Navajo Preservation Quarterly* 1, no. 4.

Hart, Richard, ed. *Zuni and the Grand Canyon: A Glen Canyon Environmental Studies Report—Zuni GCES Ethnohistorical Report*. Seattle: Institute of the NorthAmerican West, July 21, 1996.

Hart, Richard, and T. J. Ferguson, eds. *Traditional Cultural Properties of Four Tribes: The Fence Lake Mine Project*, vols. 1 and 2. Prepared for the Salt River Project. Seattle: Institute of the NorthAmerican West, August 12, 1993.

Hopi Tribe. "Office of Historic and Cultural Preservation and Protection—Protocol for Research, Publications and Recordings: Motion, Visual, Sound, Multimedia and Other Mechanical Devices," n.d.

Hustito, Charles, Perry Tsadiasi, and T. J. Ferguson. *Zuni History: Victories in the 1990s*. Tucson: Institute of the NorthAmerican West, 1991.

Indian Affairs: Special Supplement—American Indian Religious Freedom, no. 116 (Summer 1988).

Inter-Tribal Bison Cooperative. *Annual Report*. Rapid City, SD, 1993–1994.

Johnson, John F.C. *Chugach Legends: Stories and Photographs of the Chugach Region*. Anchorage: Chugach Alaska Corporation, 1984.

Klesert, Anthony L., and Alan S. Downer, eds. *Preservation on the Reservation: Native Americans, Native American Lands and Archaeology*. Navajo Nation Papers in Anthropology no. 26. Navajo Nation Historic Preservation Department, Window Rock, AZ, 1990.

Larsen Bay Tribal Council. Resolution no. 87-89. Larsen Bay, AK, May 29, 1987.

Mundell, Kathleen. *Basket Trees/Basket Makers*. Augusta: Maine Arts Commission, 1992.

Museum of New Mexico. "Collection and Display of Culturally Sensitive Materials." MNM Rule 11, adopted January 17, 1991, Santa Fe, NM.

Native American Committee. *Idaho Indians Tribal Histories*. Boise: Idaho Centennial Commission, 1990.

Navajo Nation Historic Preservation Department. Annual permit package information. Navajo Nation Policy to Protect Traditional Cultural Properties, 1/24/91. Available from the Navajo Nation Historic Preservation Department, Window Rock, AZ.

———. Guidelines for Implementation of the Navajo Nation Policies and Procedures Concerning the Protection of Cemeteries, Gravesites and Human Remains (ACMA-39-86). Revised February 8, 1996, as Navajo Nation Policy for the Protection of Jishehaá: Gravesites, Human Remains and Funerary Items.

Osage Nation. *Osage Language Class, Beginning Section Workbook*, n.d.

Piper, June-el, ed. *Papers From the Third, Fourth, and Sixth Navajo Studies Con-*

ferences. Window Rock, AZ: Navajo Nation Historic Preservation De-
    partment, October 1993.
Ray, Verne F. "Ethnic Impact of the Events Incident to Federal Power Develop-
    ment on the Colville and Spokane Indian Reservations." Prepared for the
    Confederated Tribes of the Colville Reservation and the Spokane Tribe
    of Indians. Port Townsend, WA, 1977.
Red Lake Band of Chippewa Indians. Language Policy, Education Code of the
    Red Lake Band of Chippewa Indians, Red Lake School District #38, north-
    ern Minnesota, n.d.
Reeves, Brian. "The Marias Massacre Site: A Progress Report." Prepared for
    Blackfeet Tribal Business Administration and the National Park Service,
    December 1995.
Skokomish Tribe of Shelton, Washington. Resolution no. 86-37, June 4, 1986.
    Attached to a letter to Dr. Adrienne Kaeppler, chair, Department of An-
    thropology, National Museum of Natural History, Smithsonian Institu-
    tion, Washington, D.C., June 5, 1986.
Skokomish Tribe and Anne Pavel. *The Native Canoe: Gift of the Cedar People*.
    Olympia: Washington Centennial Commission, 1989.
Southern Ute Tribe. *Ute Reference Grammar*, 1st ed. Ignacio, CO: Ute Press of
    the Southern Ute Tribe, n.d.
Taos Pueblo Commemorative Committee. "The Return of Blue Lake: 20-Year
    Commemoration Celebration" booklet. September 7 and 8, 1991.
Taos Pueblo War Chief's Office. "Taos Pueblo Blue Lake Wilderness Area,"
    pamphlet, 1992.
Uelbelacker, Morris L. *Time Ball: A Story of the Yakima People and the Land*.
    Toppenish, WA: Yakama Nation, 1984.
Warm Springs Confederated Tribes, Tribal Council of the Confederated Tribes
    of the Warm Springs Reservation of Oregon. "Protection and Manage-
    ment of Archaeological, Historical and Cultural Resources." Tribal Ordi-
    nance no. 68. Warm Springs, OR, n.d.
Wyss, Patrick H. *Cankpe Taopi: Wounded Knee Feasibility Study—Final Recom-
    mendations, 1988–1990*. South Dakota Historic Preservation Center, No-
    vember 20, 1990, three volumes.
Zuni Sustainable Agricultural Project (Zuni, NM). *Zuni Farming for Today and
    Tomorrow: An Occasional Newsletter of the Zuni Sustainable Agriculture Project
    and the Zuni Folk Varieties Project*, no. 3 (Summer–Fall 1994).
Zuni Tribe. "Facts on Indian Arts and Crafts." *The Shiwi Messenger* 3, no. 32
    (October 31, 1997): 1, 4.

Oral Histories and Interviews

Adams, Robert McCormick, former secretary, Smithsonian Institution. Inter-
    view by author. Basalt, CO, August 2, 1995.
Bailey, David, curator of the Museum of Western Colorado. Interview by au-
    thor. Grand Junction, CO, June 26, 1998.
Beckett, Anne. Interview by author. A:Shiwi Heritage Center, Zuni, NM, No-
    vember 7, 1997.
Begay, Richard. Interview by author. Navajo Nation Historic Preservation
    Department, Window Rock, AZ, November 6, 1997.
Bergie, Pat, director, Shoshone Tribal Cultural Center. Interview by author.
    Fort Washakie, WY, July 21, 1992.
Chapman, Fred, applied archaeologist, Native American liaison for the Wyo-
    ming State Historic Preservation Office. Interview by author. Lander, WY,
    July 21, 1992.
Chapoose, Betsy, cultural resources manager, Northern Ute. Interview by au-
    thor. Near Whiterocks, UT, August 14, 1992.

Craig, Rachel, Keepers of the Treasures—Alaska Chapter. Interview by author. Anchorage, AK, August 7, 1992.

Fredin, Adeline, cultural resources manager, Colville Confederated Tribes. Interview by author. Colville, WA, July 30, 1992.

Frost, Kenny, Ute Indian liaison to the White River National Forest, Glenwood Springs, CO. Speech before the Glenwood Springs chapter of the Sierra Club. June 9, 1993. Telephone interview by author, May 15, 1996.

Good, Diane, anthropologist-educator with the Kansas State Historical Society. Interview by author. Topeka, KS, June 8, 1998.

Hammond, Michael, executive director of the Museum at Warm Springs. Interview by author. Museum at Warm Springs, Warm Springs, OR, August 12, 1992.

Hart, Lawrence, director of the Southern Cheyenne Cultural Center. Interview by author. Denver, CO, October 3, 1997.

Hayes, Ellen, director of the Southeast Alaska Indian Cultural Center. Interview by author. Anchorage, AK, August 5, 1992.

Hill, John, Crow elder. Interview by author. Crow Agency, MT, July 22, 1992.

Hoosava, Yvonne. Interview by author. Hopi Cultural Preservation Office, Kykotsmovi, AZ. November 4, 1997.

Horsechief, Vance. Telephone interview by author, June 8, 1998.

Hutchinson, Perry, Lt. Col. Telephone interview by author, January 18, 1998.

Kight, William, heritage resource manager, White River National Forest, Glenwood Springs, CO. Extended conversations with author, summer 1993 and 1994.

King, Thomas F., cultural resources consultant. Interview by author. Nashville, TN, October 30, 1992.

Kipp, George, Blackfeet language and culture specialist. Interview by author. Browning, MT, July 27, 1992.

Kuwanwisiwma, Leigh, Hopi Cultural Preservation Office. Interview by author. Hopi Cultural Preservation Office, Kykotsmovi, AZ, November 4, 1997.

Lehi, Bryant, tour guide. Interview by author. Ute Mountain Ute Tribal Park, Colorado, September 9, 1997.

Lujan, Vince, Taos War Chief's Office. Interview by author. Taos, NM, September 8, 1997.

Makua, Chris, Keepers of the Treasures—Alaska Chapter. Interview by author, August, 6, 1992.

Martin, Rena. Interview by author. Navajo Nation Historic Preservation Department, Window Rock, AZ, November 5, 1997.

Platt, Geoffrey, legislative adviser, American Association of Museums. Interview by author. Washington, D.C., April 29, 1991.

Pullar, Gordon, Keepers of the Treasures—Alaska Chapter. Interview by author. Anchorage, AK, August 4, 1992. Telephone interview by author, November 10, 1995.

Quam, Vernon, curator, A:shiwi A:wan Museum and Heritage Center. Interview by author. Zuni, NM, November 7, 1997.

Sackler, Elizabeth. Telephone interview by author, April 4, 1992.

Sam, Robert, Sitka Tribe of Alaska. Interview by author. Denver, CO, October 4, 1997.

Selles, Michael, archaeologist, White River Resource Area of the Bureau of Land Management, Meeker, CO. Conversations with author, 1996.

Speaker, Stewart, Repatriation Office, National Museum of Natural History, Smithsonian Institution. Telephone interview by author, November 15, 1995.

Sutteer, Barbara Booher, superintendent at Little Bighorn National Battlefield Park (LBNBP), Montana. Interview by author. Park headquarters, LBNBP, July 23, 1992.

Wagner, Curly Bear, cultural specialist and tour guide. Interview by author. Glacier Park Lodge, East Glacier Park, MT, July 26, 1992.

Windy Boy, Janine Pease, president, Little Big Horn College. Interview by author. Crow Agency, MT, July 23, 1992.

Wise, Haman. Interview by author. Shoshone Tribal Cultural Center, Fort Washakie, WY, January 5 and 6, 1994.

Yallup, William F., Sr. Interview by author. Yakama Indian Nation headquarters, Toppenish, WA, August 10, 1992.

Unpublished Conference Papers, Theses, and Dissertations

Alexander, Craig, Office of Tribal Justice, United States Department of Justice, Washington, D.C. "Protection of Indian Sacred Places and the Religious Accommodation Doctrine." Sovereignty Symposium X, Tulsa, OK, June 9–11, 1997, pp. 1–14.

Chapman, Fred. "The Bighorn Medicine Wheel 1988–1996: Conflict and Resolution." Paper presented at the Society of American Archaeologists annual meeting, Seattle, WA, April 1998.

Conley, Manuel. "Indians and Academia: How the Post–World War II Revival of Interest in Native Americans Influenced the Teaching of Indian History in North Carolina Education." Doctor of Arts diss., Middle Tennessee State University, 1997.

Corbett, William. "A History of the Red Pipestone Quarry and Pipestone National Monument." Master's thesis, University of South Dakota, 1976.

Fearnbach, Heather. "Native American Sacred Sites: Case Studies in Preservation and Protection." Master's thesis, Middle Tennessee State University, 1997.

Fink, Jameson. "Hart Prairie and the Snow Bowl Conflict." Master's thesis, Northern Arizona University, 1997.

Gulliford, Andrew, chair. Bighorn Medicine Wheel panel, with presenters Mary Randolph, Big Horn National Forest; Fred Chapman, Wyoming State Historic Preservation Office; and Francis P. Brown, Medicine Wheel Coalition. American Places Symposium, American Heritage Center, University of Wyoming, September 1997.

Gulliford, Andrew, chair. Devils Tower National Monument panel, with presenters Deborah Liggett, superintendent, Devils Tower; Steven Emery, attorney general, Cheyenne River Sioux Tribe; and Mary Fladerka, Bear Lodge Multiple Use Association. American Places Symposium, American Heritage Center, University of Wyoming, September 1997.

Hart, Richard. "The Trail to Zuni Heaven." Paper presented at "Law for the Elephant, Law for the Beaver," Transboundary Conference on the Legal History of the West and North-West of North America, University of Victoria, British Columbia, February 23, 1991.

Mills, Kara Elizabeth. "Back to the Basics: Case Studies of the History of Native Peoples' Subsistence Practices in Yellowstone and Denali National Parks." Master's thesis, Middle Tennessee State University, 1999.

Wesler, Kit. "The Wickliffe Mounds Cemetery: Educating the Public in a Changing Exhibit." Paper presented at the symposium "Public Education at Archaeological Parks: Doing It Every Day," Society for American Archaeology, Pittsburgh, PA, April 10, 1992.

Yellowhair, Gordon. Comments in a session on NAGPRA and curation at the annual meeting of the American Association for State and Local History, Denver, CO, October 1997.

Newsletters

Alvarez, Michelle. "Mount Shasta: A Question of Power." *News From Native California* 8, no. 3 (Winter 1994–1995): 4–7.

California Indian Basketweavers. California Indian Basketweavers Association. P.O. Box 2397 (317 Spring St.), Nevada City, CA 95959.

Cummings, Patricia. "Native Religions, New-Agers, and the Forest Service." *Inner Voice* (September–October 1992): 8–9, 14.

Governors' Interstate Indian Council Newsletter on teen suicide (Summer 1992). Wyoming Indian Affairs Council, 115 N. 5th E., Riverton, WY 82501.

Masayesva, Vernon. Quoted in materials from the Association on American Indian Affairs, American Indian Religious Freedom Project, 95 Madison Ave., New York 10016.

National Park Service. *Special Resource Study, The Bear River Massacre Site Newsletter,* May 1996.

Rieger, Ted. "Discontent Lingers After Decision on Mt. Shasta's Historic Status." *Historic Preservations News,* February–March 1995, pp. 12, 14.

Contemporary Newspaper Articles

Alexie, Sherman. "White Men Can't Drum." *New York Times Magazine,* October 4, 1992.

Anderson, Mary. "Apache Woman Fights to Preserve Sacred Site." *Indian Country Today,* January 14, 1993.

Anquoe, Bunty. "Federal Government Planning Bombing Range on Sacred Site." *Indian Country Today,* June 29, 1994.

Baird, Ron. "Indians Seek Protection From Religious Suppression." *High Country News,* June 15, 1992.

Barringer, Felicity. "Smithsonian Accord Is Likely on Return of Indian Remains." *New York Times,* August 20, 1989.

"Blackfeet File Injunction Over Badger–Two Medicine Drilling." *Browning (MT) Glacier Reporter,* March 7, 1991.

Buchta, Shari. "Tribal Elders to Visit Sites in Nebraska." *Fremont (NE) Tribune,* June 8, 1994.

"Buffalo Kill Ceremony." *Indian Country Today,* November 25–December 2, 1996.

Chasing Horse, Joe. "Ancient Prophecies, Ceremonies, Have Connections to the Land." *Indian Country Today,* June 4–11, 1996.

Clay, Rebecca. "New Law Lets Tribes Ask for Return of Artifacts." *Christian Science Monitor,* January 3, 1991.

———. "Thefts Unsettle the Zuni." *High Country News,* January 28, 1991.

———. "Who Owns Indian Artifacts?" *Christian Science Monitor,* August 28, 1990.

Couglin, Ellen. "Returning Indian Remains." *Chronicle of Higher Education,* March 16, 1994.

Dawson, Pat. "Gold Company Stymied in Montana's Sweet Grass Hills." *High Country News,* August 9, 1993.

Diefenderfer, Heida. "Culture of the Whale: Makah Seek Annual Hunting Quota." *Indian Country Today,* February 3–10, 1997.

Donahue, Bill. "Oregon's Enola Hill: 'Diseased Forest' or Sacred Site?" *High Country News,* February 25, 1990.

Donovan, Bill. "Faker Healers Plague Navajo Nation." *High Country News,* June 10, 1996.

Dougherty, John. "The Long, Bitter Battle Over Mount Graham." *High Country News,* July 24, 1995.

Easley, Billy. "Red Cloud's Rifle Returned to Family." *The Tennessean*, December 12, 1990.

"An Ecumenical Group Fights for an Indian Spiritual Site." *High Country News*, December 2, 1991.

Farmer, Jared. "Devils Tower May Get a Second Name." *High Country News*, September 2, 1996.

Folstrom, Jacob John. Letter to the editor. *Indian Country Today*, April 6, 1994.

Fruhling, Larry. "Burial Dispute Pits Indians vs. Scientists." *Des Moines State Register*, April 16, 1989.

Giarelli, Andrew L. "The Return of Cheyenne Skulls Brings a Bloody Western Story to a Close." *High Country News*, November 15, 1993.

Gibson, Stan, and Jack Hayne. "Mayhem on the Marias." *Great Falls (MT) Tribune*, April 28, 1996.

Glass-Coffin, Bonnie. "Anthropology, Shamanism, and the 'New Age.'" *Chronicle of Higher Education*, June 15, 1994.

Gottlieb, Alan. "Spiritual Use of Site Debated: Indian Activists Say Parcel Sacred." *Denver Post*, December 13, 1993.

"Group Proposes Saving Yellowstone Bison." *Indian Country Today*, September 14, 1994.

Hardeen, George. "Navajos Oppose Roadside Additions in San Francisco Peaks." *High Country News*, June 17, 1991.

Johnson, Nan. "'New Agers' Damage Ute Sites." *Glenwood Springs (CO) Glenwood Post*, September 13, 1995.

———. "New-Agers Destroy Utes' Spiritual Sites: Rocky Mountain Remnants Rearranged." *Indian Country Today*, April 30–May 7, 1996.

Johnson, Richard. "Bones of Their Fathers." *Denver Post, Contemporary Magazine*, February 4, 1990.

Johnson, Terry. "Buffalo Gathering at Slim Buttes." *Indian Country Today*, October 27, 1993.

Knickerbocker, Brad. "Indians Fight for Religious Freedom." *Christian Science Monitor*, April 1, 1992.

Levendosky, Charles. "Face Off at Devils Tower: Climbers vs. Religion." *Casper (WY) Star-Tribune*, March 24, 1996.

———. "How Can a Place Named 'Devils' Be Holy?" *Casper (WY) Star-Tribune*, August 18, 1996.

Lindler, Bert. "A Vietnam Vet Tries to Preserve the Blackfeet Culture." *High Country News*, May 20, 1991.

Little Eagle, Avis. "After the Sweat: Caviar, Wine & Cheese." *Indian Country Today*, July 24, 1991.

———. "Ceremony Days Set Aside at Medicine Wheel." *Indian Country Today*, July 21, 1993.

———. "Controversy Chips Away at Pipestone." *Indian Country Today*, July 21, 1993.

———. "Lakota Rituals Being Sold." *Indian Country Today*, July 2, 1991.

———. "Medicine Men for Rent." *Indian Country Today*, July 1, 1991.

———. "Methodists Apologize for Sand Creek Massacre." *Indian Country Today*, April 30–May 4, 1996.

———. "Non-Indian Sun Dancers Bring Ohio Indian Protest." *Indian Country Today*, July 14, 1993.

———. "Oh Shinnah: Prophet for Profit." *Indian Country Today*, August 2, 1991.

———. "Paid Ads Call Her 'Medicine Woman.'" *Indian Country Today*, August 14, 1991.

———. "Sacred Pipe Keeper Fears Feds Will Step In." *Indian Country Today*, July 17, 1991.

———. "Sacred Site Protection." *Indian Country Today*, June 4–11, 1996.

———. "Tribes Fight to Keep Pipeline Away From Bear Butte." *Indian Country Today*, June 22, 1994.

Magnuson, Jon. "Selling Native American Soul." *Christian Century*, November 22, 1989.

Masayesva, Vernon. "We Can Have Electricity, Jobs and Clean Air." *High Country News*, March 30, 1998.

McCullen, Kevin. "Devils Tower for Scale." *Rocky Mountain News*, June 11, 1996.

———. "Vandals Disturb Sacred Indian Site." *Rocky Mountain News*, September 13, 1995.

McDonald, Kim A. "Construction of Observatory on Mount Graham Would Violate Sacred Site, Indian Tribes Say." *Chronicle of Higher Education*, July 17, 1991.

McMahon, Patrick. "Whale Hunt Pits Old Ways vs. New: Tribe's Plans Draw Flotilla of Protest." *USA Today*, October 2, 1998.

"Medicine Wheel Remains Unprotected." *High Country News*, May 3, 1993.

Melmer, David. "State Seeks Advice on Bear Butte Plan." *Indian Country Today*, November 23, 1994.

———. "The Sweet Grass Hills: Where Gold Weighs Heavier Than Spirituality." *Indian Country Today*, July 27, 1995.

Meyer, Eugene. "Bones of American Indians in Limbo." *Washington Post*, April 4, 1994.

Milstein, Michael. "Signing Ceremony Ends Long Dispute Over Sacred Site." *Billings (MT) Gazette*, September 30, 1996.

Newcomer, Kris. "Museum Returns Carving to Zunis." *Rocky Mountain News*, March 22, 1991.

"Nez Perce Ranger Feels Battlefield's Ghosts." *Billings (MT) Gazette*, August 14, 1993.

Noel, Tom. "Don't Erase Sand Creek: Leave Record Intact for Next Generations." *Denver Post*, July 5, 1998.

Onderdonk, Amy. "Indians Hope Buffalo Can Revive Tribes' Fortunes." *High Country News*, May 4, 1992.

Parham, Jennifer. "Three Arrested in Blockade: Logging Road Invades Yurok, Tolowa, and Karuk Sacred Sites." *Indian Country Today*, August 4–11, 1997.

Peterson, Brenda. "Saving the Makah Way of Life: Whales Are the Key to a Tribe's Culture but Will They Exist to Hunt or Watch?" *Seattle Times*, October 19, 1997.

Porterfield, K. Marie. "Pine Ridge May Face Referendum Over Sun Dance." *Indian Country Today*, August 4–11, 1997.

———. "The Selling of the Sun Dance: Spiritual Exploitation at Heart of Pine Ridge Controversy." *Indian Country Today*, July 28–August 4, 1997.

"Protecting Sacred Sites a Job for Land Managers." *Pocatello (ID) ShoBan News*, August 8, 1996.

Rambler, Sandra. "Apache Protest Telescope Bill." *Indian Country Today*, March 7, 1996.

Raymond, Chris. "Historic Bible to Be Returned to Tribe." *Washington Post*, April 21, 1990.

———. "Reburial of Indian Remains Stimulates Studies, Friction Among Scholars." *Chronicle of Higher Education*, October 3, 1990.

———. "Some Scholars Upset by Stanford's Decision to Return American Remains for Re-Burial by Tribe." *Chronicle of Higher Education*, July 5, 1989.

Reif, Rita. "Buyer Vows to Return Masks to Indians." *New York Times*, May 22, 1991, p. B1.

Roach, Jean. "Tribes Press State About Bear Butte." *Indian Country Today*, April 28–May 5, 1997.

Rushio, Michelle. "State's Job Boom Stops at Reservations." *Arizona Republic*, May 14, 1997.

Sherk, Mary L. "Dancing Leaves Still Whisper of Prairie's Ancient Past." *Denver Post*, July 7, 1996.

Silva, Samantha. "A Famous Skeleton Returns to the Earth." *High Country News*, March 8, 1993.

Smith, Loyd. "Remains of 35 Blackfeet to Be Returned to Nearby Reservation." *Browning (MT) Glacier Reporter*, June 20, 1991.

Smith, Paul. "How Do You Define Sacred?" *High Country News*, May 26, 1997.

Stillman, Pamela. "Did Fire Purify Mato Paha?" *Indian Country Today*, September 9–16, 1996.

Stoll, Michael. "Tribes Use New Riches to Recast History." *Christian Science Monitor*, August 11, 1998.

Sullivan, Robert. "Permission Granted to Kill a Whale, Now What?" *New York Times Sunday Magazine*, August 9, 1998.

Suro, Robert. "Zuni Tribe Winning Right to Restore Its War God Idols." *Denver Post*, August 19, 1990.

Swisher, Karen. "Indian Museum Board Picked." *Washington Post*, January 27, 1990.

———. "Skeletons in the Closet." *Washington Post*, October 3, 1989.

Taliman, Valerie. "Aspen Sweatlodgers Get Heat From Utes." *Indian Country Today*, May 12, 1993.

Taylor, Bill. "Salvage Rider Will Destroy Sacred Sites." *High Country News*, May 27, 1996.

Tizon, Alex. "A Calling at Wounded Knee." *Seattle Times*, October 19, 1997.

Tomsho, Robert. "Indian Burial Site Becomes Big Issue in Little Salina, Kansas." *Wall Street Journal*, May 17, 1989.

"Tribes Must Do the Research to Protect Their Sacred Sites." *Indian Country Today*, May 26–June 2, 1997.

Uhlenbrock, Tom. "Bones of Contention." *St. Louis Post-Dispatch*, April 7, 1991.

"UNPO Supports Lakota Call for Peace and Unity." *Indian Country Today*, July 2–15, 1996.

Walker, Deward E. "Anthropologists Must Allow American Indians to Bury Their Dead." *Chronicle of Higher Education*, September 12, 1990.

Webster, Tom. Letter to the editor. *Indian Country Today*, December 7, 1994.

Weinraub, Judith. "Indian Museum Director Named." *Washington Post*, May 22, 1990.

Wilford, John Noble. "8,000 Year-Old Human Bones Are Found in Cave." *New York Times*, October 3, 1993.

Wilkinson, Todd. "U.S. Agency Raps Medicine Wheel." *Billings (MT) Gazette*, July 9, 1991.

Young, John. "Grey Eagles to Oppose Devils Tower Climbing." *Indian Country Today*, August 31, 1994.

———. "Lakota Adamant: No Climbing on Mahto Tipi." *Indian Country Today*, September 14, 1994.

———. "National Park Service Reviews Current Devils Tower Climb Policy." *Indian Country Today*, August 10, 1994.

———. "New Agers Assault on Bear Butte Decried." *Indian Country Today*, June 29, 1994.

———. "Rock Climbing Ban Termed Successful." *Indian Country Today*, July 27, 1995.

———. "Wounded Knee Occupied by Protesters Who Oppose Tribal Park Designation." *Indian Country Today*, March 30, 1995.

―――. "Wounded Knee Park Plan Stalled in Congress." *Indian Country Today*, June 22, 1994.

Museum and Historical Society Documents and Publications

Adams, Robert McCormick. "Smithsonian Horizons: Recent Discussions With Indian Leaders Have Raised Questions About Repatriation of Skeletal Remains and Sacred Objects." *Smithsonian* 18 (November 1987): 12.

―――. "Smithsonian Horizons: Steps Are Under Way to Restore the American Indian's Cultural Patrimony, a Complex and Long-Overdue Process." *Smithsonian* 21 (October 1990): 10.

―――. "Smithsonian Horizons: We Have an Obligation to Return the Skeletal Remains in Our Collections to Tribal Descendants." *Smithsonian* 18 (May 1987): 12.

Baker, Charles. "In My Opinion: Indian Artifacts and Museums—A Question of Ownership." *History News* 40 (April 1985).

Bond, Constance. "An American Legacy." *Smithsonian* (October 1989): 43.

Cahokia Mounds Historic Site. Museum Assessment Program Documentation Package. 1990.

―――. Update—Cahokia Mounds Master Management Plan. 1990.

Chapman, Fred. "The Medicine Wheel: Tourism, Historic Preservation, and Native American Rights." *Wyoming Annals* 65, no. 1 (Spring 1993): 4–5.

Cosgrove, Cornelius B., and Harriet S. Cosgrove. *The Swarts Ruin: A Typical Mimbres Site of Southwestern New Mexico*. Papers of the Peabody Museum of Anthropology and Ethnology, vol. 15, no. 1. Cambridge, MA: Peabody Museum of Anthropology and Ethnology, 1932.

Cunningham, Don. "Pahuk Place." *NEBRASKAland* (June 1985).

Dongoske, Kurt, Leigh Jenkins, and T. J. Ferguson. "Understanding the Past Through Hopi Oral Tradition." *Native Peoples* 6, no. 2 (Winter 1993): 24–35.

Eriacho, Wilfred, and T. J. Ferguson. "Ahayu: da—Zuni War Gods Cooperation and Repatriation." *Native Peoples* (Fall 1990): 6–12.

Farr, William E. "Troubled Bundles, Troubled Blackfeet: The Travail of Cultural and Religious Renewal." *Montana: The Magazine of Western History* 43, no. 4 (Autumn 1993): 2–17.

Floyd, Candace. "The Repatriation Blues." *History News* 40 (April 1985).

Flynn, Gillian. "Annual Report on Repatriation Office Activities at the National Museum of Natural History, June 1994 to May 1995." Repatriation Office, National Museum of Natural History, MRC 138. Washington, D.C.

Garfield, Donald. "Cultural Chronology." *Museum News* 70, no. 1 (January–February 1991): 55–56.

Good, Diane L. *Birds, Beads & Bells: Remote Sensing of a Pawnee Sacred Bundle*. Anthropological Series no. 15. Topeka: Kansas State Historical Society, 1989.

―――. "Sacred Bundles: History Wrapped Up in Culture." *History News* 45, no. 4 (August 1990): 13–14, 27.

Green, Jerry. "The Medals of Wounded Knee." *Nebraska History* 75, no. 2 (1994): 200–208.

Gulliford, Andrew. "Bones of Contention: Wickliffe Mounds & the Evolution of Public Archaeology at a Prehistoric Mississippian Village." Report for the Museum Assessment Program, American Association of Museums. September 1991, pp. 5–6.

―――. "Museums and the Mimbres People: Interpreting the Mogollon Culture." In *Mogollon V: Proceedings of the Fifth Mogollon Conference*, edited by Patrick H. Beckett. Las Cruces, NM: Coas Publishing, 1991, pp. 28–33.

Gwinn, Vivian R., and Marilyn Norcini. "Help for the Asking." In "Museums and Native Americans: Renegotiating the Contract," special issue of *Museum News* (January–February 1991).

Halaas, David Fridtjof. " 'All the Camp Was Weeping': George Bent and the Sand Creek Massacre." *Colorado Heritage* (Summer 1995): 2–17.

Harney, Thomas, and Dan Agent. "Cheyenne Ancestors Interred in Concho, Oklahoma." *Smithsonian Runner*, no. 93-5 (September–October 1993): 6.

Hill, Richard. "Reclaiming Cultural Artifacts." *Museum News* 55 (May–June 1977): 43–46.

Horse Capture, George P. "Some Observations on Establishing Tribal Museums." American Association for State and Local History, Technical Leaflet 134. Published in *History News* 36 (January 1981).

Horse Capture, George P., ed. *The Concept of Sacred Materials and Their Place in the World.* Cody, WY: Plains Indian Museum, Buffalo Bill Historical Center, 1989.

———. "Survival of Culture." *Museum News* 70, no. 1 (January–February 1991): 49–51.

Karpan, Robin, and Arlene Karpan. "Saskatchewan Indians Tell Their Own Story." *History News* (May–June 1990).

Kwapil, Bryan W. "Coping With a Shady Past." *History News* 42, no. 2 (1987): 13–17.

Lowawaima, Hartman H. "Native American Collections: Legal and Ethical Concerns." *History News* 45 (May–June 1990): 6–8.

MacLeish, William H. "1492 America: The Land Columbus Never Saw," *Smithsonian* 22 (November 1991): 34–51.

Museum of New Mexico, Office of Cultural Affairs. "Policy on Collection, Display and Repatriation of Culturally Sensitive Materials." Rule no. 11, adopted January 17, 1991.

National Museum of the American Indian, Smithsonian Institution. Collections Policy. September 11, 1992.

———. Meeting minutes, museum directors, administrators and designers consultation, May 2–September 10, 1991.

Parkman, Alice. "A Joint Effort: Planning Exhibits for the Museum at Warm Springs." *History News* 54, no. 3 (Summer 1998): 20–23.

Quimby, George I., and James D. Nason. "New Staff for a New Museum." *Museum News* 55 (May–June 1977).

Roth, Evan. "Success Stories." *Museum News* 70, no. 1 (January–February 1991): 45.

Sletto, Jacqueline Wiora. "Pipestone." *Native Peoples* 5, no. 2 (Winter 1992): 20–24.

Sletto, Jacqueline Wiora, and Bjorn Sletto. "Prairie Tribes and the Buffalo." *Native Peoples* 6, no. 2 (Winter 1993): 36–45.

Smith, Ben. "Return of the Great Canoes." *Native Peoples* 6, no. 2 (Winter 1993): 12.

Stark, Peter. "The Old North Trail." *Smithsonian* (July 1997): 54–66.

"Study at Indian Burial Pit." *Kansas State Historical Society Mirror* 36, no. 3 (April 1990).

"Studying Sand Creek Site." *Colorado History News* (November 1996): 7.

Articles, Essays, and Book Chapters

Adams, David Wallace. "From Bullets to Boarding Schools: The Educational Assault on the American Indian Identity." In *The American Indian Experience*, edited by Philip Weeks. Wheeling, IL: Forum Press, 1988, pp. 218–239.

Anyon, Roger. "Zuni Protection of Cultural Resources and Religious Freedom." *Cultural Survival Quarterly* 19, no. 4 (1996): 46–49.

Anyon, Roger, and T. J. Ferguson. "Cultural Resources Management at the Pueblo of Zuni, New Mexico, USA." *Antiquity* 69, no. 266 (December 1996): 913–931.

Arden, H. "Who Owns Our Past?" *National Geographic* 175 (March 1989): 376–393.

Begay, Richard. "The Role of Archaeology on Indian Lands." In *Native Americans and Archaeologists*, edited by Nina Swidler et al. Walnut Creek, CA: AltaMira Press, 1997, pp. 161–166.

Bieder, Robert E. "The Representation of Indian Bodies in Nineteenth-Century American Anthropology." *American Indian Quarterly* 20, no. 2 (1995): 165–178.

Brandt, Elizabeth A. "The Fight for Dzil Nchaa Si An, Mt. Graham: Apaches and Astrophysical Development in Arizona." *Cultural Survival Quarterly* 19, no. 4 (1996): 50–57.

Brower, Montgomery, and Conan Putnam. "Walter Echo-Hawk Fights for His People's Right to Rest in Peace." *People* 4 (September 1984): 43.

Brown, Brian Edward. "Native American Religions, the First Amendment, and the Judicial Interpretation of Public Land." *Environmental History Review* 15, no. 4 (Winter 1991): 19–44.

Brown, Michael F. "Can Culture Be Copyrighted?" *Current Anthropology* 39, no. 2 (April 1998): 193–206.

Clifford, James. "Four Northwest Coast Museums: Travel Reflections." In *Exhibiting Cultures: The Poetics and Politics of Museum Display*, edited by Ivan Karp and Steven D. Levine. Washington, D.C.: Smithsonian Institution Press, 1991, pp. 212–254.

Collins, Susan M. "Review of *Kunaitupii: Coming Together on Native Saved Sites—Their Sacredness, Conservation, and Interpretation*, ed. by Society for American Archaeology." *American Antiquity* 60, no. 2 (1995): 374–377.

"Court Rules for Religious Freedom." *Native American Rights Fund Legal Review* 23, no. 1 (Winter–Spring 1998): 1–4.

Crosby, Alfred. "Ecological Imperialism: The Overseas Migration of Western Europeans as a Biological Phenomenon." *Texas Quarterly* 21 (Spring 1978): 10–22.

Cross, Raymond, and Elizabeth Brenneman. "Devils Tower at the Crossroads: The National Park Service and the Preservation of Native American Cultural Resources in the 21st Century." *Public Land & Resources Law Review* 18 (1997): 6–45.

Deloria, Philip S. "The Preservation of Indian Culture." *Historic Preservation Forum* (January–February 1993): 42–47.

Donahue, Bill. "Hey, Get Your Ropes off My Cathedral!" *Outside* (June 1997): 29.

Dongoske, Kurt E., Leigh Jenkins, and T. J. Ferguson. "Issues Relating to the Use and Preservation of Hopi Sacred Sites." *Historic Preservation Forum* (March–April 1994): 12–14.

Dormaar, J. F. "Sweetgrass Hills, Montana, USA." *Alberta Archaeological Review* (April 1997): 4–28.

Downer, Al. "A Decade of Change." *Common Ground: Archaeology and Ethnography in the Public Interest*, ed. C. Timothy McKeown (Fall 1999): 14–19.

Downer, Alan S., and Alexandra Roberts. "The Navajo Experience With the Federal Historic Preservation Program." *Natural Resources & Environment* 10, no. 3 (Winter 1996): 39–42, 78–79.

Eastman, Charles Alexander. "The Ghost Dance War." In *Visions of America*, edited by Wesley Brown and Amy Ling. New York: Persea Books, 1993, pp. 1–7.

Echo-Hawk, Roger. "Forging a New Ancient History for Native America." In
    Native Americans and Archaeologists, edited by Nina Swidler et al. Walnut
    Creek, CA: AltaMira Press, 1997, pp. 88–102.

Echo-Hawk, Walter R. "Loopholes in Religious Liberty: The Need for a Fed-
    eral Law to Protect Freedom of Worship for Native People." *Native Ameri-
    can Rights Fund Legal Review* 16, no. 2 (1991): 7–12.

———. "Native American Religious Liberty: 500 Years After Columbus."
    American Indian Culture and Research Journal 17, no. 3 (1993): 33–52.

Eddy, John A. "Probing the Mystery of the Medicine Wheels." *National Geo-
    graphic* 151, no. 1 (January 1977): 140–146.

Evans, Michael. "The Many Voices of Sacred Geography." *Common Ground* 3,
    no. 2–3 (1998): 64–65.

Fenton, William N. "Return of Eleven Wampum Belts to the Six Nations
    Iroquois Confederacy on Grand River, Canada." *Ethnohistory* 36, no. 4
    (Fall 1989): 392–411.

Forbes-Boyte, Kari. "Respecting Sacred Perspectives: The Lakotas, Bear Butte,
    and Land-Management Strategies." *Public Historian* 18, no. 4 (1996): 99–
    118.

Gillette, Jane Brown. "Sweetgrass Saga." *Historic Preservation* (September–
    October 1994): 28–33, 90–92.

Gonzales, Mario. "The Black Hills: The Sacred Land of the Lakota and Tsis-
    tsistas." *Cultural Survival Quarterly* 19, no. 4 (1996): 63–67.

Greer, Sandy. "Intellectual Property Rights: Where Do Indians Draw the Line?"
    Winds of Change (Winter 1995): 76–81.

Grimm, Lydia T. "Sacred Lands and the Establishment Clause: Indian Reli-
    gious Practices on Federal Lands." *Natural Resources and Environment* 12,
    no. 1 (1997): 19–78.

Gulliford, Andrew. "Bones of Contention: The Repatriation of Native Ameri-
    can Human Remains." *Public Historian* 18, no. 4 (1996): 119–143.

———. "Interpreting Historic Photographs of Native Americans." *Hayes Histori-
    cal Journal: A Journal of the Gilded Age* 11, no. 4 (Summer 1992): 19–35.

———. "Native Americans and Museums: Curation and Repatriation of Sa-
    cred and Tribal Objects." *Public Historian* 14, no. 3 (1992): 23–45.

———. "Tribal Preservation: An Overview of Cultural Management." *Preser-
    vation Forum* 6, no. 6 (1992): 33–43.

Gysin, Catherine. "The Lost Horizon." *Utne Reader* (May–June 1993): 21, 24.

Hagan, William T. "Reformers' Images of the Native Americans: The Late
    Nineteenth Century." In *The American Indian Experience,* edited by Philip
    Weeks. Arlington, IL: Forum Press, 1988, pp. 207–217.

Hawkins, Janet. "Resting in Pieces." *Harvard Magazine* (November–December
    1991): 43.

Hernandez-Avila, Ines. "Meditations of the Spirit: Native American Religious
    Traditions and the Ethics of Representation." *American Indian Quarterly*
    20, no. 3–4 (Summer and Fall 1996): 329–353.

Hodgson, Bryan. "Buffalo: Back Home on the Range." *National Geographic*
    186, no. 5 (November 1994): 64–89.

Horse Capture, George. "Richard A. Pohrt." In *Art of the American Indian Frontier:
    The Chandler-Pohrt Collection,* edited by David W. Penny. Seattle: University
    of Washington Press and the Detroit Institute of Arts, 1992, pp. 323–337.

Hoxie, Frederick E. "The Curious Story of Reformers and the American Indi-
    ans." In *Indians in American History,* edited by Frederick E. Hoxie. Wheel-
    ing, IL: Harlan Davidson, 1988, pp. 205–230.

Jenkins, Leigh, Kurt E. Dongoske, and T. J. Ferguson. "Managing Hopi Sacred
    Sites to Protect Religious Freedom." *Cultural Survival Quarterly* 19, no. 4
    (1996): 36–39.

Jett, Stephen C. "Navajo Sacred Places: The Management and Interpretation of Mythic History." *Public Historian* 17, no. 2 (Spring 1995): 39–47.

Jocks, Christopher Ronwanien:te. "Spirituality for Sale: Sacred Knowledge in the Consumer Age." *American Indian Quarterly* 20, no. 3 (1996): 415–431.

Johnson, Jessica. "Masked Hazard." *Common Ground: Archaeology and Ethnography in the Public Interest,* ed. C. Timothy McKeown (Fall 1999): 26–31.

Keister, Kim. "In the Native Tongue." *Historic Preservation* 44, no. 4 (July–August 1992): 38.

LaFarge, Oliver. "The Little Stone Man." In *Yellow Sun/Bright Sky,* edited by David L. Caffey. Albuquerque: University of New Mexico Press, 1988, pp. 181–192.

Lassiter, Luke E. "Southeastern Oklahoma, the Gourd Dance, and 'Charlie Brown.'" In *Contemporary Native American Cultural Issues,* edited by Duane Champagne. Walnut Creek, CA: AltaMira Press, 1999, pp. 145–166.

Lewis, David Rich. "Still Native: The Significance of Native Americans in the History of the Twentieth-Century American West." *Western Historical Quarterly* 24, no. 2 (May 1993): 203–228.

Limerick, Patricia. "Haunted America." In *Sweet Medicine: Sites of Indian Massacres, Battlefields and Treaties,* edited by Drex Brooks. Albuquerque: University of New Mexico Press, 1995, pp. 119–161.

———. "The Repression of Indian Religious Freedom." *Native American Rights Fund Legal Review* 18, no. 2 (1993): 9–13.

Mattern, Mark. "The Powwow as a Public Arena for Negotiating Unity and Diversity in American Life." In *Contemporary Native American Cultural Issues,* edited by Duane Champagne. Walnut Creek, CA: AltaMira Press, 1999, pp. 129–144.

May, Philip A. "The Epidemiology of Alcohol Abuse Among Native Americans: The Mythical and Real Properties." In *Contemporary Native American Cultural Issues,* edited by Duane Champagne. Walnut Creek, CA: AltaMira Press, 1999, pp. 227–244.

McCarty, Teresa L., and Lucille J. Watahomigie. "Reclaiming Indigenous Languages." *Common Ground: Archaeology and Ethnography in the Public Interest,* ed. C. Timothy McKeown (Fall 1999): 33–43.

McGowan, Janet. "What's in a Name? Can Native America Control Outsiders' Use of Their Tribal Names?" *Cultural Survival Quarterly* 18, no. 4 (Winter 1995): 11–15.

McKeown, Timothy C. "Preservation on the Reservation (Revisited)." *Common Ground: Archaeology and Ethnography in the Public Interest* (Fall 1999): 10–13.

McManamon, Francis P. "Changing Relationships Between Native Americans and Archaeologists." *Historic Preservation Forum* (March–April 1994): 15–20.

Merrill, William L., Edmund J. Ladd, and T. J. Ferguson. "The Return of the *Ahayu:da:* Lessons for Repatriation From Zuni Pueblo and the Smithsonian Institution." *Current Anthropology* 13, no. 5 (December 1993): 523–567.

Michaelsen, Robert S. "Dirt in the Court Room: Indian Land Claims and American Property Rights." In *American Sacred Space,* edited by David Chidester and Edward T. Linenthal. Bloomington: Indiana University Press, 1995, pp. 43–96.

Mihesuah, Devon A., ed. "American Indian Identities: Issues of Individual Choices and Development." In *Contemporary Native American Cultural Issues,* edited by Duane Champagne. Walnut Creek, CA: AltaMira Press, 1999, pp. 13–38.

———. "Repatriation: An Interdisciplinary Dialogue." *American Indian Quarterly* 20, no. 2 (Spring 1996): 153–307.

Moore, Steven C. "Sacred Sites and Public Lands." In *Handbook of American Indian Religious Freedom*, edited by Christopher Vecsey. New York: Crossroad, 1991, pp. 81–99.

Native American Rights Fund. "Second Special Edition on Freedom of Religion: A Time for Justice." *Native American Rights Fund Legal Review* 18, no. 2 (Summer 1993).

Ortiz, Alfonso, ed. "American Indian Religious Freedom: First People and the First Amendment." *Cultural Survival Quarterly* 19, no. 4 (Winter 1996).

———. "Indian/White Relations: A View From the Other Side of the 'Frontier.'" In *Indians in American History*, edited by Frederick E. Hoxie. Wheeling, IL: Harlan Davidson, 1988, pp. 1–16.

Parks, Douglas R., and Waldo R. Wedel. "Pawnee Geography: Historical & Sacred." *Great Plains Quarterly* 5, no. 3 (Summer 1985): 143–176.

Pascua, Maria Parker. "Ozette." *National Geographic* 180 (October 1991): 38–53.

Preston, Douglas J. "The Lost Man." *New Yorker*, June 16, 1997, pp. 70–81.

———. "Skeletons in Our Museums' Closets." *Harper's*, February 1989, pp. 66–76.

Price, Nicole. "Tourism and the Bighorn Medicine Wheel: How Multiple Use Does Not Work for Sacred Land Sites." In *Sacred Sites, Sacred Places*, edited by David L. Carmichael, Jane Hubert, Brian Reeves, and Audhild Schanche. New York: Routledge, 1994, pp. 259–264.

Pullar, Gordon L. "The Quikertarmiut and the Scientist: Fifty Years of Clashing World Views." In *Reckoning With the Dead*, edited by Tamara Bray and Thomas Killion. Washington, D.C.: Smithsonian Institution Press, 1994, pp. 17, 22.

Reeves, Brian. "Ninaistakis—The Nitsiapii's Sacred Mountain: Traditional Native Religious Activities and Land Use/Tourism Conflicts" (Blackfeet in Glacier National Park). In *Sacred Sites, Sacred Places*, edited by David L. Carmichael, Jane Hubert, Brian Reeves, and Audhild Schanche. New York: Routledge, 1994, pp. 265–294.

Reimensnyder, Barbara L. "Cherokee Sacred Sites in the Appalachians." In *Cultural Heritage Conservation in the American South*, edited by Benita J. Howell. Athens: University of Georgia Press, 1990, pp. 107–117.

Rudner, Ruth. "Sacred Geographies: Indian Country, Where Time, Land, Tradition, and Law Are Joined—Or Should Be." *Wilderness* 58, no. 206 (Fall 1994): 10–27.

Ruppert, David. "Buying Secrets: Federal Government Procurement of Intellectual Cultural Property." In *Intellectual Property Rights for Indigenous Peoples*, edited by Tom Greaves. Oklahoma City, OK: Society for Applied Anthropology, 1994, pp. 111–128.

Simon, David J. "Healing the Sacred Hoop." *National Parks* 65 (September–October 1991): 24–29.

Smith, Allison A. Chun. "Kaho'olawe: The Sacred Isle." In *Hawai'i: New Geographies*, edited by D. W. Woodcock. Honolulu: Department of Geography, University of Hawai'i at Manoa, 1999, pp. 133–152.

Steiner, Stan. "Sacred Objects, Secular Laws." *Perspectives* 13, no. 2 (1981): 12–15.

Stern, Walter E., and Lynn H. Slade. "Effects of Historic, Cultural Resources, and Indian Religious Freedom on Public Lands: A Practical Primary." *Natural Resources* 35 (Winter 1995): 133–181.

Stokes, Samuel. "Hanalei, Hawai'i: The Cultural Landscape." In Samuel N. Stokes and A. Elizabeth Watson, *Saving America's Countryside*. Baltimore, MD: Johns Hopkins University Press, 1989, pp. 112–113.

Stolzenburg, William. "Sacred Peaks Common Grounds: American Indians and Conservationists Meet at a Cultural Crossroads." *Nature Conservancy* 42, no. 5 (September–October 1992): 17–23.

Tallbull, William V., and Sherri Deaver. "Living Human Values." Foreword to *Native Americans and Archaeologists*, edited by Nina Swidler et al. Walnut Creek, CA: AltaMira Press, 1997, pp. 9–10.

Taylor, Bron. "Resacralizing Earth: Pagan Environmentalism and the Restoration of Turtle Island." In *American Sacred Space*, edited by David Chidester and Edward T. Linenthal. Bloomington: Indiana University Press, 1995.

Trennert, Robert A. "Educating Indian Girls at Nonreservation Boarding Schools, 1878–1920." In *The American Indian Past and Present*, edited by Roger Nichols. New York: Knopf, 1986, pp. 218–231.

Trillin, Calvin. "U.S. Journal: Louisiana—The Tunica Treasure." *New Yorker*, July 27, 1981, pp. 41–51.

Trope, Jack F. "Existing Federal Law and the Protection of Sacred Sites: Possibilities and Limitations." *Cultural Survival Quarterly* 19, no. 4 (1996): 30–35.

Trope, Jack F., and Walter R. Echo-Hawk. "The Native American Graves Protection and Repatriation Act: Background and Legislative History." *Arizona State Law Journal* 24, no. 1 (Spring 1992): 35–77.

Tsosie, Rebecca. "Indigenous Rights and Archaeology." In *Native Americans and Archaeologists*, edited by Nina Swidler et al. Walnut Creek, CA: AltaMira Press, 1997, pp. 64–76.

Ubelaker, Douglas, and Laurym Guttenplan-Grant. "Human Skeletal Remains—Preservation or Reburial?" In *1989 Yearbook of Physical Anthropology*, vol. 32. New York: Alan R. Liss, 1989, pp. 249–287.

Vest, Jay Hansford C. "Traditional Blackfeet Religion and the Sacred Badger–Two Medicine Wildlands." *Journal of Law and Religion* 6, no. 2 (1988): 455–489.

Vizenor, Gerald. "Bone Courts: The Natural Rights of Tribal Bones." In his *Crossbloods: Bone Courts, Bingo, and Other Reports*. Minneapolis: University of Minnesota Press, 1990, p. 62.

Vollers, Maryanne. "Indian Summer." *Time*, August 26, 1996, p. 38.

Walker, Deward. "American Indian Sacred Geography." *Indian Affairs: Special Supplement—American Indian Religious Freedom*, no. 116 (Summer 1988): ii, vi–vii.

Waller, David. "Friendly Fire: When Environmentalists Dehumanize American Indians." In *Contemporary Native American Cultural Issues*, edited by Duane Champagne. Walnut Creek, CA: AltaMira Press, 1999, pp. 277–292.

Welch, John. "White Eyes' Lies and the Battle for Dzi Nchaa Si'an." *American Indian Quarterly* 21, no. 1 (Winter 1997): 75–109.

Wesler, Kit. "The King Project at Wickliffe Mounds: A Private Excavation in the New Deal Era." In *New Deal Era Archaeology and Current Research in Kentucky*, edited by D. Polloack and M. L. Powell. Frankfort: Kentucky Heritage Council, 1988, pp. 83–96.

White Deer, Gary. "Return of the Sacred." In *Native Americans and Archaeologists*, edited by Nina Swidler et al. Walnut Creek, CA: AltaMira Press, 1997, pp. 37–43.

Whittemore, Katharine. "To Converse With Creation: Saving California Indian Languages." *Native Americas* 14, no. 3 (Fall 1997): 46–53.

Wilkinson, Charles F. "Indian Tribes and the American Constitution." In *Indians in American History*, edited by Frederick E. Hoxie. Wheeling, IL: Harlan Davidson, 1988, pp. 117–136.

Books

Akens, Jean. *Ute Mountain Tribal Park: The Other Mesa Verde*. Moab, UT: Four Corners Publications, 1995.

Ambrose, Stephen. *Crazy Horse and Custer*. New York: Doubleday, 1975.

————. *Undaunted Courage: Meriwether Lewis, Thomas Jefferson and the Opening of the American West.* New York: Simon & Schuster, 1996.

Basso, Keith M. *Wisdom Sits in Places.* Albuquerque: University of New Mexico Press, 1996.

Bieder, Robert E. *Science Encounters the Indian, 1820–1880: The Early Years of American Ethnology.* Norman: University of Oklahoma Press, 1986.

Blackburn, Fred M., and Ray A. Williamson. *Cowboys & Cave Dwellers: Basketmaker Archaeology in Utah's Grand Gulch.* Santa Fe, NM: School of American Research Press, 1997.

Brain, Jeffrey P. *Tunica Treasure.* Cambridge, MA: Harvard University Peabody Museum of Archaeology and Ethnology, and the Peabody Museum of Salem, Massachusetts, 1979.

————. *The Tunica-Biloxi.* New York: Chelsea House, 1989.

Bray, Tamara L., and Thomas W. Killion, eds. *Reckoning With the Dead: The Larsen Bay Repatriation and the Smithsonian Institution.* Washington, D.C.: Smithsonian Institution Press, 1994.

Brody, J. J. *Mimbres Painted Pottery.* Santa Fe, NM: School of American Research, and Albuquerque: University of New Mexico Press, 1977.

Brooks, Drex. *Sweet Medicine: Sites of Indian Massacres, Battlefields, and Treaties.* Albuquerque: University of New Mexico Press, 1995.

Brown, Joseph Epes. *The Sacred Pipe.* Norman: University of Oklahoma Press, 1953.

Bruchac, Joseph. *The Native American Sweat Lodge: History and Legends.* Freedom, CA: Crossing Press, 1993.

Bucko, Raymond A. *The Lakota Ritual of the Sweat Lodge.* Lincoln: University of Nebraska Press, 1998.

Carmichael, David L., Jane Hubert, Brian Reeves, and Audhild Schanche, eds. *Sacred Sites, Sacred Places.* New York: Routledge, 1994.

Carr, Pat. *Mimbres Mythology.* El Paso: Texas Western Press, 1982.

Case, David S. *Alaska Natives and American Laws.* Fairbanks: University of Alaska Press, 1984.

Catlin, George. *Letters and Notes on the Manners, Customs, and Condition of the North American Indians,* vol. 1. London: published by the author and printed by Tosswill and Myers, 1841.

Chamberlin, Russell. *Loot! The Heritage of Plunder.* New York: Facts on File, 1983.

Chidester, David, and Edward T. Linenthal, eds. *American Sacred Space.* Bloomington: Indiana University Press, 1995.

Cole, Douglas. *Captured Heritage: The Scramble for Northwest Coast Artifacts.* Norman: University of Oklahoma Press, 1995.

Crawford, James T. *Hold Your Tongue: Bilingualism and the Politics of English Only.* New York: Addison Wesley, 1992.

Crummett, Michael. *Sun Dance.* Helena, MT: Falcon Press, 1993.

de Voto, Bernard, ed. *The Journals of Lewis and Clark.* Boston: Houghton Mifflin, 1997.

Delaney, Robert W. *The Ute Mountain Utes.* Albuquerque: University of New Mexico Press, 1989.

Deloria, Vine, Jr. *God Is Red: A Native View of Religion.* Golden, CO: Fulcrum Publishing, 1994.

DeMallie, Raymond J. *The Sixth Grandfather: Black Elk's Teachings Given to John G. Neihardt.* Lincoln: University of Nebraska Press, 1995.

Doll, Don. *Vision Quest: Men, Women and Sacred Sites of the Sioux Nation.* New York: Crown Publishers, 1994.

Dougherty, Michael. *To Steal a Kingdom: Probing Hawaiian History.* Waimanalo, HI: Island Style Press, 1992.

Echo-Hawk, Roger C., and Walter R. Echo-Hawk. *Battlefields and Burial Grounds: The Indian Struggle to Protect Ancestral Graves in the United States*. Minneapolis, MN: Lerner Publications, 1994.

Emmitt, Robert. *The Last War Trail*. Boulder: University Press of Colorado, 2000.

Evans, Steven Ross. *Voice of the Old Wolf: Lucullus Virgil McWhorter and the Nez Perce Indians*. Pullman: Washington State University Press, 1996.

Fewkes, J. Walter. *The Mimbres Art and Archaeology*. Albuquerque, NM: Avanyu Publishing, 1989.

Giammettei, Victor M., and Nanci Greer Reichert. *Art of a Vanished Race: The Mimbres Classic Black-on-White*. Silver City, NM: High-Lonesome Books, 1990.

Gordon-McCutchan, R. C. *The Taos Indians and the Battle for Blue Lake*. Santa Fe, NM: Red Crane Books, 1991.

Greaves, Tom, ed. *Intellectual Property Rights for Indigenous Peoples: A Sourcebook*. Oklahoma City, OK: Society for Applied Anthropology, 1994.

Guyette, Susan. *Planning for Balanced Development: A Guide for Native American and Rural Communities*. Santa Fe, NM: Clear Light Publishers, 1996.

Hampton, Bruce. *Children of Grace: The Nez Perce War of 1877*. New York: Avon Books, 1994.

Harper, Kenn. *Give Me My Father's Body: The Life of Minik, the New York Eskimo*. Frobisher Bay, Northwest Territory: Blacklead Books, 1986.

Hart, Richard E., ed. *Zuni and the Courts: A Struggle for Sovereign Land Rights*. Lawrence: University Press of Kansas, 1995.

Hill, Tom, and Richard W. Hill Sr. *Creation's Journey: Native American Identity and Belief*. Washington, D.C.: Smithsonian Institution Press, 1994.

Hillerman, Tony. *Talking God*. New York: Harper & Row, 1989.

———. *A Thief of Time*. New York: Harper & Row, 1988.

Hinsley, Curtis M. *The Smithsonian and the American Indian: Making a Moral Anthropology in Victorian America*. Washington, D.C.: Smithsonian Institution Press, 1981.

Hoxie, Frederick, ed. *Indians in American History*. Wheeling, IL: Harlan Davidson, 1988.

Hutt, Sherry, Elwood W. Jones, and Martin E. McAllister. *Archaeological Resources Protection*. Washington, D.C.: Preservation Press, 1992.

Jennings, Francis. *The Invasion of America*. Chapel Hill, NC: Duke University Press, 1976.

Jensen, Richard E., R. Eli Paul, and John E. Carter. *Eyewitness at Wounded Knee*. Lincoln: University of Nebraska Press, 1991.

Jorgensen, Joseph G. *The Sun Dance Religion: Power for the Powerless*. Chicago: University of Chicago Press, 1972.

Josephy, Alvin M., Jr. *Now That the Buffalo's Gone*. Norman: University of Oklahoma Press, 1984.

Josephy, Alvin M., Jr., ed. *America in 1492: The World of the Indian Peoples Before the Arrival of Columbus*. New York: Vintage Books, 1991.

Karp, Ivan, and Steven D. Lavine. *Exhibiting Cultures: The Poetics and Politics of Museum Display*. Washington, D.C.: Smithsonian Institution Press, 1991.

Kelley, Klara Bonsack, and Harris Francis. *Navajo Sacred Places*. Bloomington: Indiana University Press, 1994.

Kennedy, Roger G. *Hidden Cities: The Discovery and Loss of Ancient North American Civilization*. New York: Free Press, 1994.

King, Thomas F. *Cultural Resource Laws & Practice: An Introductory Guide*. Walnut Creek, CA: AltaMira Press, 1998.

Kirch, Patrick Vinton. *Legacy of the Landscape: An Illustrated Guide to Hawaiian Archaeological Sites*. Honolulu: University of Hawai'i Press, 1996.

Krech, Shephard, III, and Barbara A. Hail, eds. *Collecting Native America*. Washington, D.C.: Smithsonian Institution Press, 1999.

Krinsky, Carol Herselle. *Contemporary Native American Architecture: Cultural Regeneration and Creativity*. New York: Oxford University Press, 1996.

Kroeber, Karl, ed. *American Indian Persistence and Resurgence*. Durham, NC: Duke University Press, 1994.

L'Amour, Louis. *Haunted Mesa*. New York: Bantam Books, 1987.

Lewis, David Rich. *Neither Wolf nor Dog: American Indians, Environment & Agrarian Change*. New York: Oxford University Press, 1994.

Limerick, Patricia Nelson. *The Legacy of Conquest: The Unbroken Past of the American West*. New York: W. W. Norton, 1987.

Mails, Thomas E. *Fools Crow*. Lincoln: University of Nebraska Press, 1979.

Manning, Richard. *Grassland*. New York: Penguin Books, 1995.

Matthiessen, Peter. *Indian Country*. New York: Penguin, 1979.

McKenzie, Melody Kapilialoha, ed. *Native Hawaiian Rights Handbook*. Honolulu: University of Hawai'i Press, 1991.

McNickle, D'Arcy. *Native American Tribalism: Indian Survivals and Renewals*. New York: Oxford University Press, 1973.

McPherson, Robert S. *Sacred Land, Sacred View: Navajo Perceptions of the Four Corners Region*. Provo, UT: Brigham Young University, Charles Redd Center for Western Studies, 1992.

Milne, Courtney. *Sacred Places in North America: A Journey Into the Medicine Wheel*. New York: Stewart, Tabori & Chang, 1994.

Molyneaux, Brian Leigh. *The Sacred Earth*. Boston: Little, Brown, 1995.

Momaday, N. Scott. *The Way to Rainy Mountain*. Albuquerque: University of New Mexico Press, 1969.

Mundell, Kathleen. *Basket Trees/Basket Makers*. Augusta: Maine Arts Commission, 1992, p. 10.

Nabokov, Peter. *Native American Testimony*. New York: Penguin, 1991.

Neihardt, Hilda. *Black Elk and Flaming Rainbow: Personal Memories of the Lakota Holy Man and John Neihardt*. Lincoln: University of Nebraska Press, 1995.

Neihardt, John G. *Black Elk Speaks*. New York: Pocket Books, 1975.

Nichols, Roger L. *The American Indian Past and Present*. New York: Knopf, 1986.

Ortiz, Alfonso. *The Tewa World: Space, Time, Being & Becoming in a Pueblo Society*. Chicago: University of Chicago Press, 1969.

Paper, Jordan. *Offering Smoke: The Sacred Pipe and Native American Religion*. Moscow: University of Idaho Press, 1988.

Patterson, Alex. *A Field Guide to Rock Art Symbols of the Greater Southwest*. Boulder, CO: Johnson Books, 1992.

Powell, Peter J. *Sweet Medicine: The Continuing Role of the Sacred Arrows, the Sun Dance, and the Sacred Buffalo Hat in Northern Cheyenne History*. Norman: University of Oklahoma Press, 1998.

Price, Marcus. *Disputing the Dead: U.S. Law on Aboriginal Remains and Grave Goods*. Columbia: University of Missouri Press, 1991.

Ransom, Jay Ellis. *The Bighorn Medicine Wheel: The Birth and Death of Humanity*. Cody, WY: Yellowstone Printing & Publishing, 1992.

Rice, Julian. *Black Elk's Story: Distinguishing Its Lakota Purpose*. Albuquerque: University of New Mexico Press, 1991.

Ridington, Robin, and Dennis Hastings. *Blessing for a Long Time: The Sacred Pole of the Omaha Tribe*. Lincoln: University of Nebraska Press, 1997.

Rohner, Ronald P. *The Ethnography of Franz Boas*. Chicago: University of Chicago Press, 1969.

Rothman, Hal. *America's National Monuments: The Politics of Preservation*. Lawrence: University Press of Kansas, 1989.

Schaafsma, Polly. *Indian Rock Art of the Southwest*. Albuquerque: University of New Mexico Press, 1986.

———. *Rock Art in New Mexico*. Santa Fe: Museum of New Mexico Press, 1991.

———. *Rock Art in Utah*. Salt Lake City: University of Utah Press, 1993.

Simmons, William. *The Narragansett*. New York: Chelsea House, 1989.

Smith, George S., and John E. Ehrenard, eds. *Protecting the Past*. Boca Raton, FL: CRC Press, 1991.

Spence, Mark David. *Dispossessing the Wilderness: Indian Removal and the Making of the National Parks*. New York: Oxford University Press, 1999.

Sprague, Marshall. *Massacre: The Tragedy at White River*. Lincoln: University of Nebraska Press, 1980.

Stokes, John F.G. *Heiau of the Island of Hawai'i: A Historic Survey of Native Hawaiian Temple Sites*. Honolulu, HI: Bishop Museum Press, 1991.

Stowell, Cynthia D. *Faces of a Reservation: A Portrait of the Warm Springs Reservation*. Portland: Oregon Historical Society Press, 1987.

Swan, James A. *Sacred Places: How the Living Earth Seeks Our Friendship*. Santa Fe, NM: Bear, 1990.

Swidler, Nina, Kurt E. Dongoske, Roger Anyon, and Alan S. Downer, eds. *Native Americans and Archaeologists*. Walnut Creek, CA: AltaMira Press, 1997.

Thomas, David Hurst. *Exploring Ancient North America: An Archaeological Guide*. New York: Macmillan, 1994.

Trenholm, Virginia Cole, and Maurine Carley. *The Shoshonis, Sentinels of the Rockies*. Norman: University of Oklahoma Press, 1964.

Utley, Robert M. *The Indian Frontier of the American West, 1846–1890*. Albuquerque: University of New Mexico Press, 1984.

Vecsey, Christopher, ed. *Handbook of American Indian Religious Freedom*. New York: Crossroads, 1991.

Vizenor, Gerald. *Crossbloods: Bone Courts, Bingo, and Other Reports*. Minneapolis: University of Minnesota Press, 1990.

Waters, Frank. *The Man Who Killed the Deer*. New York: Pocket Books, 1975.

Weeks, Philip, ed. *The American Indian Experience*. Arlington Heights, IL: Forum Press, 1988.

Welch, James. *Killing Custer*. New York: W. W. Norton, 1994.

Williamson, Ray A. *Living the Sky: The Cosmos of the American Indian*. Norman: University of Oklahoma Press, 1984.

Woodcock, D. W., ed. *Hawai'i: New Geographies*. Honolulu: Department of Geography, University of Hawai'i at Manoa, 1999.

About the Author

Andrew Gulliford has researched Native American sacred objects and sacred places throughout the West, Alaska, and Hawai'i. A graduate of Colorado College (B.A., M.A.T.) and Bowling Green State University in Ohio (Ph.D.), he is a professor of Southwest Studies and History and Director of the Center of Southwest Studies at Fort Lewis College in Durango, Colorado. Previously he directed the Public History and Historic Preservation Program at Middle Tennessee State University near Nashville.

His photographs of American Indian sacred sites have been published in *Nonrenewable Resources* (1994), *The Secretary of the Interior's Report to Congress: Federal Archaeological Programs and Activities, 1993* (1993), and *Advisory Council on Historic Preservation, Report to Congress and the President, 1993* (1993). His previous books include *Boomtown Blues: Colorado Oil Shale, 1885–1985* (1989) and *America's Country Schools* (1984, 1996), both published by the University Press of Colorado.

Formerly the director of the Western New Mexico University Museum in Silver City, New Mexico, Gulliford curated one of the largest prehistoric Mimbres pottery collections. He has worked with the Ute to document, preserve, and protect the Ute Trail on Colorado's Western Slope, and he now works with the Eastern Shoshone in Wyoming on museum and preservation planning. For the American Association of Museums he reviews tribal museums and historic sites with Indian collections, and for the Smithsonian Associates program, he has led tours on the Columbia and Snake Rivers in Washington and Oregon and on the Lewis and Clark Trail by canoe and horseback in Montana and Idaho.

He has received a Take Pride in America National Award from the secretary of agriculture for "outstanding contributions to America's natural and cultural resources"; the National Volunteer Award from the chief of the United States Forest Service; the Second Annual James Marston Fitch Mid-Career Award for Historic Preservation; and the Award of Merit from the American Association for State and Local History.

In summers, he backpacks, hikes, and canoes the West with his wife and two sons.

Index

References to indexed notes are indicated by the letter "n" following the page number. The number after the "n" indicates the note number.

Acting as a tour leader, the author brought Eastern Shoshone cultural center board members from Wyoming to meet staff at the Ak Chin Him Dak Ecomuseum in Arizona. Author is second from right.